Boarding School *Juliet*

vol. 4

YOUSUKE KANEDA

To LOVƐ, or not to LOVƐ

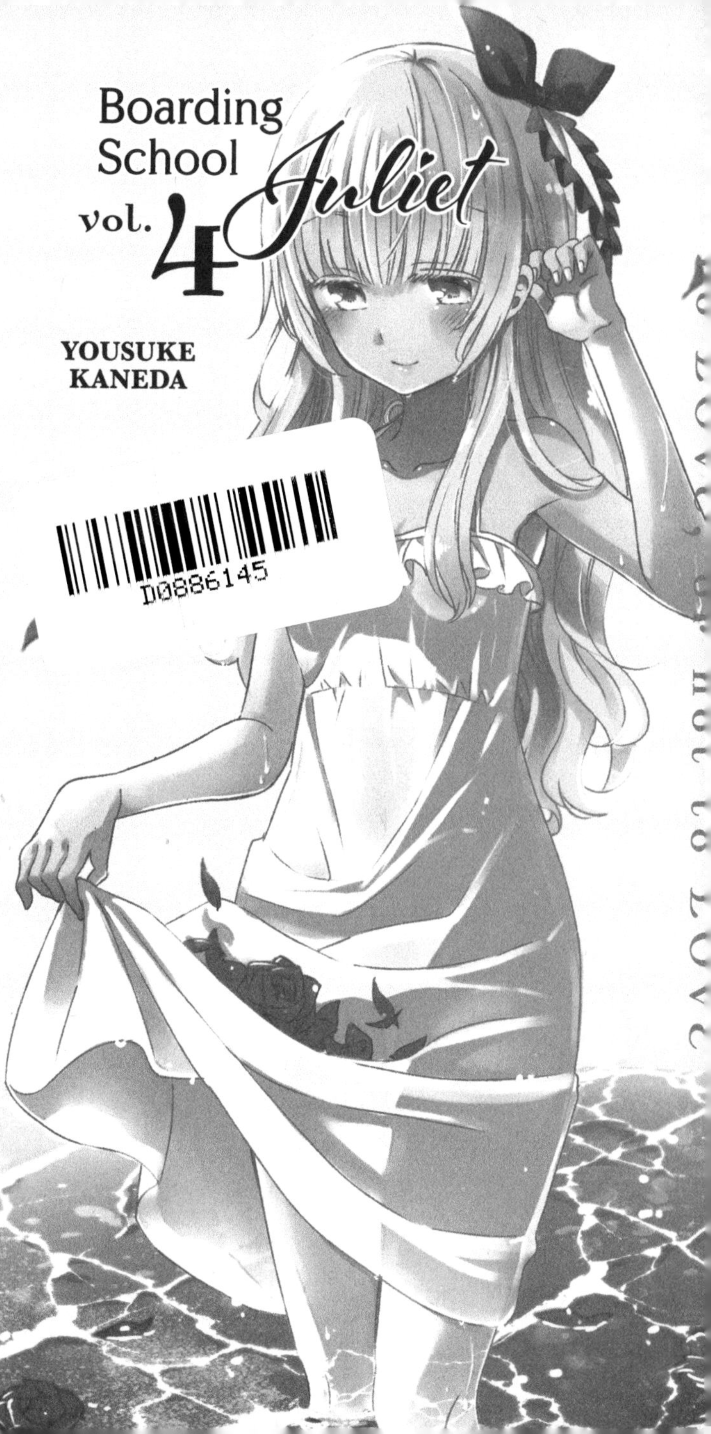

THE PLAYERS

character

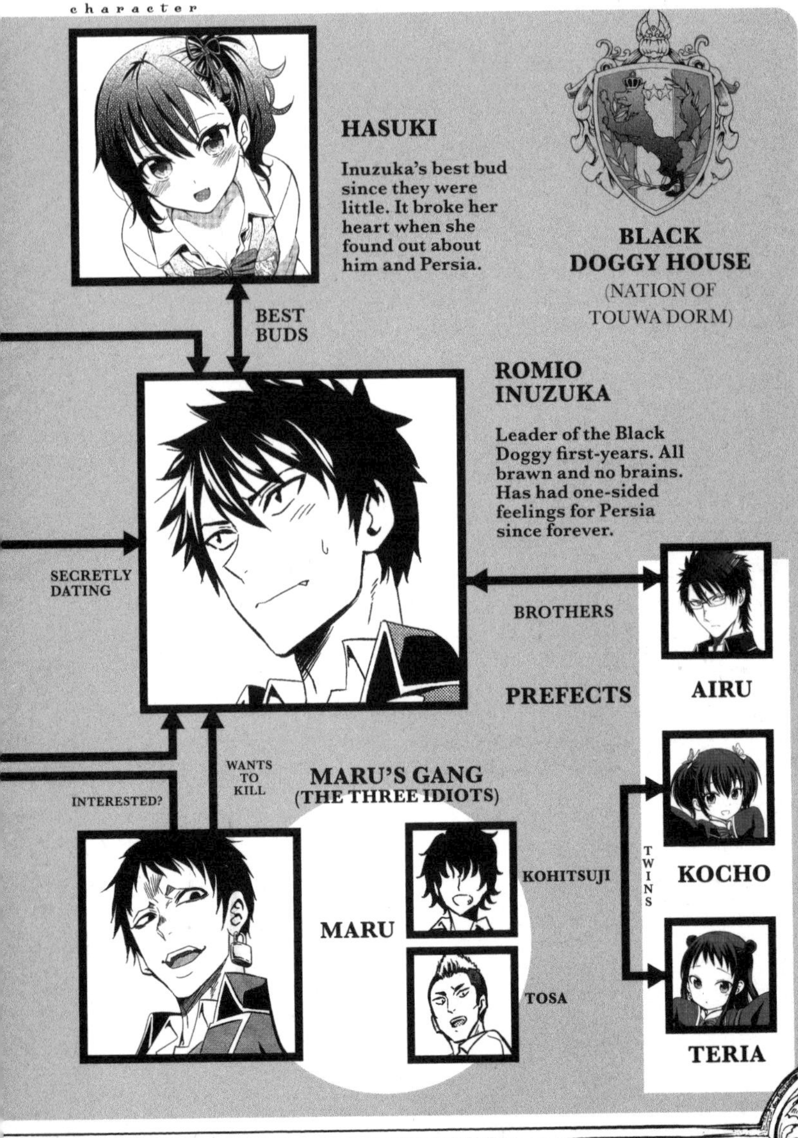
HASUKI
Inuzuka's best bud since they were little. It broke her heart when she found out about him and Persia.
BLACK DOGGY HOUSE
(NATION OF TOUWA DORM)
BEST BUDS
ROMIO INUZUKA
Leader of the Black Doggy first-years. All brawn and no brains. Has had one-sided feelings for Persia since forever.
SECRETLY DATING
BROTHERS
PREFECTS
AIRU
WANTS TO KILL
INTERESTED?
MARU'S GANG (THE THREE IDIOTS)
KOHITSUJI
TWINS
KOCHO
MARU
TOSA
TERIA

BOARDING SCHOOL JULIET

To LOVE, or not to LOVE

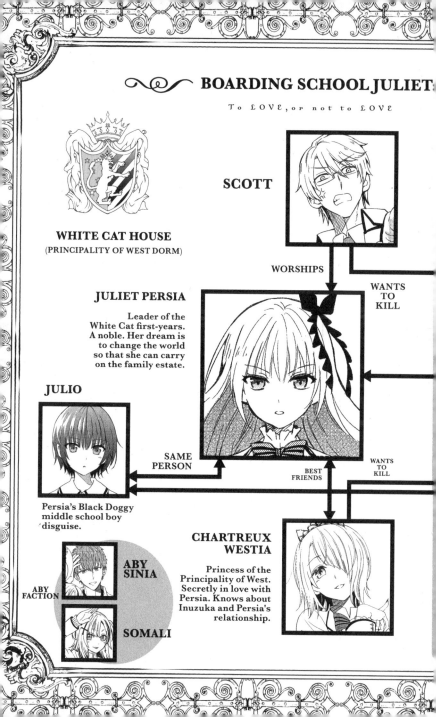

SCOTT

WHITE CAT HOUSE
(PRINCIPALITY OF WEST DORM)

WORSHIPS

WANTS
TO
KILL

JULIET PERSIA

Leader of the
White Cat first-years.
A noble. Her dream is
to change the world
so that she can carry
on the family estate.

JULIO

SAME
PERSON

BEST
FRIENDS

WANTS
TO
KILL

Persia's Black Doggy
middle school boy
disguise.

**ABY
SINIA**

**ABY
FACTION**

SOMALI

CHARTREUX
WESTIA

Princess of the
Principality of West.
Secretly in love with
Persia. Knows about
Inuzuka and Persia's
relationship.

contents

ACT 16: ROMIO & JULIET & THE BIRTHDAY II
005

ACT 17: ROMIO & JULIET & THE BIRTHDAY III
039

ACT 18: ROMIO & JULIET & THE BIRTHDAY IV
077

ACT 19: ROMIO & TERIA
115

ACT 20: THE BEACH & ROMIO & JULIET I
151

story

At boarding school Dahlia Academy, attended by students from two feuding countries, one first-year longs for a forbidden love. His name: Romio Inuzuka, leader of the Black Doggy House first-years. The apple of his eye: Juliet Persia, leader of the White Cat House first-years. It all begins when Inuzuka confesses his feelings to her. This is Inuzuka and Persia's star-crossed, secret love story...

Inuzuka and Persia promised to spend Persia's birthday eve together, but Inuzuka ended up under the close surveillance of his older brother Airu, who suspects him of conspiring with a White Cat. Inuzuka managed to slip free for their rendezvous, but the sight of his battered body wounded Persia's heart...

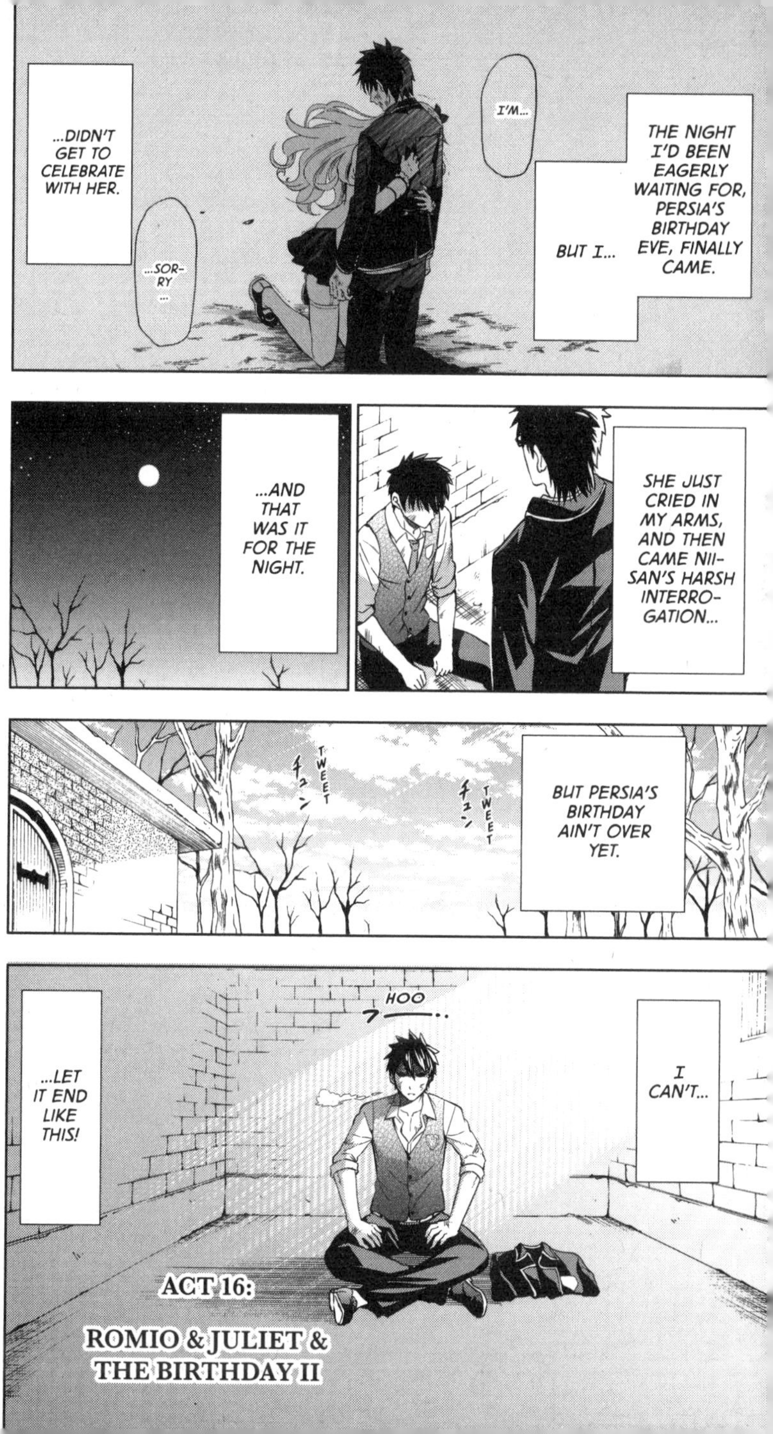
THE NIGHT I'D BEEN EAGERLY WAITING FOR, PERSIA'S BIRTHDAY EVE, FINALLY CAME.
BUT I...
I'M...
...DIDN'T GET TO CELEBRATE WITH HER.
...SOR-RY...
SHE JUST CRIED IN MY ARMS, AND THEN CAME NII-SAN'S HARSH INTERRO-GATION...
...AND THAT WAS IT FOR THE NIGHT.
BUT PERSIA'S BIRTHDAY AIN'T OVER YET.
チュン TWEET
チュン TWEET
I CAN'T...
HOO
...LET IT END LIKE THIS!
ACT 16:
ROMIO & JULIET & THE BIRTHDAY II

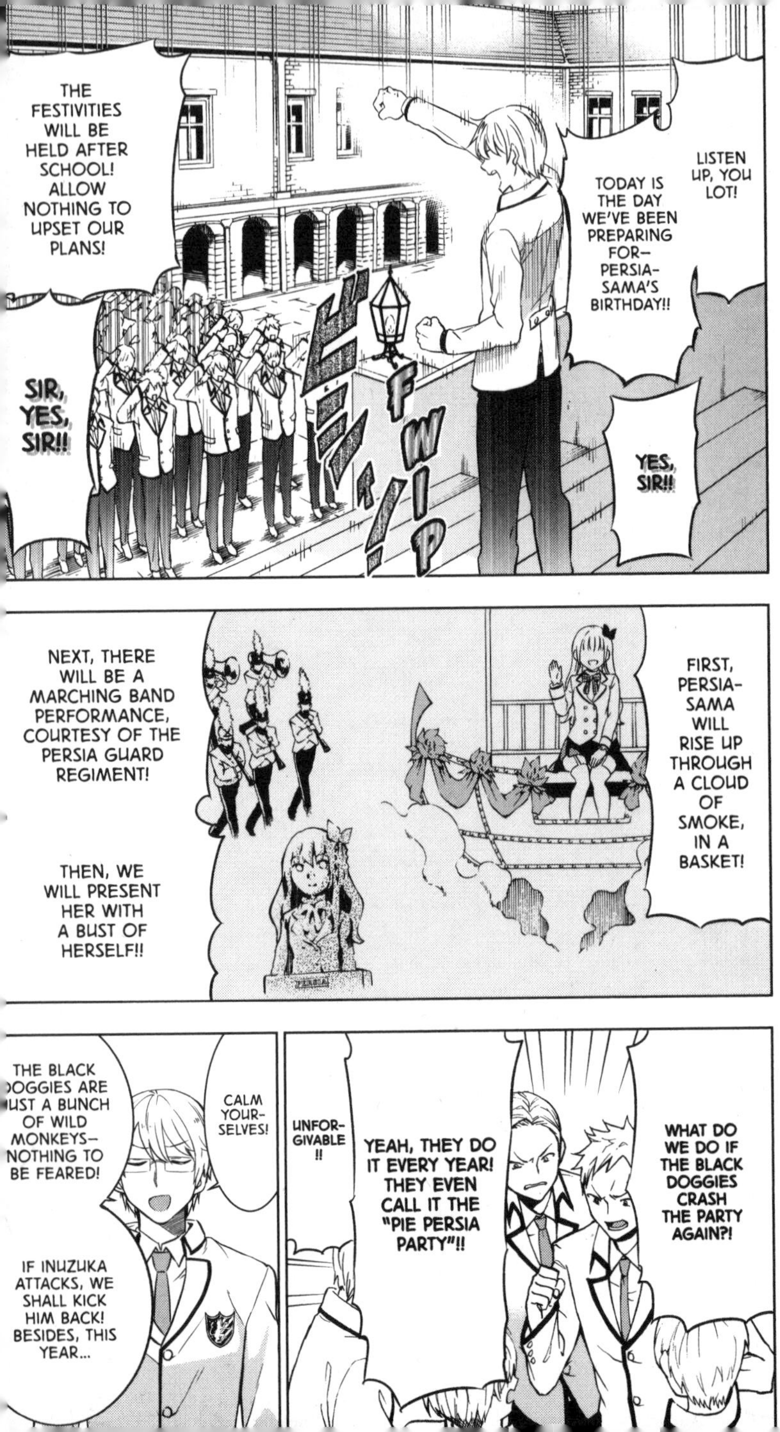
LISTEN UP, YOU LOT!
TODAY IS THE DAY WE'VE BEEN PREPARING FOR— PERSIA-SAMA'S BIRTHDAY!!
THE FESTIVITIES WILL BE HELD AFTER SCHOOL! ALLOW NOTHING TO UPSET OUR PLANS!
YES, SIR!!
FWIP
SIR, YES, SIR!!
FIRST, PERSIA-SAMA WILL RISE UP THROUGH A CLOUD OF SMOKE, IN A BASKET!
NEXT, THERE WILL BE A MARCHING BAND PERFORMANCE, COURTESY OF THE PERSIA GUARD REGIMENT!
THEN, WE WILL PRESENT HER WITH A BUST OF HERSELF!!
PERSIA
WHAT DO WE DO IF THE BLACK DOGGIES CRASH THE PARTY AGAIN?!
YEAH, THEY DO IT EVERY YEAR! THEY EVEN CALL IT THE "PIE PERSIA PARTY"!!
UNFORGIVABLE!!
CALM YOURSELVES!
THE BLACK DOGGIES ARE JUST A BUNCH OF WILD MONKEYS—NOTHING TO BE FEARED!
IF INUZUKA ATTACKS, WE SHALL KICK HIM BACK! BESIDES, THIS YEAR...

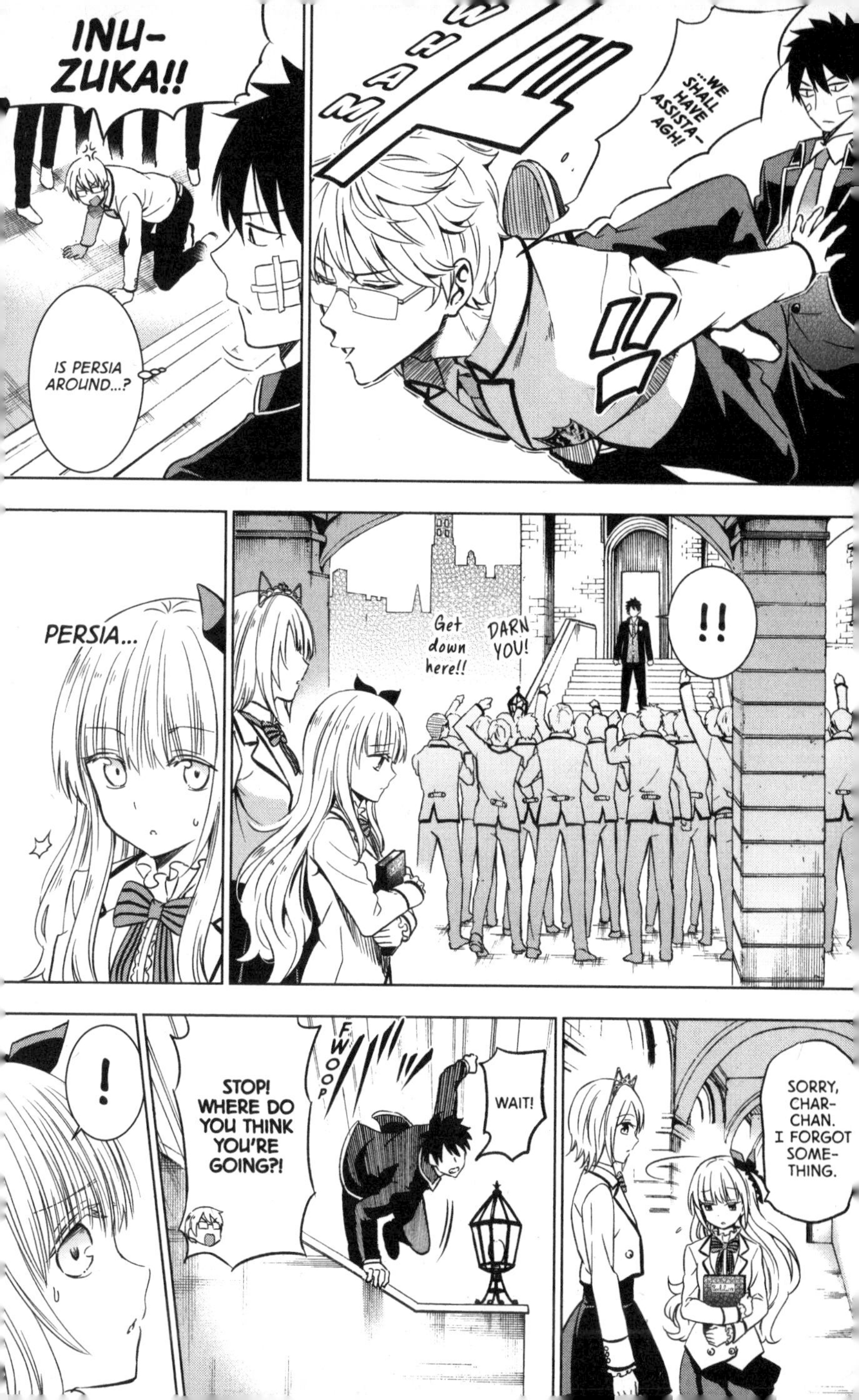
...WE SHALL HAVE ASSISTA— AGH!
WHAM
INU-ZUKA!!
IS PERSIA AROUND...?
!!
DARN YOU!
Get down here!!
PERSIA...
SORRY, CHAR-CHAN. I FORGOT SOME-THING.
WAIT!
FWOOP
STOP! WHERE DO YOU THINK YOU'RE GOING?!
!

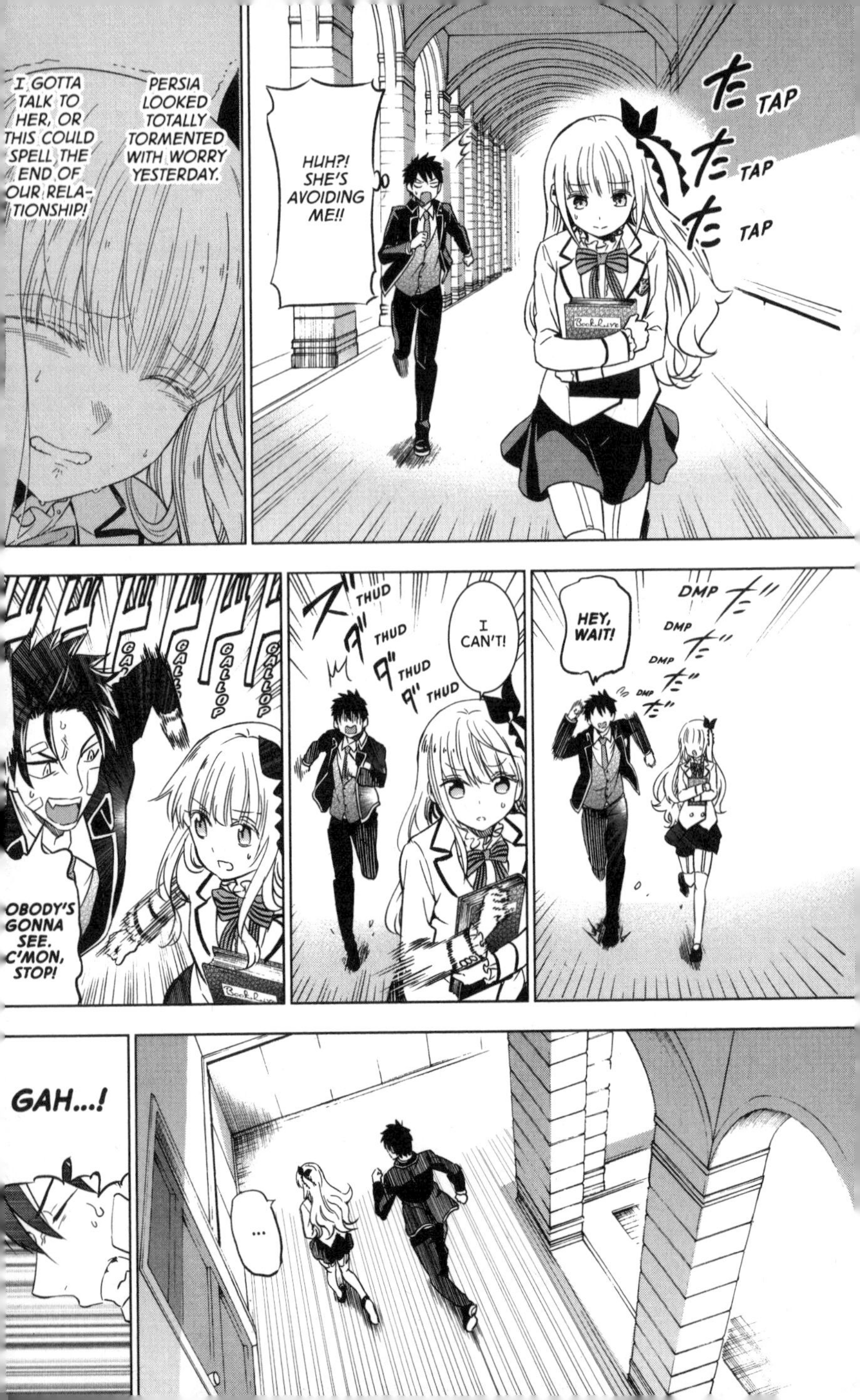
たたた
TAP TAP TAP
HUH?! SHE'S AVOIDING ME!!
PERSIA LOOKED TOTALLY TORMENTED WITH WORRY YESTERDAY.
I GOTTA TALK TO HER, OR THIS COULD SPELL THE END OF OUR RELATIONSHIP!
DMP DMP DMP DMP
HEY, WAIT!
THUD THUD THUD THUD
I CAN'T!
GALLOP GALLOP GALLOP GALLOP
OBODY'S GONNA SEE. C'MON, STOP!
...
GAH...!

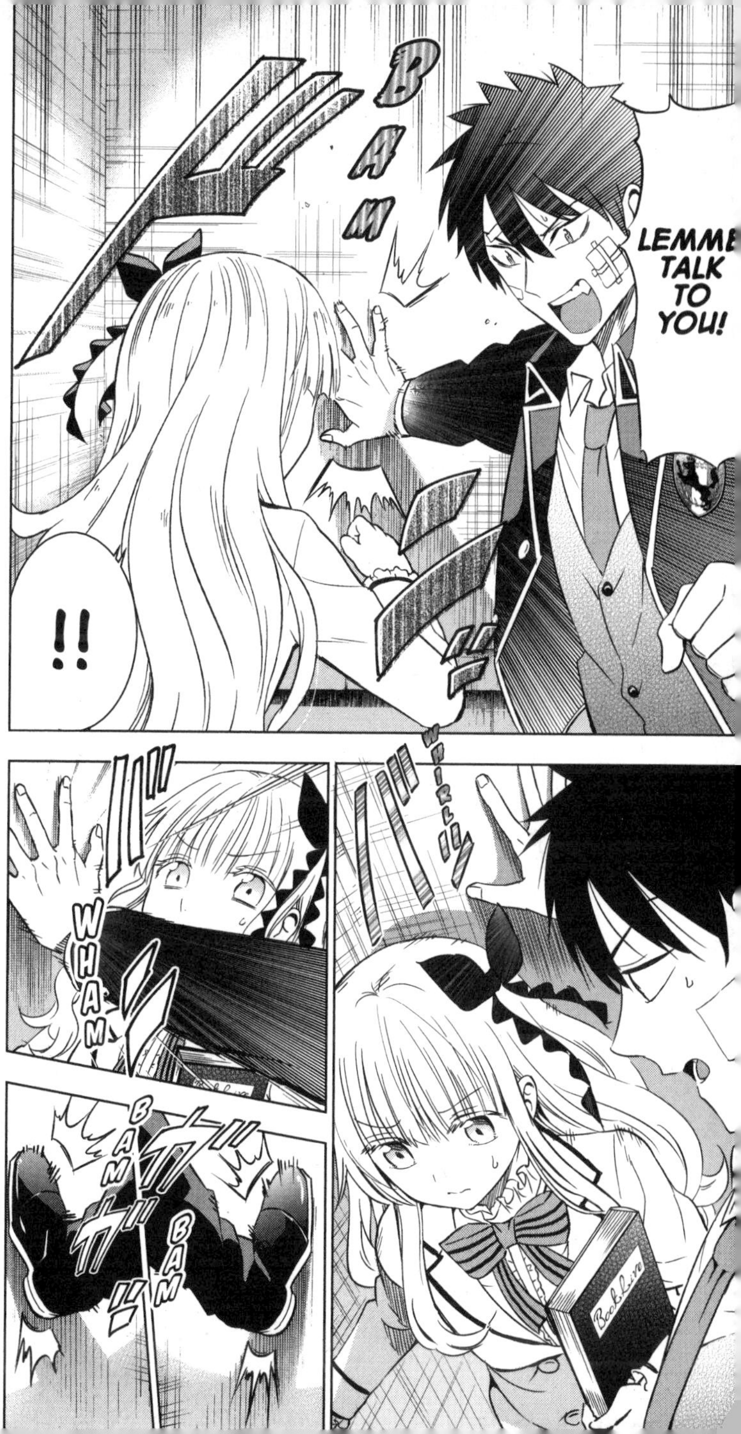
BAM
LEMME TALK TO YOU!
!!
WHIRL
WHAM
BAM
BAM

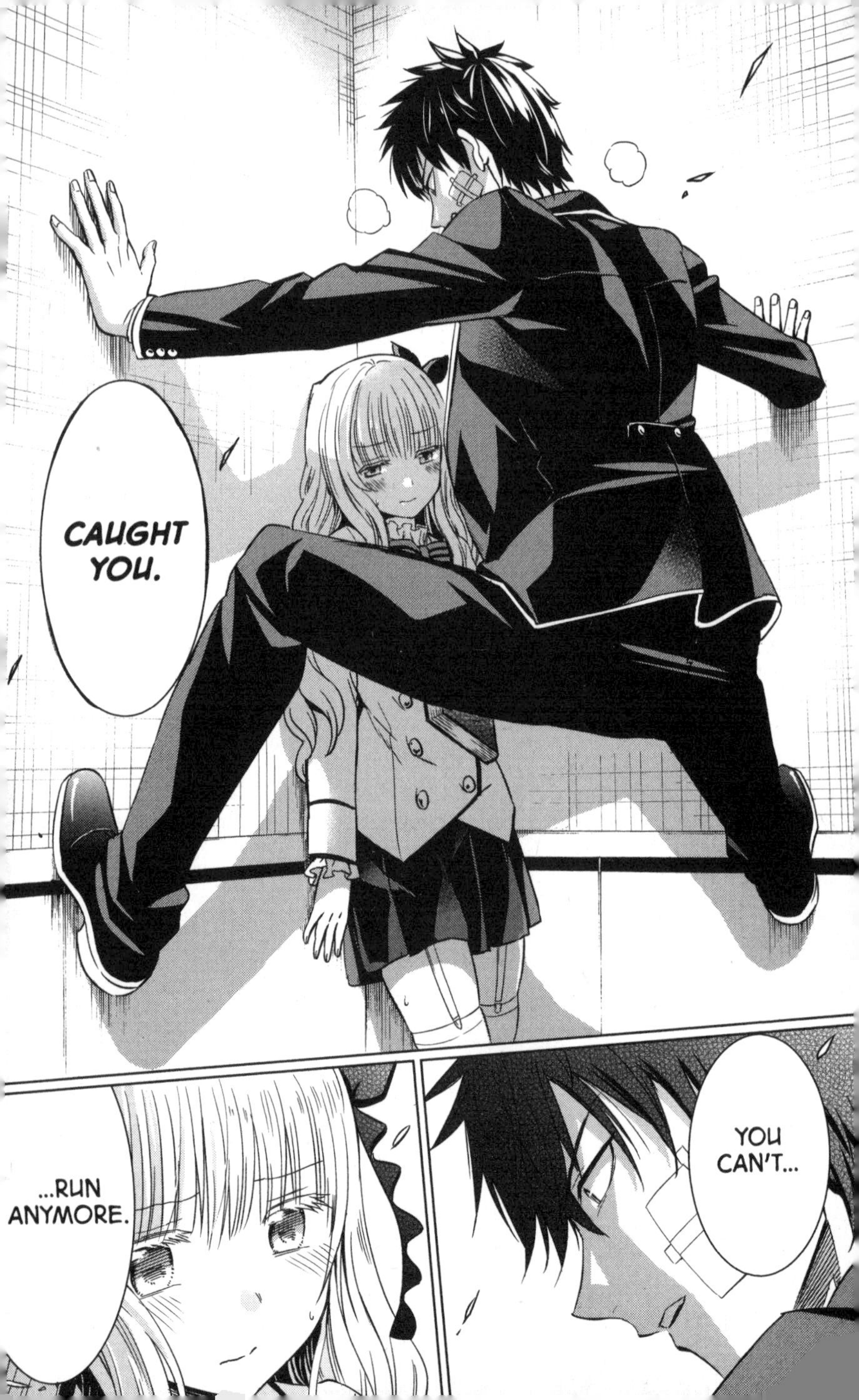
CAUGHT YOU.
YOU CAN'T...
...RUN ANYMORE.

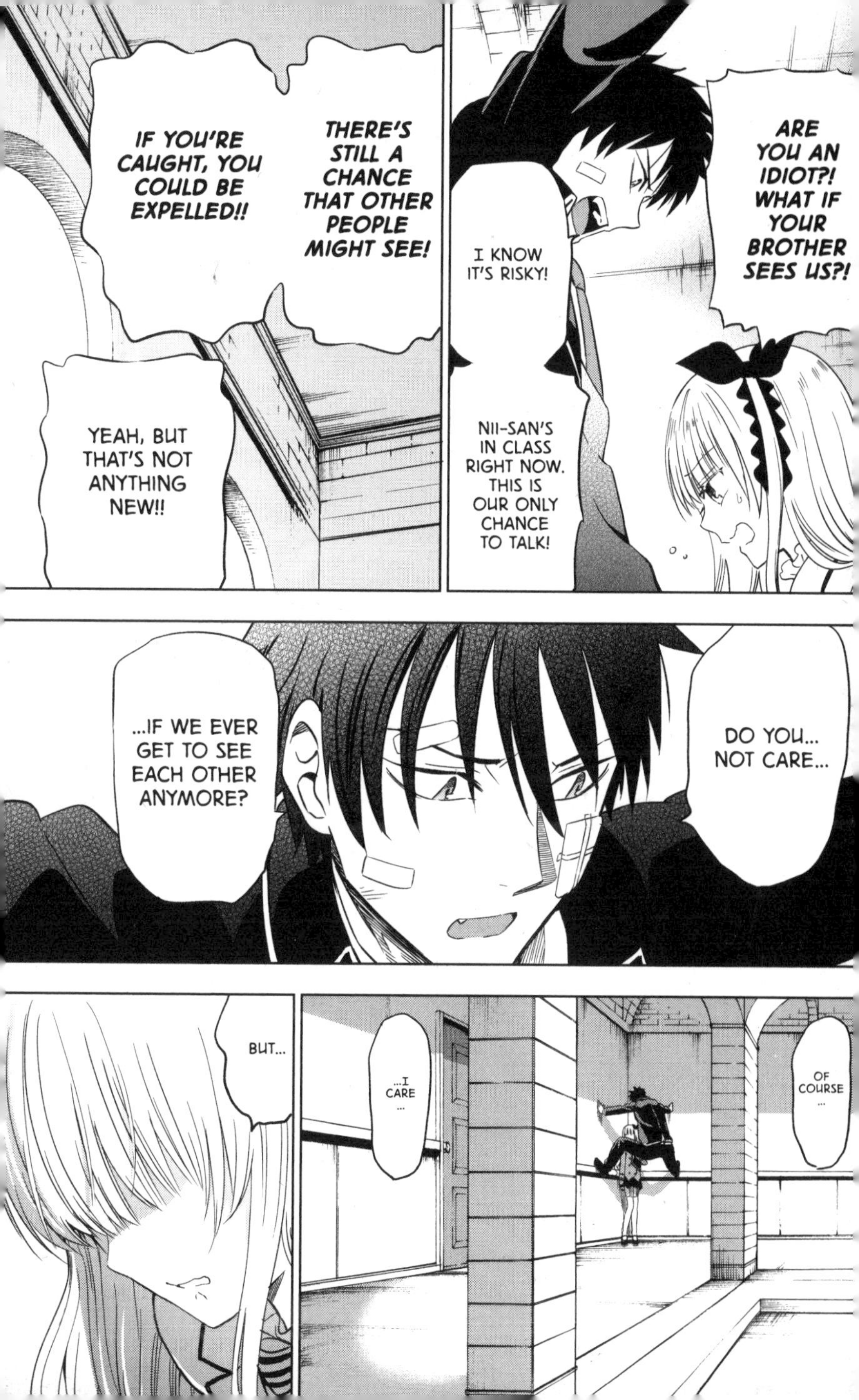
ARE YOU AN IDIOT?! WHAT IF YOUR BROTHER SEES US?!
I KNOW IT'S RISKY!
NII-SAN'S IN CLASS RIGHT NOW. THIS IS OUR ONLY CHANCE TO TALK!
THERE'S STILL A CHANCE THAT OTHER PEOPLE MIGHT SEE!
IF YOU'RE CAUGHT, YOU COULD BE EXPELLED!!
YEAH, BUT THAT'S NOT ANYTHING NEW!!
DO YOU... NOT CARE...
...IF WE EVER GET TO SEE EACH OTHER ANYMORE?
OF COURSE ...
...I CARE ...
BUT...

WHUMP

PUSH

I'M SORRY...

PERSIA ...

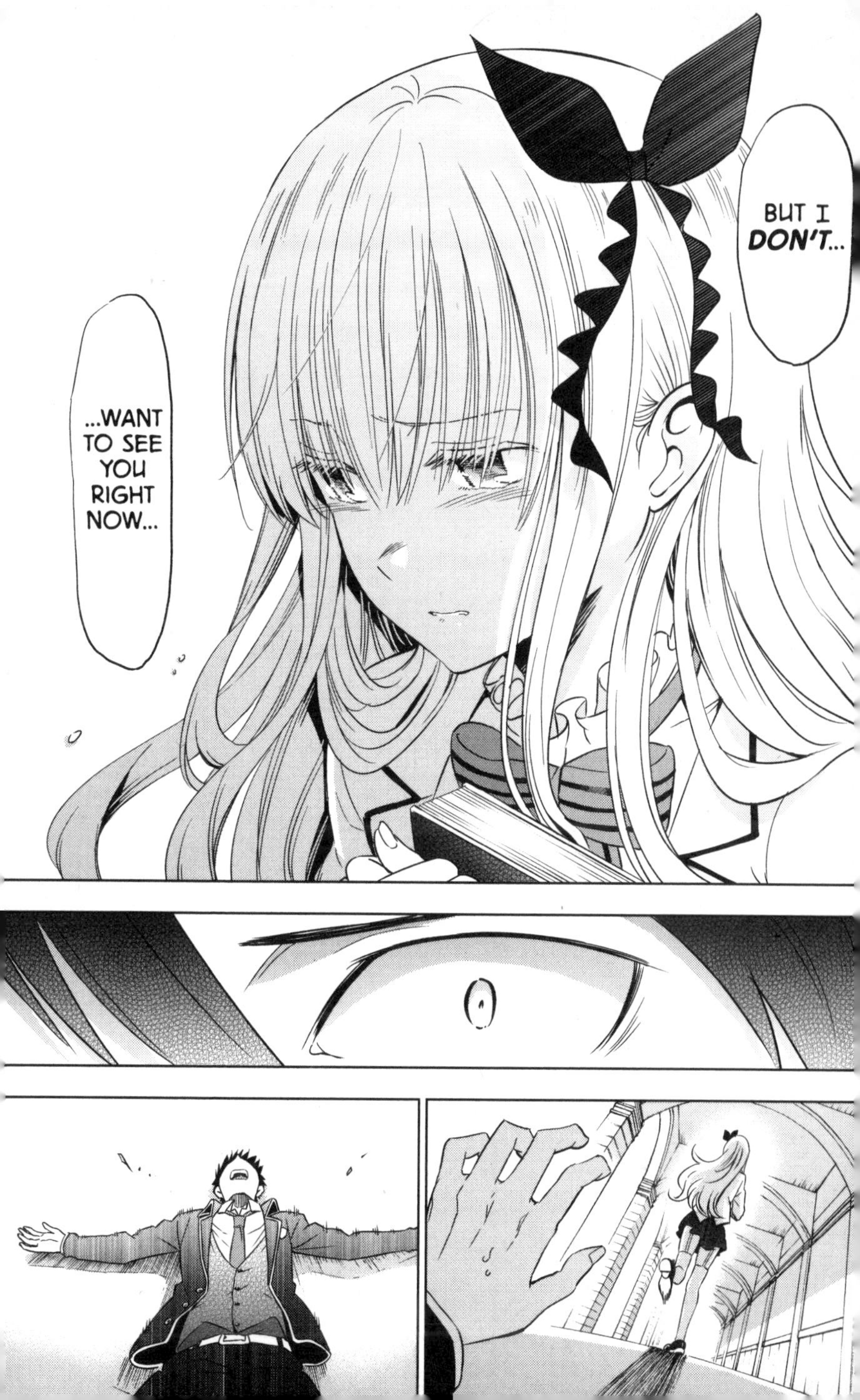
BUT I DON'T...
...WANT TO SEE YOU RIGHT NOW...

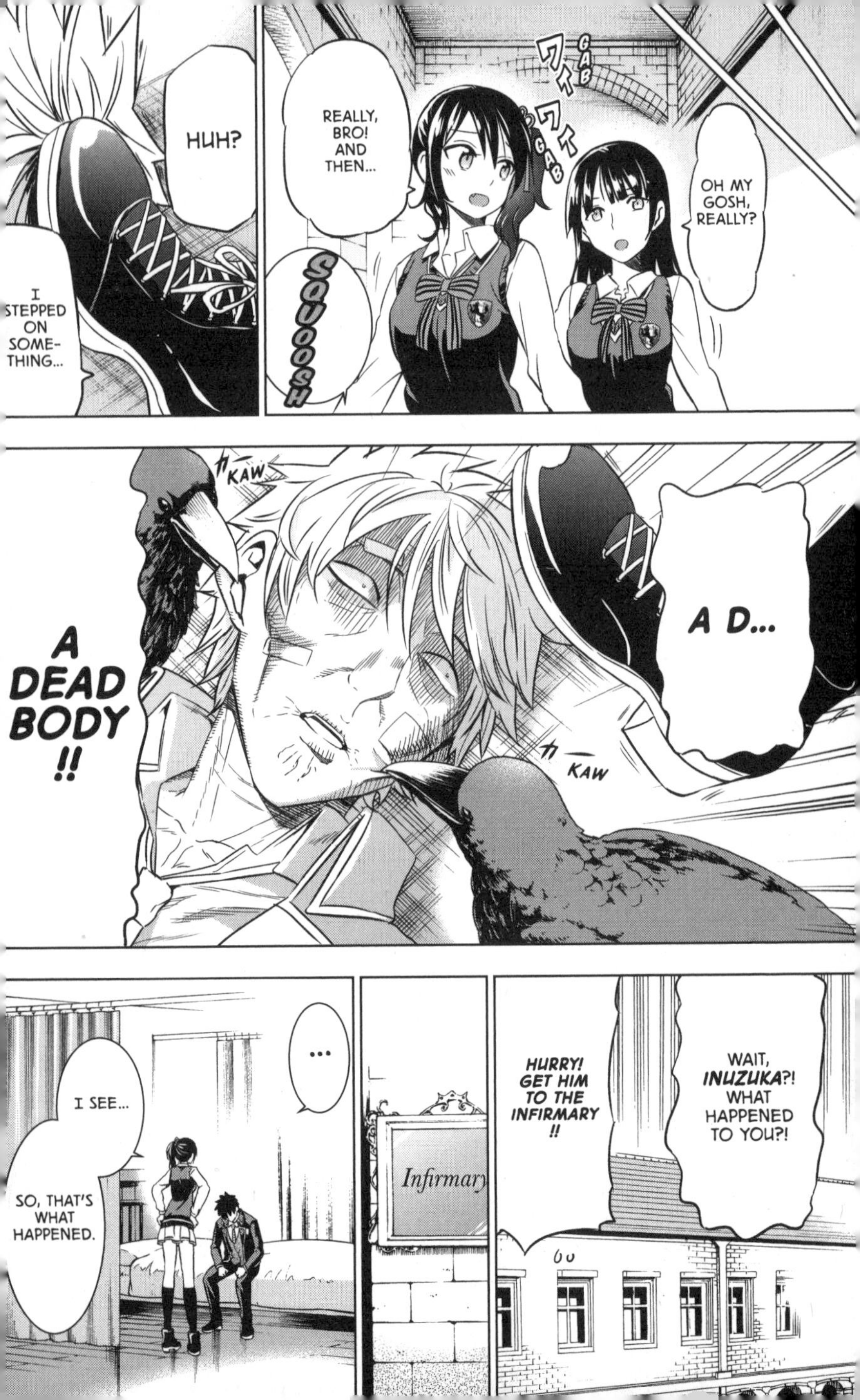
OH MY GOSH, REALLY?
ワイ ワイ
GAB GAB
REALLY, BRO! AND THEN...
SQUOOOSH
HUH?
I STEPPED ON SOME-THING...
A D...
KAW
KAW
A DEAD BODY!!
WAIT, INUZUKA?! WHAT HAPPENED TO YOU?!
HURRY! GET HIM TO THE INFIRMARY!!
Infirmary
...
I SEE...
SO, THAT'S WHAT HAPPENED.

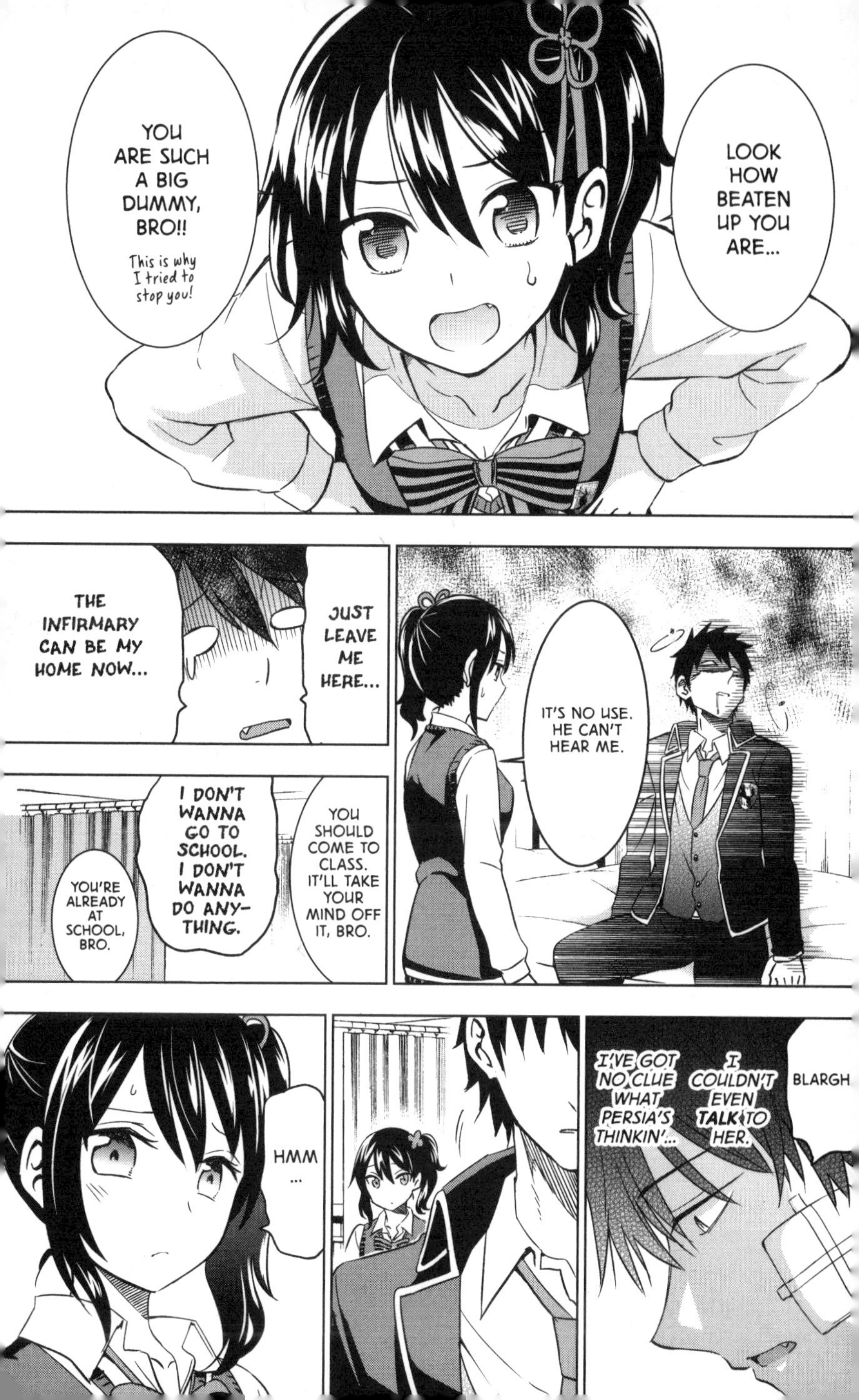
LOOK HOW BEATEN UP YOU ARE...
YOU ARE SUCH A BIG DUMMY, BRO!!
This is why I tried to stop you!
IT'S NO USE. HE CAN'T HEAR ME.
JUST LEAVE ME HERE...
THE INFIRMARY CAN BE MY HOME NOW...
YOU SHOULD COME TO CLASS. IT'LL TAKE YOUR MIND OFF IT, BRO.
I DON'T WANNA GO TO SCHOOL. I DON'T WANNA DO ANY-THING.
YOU'RE ALREADY AT SCHOOL, BRO.
BLARGH
I COULDN'T EVEN TALK TO HER.
I'VE GOT NO CLUE WHAT PERSIA'S THINKIN'...
HMM ...

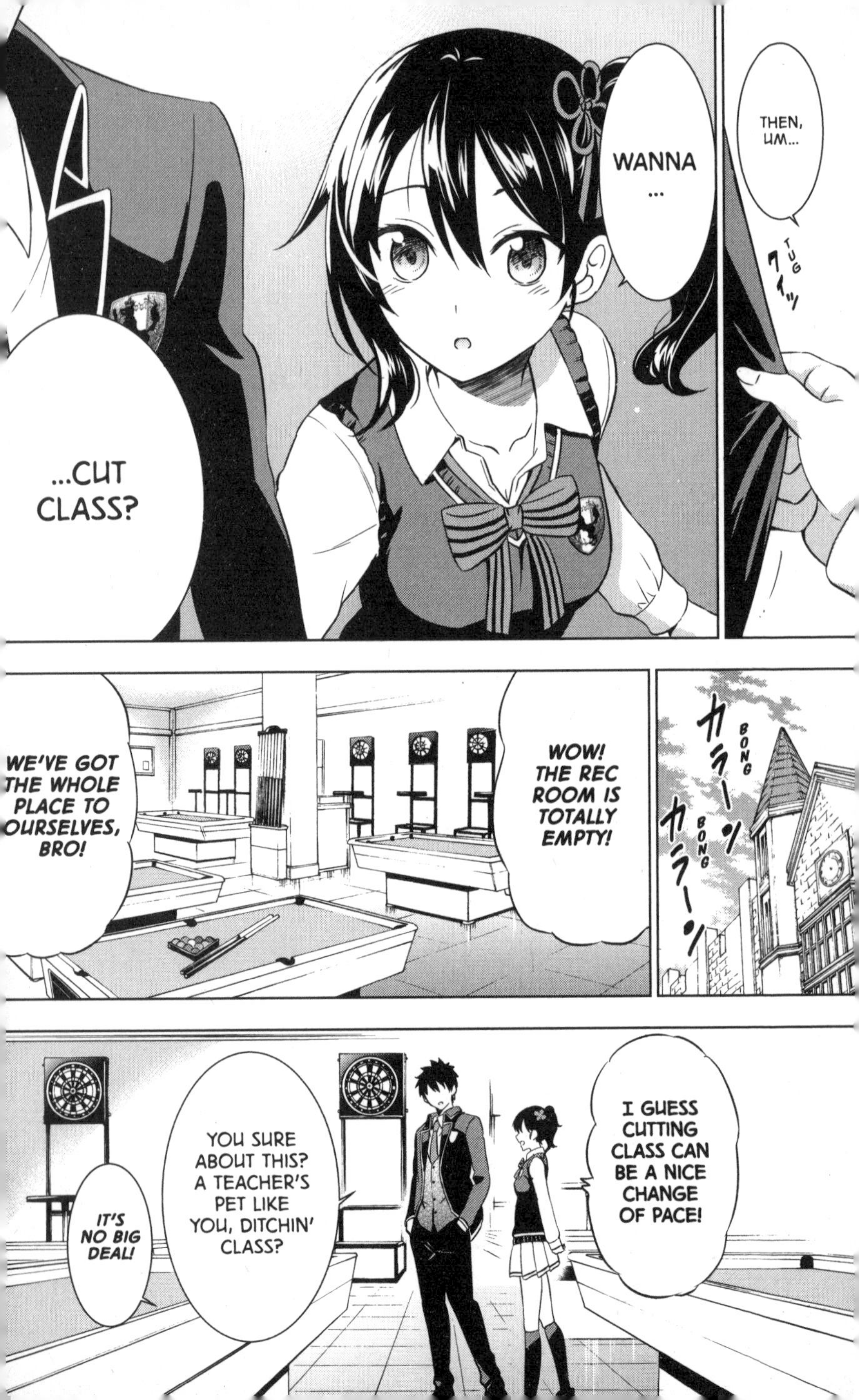
THEN, UM...
クイッ
TUG
WANNA ...
...CUT CLASS?
カラーン
BONG
カラーン
BONG
WOW! THE REC ROOM IS TOTALLY EMPTY!
WE'VE GOT THE WHOLE PLACE TO OURSELVES, BRO!
I GUESS CUTTING CLASS CAN BE A NICE CHANGE OF PACE!
YOU SURE ABOUT THIS? A TEACHER'S PET LIKE YOU, DITCHIN' CLASS?
IT'S NO BIG DEAL!

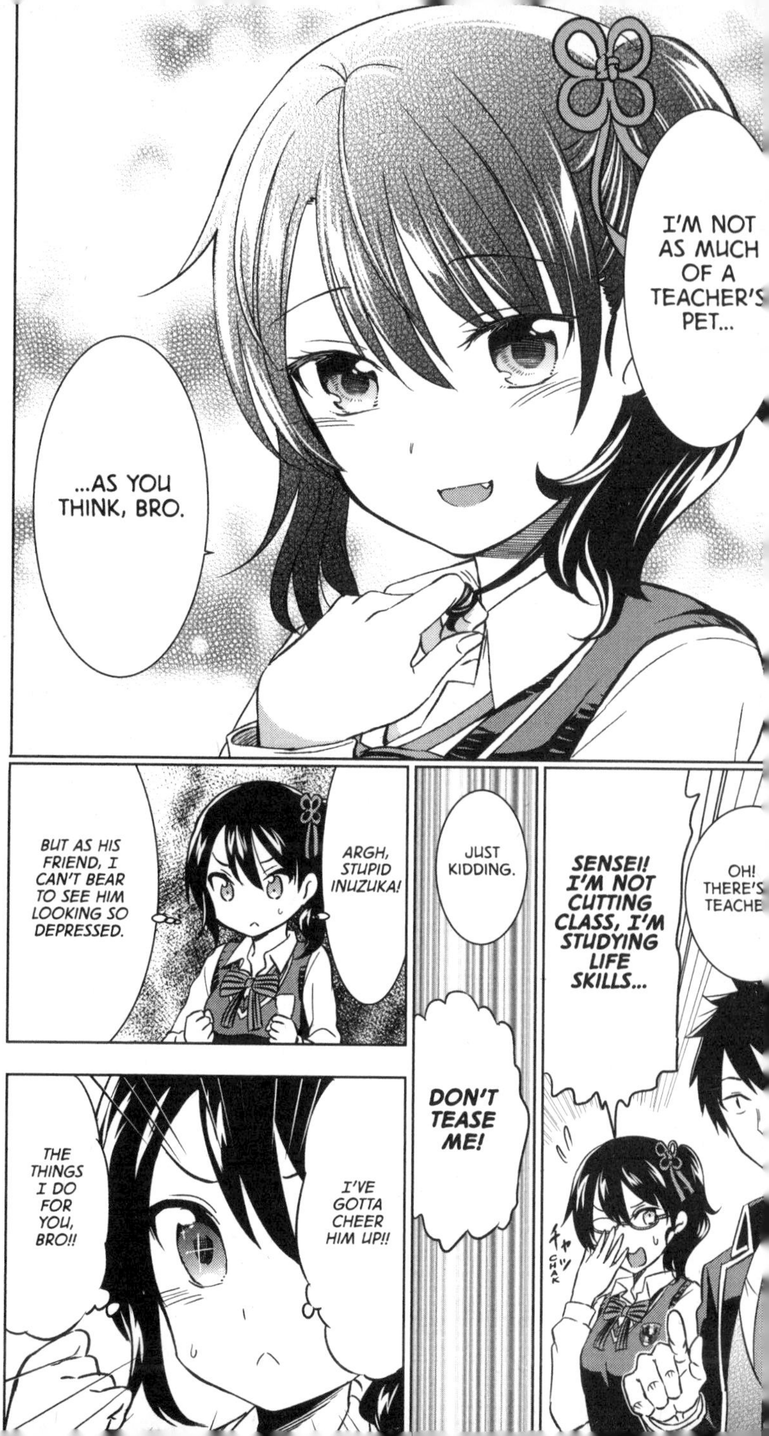
I'M NOT AS MUCH OF A TEACHER'S PET...
...AS YOU THINK, BRO.
OH! THERE'S TEACHE
SENSEI! I'M NOT CUTTING CLASS, I'M STUDYING LIFE SKILLS...
CHAK
JUST KIDDING.
DON'T TEASE ME!
ARGH, STUPID INUZUKA!
BUT AS HIS FRIEND, I CAN'T BEAR TO SEE HIM LOOKING SO DEPRESSED.
I'VE GOTTA CHEER HIM UP!!
THE THINGS I DO FOR YOU, BRO!!

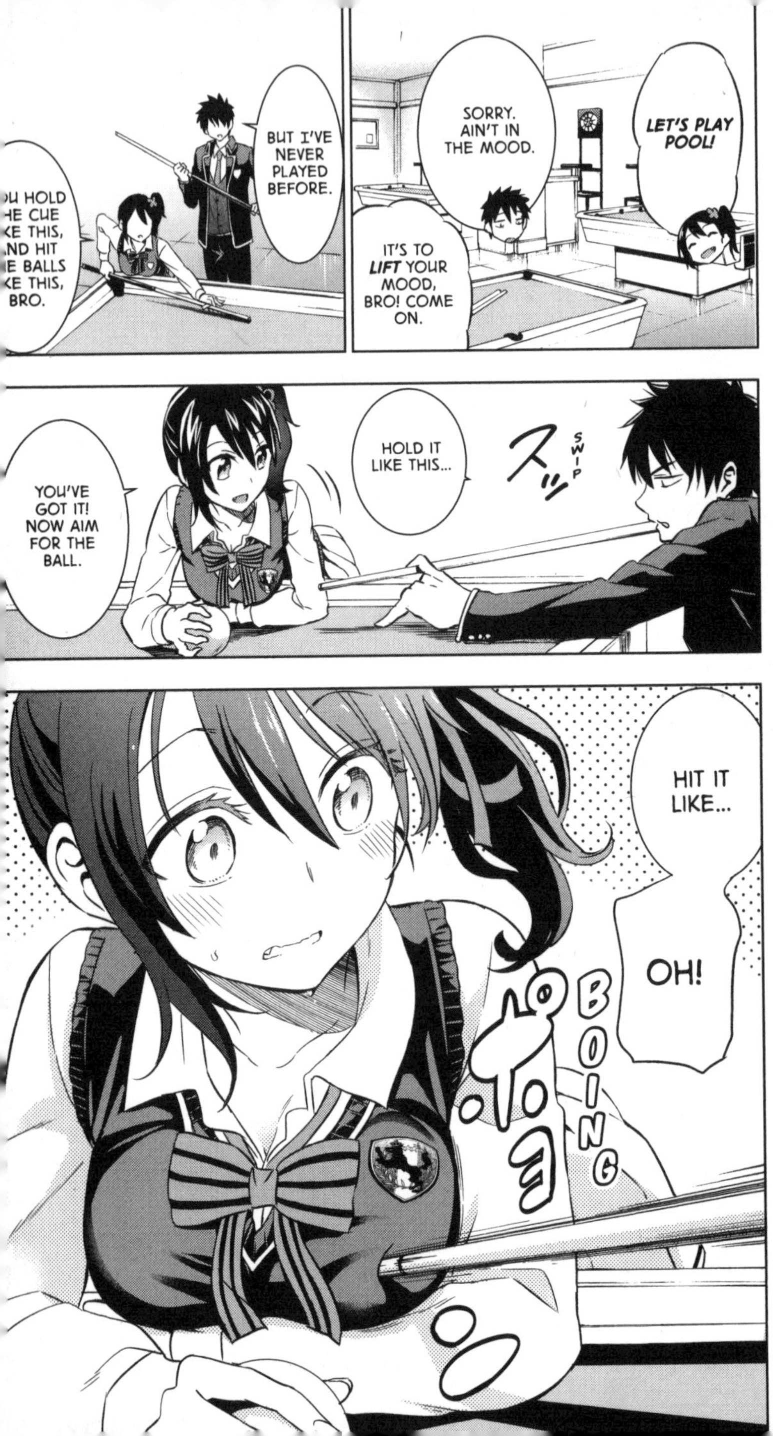
LET'S PLAY POOL!
SORRY. AIN'T IN THE MOOD.
IT'S TO LIFT YOUR MOOD, BRO! COME ON.
BUT I'VE NEVER PLAYED BEFORE.
OU HOLD HE CUE KE THIS, ND HIT E BALLS KE THIS, BRO.
SWIP
HOLD IT LIKE THIS...
YOU'VE GOT IT! NOW AIM FOR THE BALL.
HIT IT LIKE...
OH!
BOING

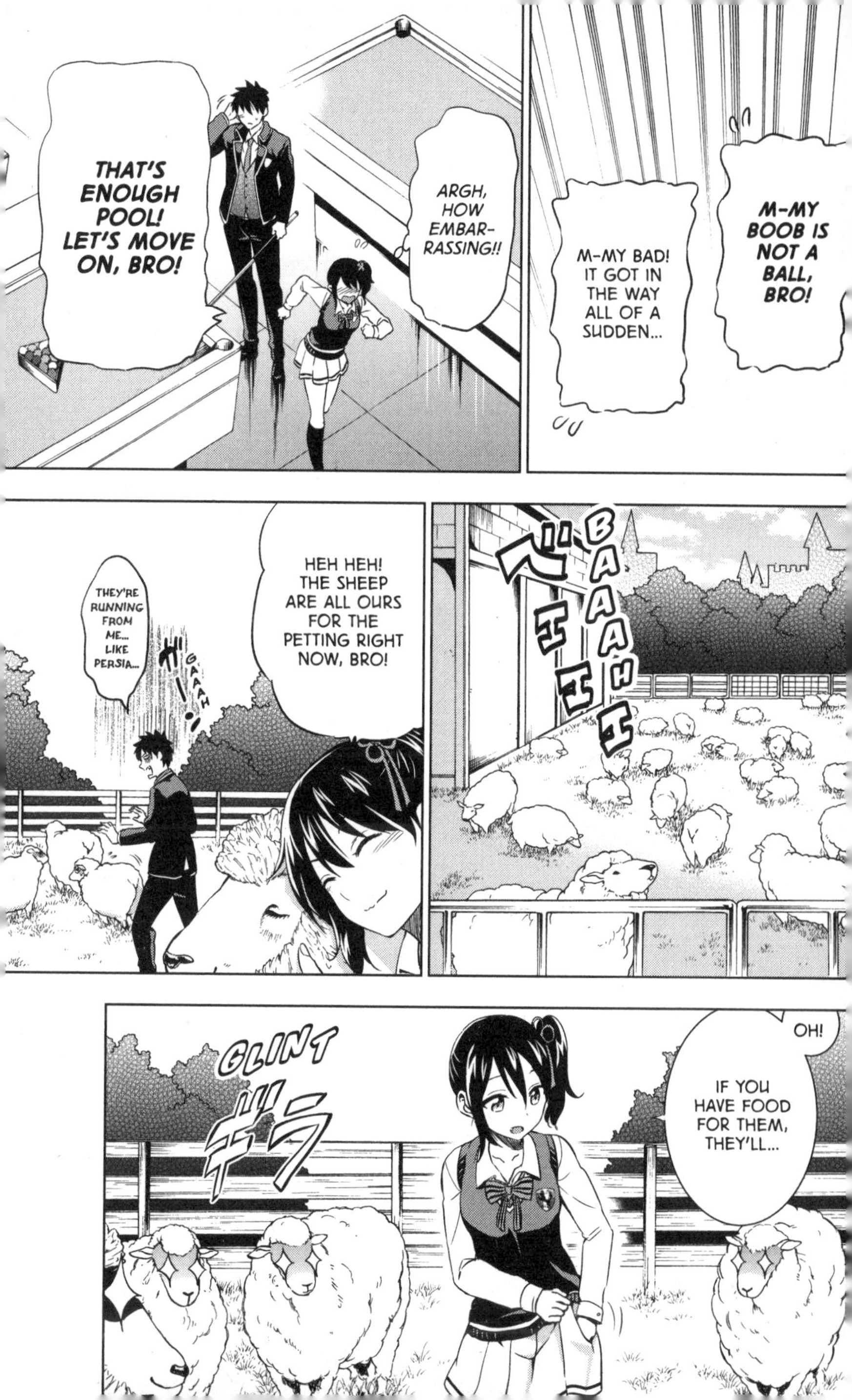
M-MY BOOB IS NOT A BALL, BRO!
M-MY BAD! IT GOT IN THE WAY ALL OF A SUDDEN...
ARGH, HOW EMBARRASSING!!
THAT'S ENOUGH POOL! LET'S MOVE ON, BRO!
BAAAAH
ベエエエ
HEH HEH! THE SHEEP ARE ALL OURS FOR THE PETTING RIGHT NOW, BRO!
THEY'RE RUNNING FROM ME... LIKE PERSIA...
GAAAH
ガー
OH!
IF YOU HAVE FOOD FOR THEM, THEY'LL...
GLINT
ギラ

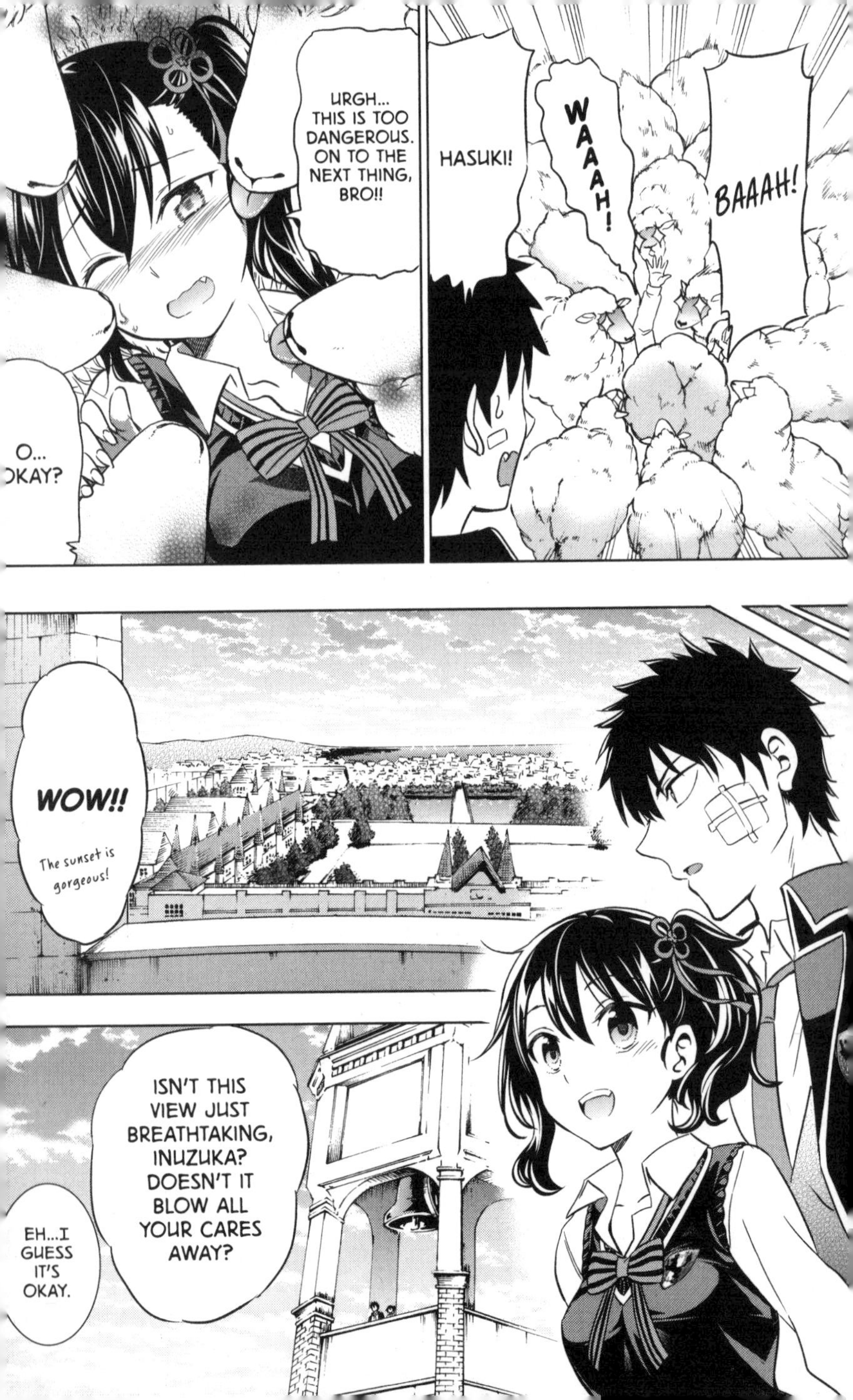
BAAAH!
WAAAAH!
HASUKI!
URGH... THIS IS TOO DANGEROUS. ON TO THE NEXT THING, BRO!!
O... OKAY?
WOW!!
The sunset is gorgeous!
ISN'T THIS VIEW JUST BREATHTAKING, INUZUKA? DOESN'T IT BLOW ALL YOUR CARES AWAY?
EH...I GUESS IT'S OKAY.

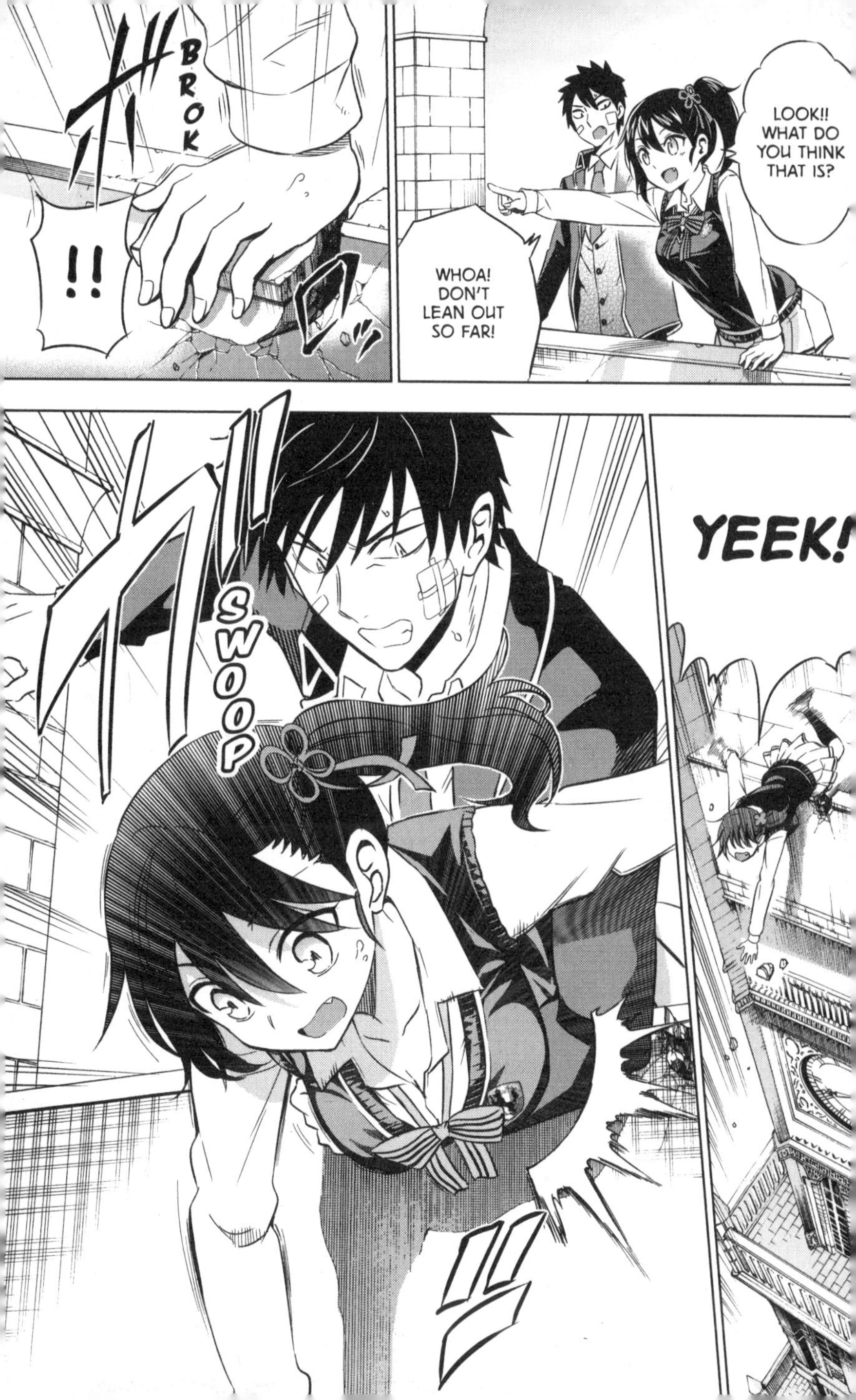
LOOK!! WHAT DO YOU THINK THAT IS?
WHOA! DON'T LEAN OUT SO FAR!
BROK
!!
YEEK!
SWOOP

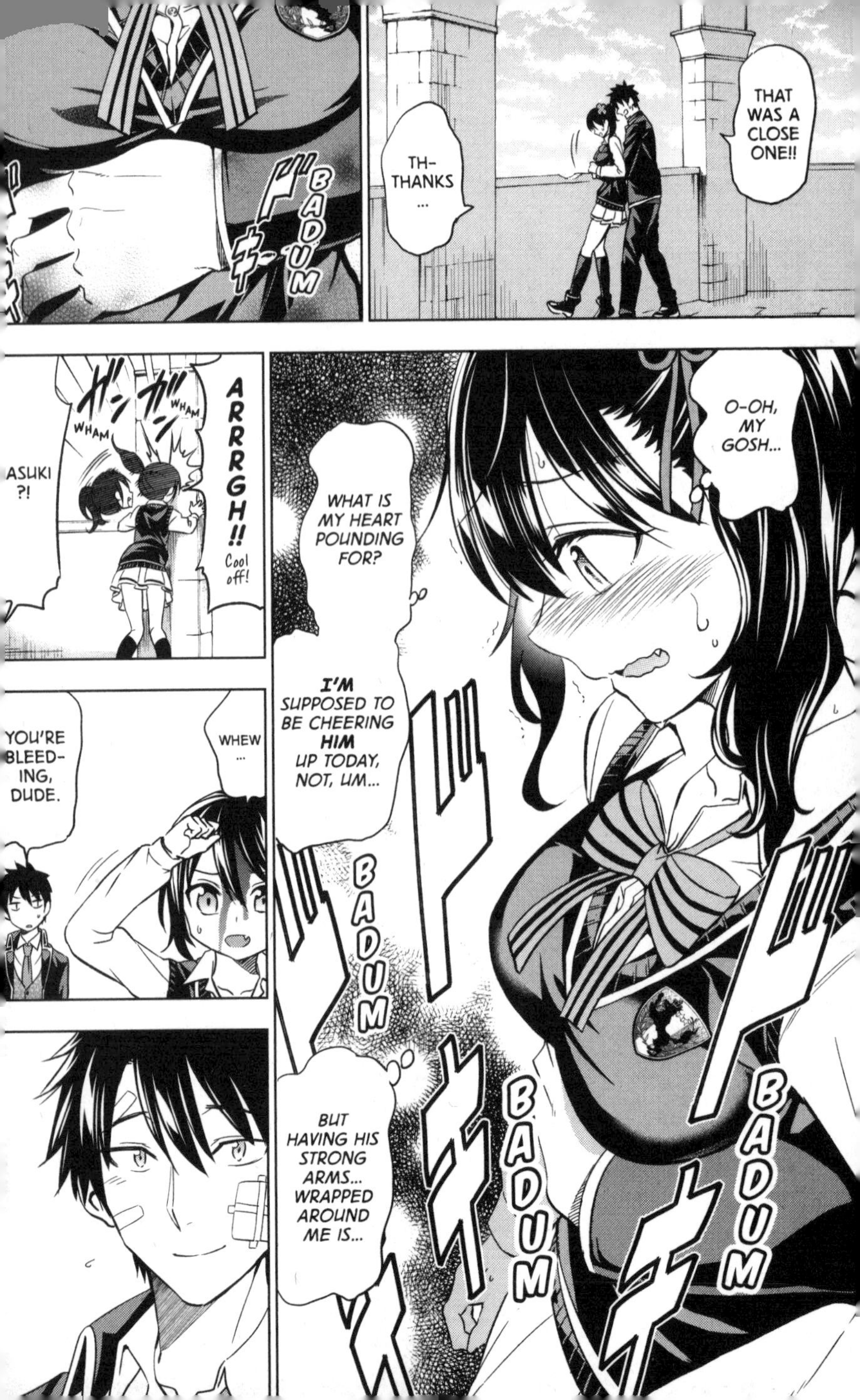

THAT WAS A CLOSE ONE!!
TH-THANKS...
BADUM
O-OH, MY GOSH...
WHAT IS MY HEART POUNDING FOR?
I'M SUPPOSED TO BE CHEERING HIM UP TODAY, NOT, UM...
BADUM
BUT HAVING HIS STRONG ARMS... WRAPPED AROUND ME IS...
BADUM
BADUM
ARRRGH!!
WHAM
WHAM
Cool off!
ASUKI?!
WHEW...
YOU'RE BLEEDING, DUDE.

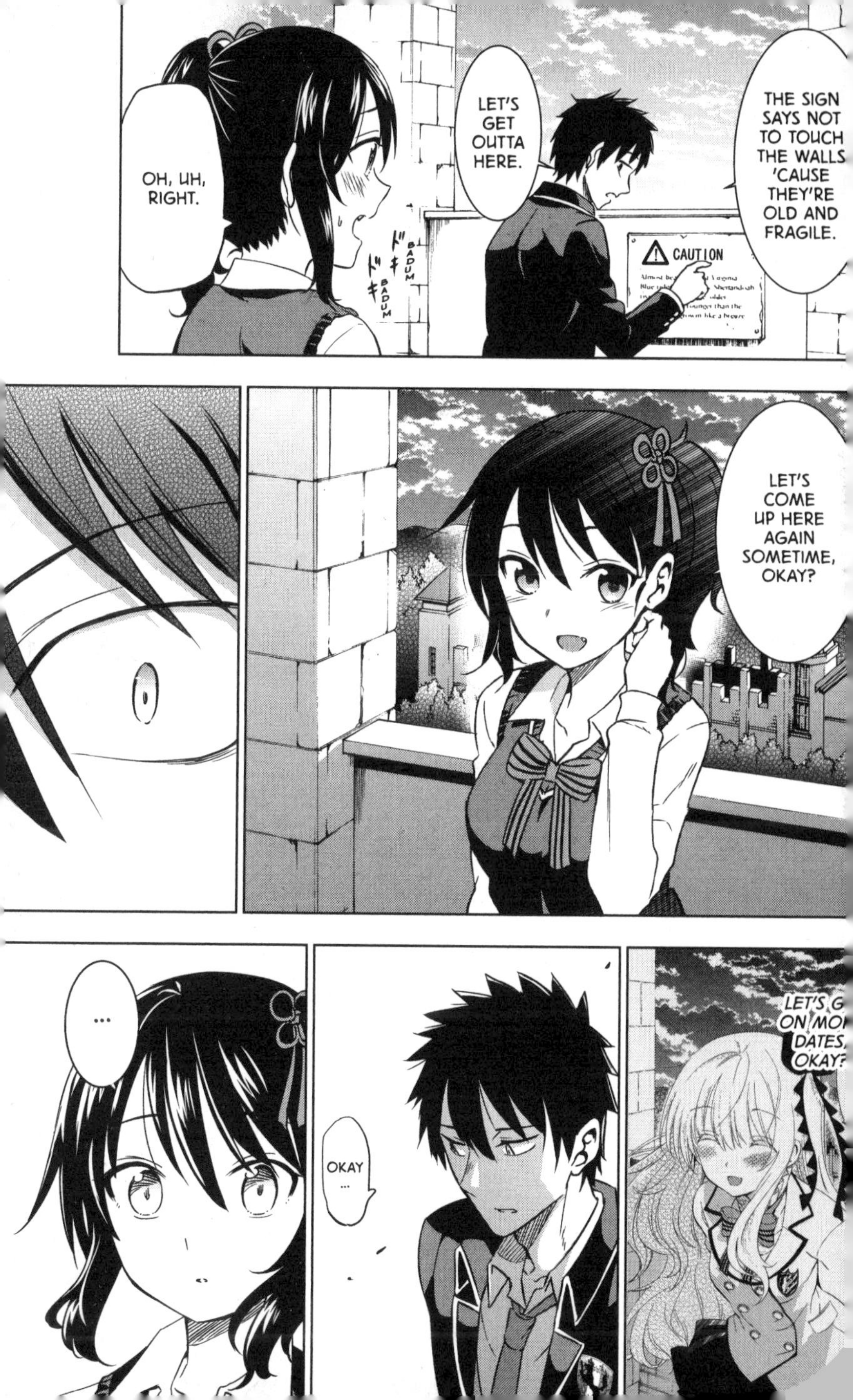
THE SIGN SAYS NOT TO TOUCH THE WALLS 'CAUSE THEY'RE OLD AND FRAGILE.
CAUTION
LET'S GET OUTTA HERE.
ドキ BADUM
ドキ BADUM
OH, UH, RIGHT.
LET'S COME UP HERE AGAIN SOMETIME, OKAY?
LET'S G ON MO DATES, OKAY?
OKAY ...
...

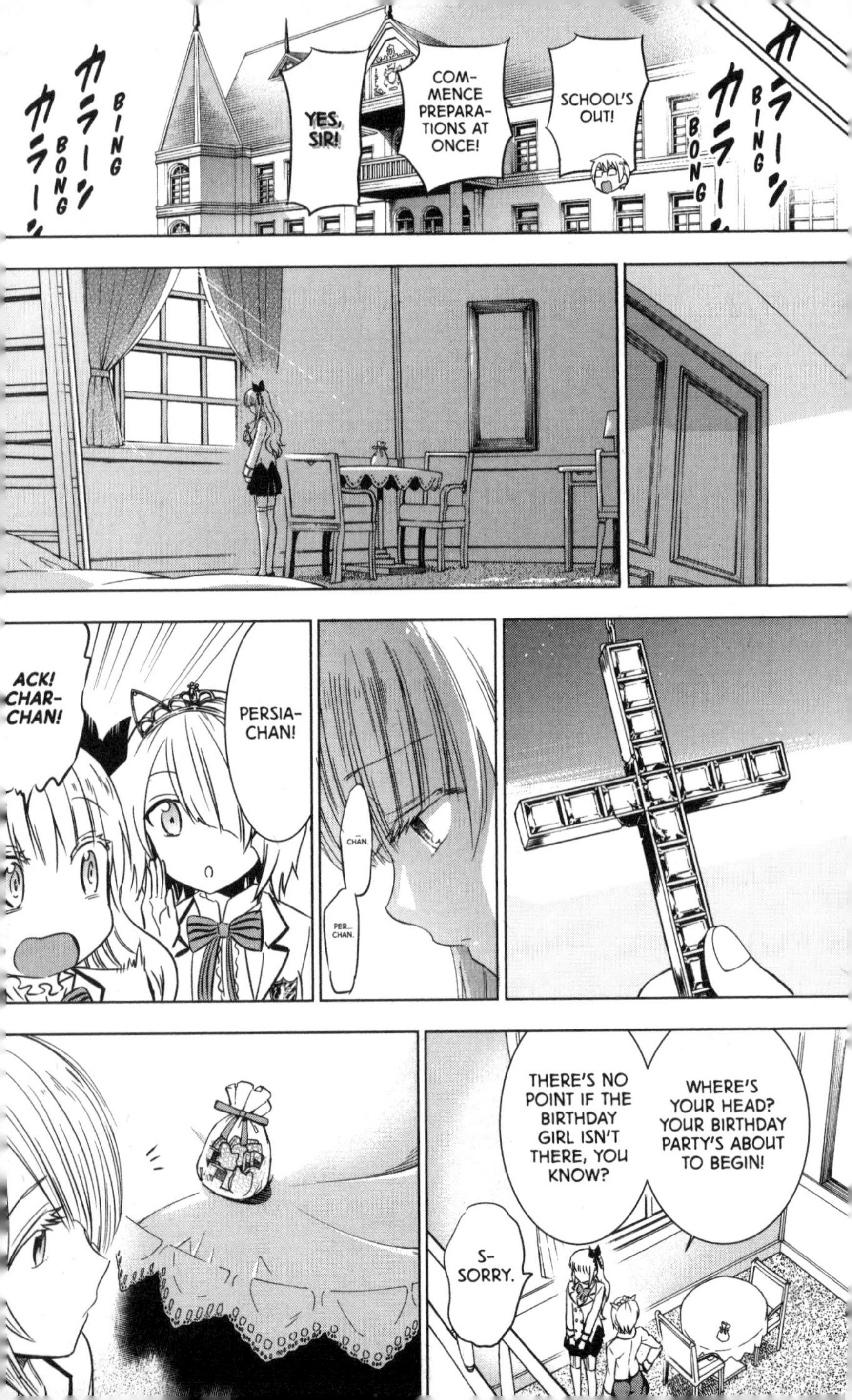
BING BONG
SCHOOL'S OUT!
COMMENCE PREPARATIONS AT ONCE!
YES, SIR!
BING BONG
...CHAN.
PER... CHAN.
PERSIA-CHAN!
ACK! CHAR-CHAN!
WHERE'S YOUR HEAD? YOUR BIRTHDAY PARTY'S ABOUT TO BEGIN!
THERE'S NO POINT IF THE BIRTHDAY GIRL ISN'T THERE, YOU KNOW?
S-SORRY.

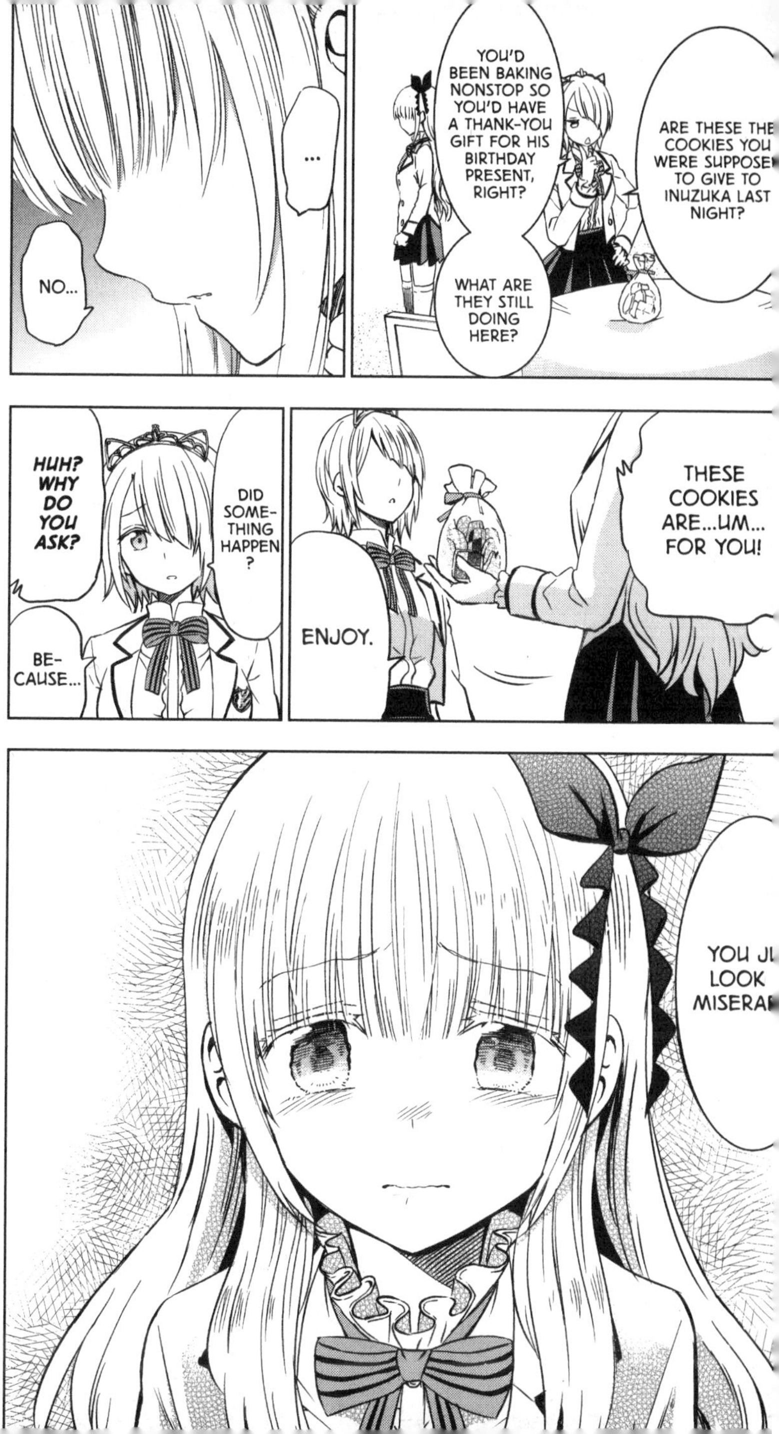
ARE THESE THE COOKIES YOU WERE SUPPOSE TO GIVE TO INUZUKA LAST NIGHT?
YOU'D BEEN BAKING NONSTOP SO YOU'D HAVE A THANK-YOU GIFT FOR HIS BIRTHDAY PRESENT, RIGHT?
WHAT ARE THEY STILL DOING HERE?
...
NO...
THESE COOKIES ARE...UM... FOR YOU!
ENJOY.
DID SOME-THING HAPPEN?
HUH? WHY DO YOU ASK?
BE-CAUSE...
YOU JU LOOK MISERA

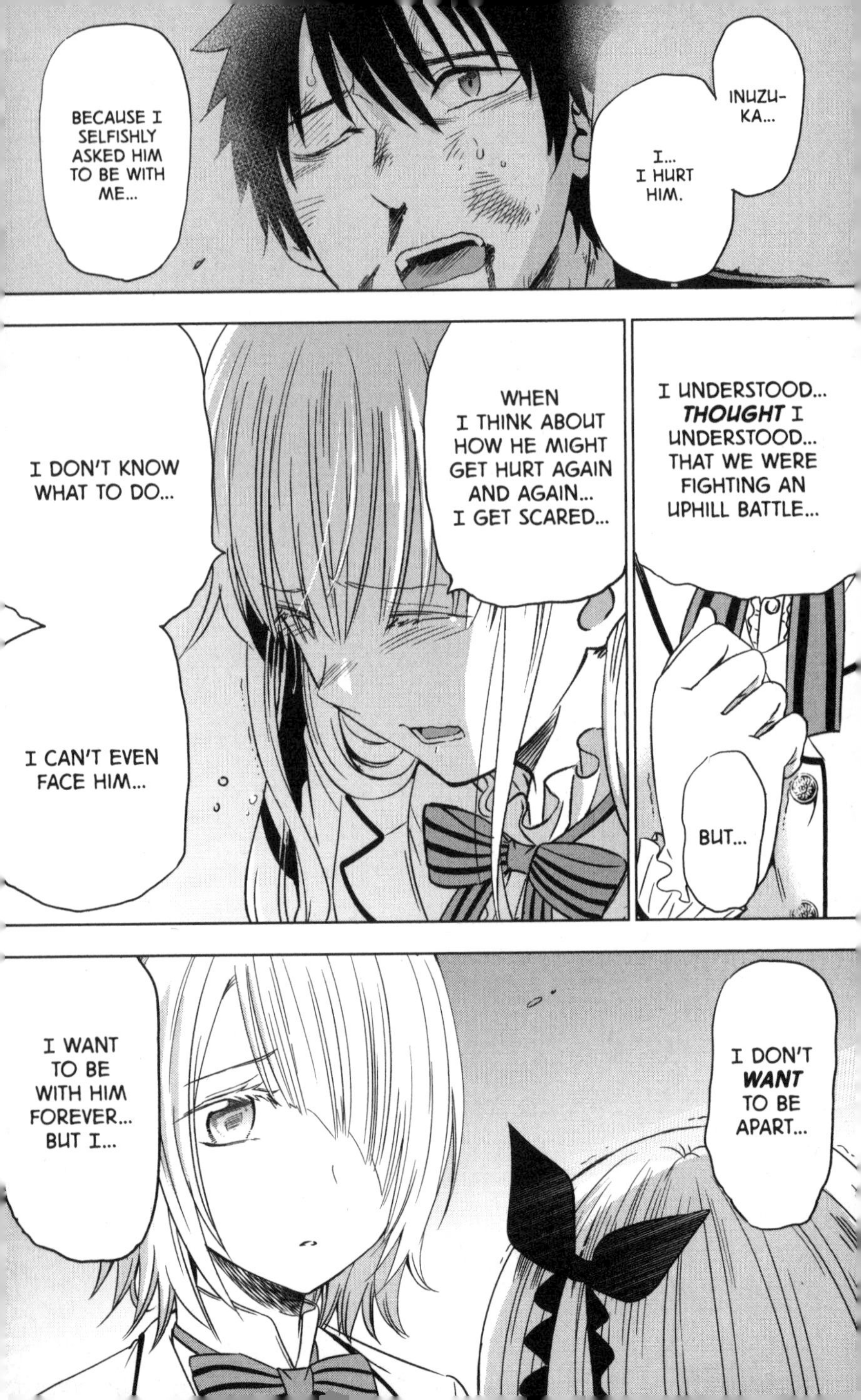
INUZUKA...
I... I HURT HIM.
BECAUSE I SELFISHLY ASKED HIM TO BE WITH ME...
I UNDERSTOOD... *THOUGHT* I UNDERSTOOD... THAT WE WERE FIGHTING AN UPHILL BATTLE...
BUT...
WHEN I THINK ABOUT HOW HE MIGHT GET HURT AGAIN AND AGAIN... I GET SCARED...
I DON'T KNOW WHAT TO DO...
I CAN'T EVEN FACE HIM...
I DON'T *WANT* TO BE APART...
I WANT TO BE WITH HIM FOREVER... BUT I...

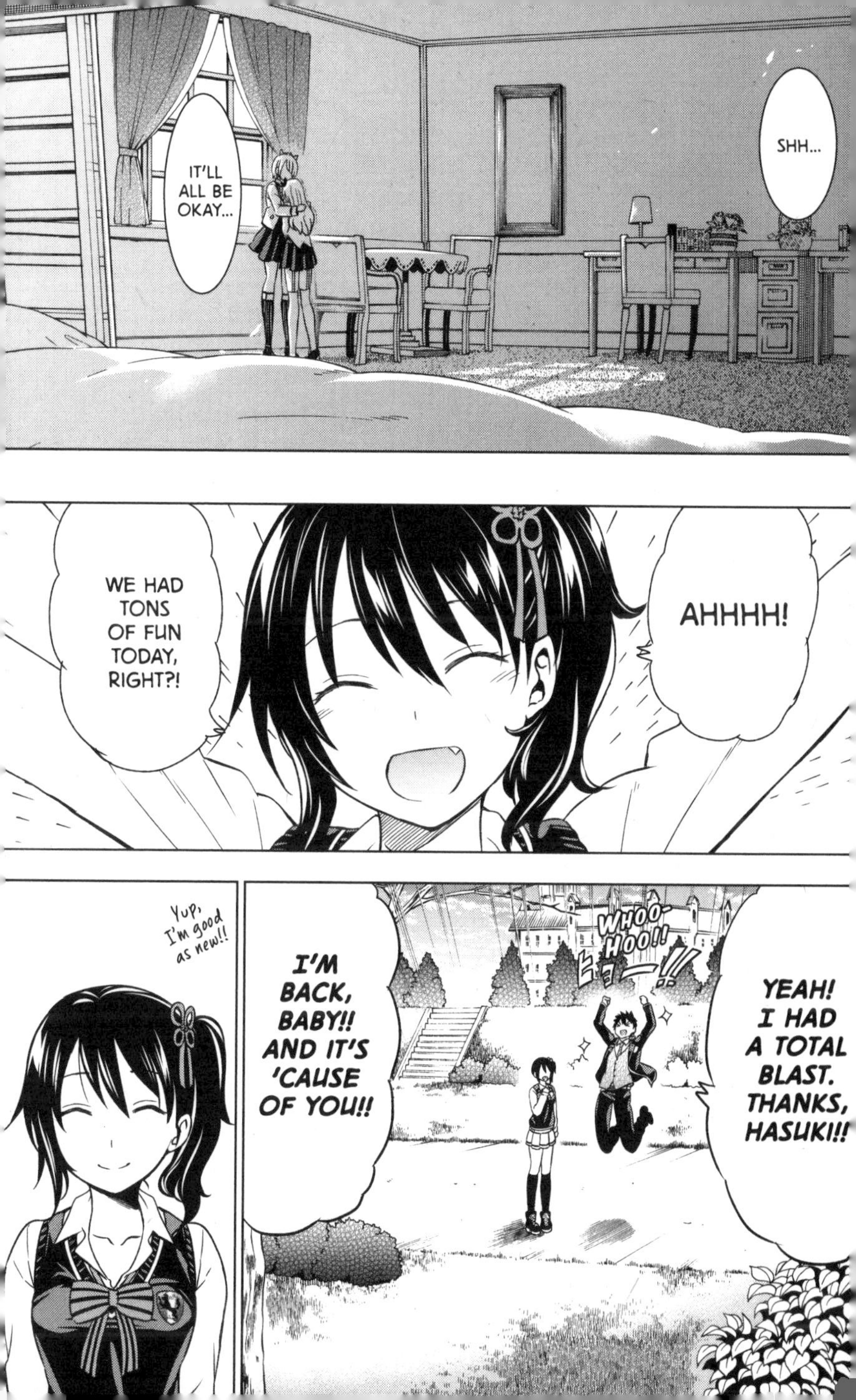
SHH...
IT'LL ALL BE OKAY...
AHHHH!
WE HAD TONS OF FUN TODAY, RIGHT?!
YEAH! I HAD A TOTAL BLAST. THANKS, HASUKI!!!
WHOO-HOO!!
ヒョー!!
I'M BACK, BABY!! AND IT'S 'CAUSE OF YOU!!
Yup, I'm good as new!!

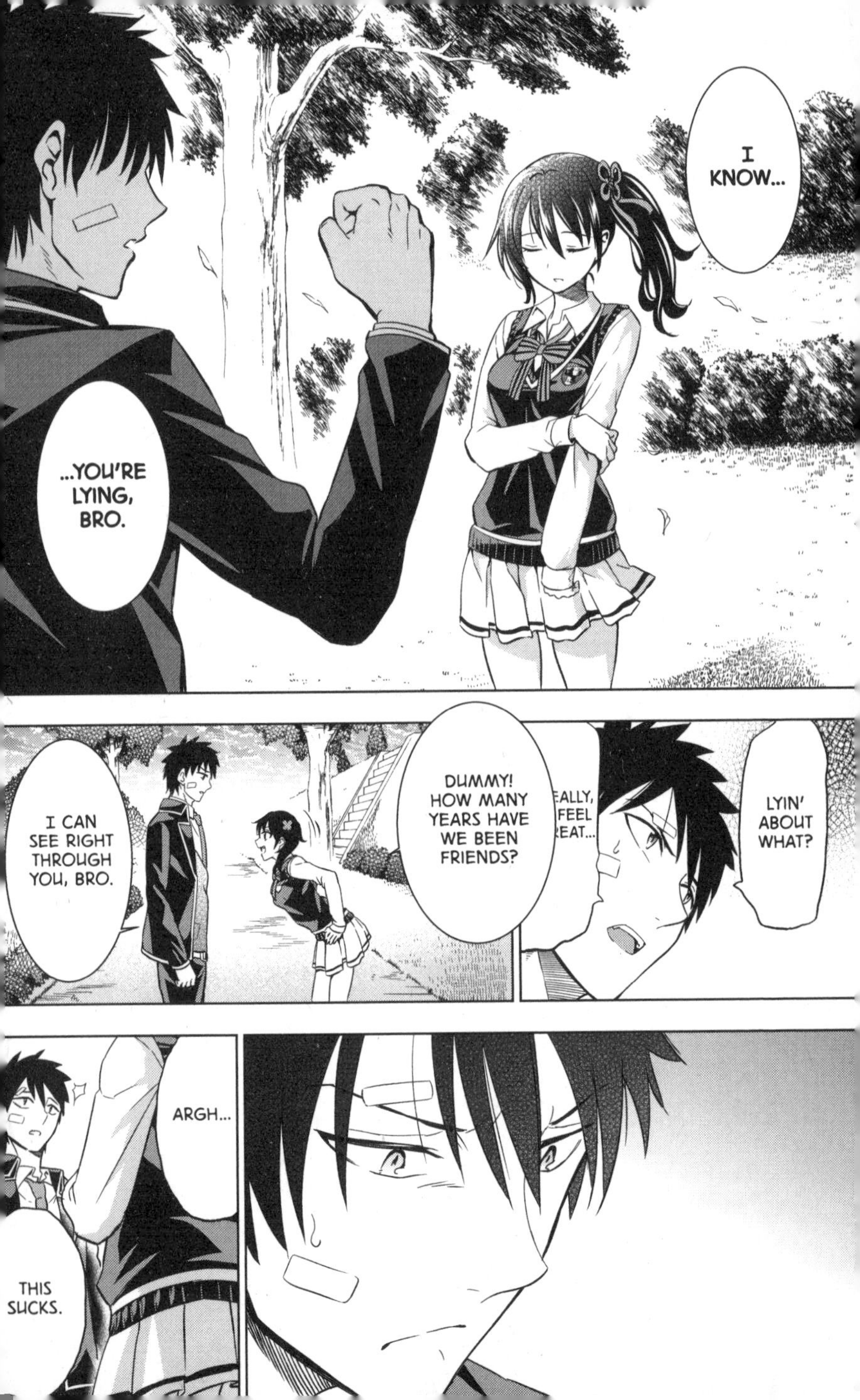
I KNOW...
...YOU'RE LYING, BRO.
LYIN' ABOUT WHAT?
DUMMY! HOW MANY YEARS HAVE WE BEEN FRIENDS?
I CAN SEE RIGHT THROUGH YOU, BRO.
ARGH...
THIS SUCKS.

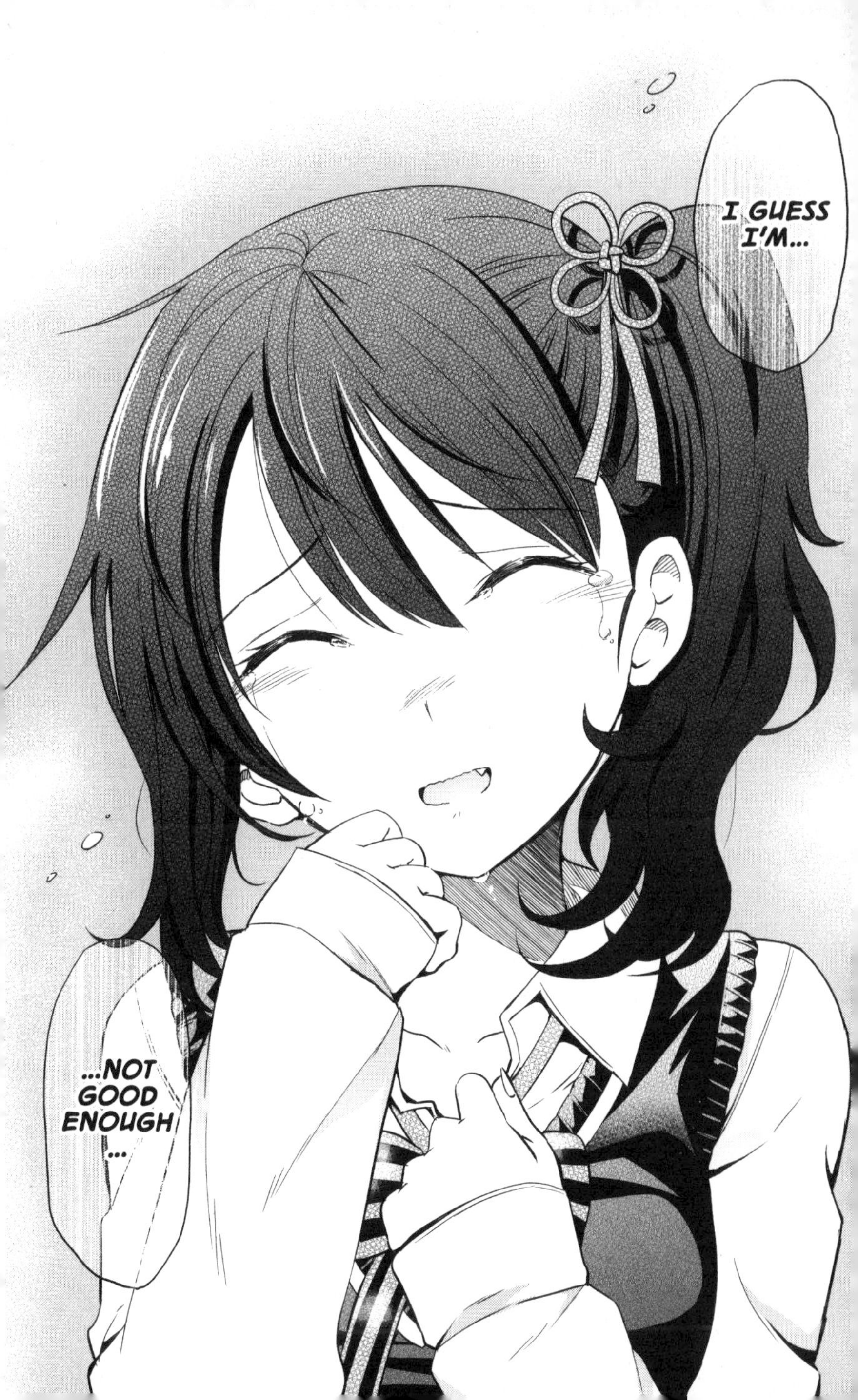
I GUESS I'M...
...NOT GOOD ENOUGH ...

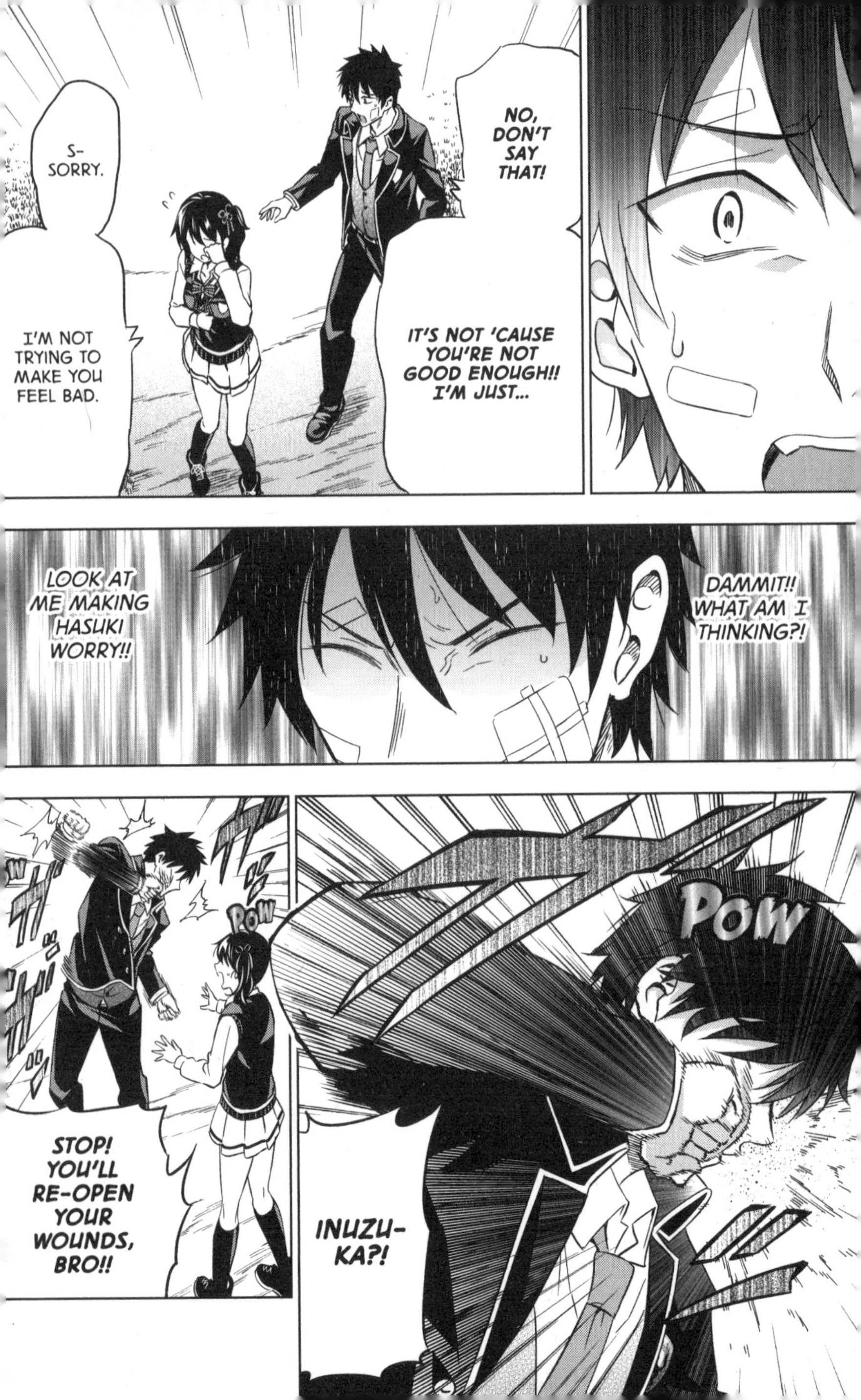

NO, DON'T SAY THAT!
IT'S NOT 'CAUSE YOU'RE NOT GOOD ENOUGH!! I'M JUST...
S-SORRY.
I'M NOT TRYING TO MAKE YOU FEEL BAD.
DAMMIT!! WHAT AM I THINKING?!
LOOK AT ME MAKING HASUKI WORRY!!
POW
INUZU-KA?!
POW
STOP! YOU'LL RE-OPEN YOUR WOUNDS, BRO!!

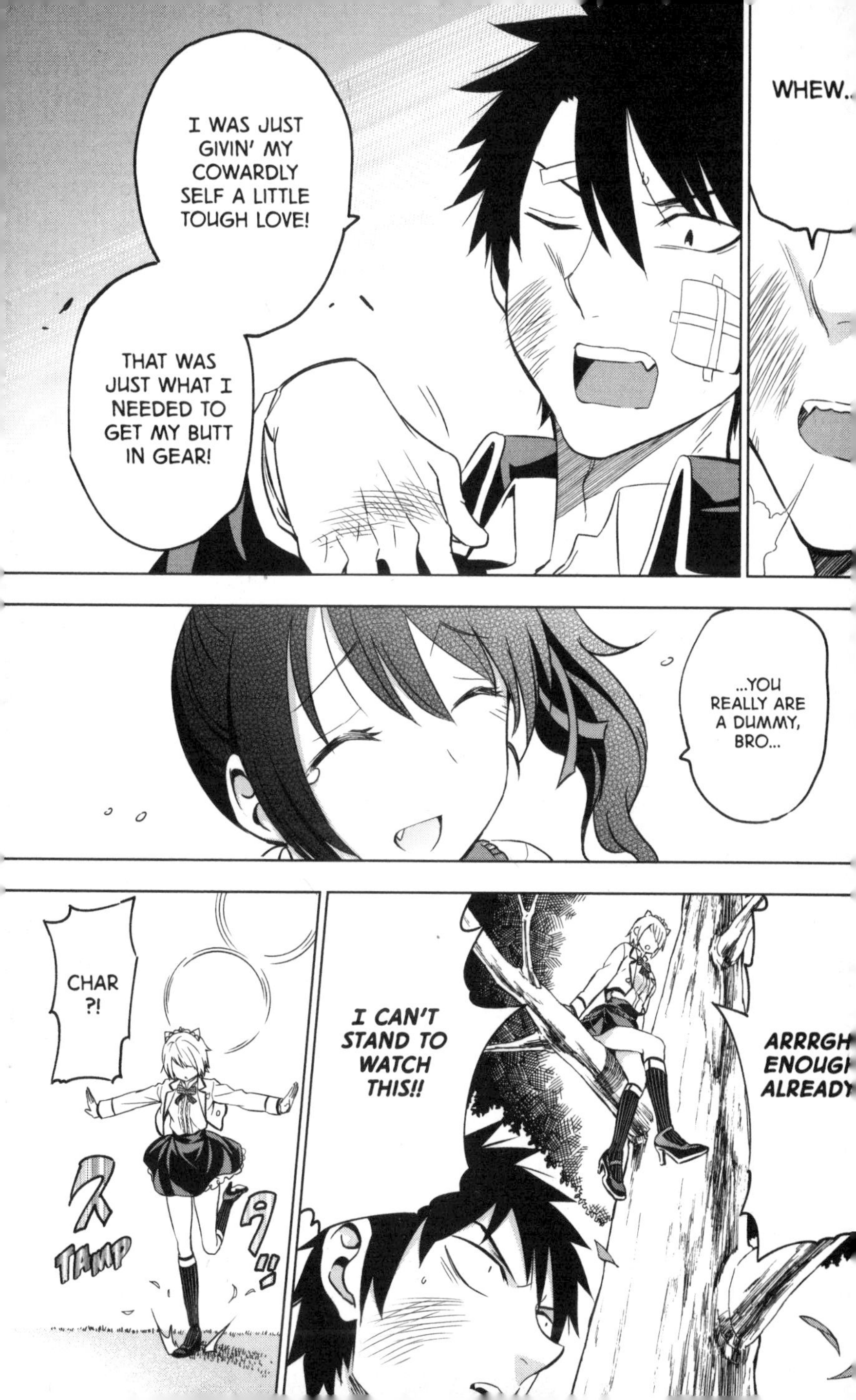
WHEW..
I WAS JUST GIVIN' MY COWARDLY SELF A LITTLE TOUGH LOVE!
THAT WAS JUST WHAT I NEEDED TO GET MY BUTT IN GEAR!
...YOU REALLY ARE A DUMMY, BRO...
ARRRGH ENOUGH ALREADY
I CAN'T STAND TO WATCH THIS!!
CHAR ?!
スタッ
TAMP

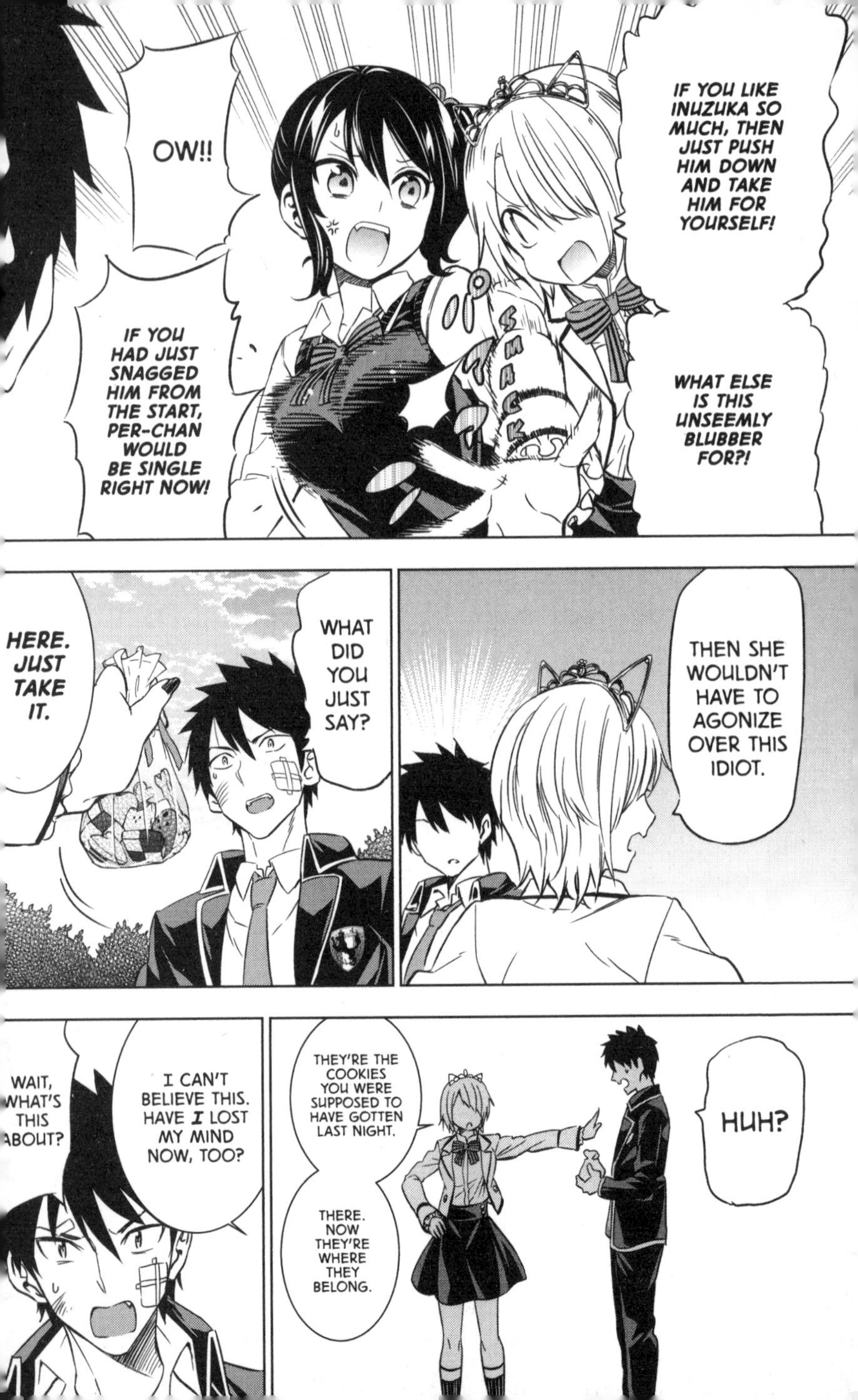
IF YOU LIKE INUZUKA SO MUCH, THEN JUST PUSH HIM DOWN AND TAKE HIM FOR YOURSELF!
WHAT ELSE IS THIS UNSEEMLY BLUBBER FOR?!
SMACK
OW!!
IF YOU HAD JUST SNAGGED HIM FROM THE START, PER-CHAN WOULD BE SINGLE RIGHT NOW!
THEN SHE WOULDN'T HAVE TO AGONIZE OVER THIS IDIOT.
WHAT DID YOU JUST SAY?
HERE. JUST TAKE IT.
HUH?
THEY'RE THE COOKIES YOU WERE SUPPOSED TO HAVE GOTTEN LAST NIGHT.
THERE. NOW THEY'RE WHERE THEY BELONG.
I CAN'T BELIEVE THIS. HAVE I LOST MY MIND NOW, TOO?
WAIT, WHAT'S THIS ABOUT?

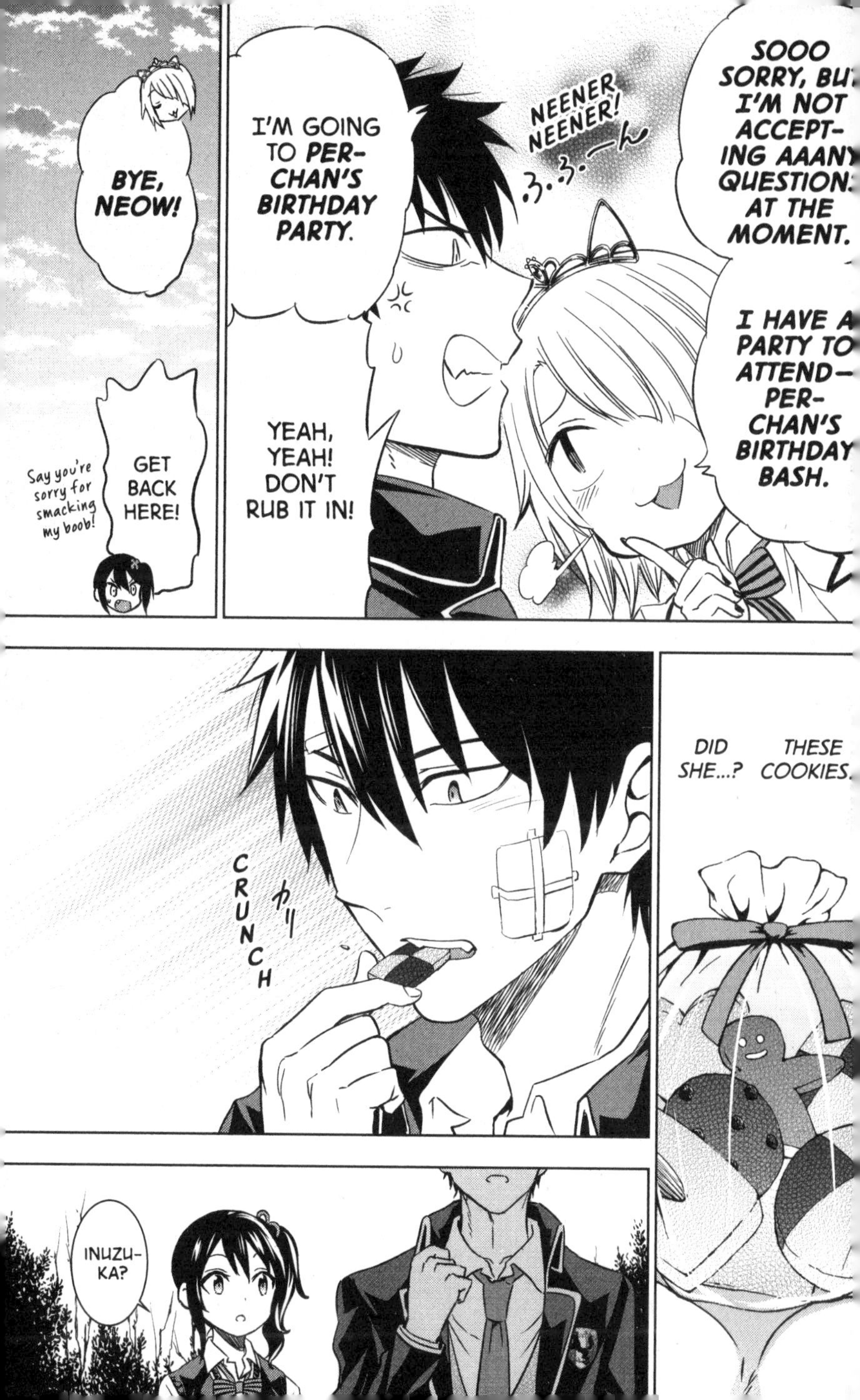
SOOO SORRY, BU I'M NOT ACCEPT-ING AAANY QUESTION AT THE MOMENT.
I HAVE A PARTY TO ATTEND—PER-CHAN'S BIRTHDAY BASH.
NEENER NEENER! ふふーん
I'M GOING TO PER-CHAN'S BIRTHDAY PARTY.
YEAH, YEAH! DON'T RUB IT IN!
BYE, NEOW!
GET BACK HERE!
Say you're sorry for smacking my boob!
THESE COOKIES.
DID SHE...?
CRUNCH
カリ
INUZU-KA?

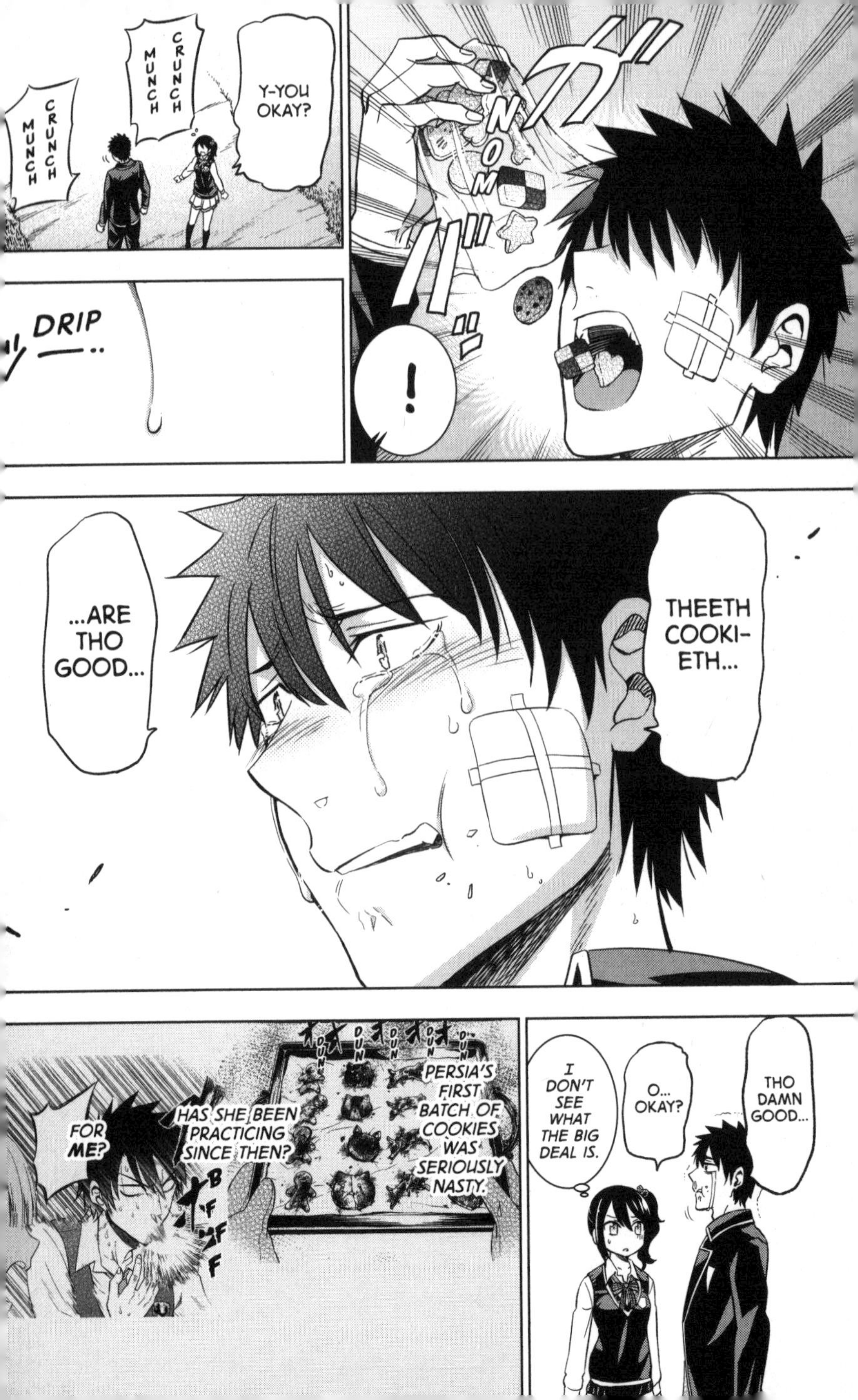
NOM
!
Y-YOU OKAY?
CRUNCH MUNCH
CRUNCH MUNCH
DRIP
THEETH COOKI-ETH...
...ARE THO GOOD...
THO DAMN GOOD...
O... OKAY?
I DON'T SEE WHAT THE BIG DEAL IS.
DUN DUN DUN DUN DUN
PERSIA'S FIRST BATCH OF COOKIES WAS SERIOUSLY NASTY.
HAS SHE BEEN PRACTICING SINCE THEN?
FOR ME?
BFFF

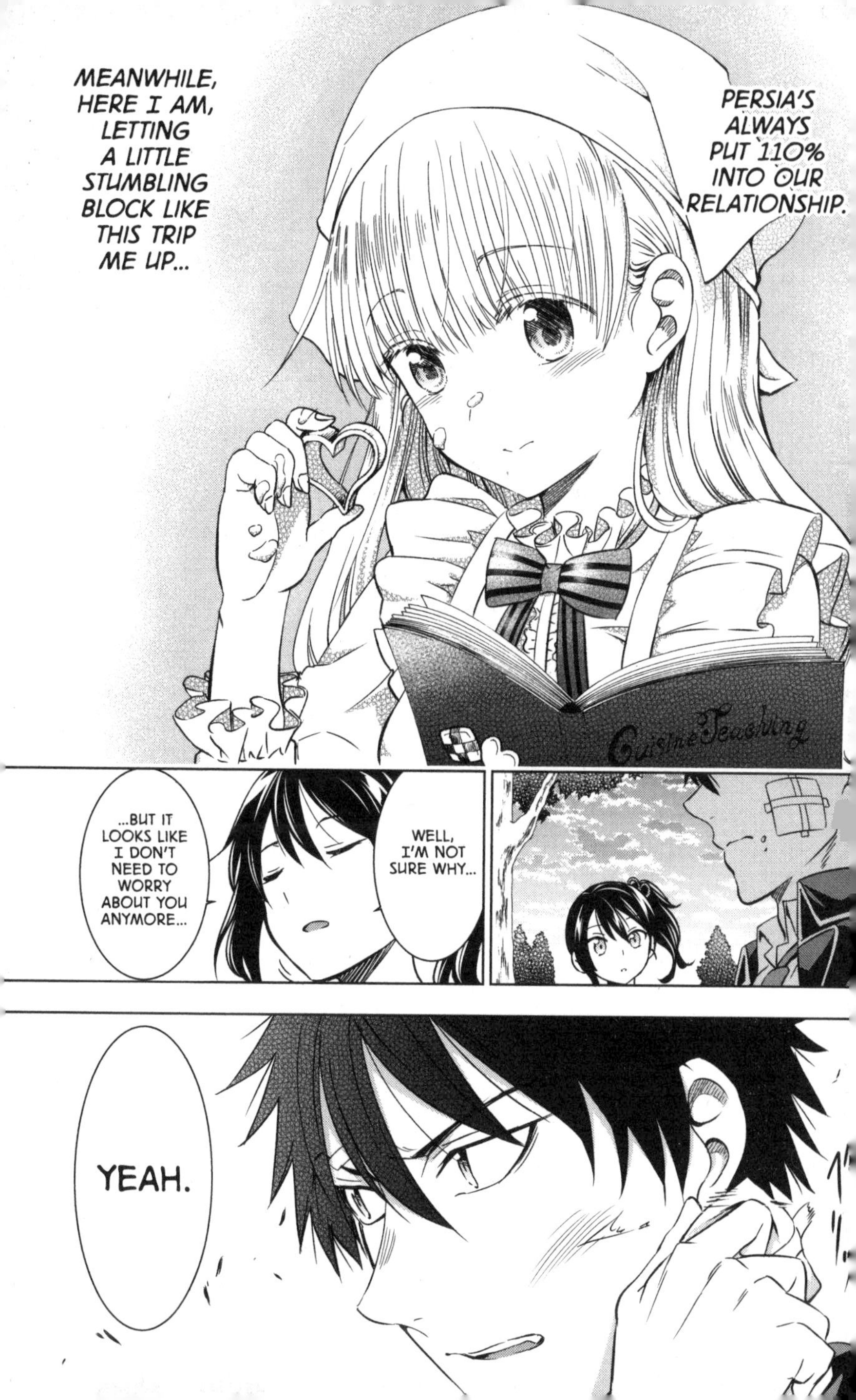
PERSIA'S ALWAYS PUT 110% INTO OUR RELATIONSHIP.
MEANWHILE, HERE I AM, LETTING A LITTLE STUMBLING BLOCK LIKE THIS TRIP ME UP...
Cuisine Teaching
WELL, I'M NOT SURE WHY...
...BUT IT LOOKS LIKE I DON'T NEED TO WORRY ABOUT YOU ANYMORE...
YEAH.

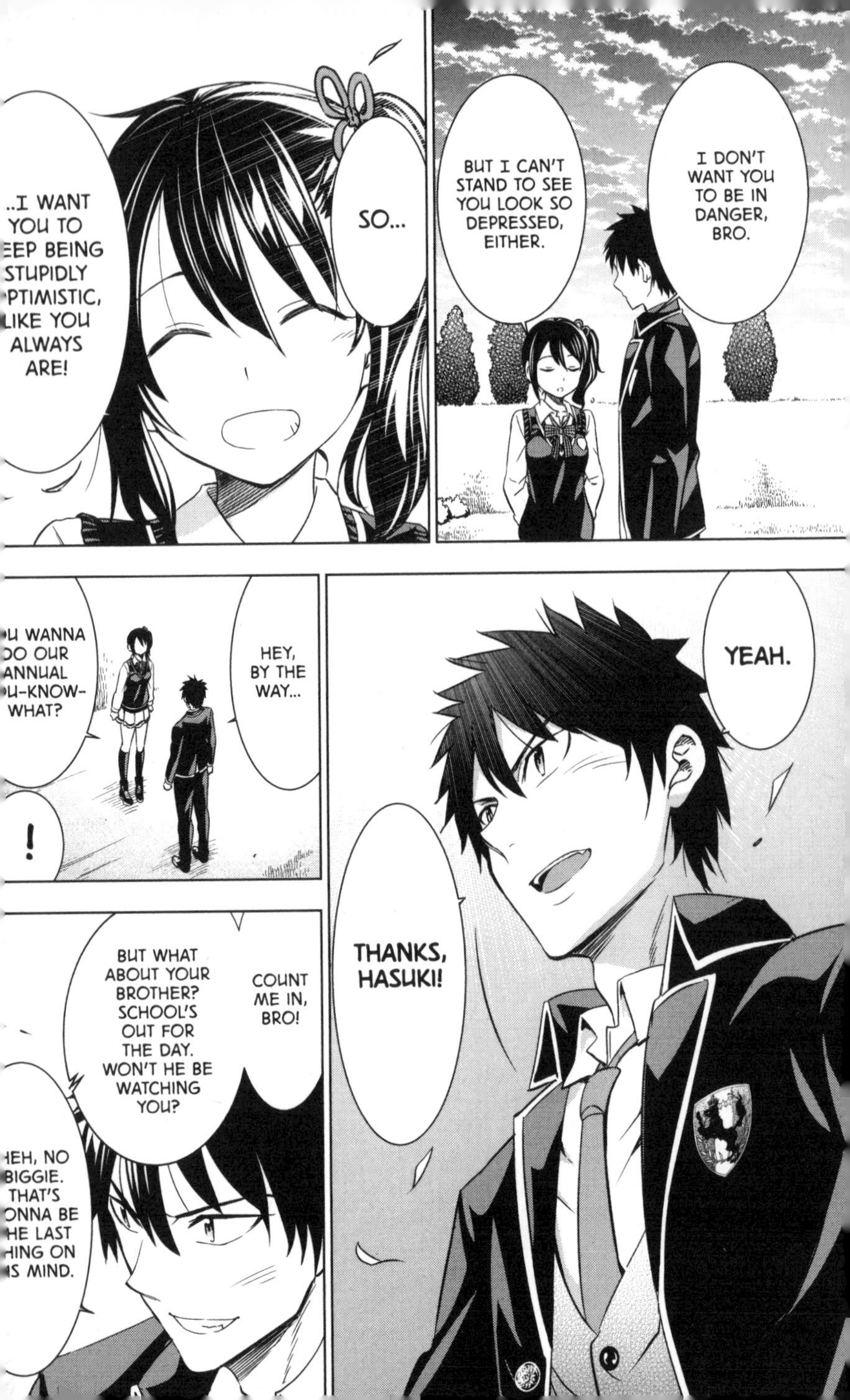
I DON'T WANT YOU TO BE IN DANGER, BRO.
BUT I CAN'T STAND TO SEE YOU LOOK SO DEPRESSED, EITHER.
SO...
..I WANT YOU TO EEP BEING STUPIDLY PTIMISTIC, LIKE YOU ALWAYS ARE!
YEAH.
THANKS, HASUKI!
HEY, BY THE WAY...
U WANNA DO OUR ANNUAL U-KNOW-WHAT?
!
COUNT ME IN, BRO!
BUT WHAT ABOUT YOUR BROTHER? SCHOOL'S OUT FOR THE DAY. WON'T HE BE WATCHING YOU?
IEH, NO BIGGIE. THAT'S ONNA BE HE LAST HING ON IS MIND.

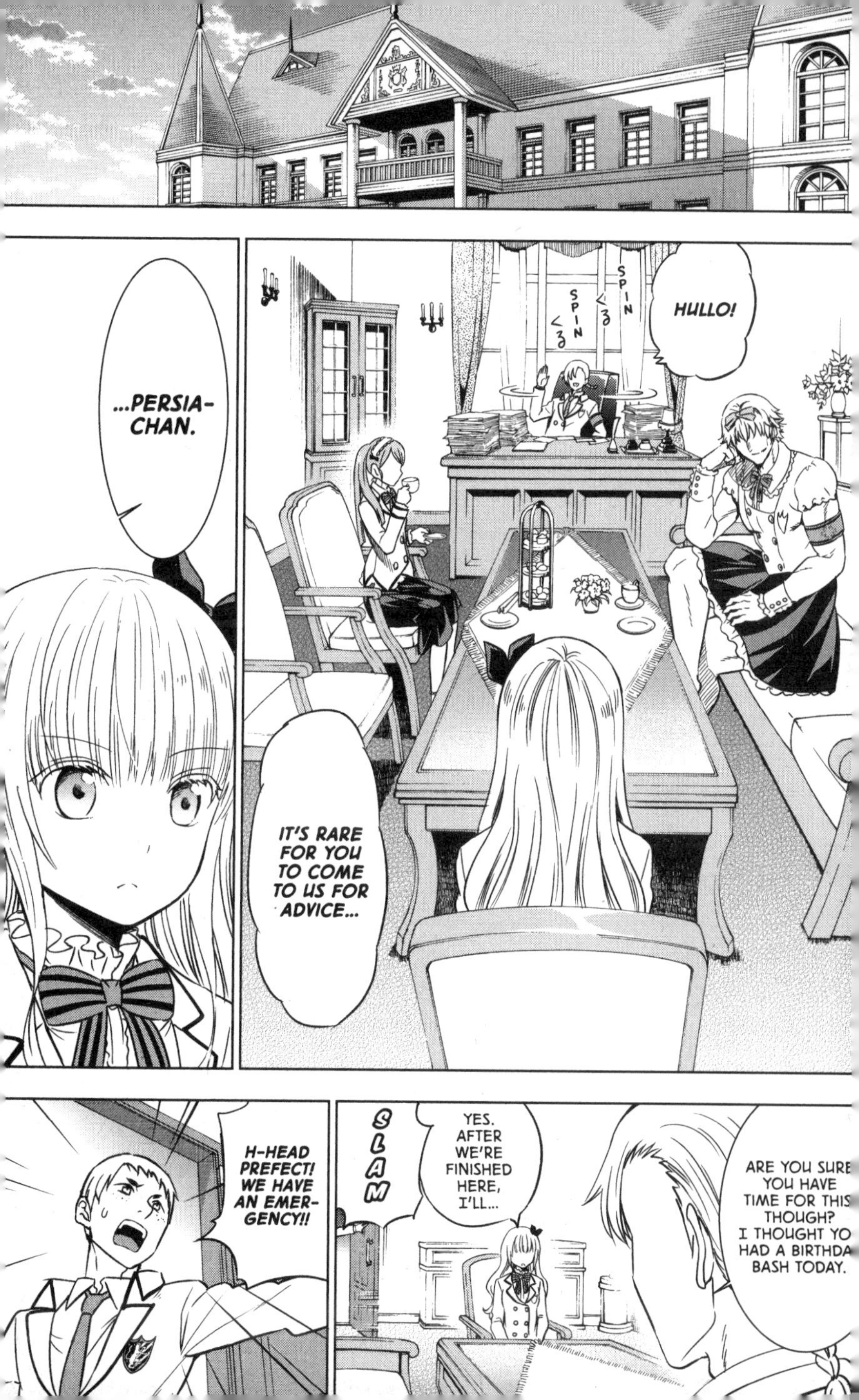
SPIN
SPIN
HULLO!
IT'S RARE FOR YOU TO COME TO US FOR ADVICE...
...PERSIA-CHAN.
ARE YOU SURE YOU HAVE TIME FOR THIS THOUGH? I THOUGHT YO HAD A BIRTHDA BASH TODAY.
YES. AFTER WE'RE FINISHED HERE, I'LL...
SLAM
H-HEAD PREFECT! WE HAVE AN EMERGENCY!!

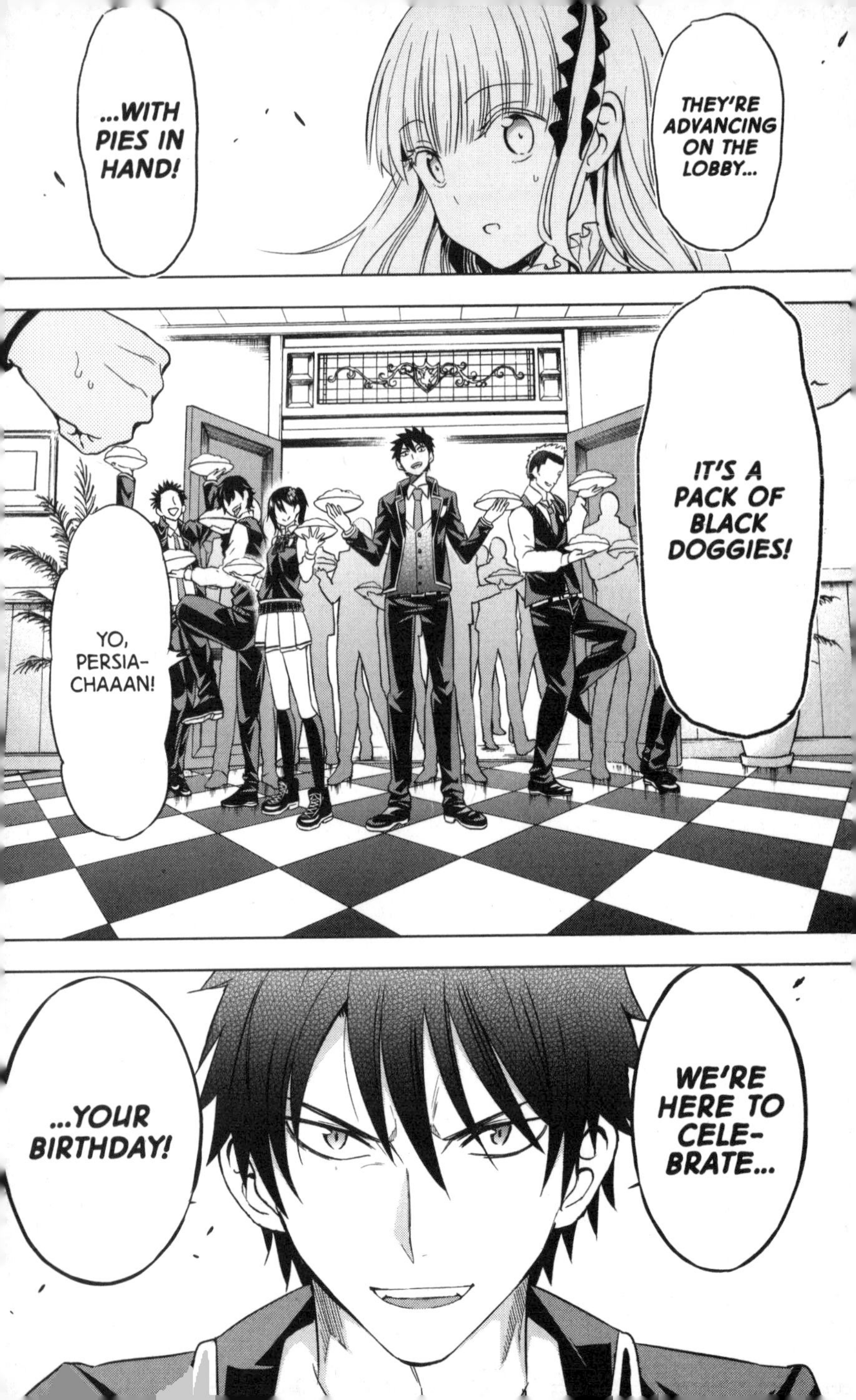
THEY'RE ADVANCING ON THE LOBBY...
...WITH PIES IN HAND!
IT'S A PACK OF BLACK DOGGIES!
YO, PERSIA-CHAAAN!
WE'RE HERE TO CELE-BRATE...
...YOUR BIRTHDAY!

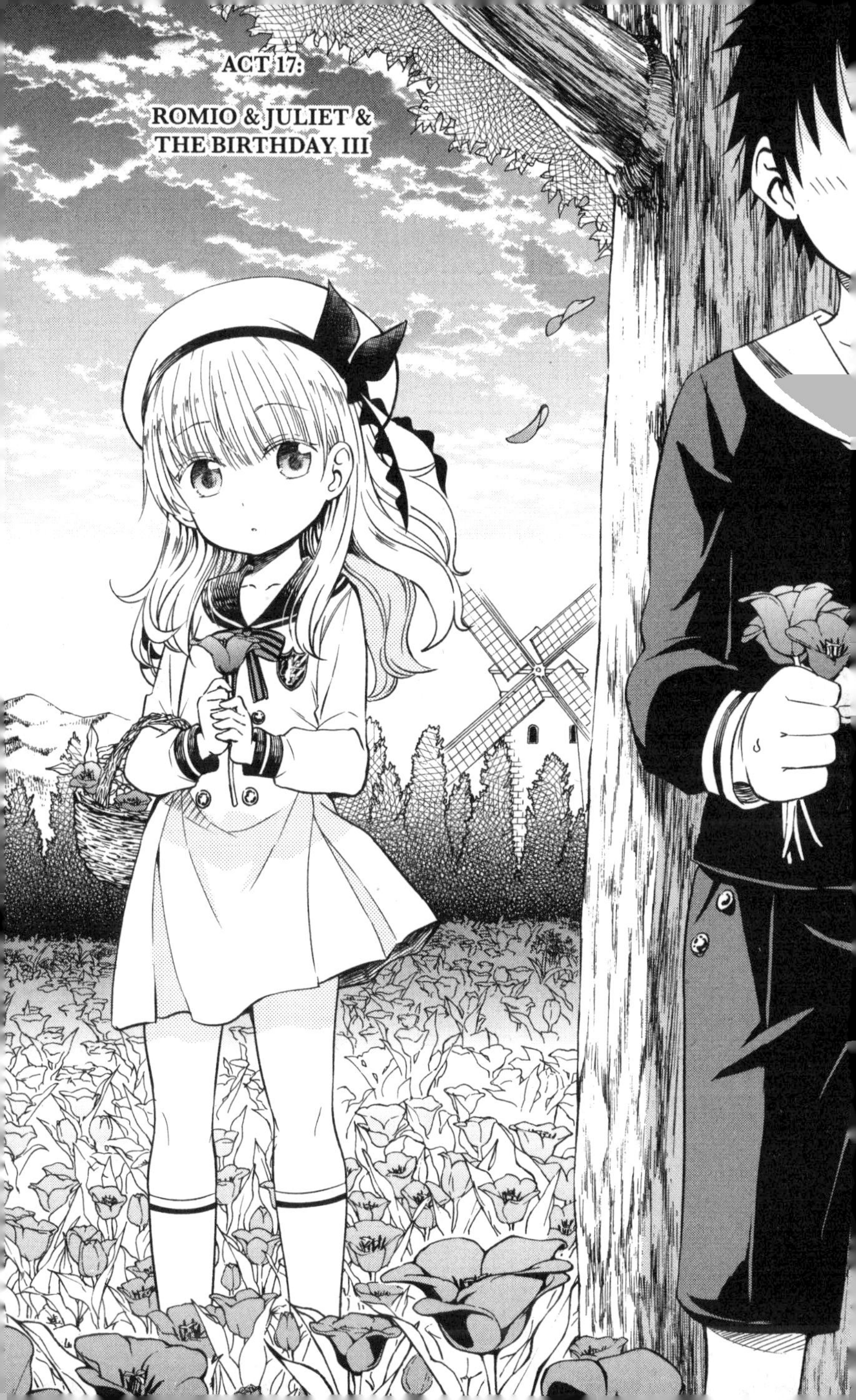
ACT 17:
ROMIO & JULIET & THE BIRTHDAY III

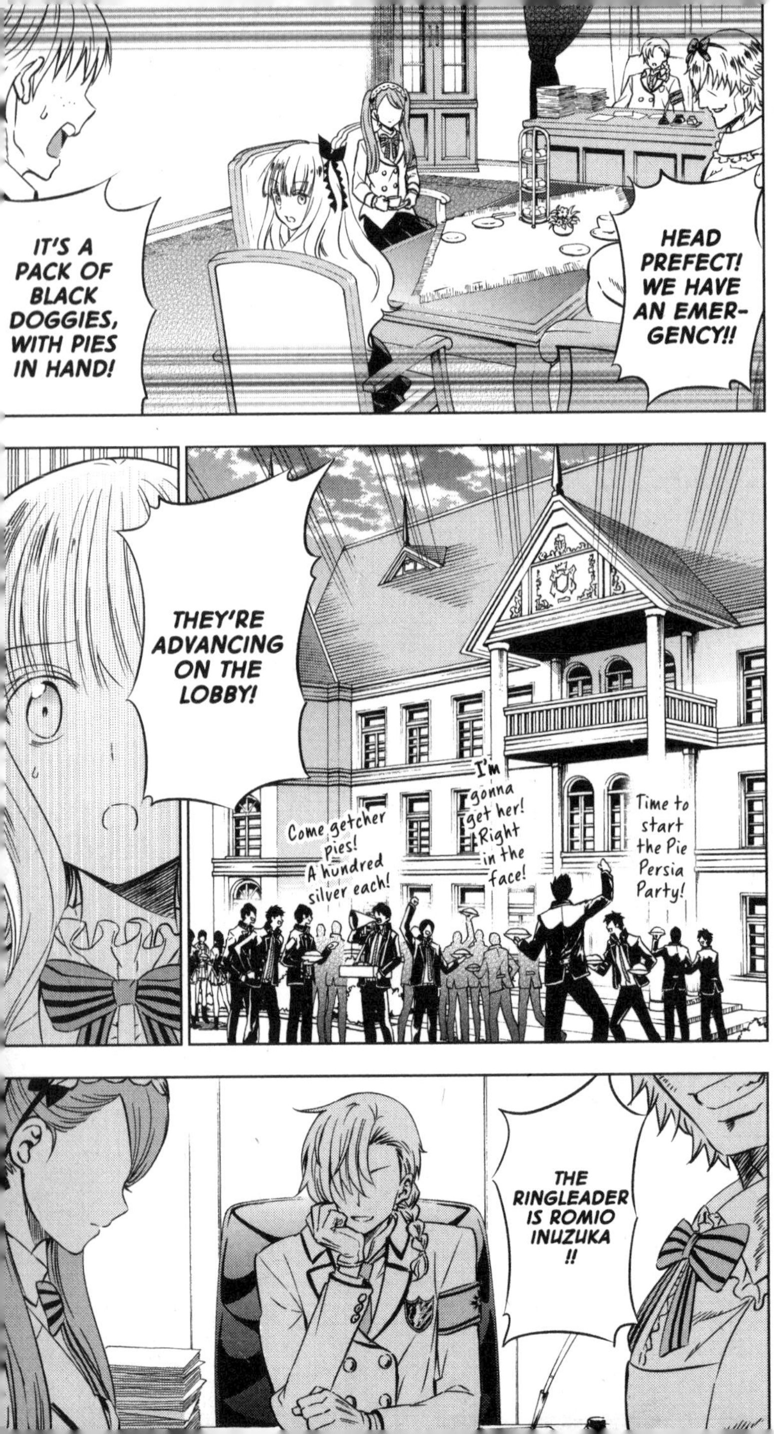
HEAD PREFECT! WE HAVE AN EMER-GENCY!!
IT'S A PACK OF BLACK DOGGIES, WITH PIES IN HAND!
THEY'RE ADVANCING ON THE LOBBY!
Time to start the Pie Persia Party!
I'm gonna get her! Right in the face!
Come getcher pies! A hundred silver each!
THE RINGLEADER IS ROMIO INUZUKA !!

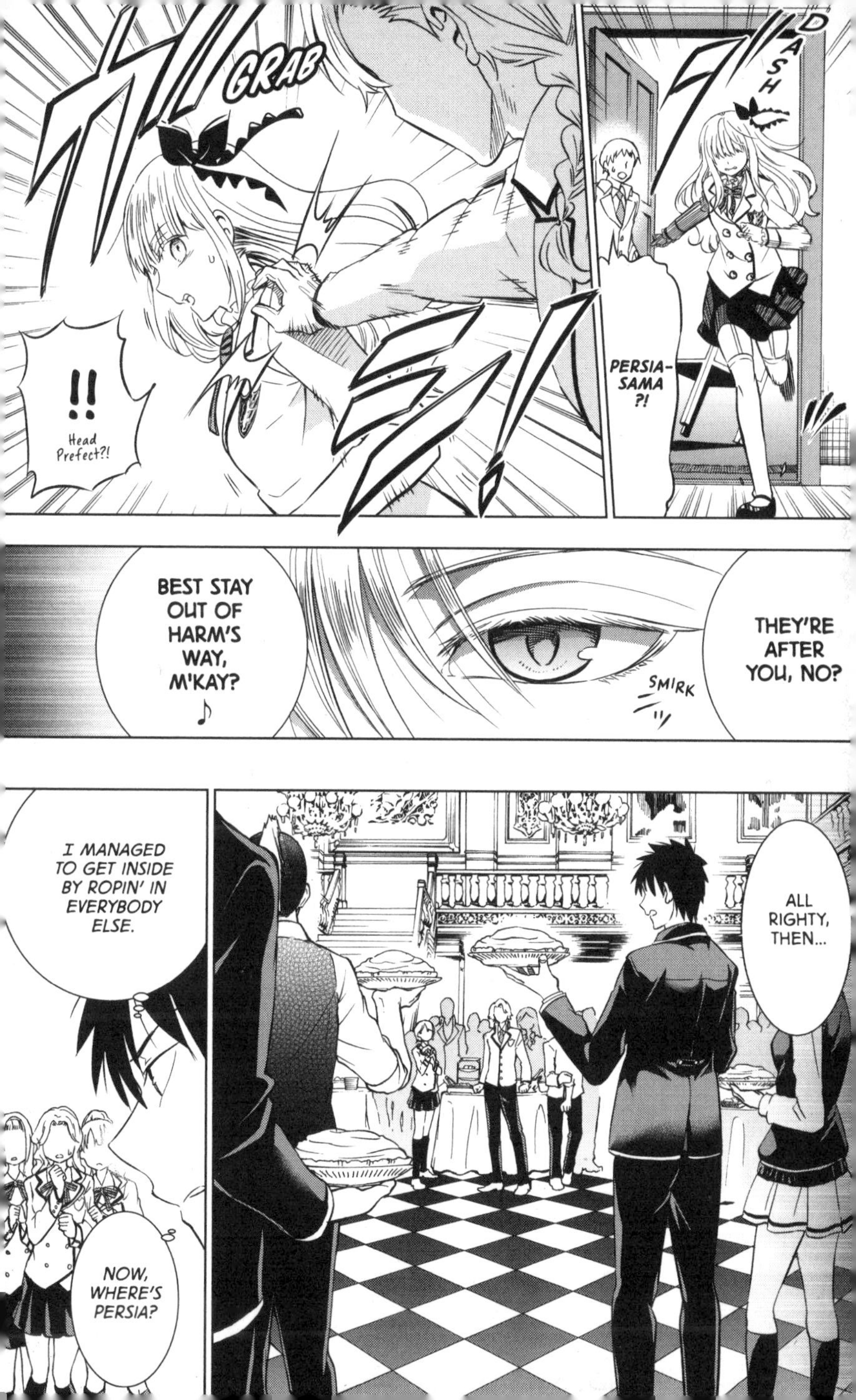
DASH
PERSIA-SAMA ?!
GRAB
!!
Head Prefect?!
THEY'RE AFTER YOU, NO?
SMIRK
BEST STAY OUT OF HARM'S WAY, M'KAY? ♪
ALL RIGHTY, THEN...
I MANAGED TO GET INSIDE BY ROPIN' IN EVERYBODY ELSE.
NOW, WHERE'S PERSIA?

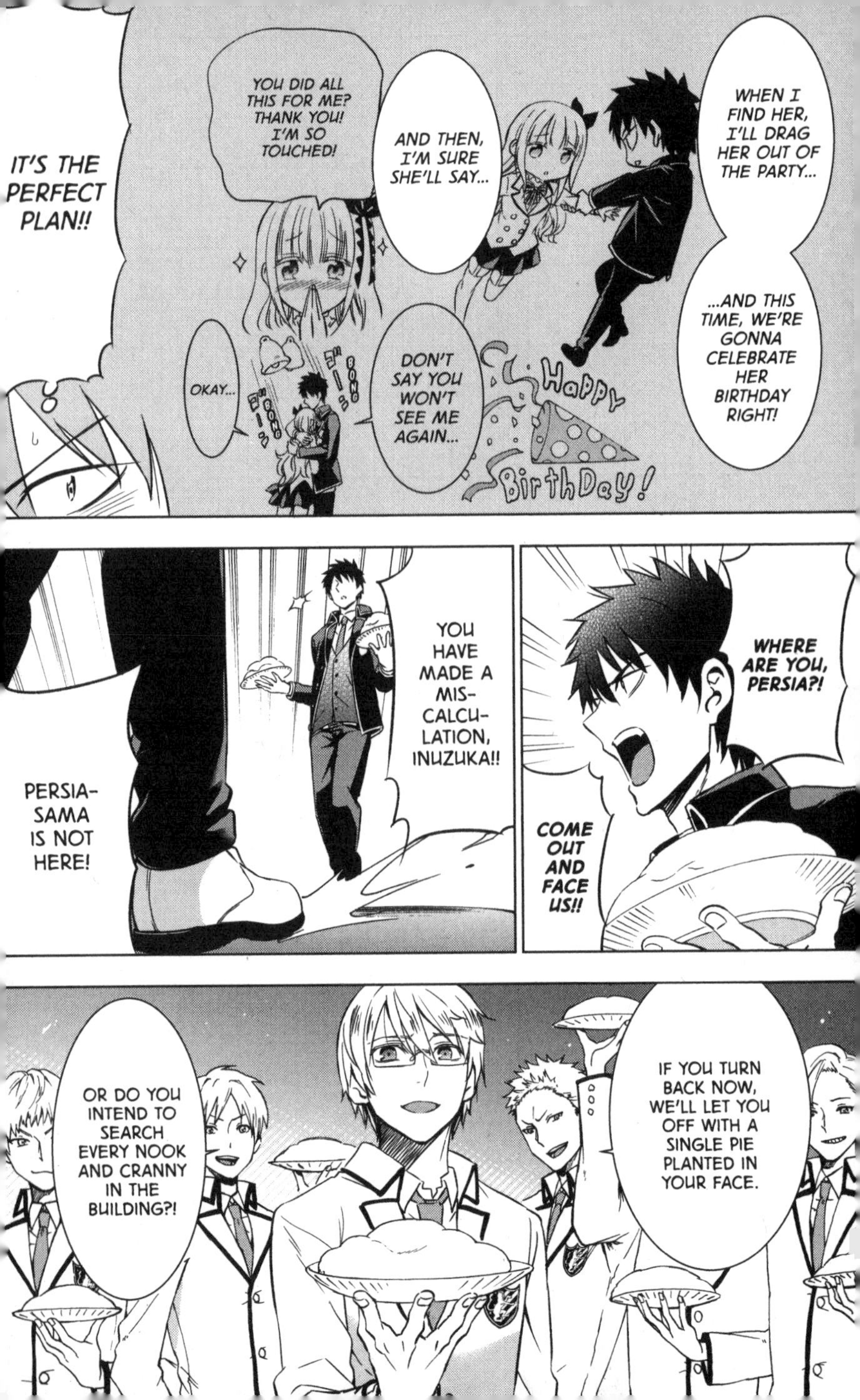
WHEN I FIND HER, I'LL DRAG HER OUT OF THE PARTY...
...AND THIS TIME, WE'RE GONNA CELEBRATE HER BIRTHDAY RIGHT!
Happy BirthDay!
AND THEN, I'M SURE SHE'LL SAY...
YOU DID ALL THIS FOR ME? THANK YOU! I'M SO TOUCHED!
DON'T SAY YOU WON'T SEE ME AGAIN...
OKAY...
IT'S THE PERFECT PLAN!!
WHERE ARE YOU, PERSIA?!
COME OUT AND FACE US!!
YOU HAVE MADE A MIS-CALCU-LATION, INUZUKA!!
PERSIA-SAMA IS NOT HERE!
IF YOU TURN BACK NOW, WE'LL LET YOU OFF WITH A SINGLE PIE PLANTED IN YOUR FACE.
OR DO YOU INTEND TO SEARCH EVERY NOOK AND CRANNY IN THE BUILDING?!

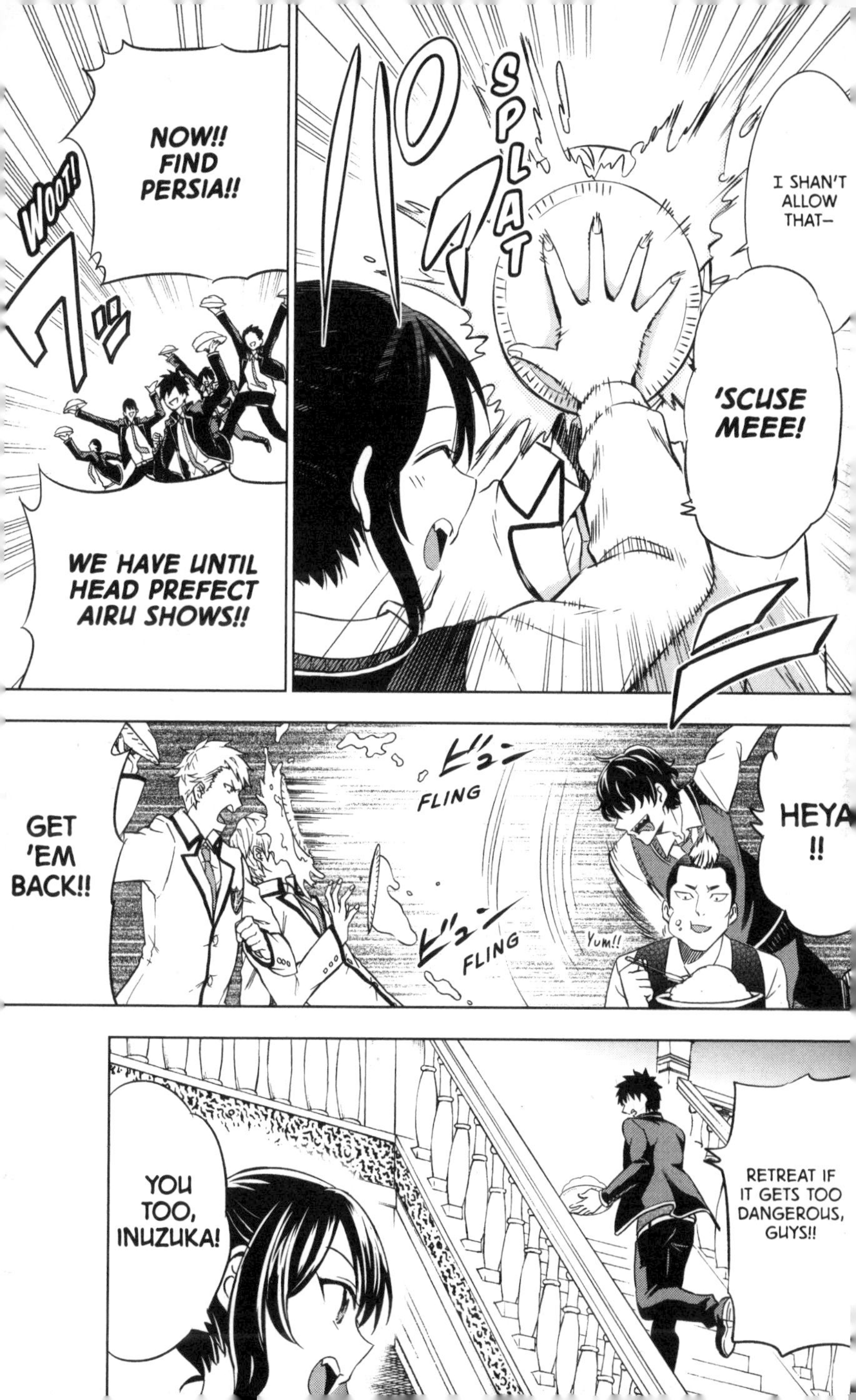
I SHAN'T ALLOW THAT—
SPLAT
'SCUSE MEEE!
WOOT!
NOW!! FIND PERSIA!!
WE HAVE UNTIL HEAD PREFECT AIRU SHOWS!!
HEYA!!
Yum!!
FLING
FLING
GET 'EM BACK!!
RETREAT IF IT GETS TOO DANGEROUS, GUYS!!
YOU TOO, INUZUKA!

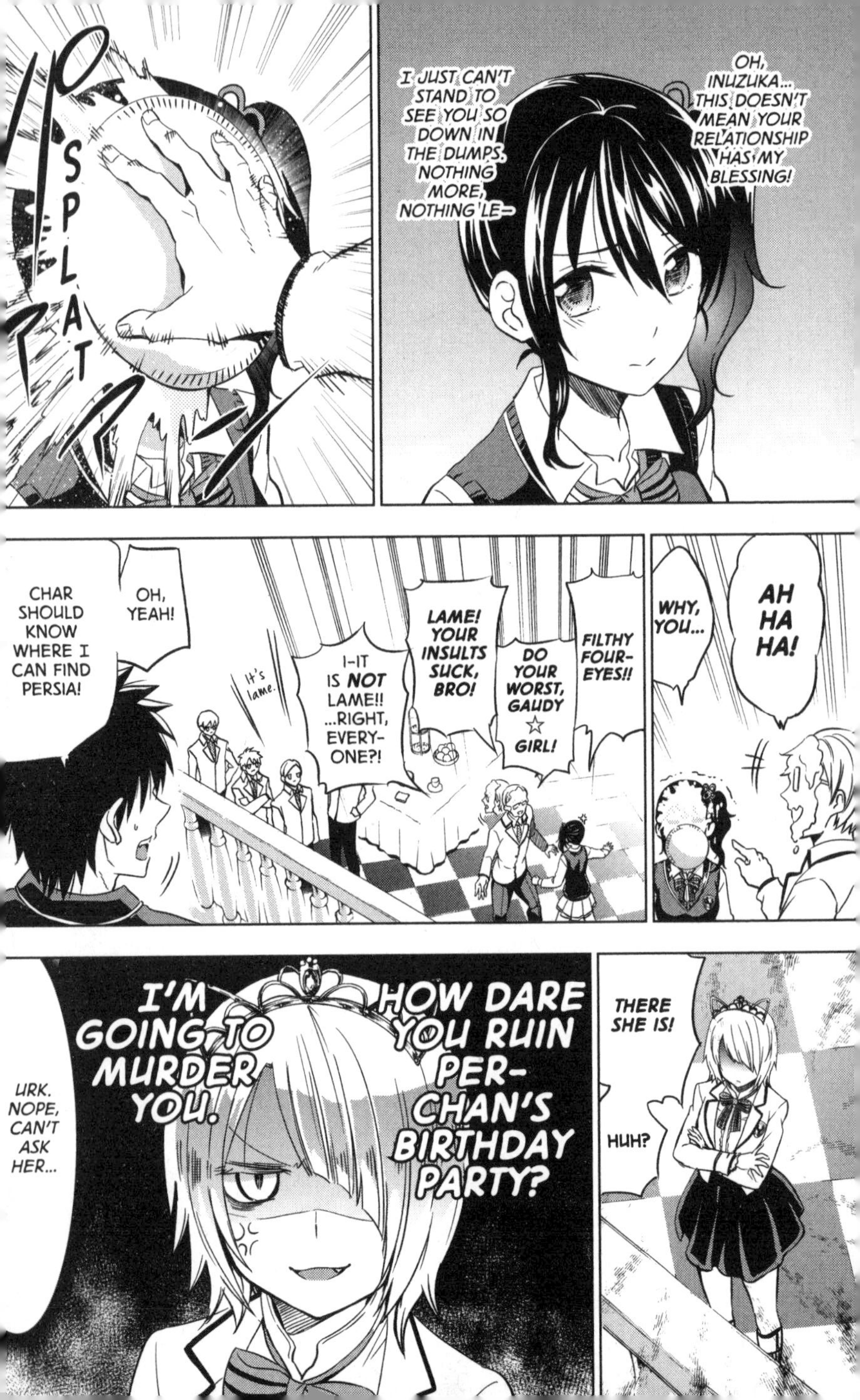
OH, INUZUKA... THIS DOESN'T MEAN YOUR RELATIONSHIP HAS MY BLESSING!
I JUST CAN'T STAND TO SEE YOU SO DOWN IN THE DUMPS. NOTHING MORE, NOTHING LE—
SPLAT
AH HA HA!
WHY, YOU...
FILTHY FOUR-EYES!!
DO YOUR WORST, GAUDY ☆ GIRL!
LAME! YOUR INSULTS SUCK, BRO!
I-IT IS NOT LAME!! ...RIGHT, EVERYONE?!
It's lame.
OH, YEAH!
CHAR SHOULD KNOW WHERE I CAN FIND PERSIA!
THERE SHE IS!
HUH?
HOW DARE YOU RUIN PER-CHAN'S BIRTHDAY PARTY?
I'M GOING TO MURDER YOU.
URK. NOPE, CAN'T ASK HER...

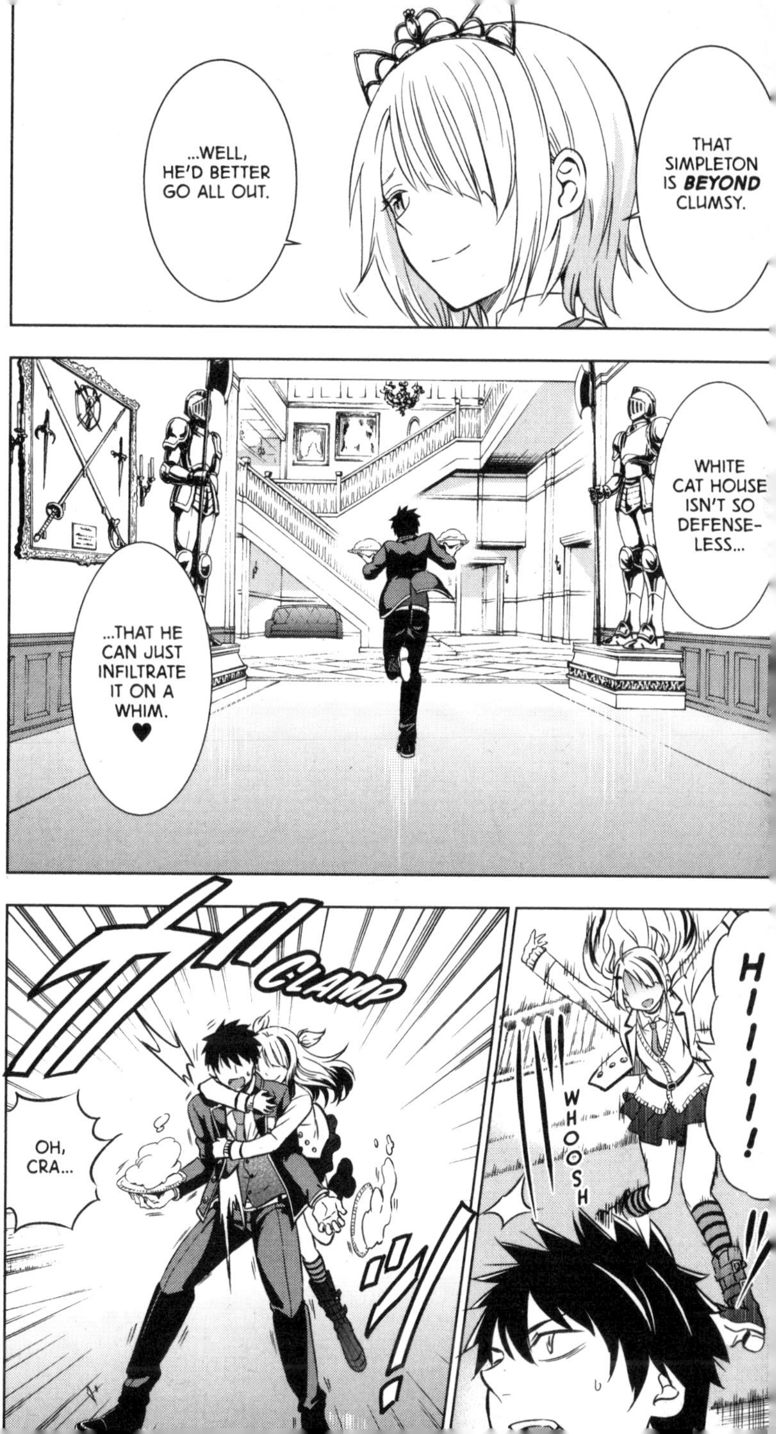
THAT SIMPLETON IS **BEYOND** CLUMSY.
...WELL, HE'D BETTER GO ALL OUT.
WHITE CAT HOUSE ISN'T SO DEFENSE-LESS...
...THAT HE CAN JUST INFILTRATE IT ON A WHIM. ♥
HIIIIII!
WHOOSH
!!
CLAMP
OH, CRA...

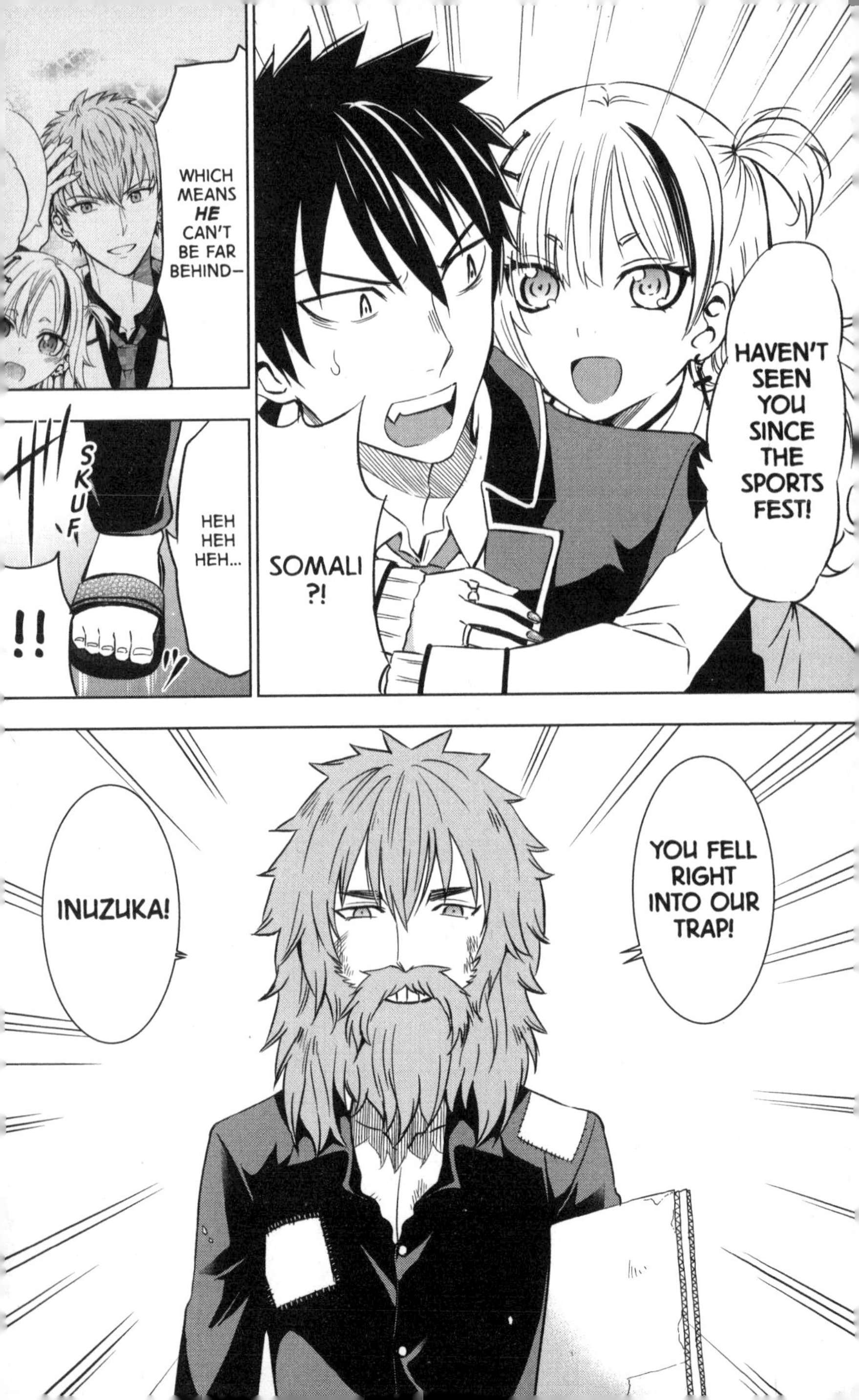
HAVEN'T SEEN YOU SINCE THE SPORTS FEST!
SOMALI ?!
WHICH MEANS *HE* CAN'T BE FAR BEHIND—
HEH HEH HEH...
SKUF
!!
YOU FELL RIGHT INTO OUR TRAP!
INUZUKA!

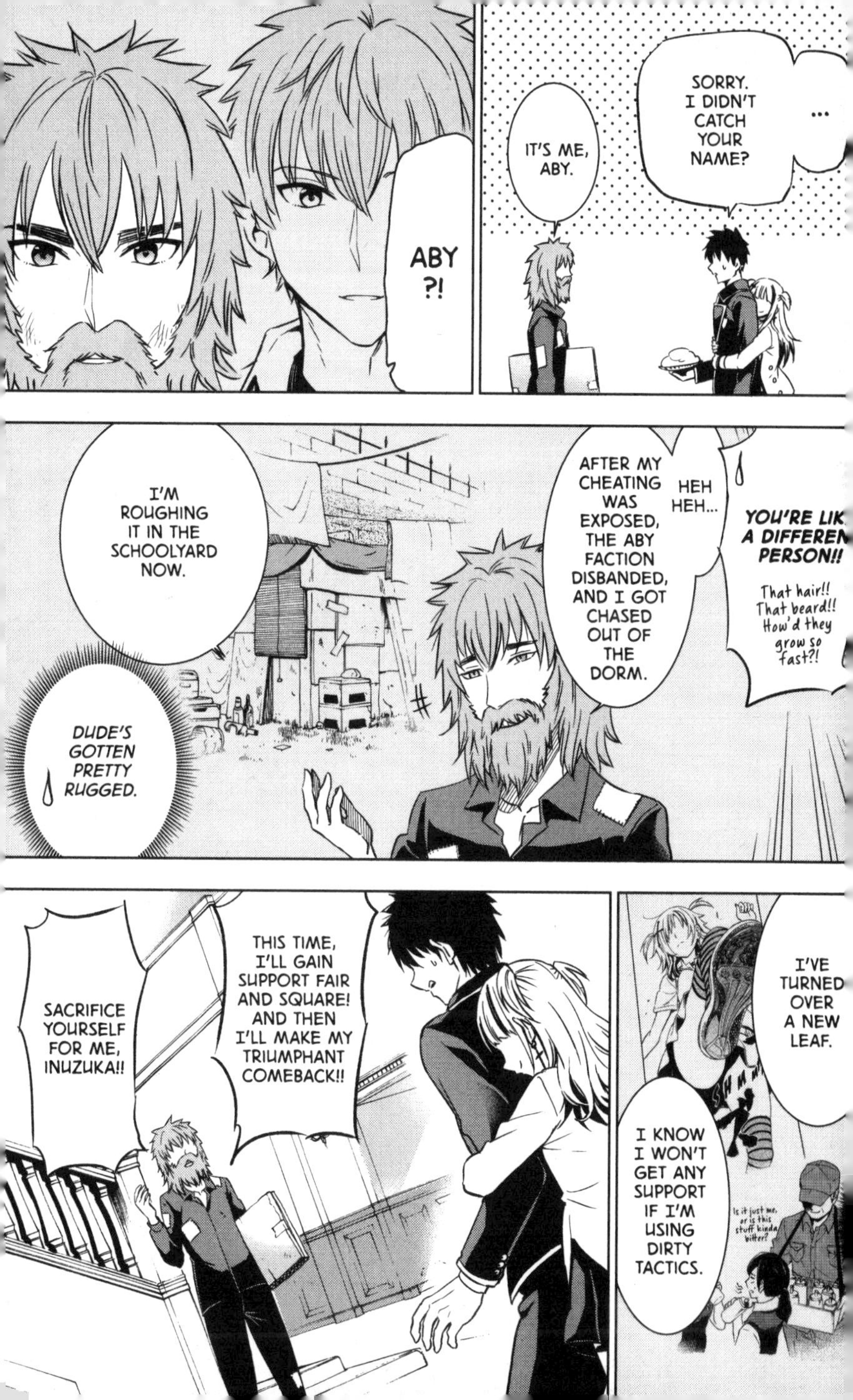

...
SORRY. I DIDN'T CATCH YOUR NAME?
IT'S ME, ABY.
ABY ?!
YOU'RE LIK A DIFFEREN PERSON!!
That hair!! That beard!! How'd they grow so fast?!
HEH HEH...
AFTER MY CHEATING WAS EXPOSED, THE ABY FACTION DISBANDED, AND I GOT CHASED OUT OF THE DORM.
I'M ROUGHING IT IN THE SCHOOLYARD NOW.
DUDE'S GOTTEN PRETTY RUGGED.
I'VE TURNED OVER A NEW LEAF.
I KNOW I WON'T GET ANY SUPPORT IF I'M USING DIRTY TACTICS.
Is it just me, or is this stuff kinda bitter?
THIS TIME, I'LL GAIN SUPPORT FAIR AND SQUARE! AND THEN I'LL MAKE MY TRIUMPHANT COMEBACK!!
SACRIFICE YOURSELF FOR ME, INUZUKA!!

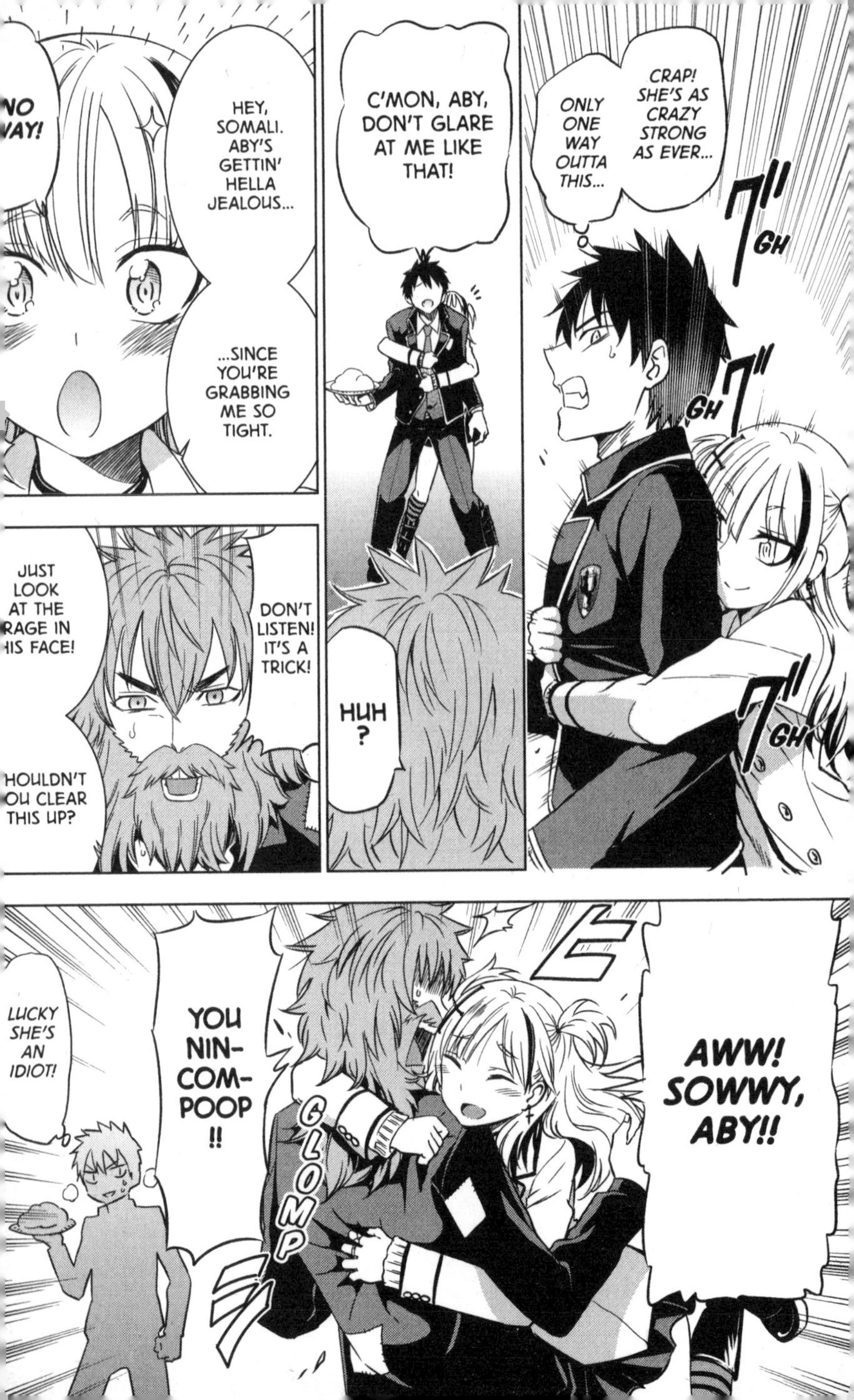
CRAP! SHE'S AS CRAZY STRONG AS EVER...
ONLY ONE WAY OUTTA THIS...
GH
GH
GH
C'MON, ABY, DON'T GLARE AT ME LIKE THAT!
HUH?
HEY, SOMALI. ABY'S GETTIN' HELLA JEALOUS...
...SINCE YOU'RE GRABBING ME SO TIGHT.
NO
AY!
DON'T LISTEN! IT'S A TRICK!
JUST LOOK AT THE RAGE IN
IS FACE!
HOULDN'T
OU CLEAR THIS UP?
AWW! SOWWY, ABY!!
YOU NIN-COM-POOP!!
GLOMP
LUCKY SHE'S AN IDIOT!

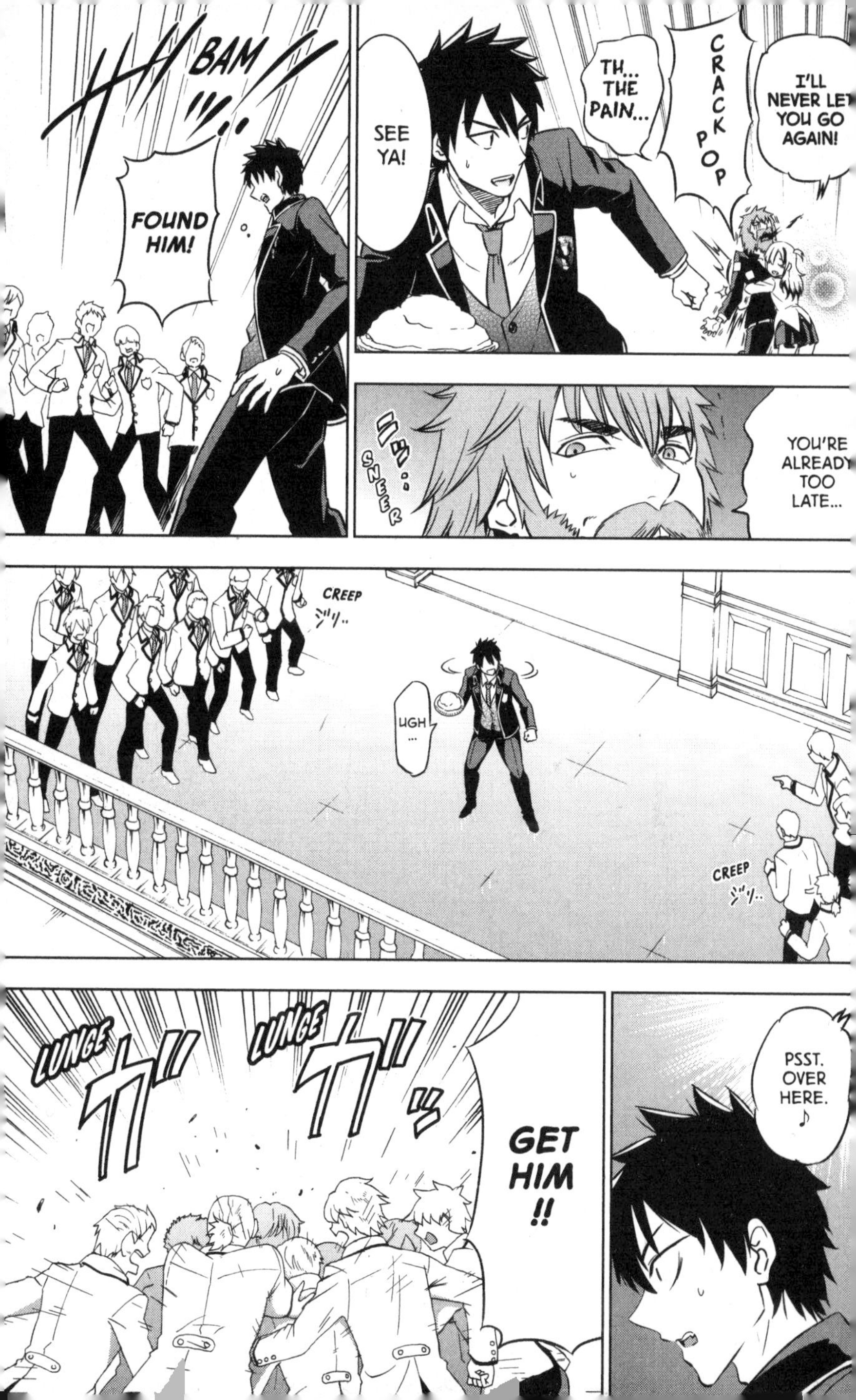
I'LL NEVER LET YOU GO AGAIN!
CRACK POP
TH... THE PAIN...
SEE YA!
YOU'RE ALREADY TOO LATE...
SNEER
BAM
FOUND HIM!
CREEP
UGH ...
CREEP
PSST. OVER HERE. ♪
GET HIM !!
LUNGE
LUNGE

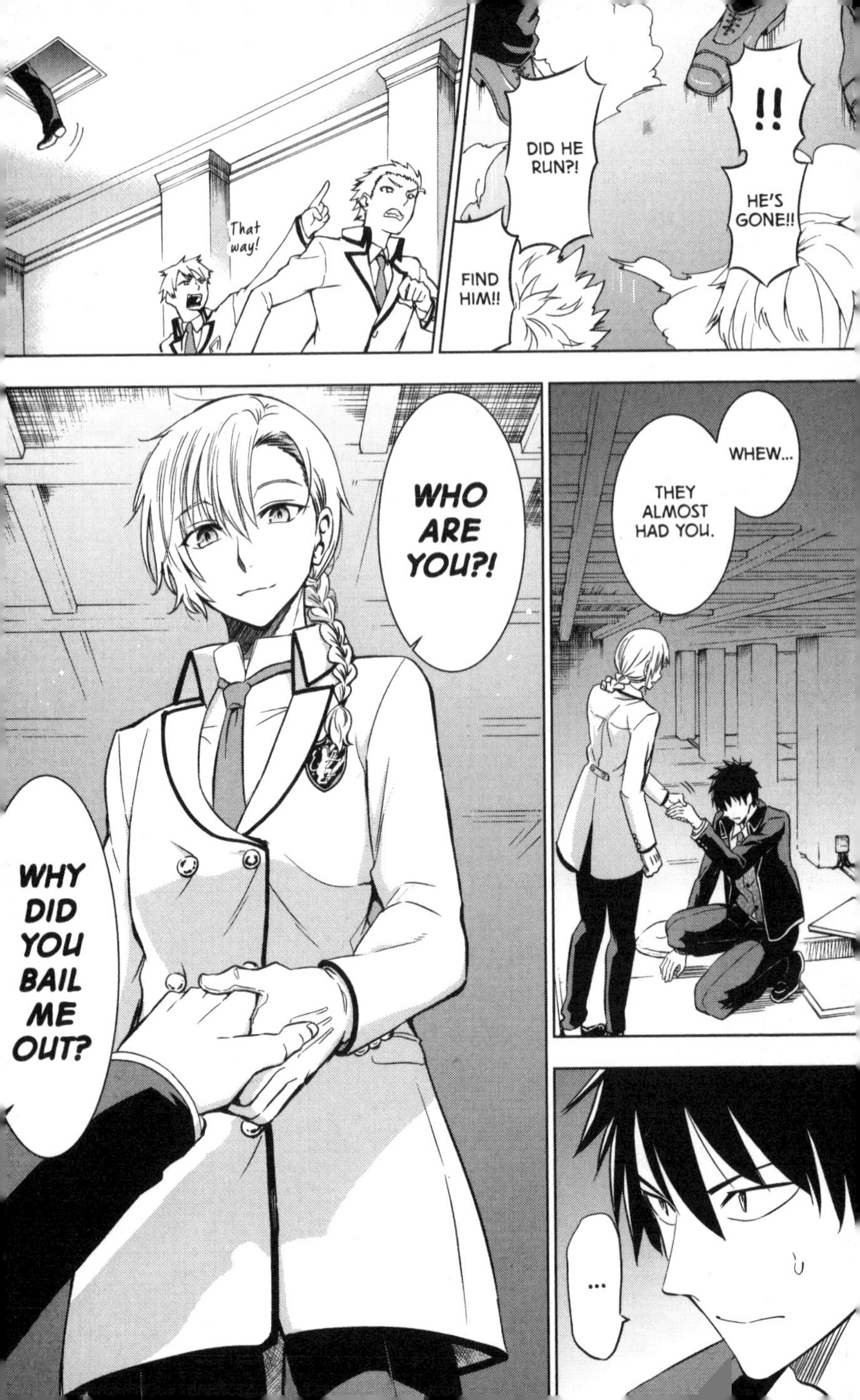
!! HE'S GONE!!
DID HE RUN?!
FIND HIM!!
That way!
WHEW...
THEY ALMOST HAD YOU.
...
WHO ARE YOU?!
WHY DID YOU BAIL ME OUT?

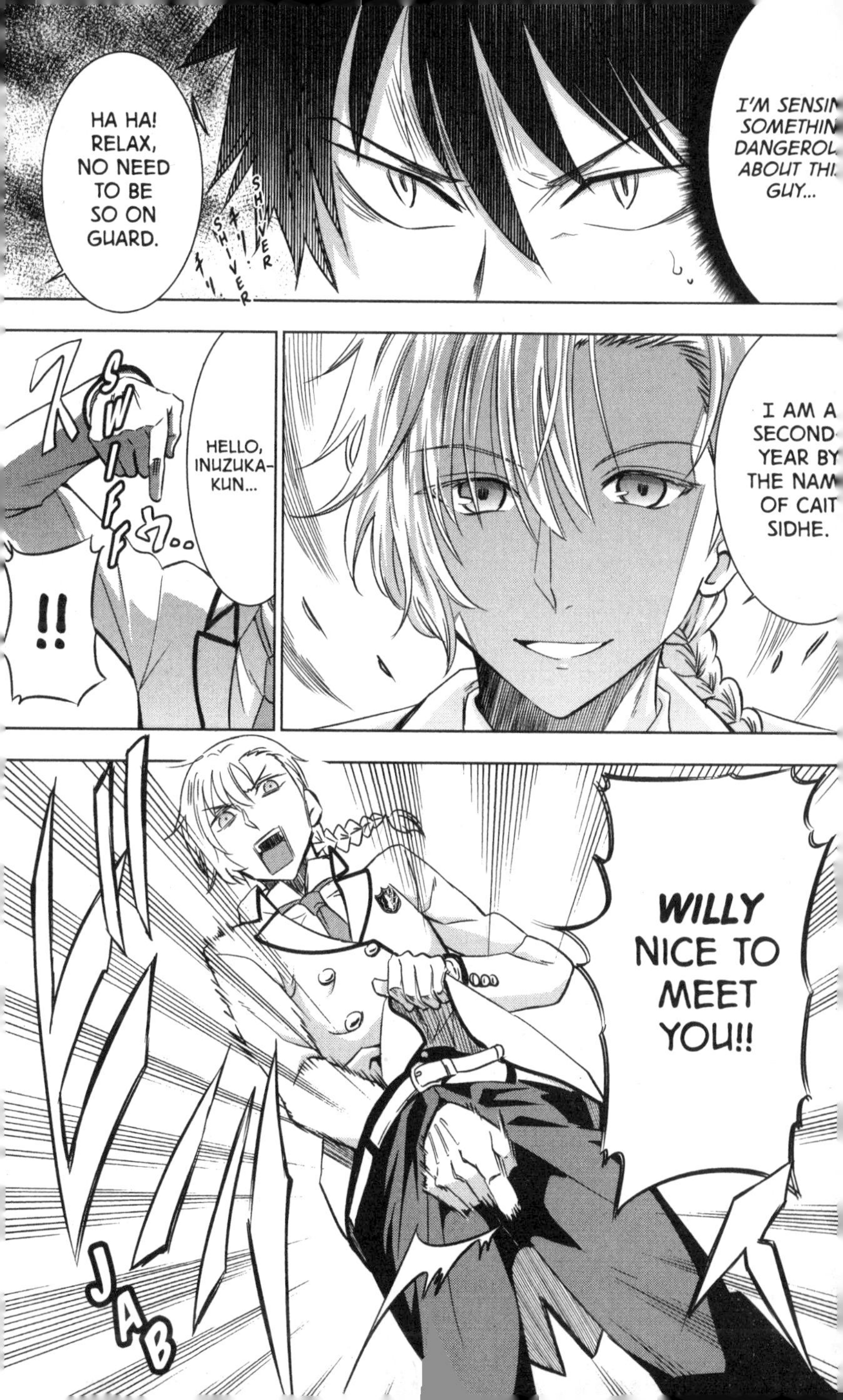
I'M SENSIN SOMETHIN DANGEROU ABOUT THI GUY...
SHIVER
SHIVER
HA HA! RELAX, NO NEED TO BE SO ON GUARD.
I AM A SECOND-YEAR BY THE NAM OF CAIT SIDHE.
HELLO, INUZUKA-KUN...
SWIFF
!!
WILLY NICE TO MEET YOU!!
JAB

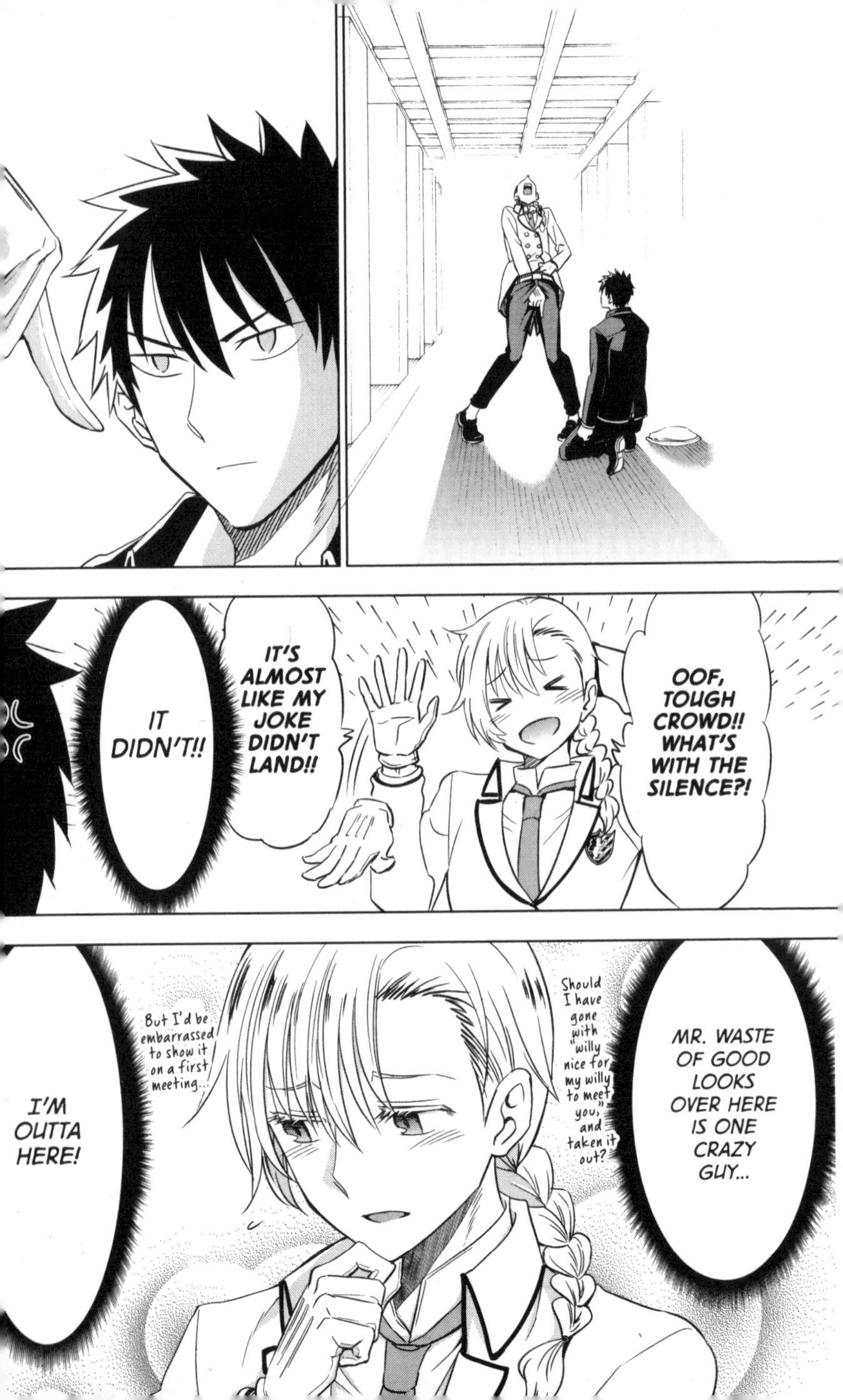
OOF, TOUGH CROWD!! WHAT'S WITH THE SILENCE?!
IT'S ALMOST LIKE MY JOKE DIDN'T LAND!!
IT DIDN'T!!
MR. WASTE OF GOOD LOOKS OVER HERE IS ONE CRAZY GUY...
Should I have gone with "willy nice for my willy to meet you," and taken it out?
But I'd be embarrassed to show it on a first meeting...
I'M OUTTA HERE!

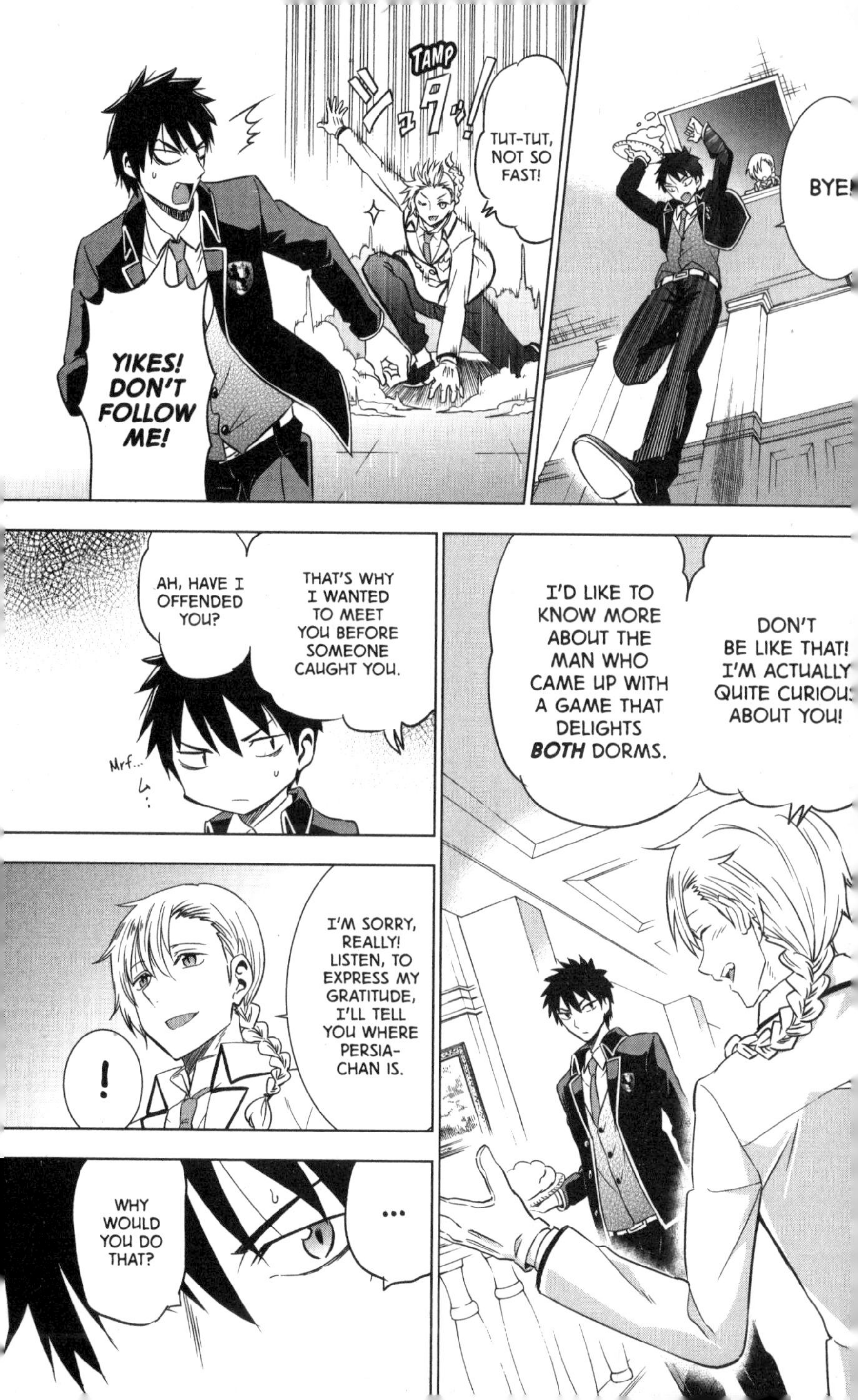
BYE!
TAMP
TUT-TUT, NOT SO FAST!
YIKES! DON'T FOLLOW ME!
DON'T BE LIKE THAT! I'M ACTUALLY QUITE CURIOUS ABOUT YOU!
I'D LIKE TO KNOW MORE ABOUT THE MAN WHO CAME UP WITH A GAME THAT DELIGHTS *BOTH* DORMS.
THAT'S WHY I WANTED TO MEET YOU BEFORE SOMEONE CAUGHT YOU.
AH, HAVE I OFFENDED YOU?
Mrf...
I'M SORRY, REALLY! LISTEN, TO EXPRESS MY GRATITUDE, I'LL TELL YOU WHERE PERSIA-CHAN IS.
!
...
WHY WOULD YOU DO THAT?

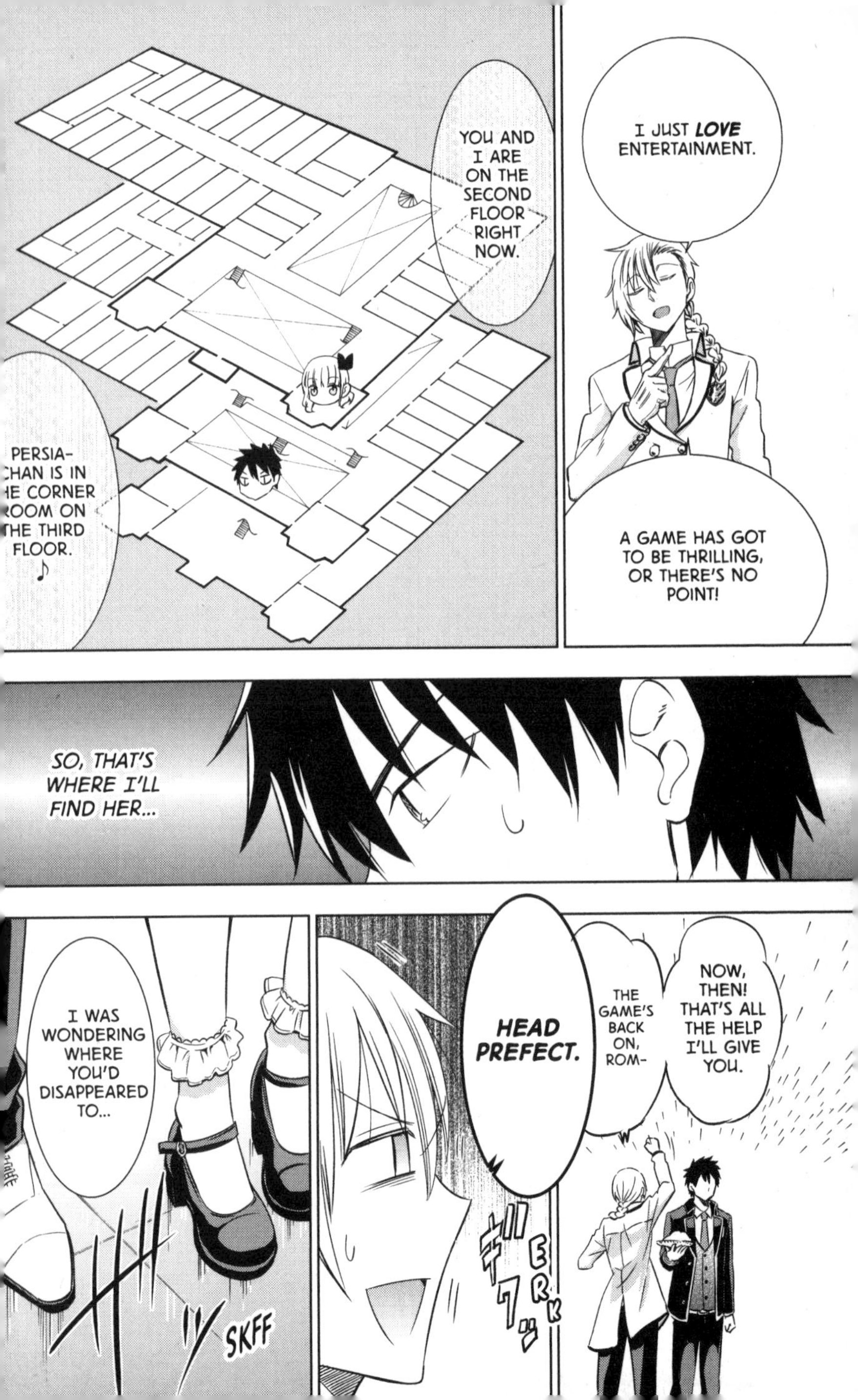
I JUST **LOVE** ENTERTAINMENT.
A GAME HAS GOT TO BE THRILLING, OR THERE'S NO POINT!
YOU AND I ARE ON THE SECOND FLOOR RIGHT NOW.
PERSIA-CHAN IS IN THE CORNER ROOM ON THE THIRD FLOOR. ♪
SO, THAT'S WHERE I'LL FIND HER...
NOW, THEN! THAT'S ALL THE HELP I'LL GIVE YOU.
THE GAME'S BACK ON, ROM-
HEAD PREFECT.
ギクッ
ERK
I WAS WONDERING WHERE YOU'D DISAPPEARED TO...
SKFF

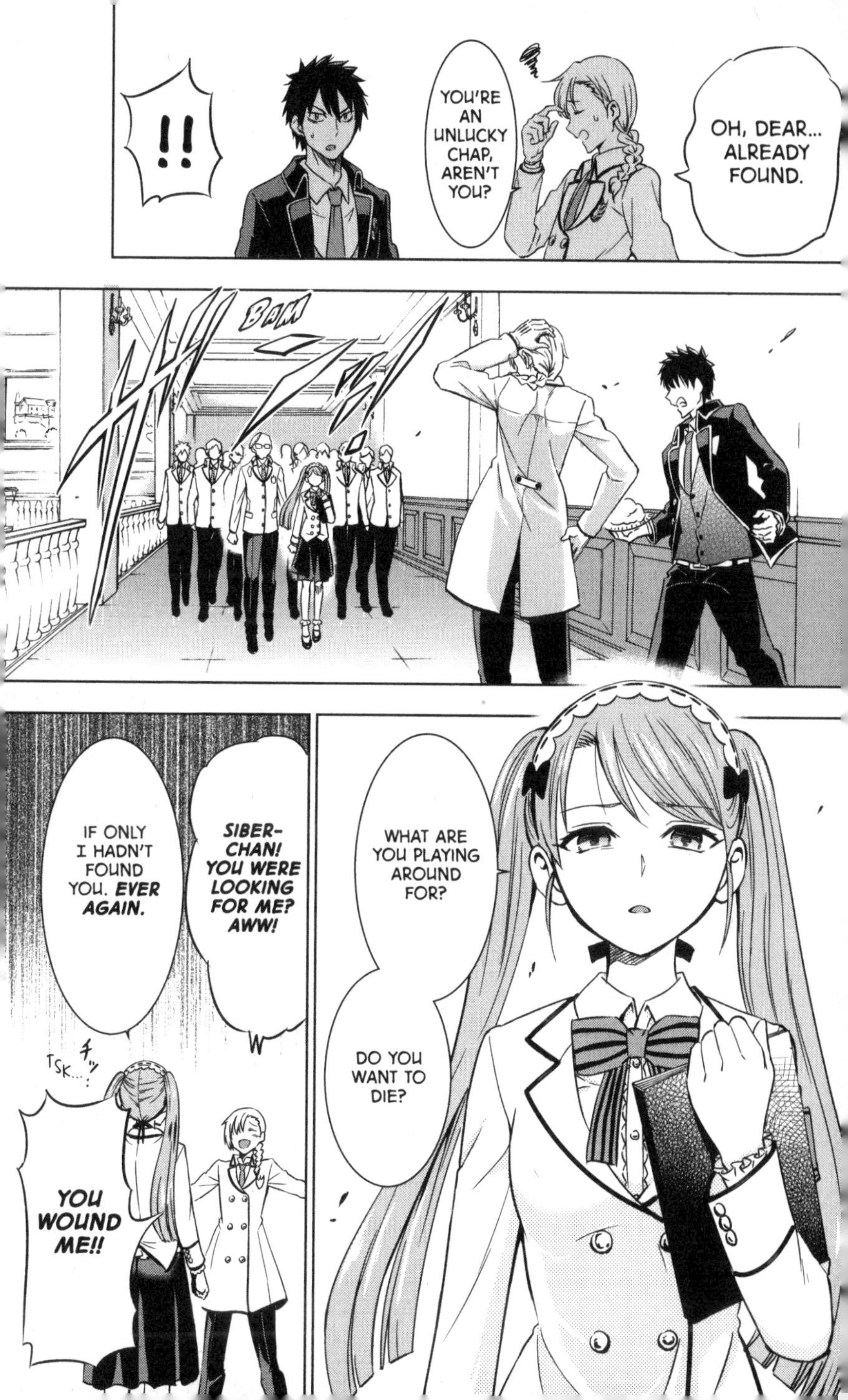
OH, DEAR... ALREADY FOUND.
YOU'RE AN UNLUCKY CHAP, AREN'T YOU?
!!
BAM
WHAT ARE YOU PLAYING AROUND FOR?
DO YOU WANT TO DIE?
SIBER-CHAN! YOU WERE LOOKING FOR ME? AWW!
IF ONLY I HADN'T FOUND YOU. EVER AGAIN.
チッ
TSK...
YOU WOUND ME!!

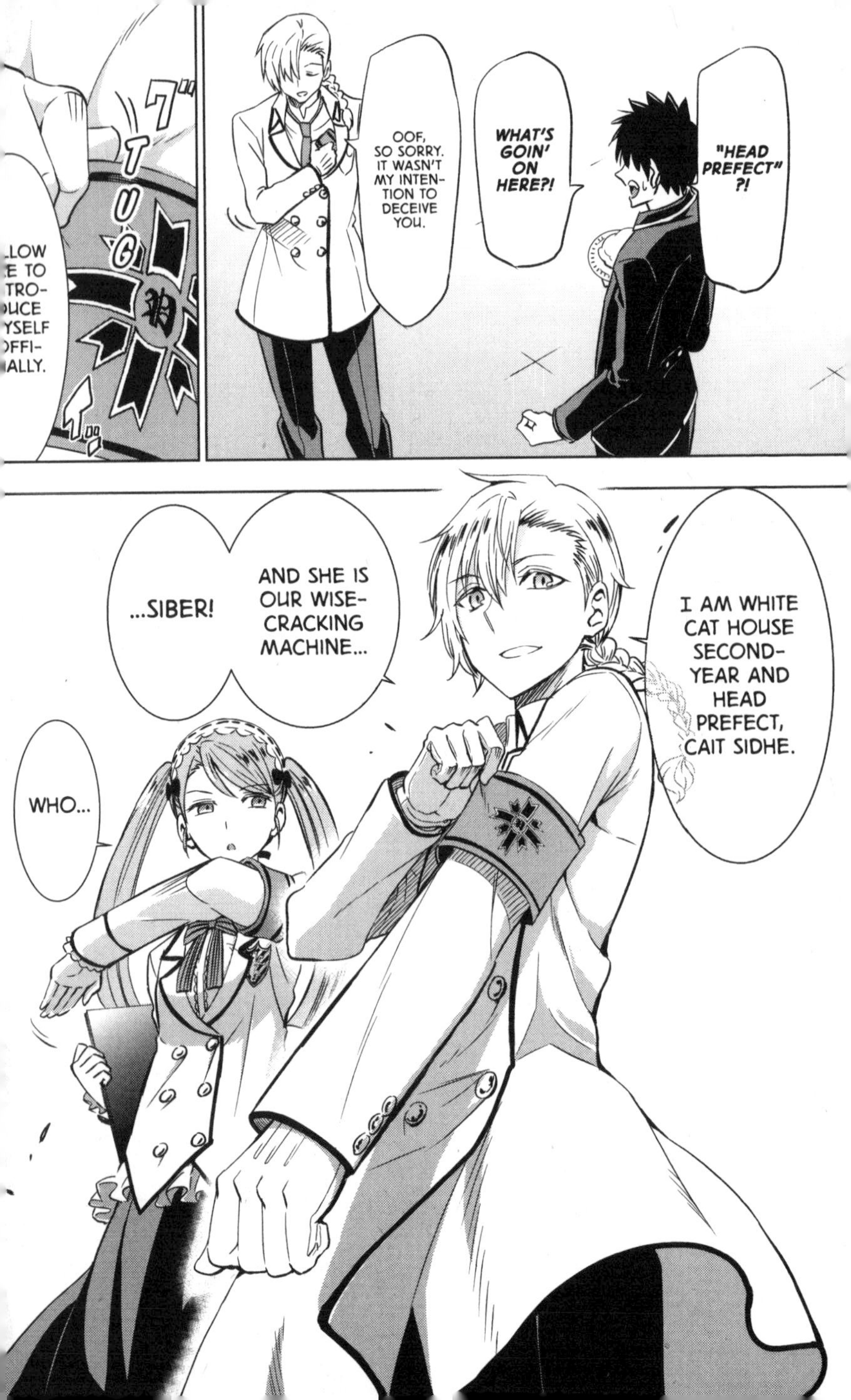
"HEAD PREFECT"?!
WHAT'S GOIN' ON HERE?!
OOF, SO SORRY. IT WASN'T MY INTEN-TION TO DECEIVE YOU.
TUG
I AM WHITE CAT HOUSE SECOND-YEAR AND HEAD PREFECT, CAIT SIDHE.
AND SHE IS OUR WISE-CRACKING MACHINE...
...SIBER!
WHO...

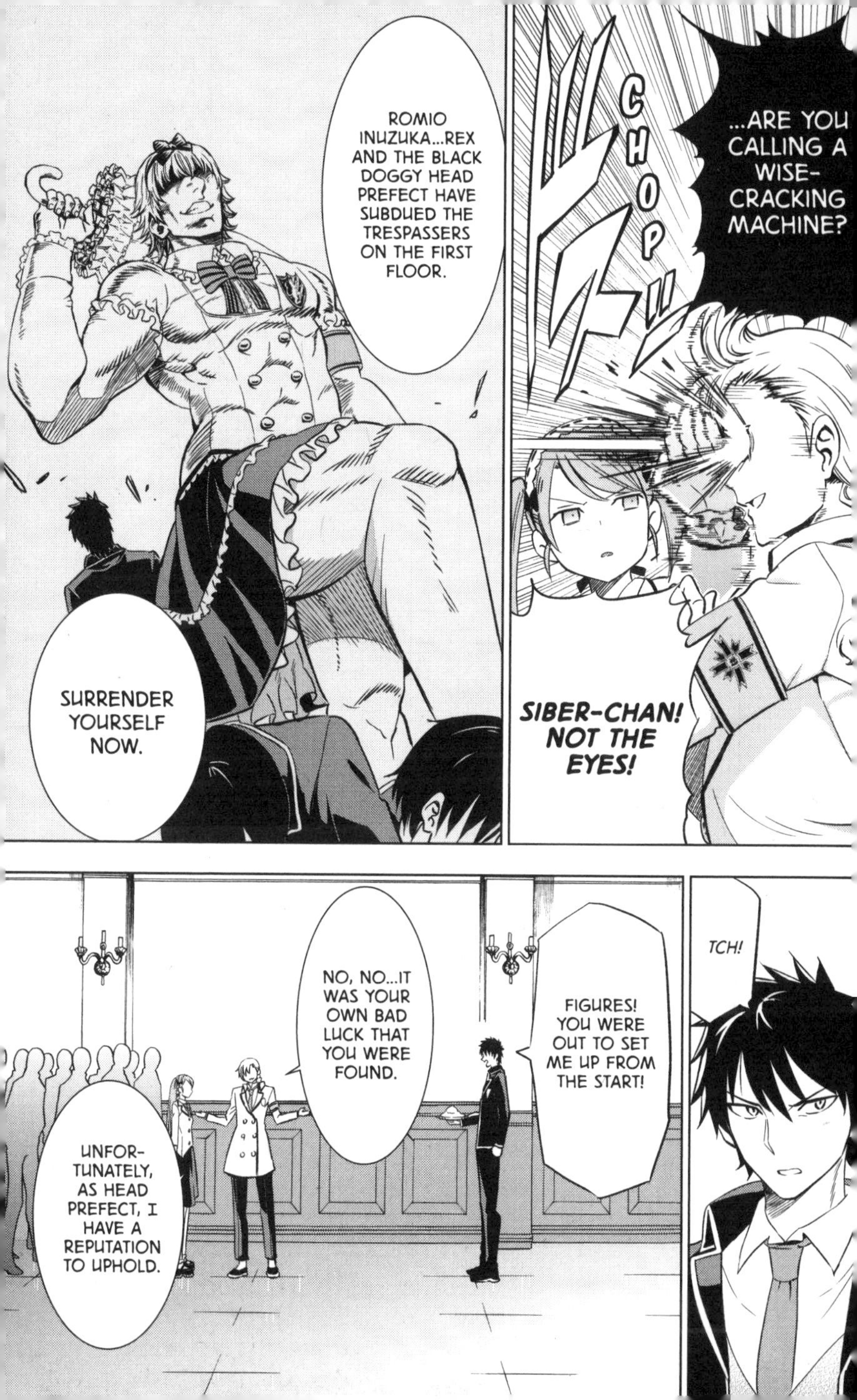
...ARE YOU CALLING A WISE-CRACKING MACHINE?
CHOP!!
SIBER-CHAN! NOT THE EYES!
ROMIO INUZUKA...REX AND THE BLACK DOGGY HEAD PREFECT HAVE SUBDUED THE TRESPASSERS ON THE FIRST FLOOR.
SURRENDER YOURSELF NOW.
TCH!
FIGURES! YOU WERE OUT TO SET ME UP FROM THE START!
NO, NO...IT WAS YOUR OWN BAD LUCK THAT YOU WERE FOUND.
UNFOR-TUNATELY, AS HEAD PREFECT, I HAVE A REPUTATION TO UPHOLD.

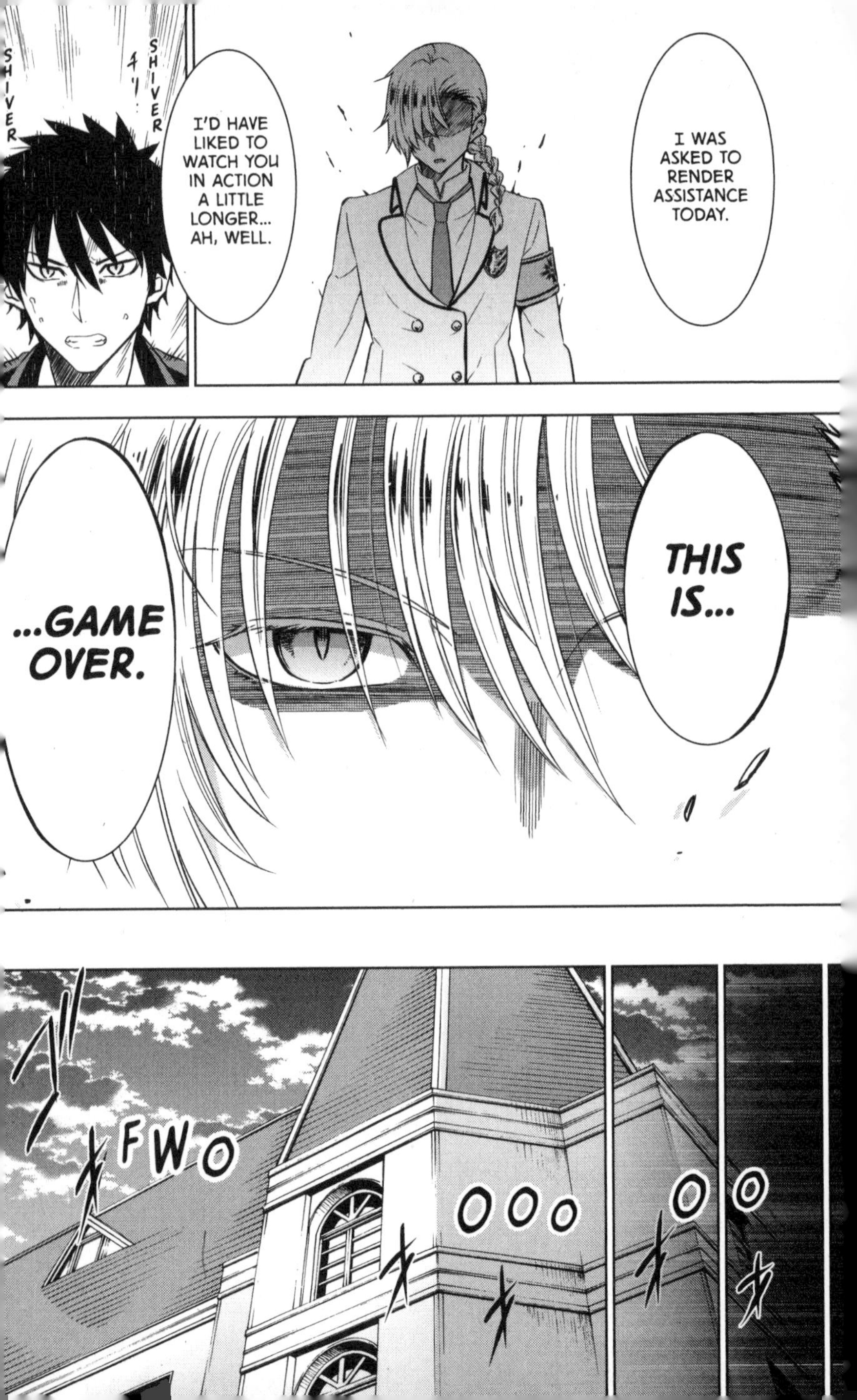
I WAS ASKED TO RENDER ASSISTANCE TODAY.
I'D HAVE LIKED TO WATCH YOU IN ACTION A LITTLE LONGER... AH, WELL.
SHIVER
SHIVER
THIS IS...
...GAME OVER.
FWOOOOOO

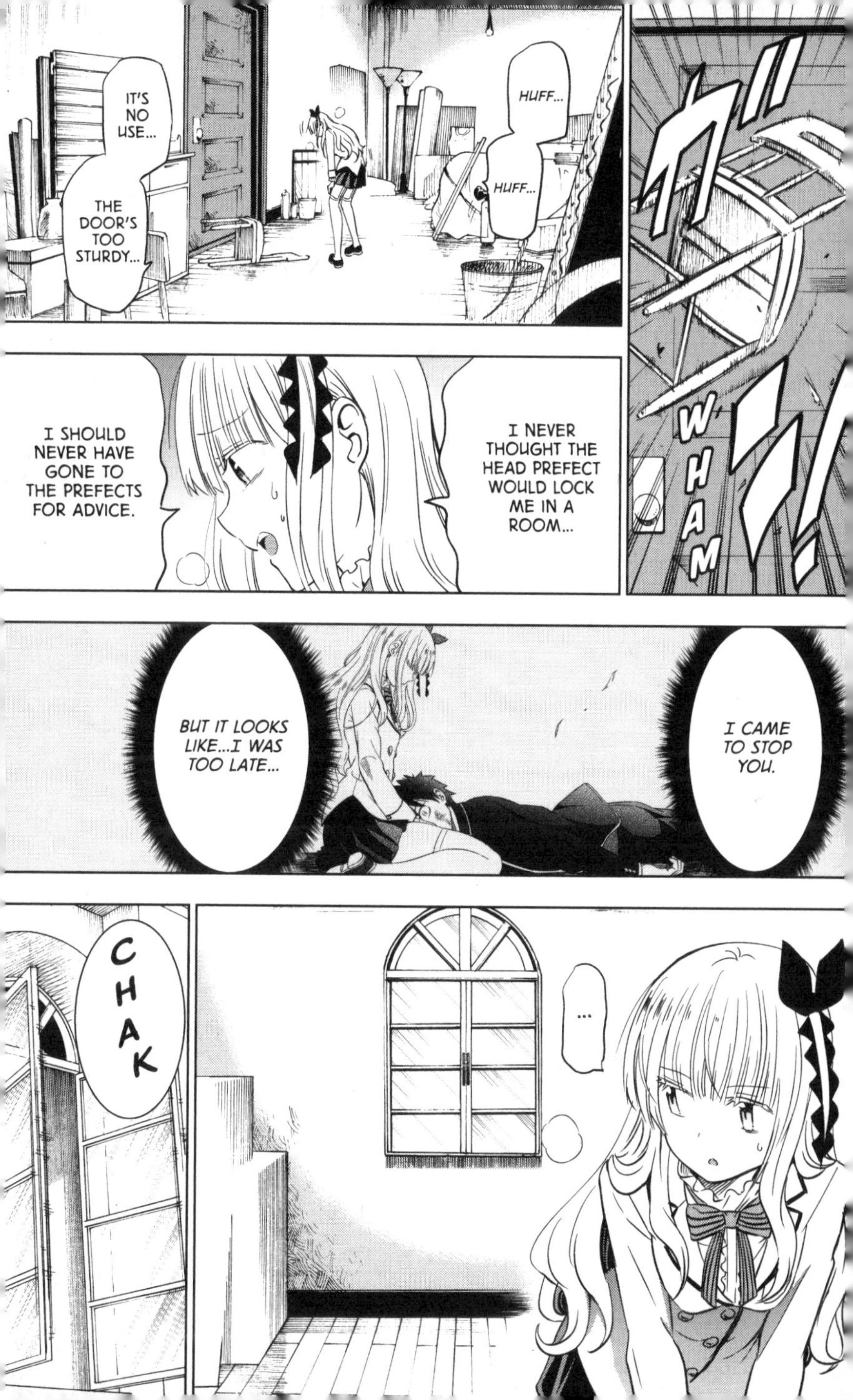
WHAM
HUFF...
HUFF...
IT'S NO USE...
THE DOOR'S TOO STURDY...
I NEVER THOUGHT THE HEAD PREFECT WOULD LOCK ME IN A ROOM...
I SHOULD NEVER HAVE GONE TO THE PREFECTS FOR ADVICE.
I CAME TO STOP YOU.
BUT IT LOOKS LIKE...I WAS TOO LATE...
...
CHAK

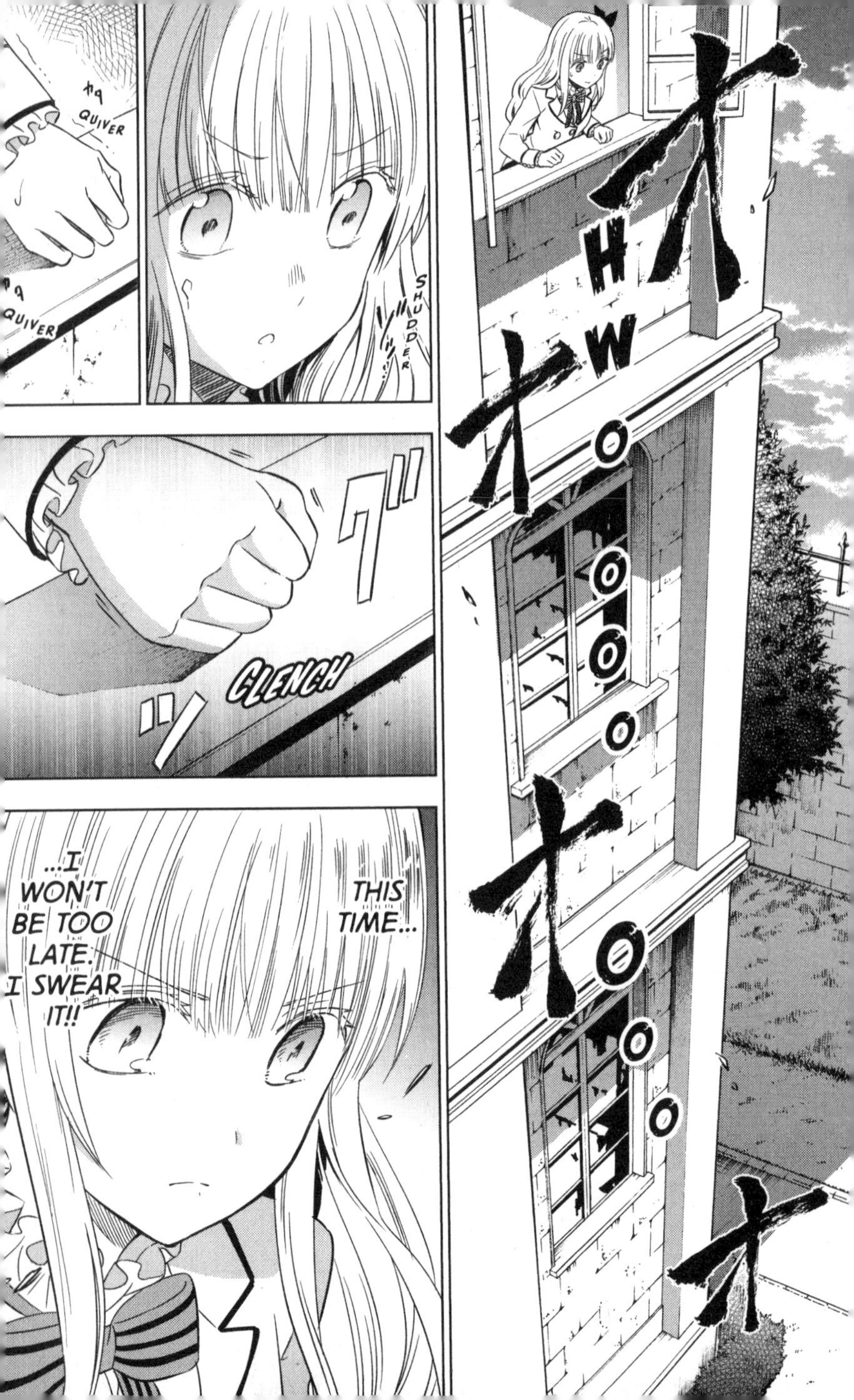
HW
SHUDDER
QUIVER
QUIVER
CLENCH
THIS TIME...
...I WON'T BE TOO LATE. I SWEAR IT!!

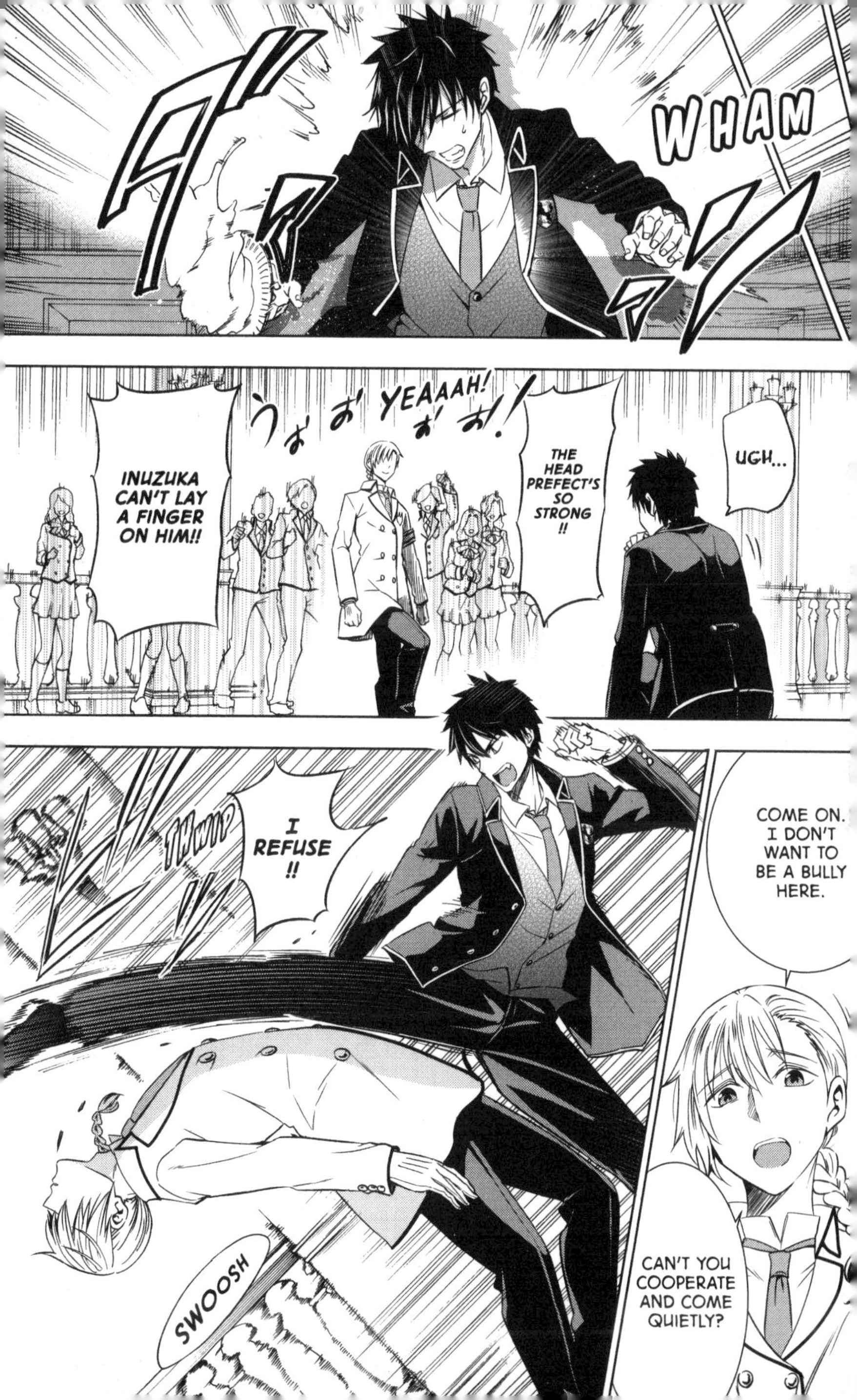
WHAM
UGH...
THE HEAD PREFECT'S SO STRONG!!
YEAAAH!
INUZUKA CAN'T LAY A FINGER ON HIM!!
COME ON. I DON'T WANT TO BE A BULLY HERE.
CAN'T YOU COOPERATE AND COME QUIETLY?
I REFUSE!!
THWIP
SWOOSH

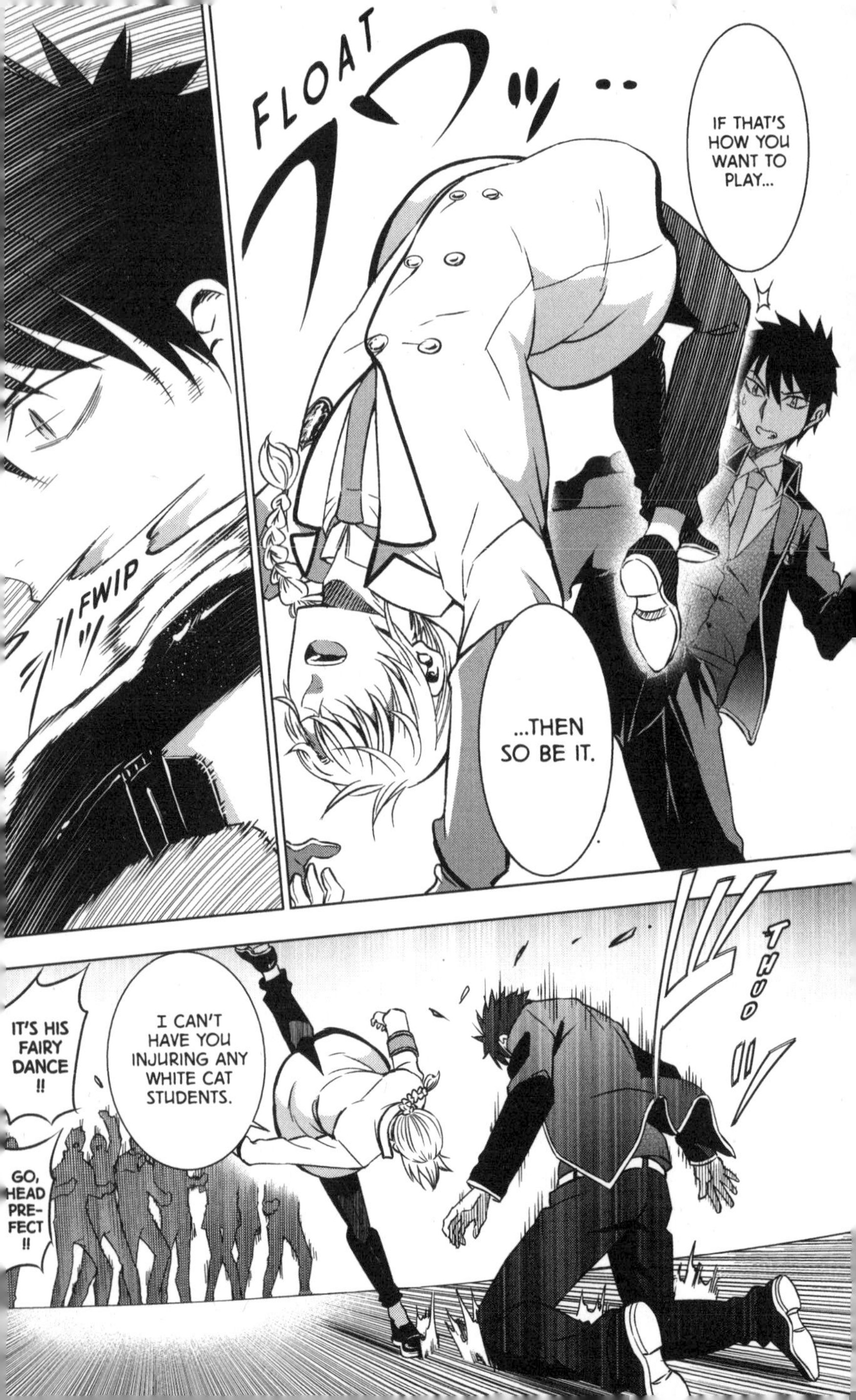
IF THAT'S HOW YOU WANT TO PLAY...
FLOAT
...THEN SO BE IT.
FWIP
THUD
I CAN'T HAVE YOU INJURING ANY WHITE CAT STUDENTS.
IT'S HIS FAIRY DANCE!!
GO, HEAD PREFECT!!

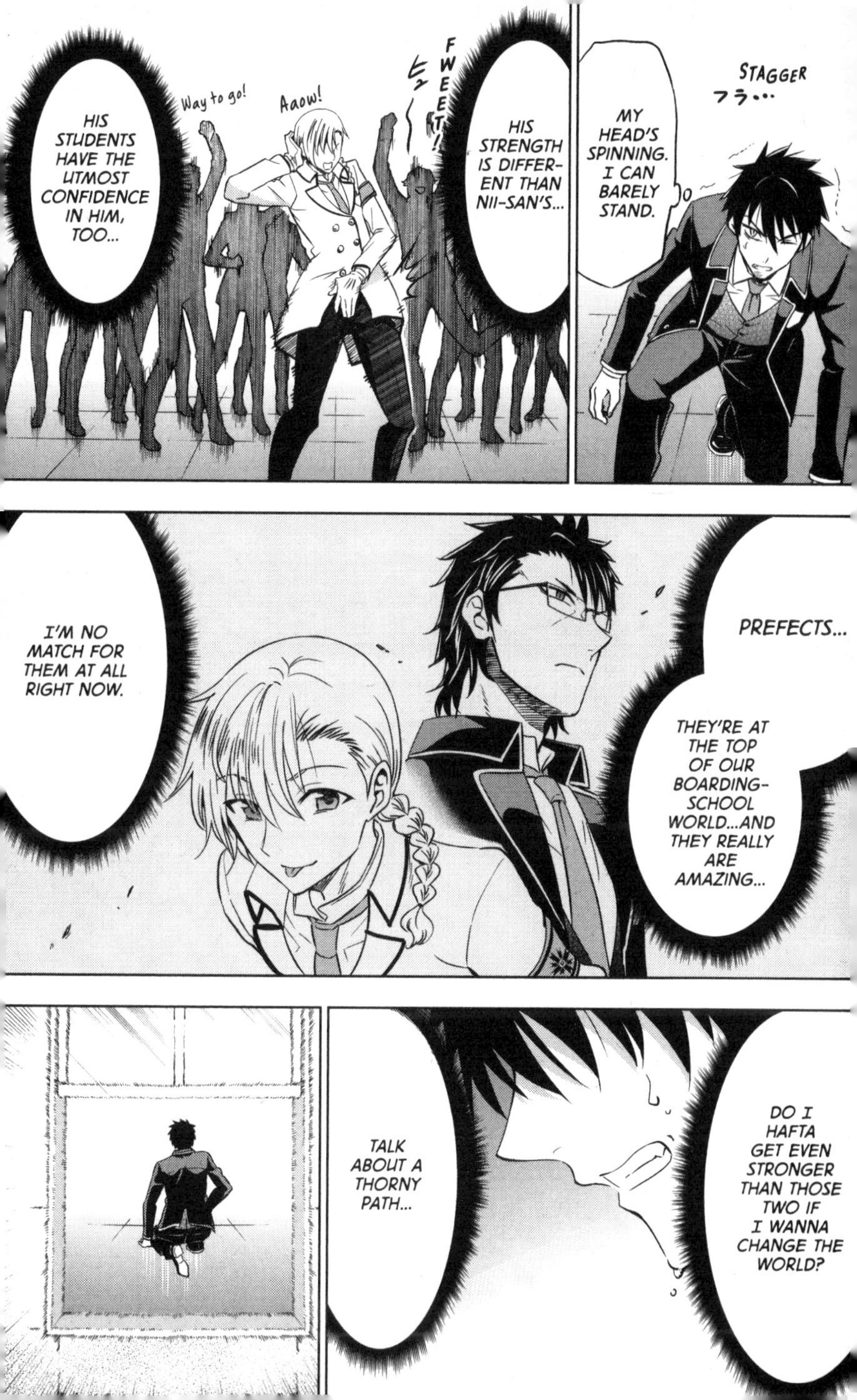
STAGGER
フラ…
MY HEAD'S SPINNING. I CAN BARELY STAND.
HIS STRENGTH IS DIFFERENT THAN NII-SAN'S...
FWEET!!
ヒュ
Aaow!
Way to go!
HIS STUDENTS HAVE THE UTMOST CONFIDENCE IN HIM, TOO...
PREFECTS...
THEY'RE AT THE TOP OF OUR BOARDING-SCHOOL WORLD...AND THEY REALLY ARE AMAZING...
I'M NO MATCH FOR THEM AT ALL RIGHT NOW.
DO I HAFTA GET EVEN STRONGER THAN THOSE TWO IF I WANNA CHANGE THE WORLD?
TALK ABOUT A THORNY PATH...

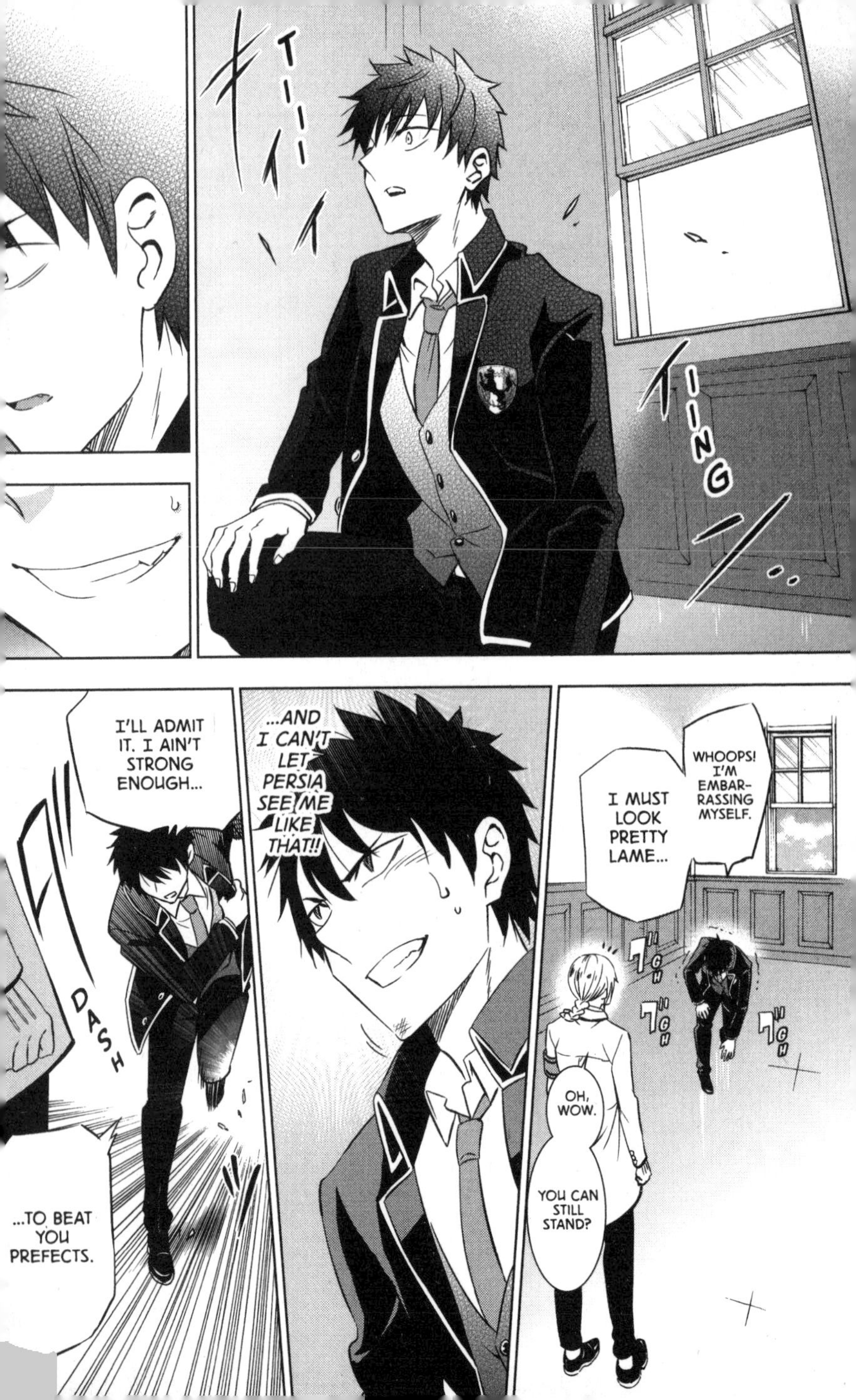
T-I-I-I
TIING
WHOOPS! I'M EMBAR-RASSING MYSELF.
I MUST LOOK PRETTY LAME...
GH
GH
GH
OH, WOW.
YOU CAN STILL STAND?
...AND I CAN'T LET PERSIA SEE ME LIKE THAT!!
I'LL ADMIT IT. I AIN'T STRONG ENOUGH...
DASH
...TO BEAT YOU PREFECTS.

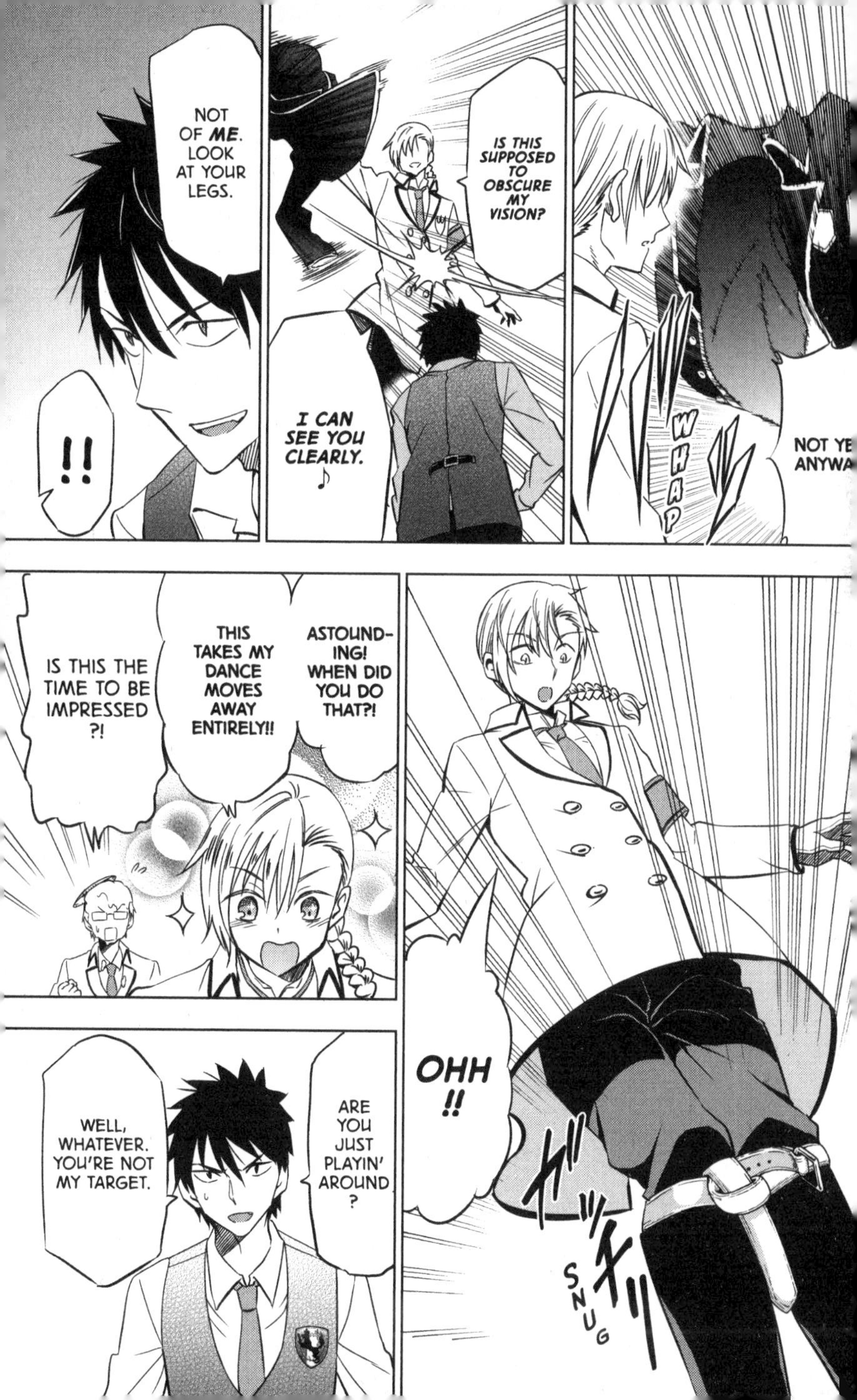
NOT YE ANYWA
WHAP
IS THIS SUPPOSED TO OBSCURE MY VISION?
I CAN SEE YOU CLEARLY. ♪
NOT OF *ME*. LOOK AT YOUR LEGS.
!!
OHH !!
SNUG
ASTOUND-ING! WHEN DID YOU DO THAT?!
THIS TAKES MY DANCE MOVES AWAY ENTIRELY!!
IS THIS THE TIME TO BE IMPRESSED ?!
ARE YOU JUST PLAYIN' AROUND ?
WELL, WHATEVER. YOU'RE NOT MY TARGET.

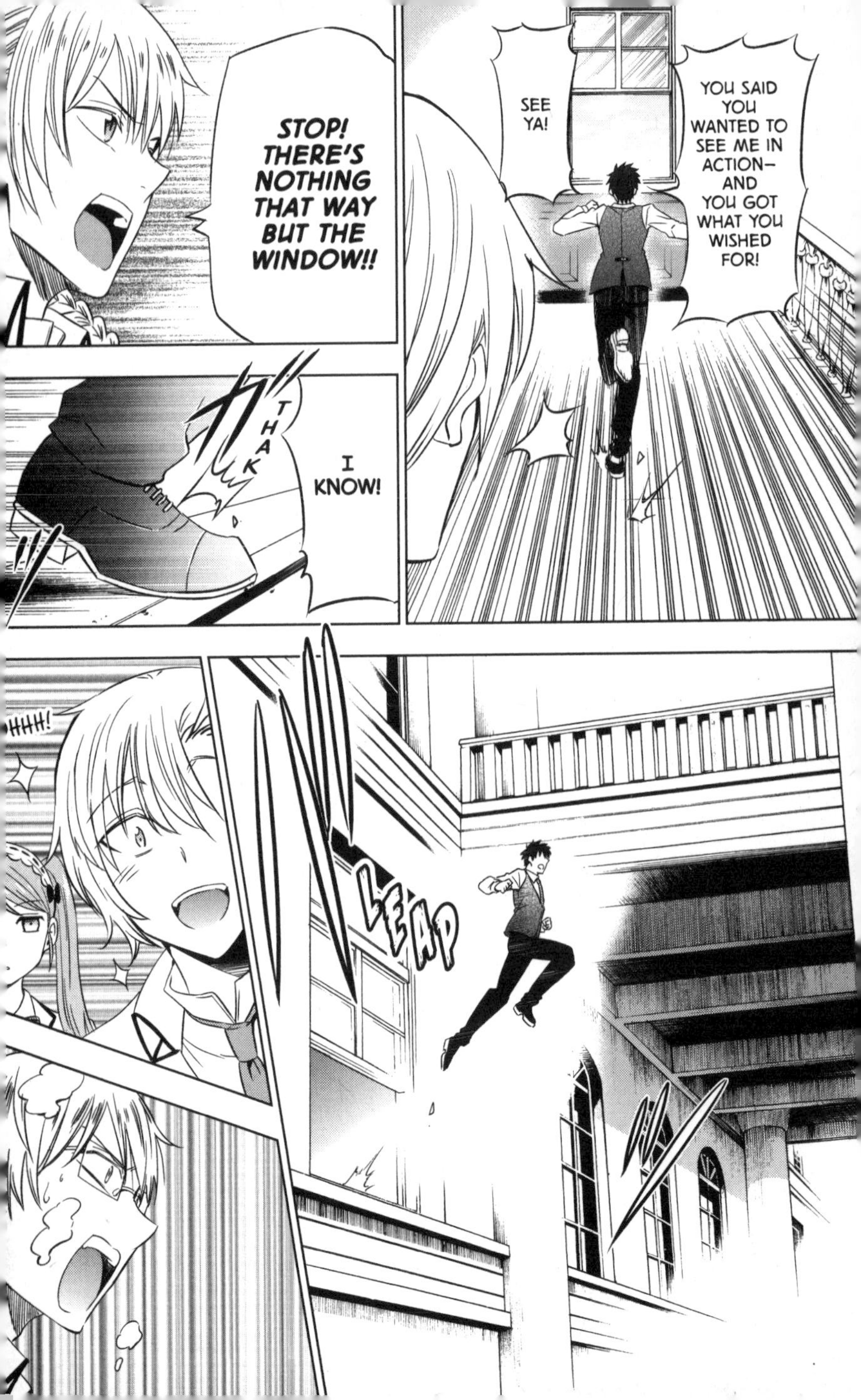
YOU SAID YOU WANTED TO SEE ME IN ACTION—AND YOU GOT WHAT YOU WISHED FOR!
SEE YA!
STOP! THERE'S NOTHING THAT WAY BUT THE WINDOW!!
THAK
I KNOW!
LEAP
HHH!

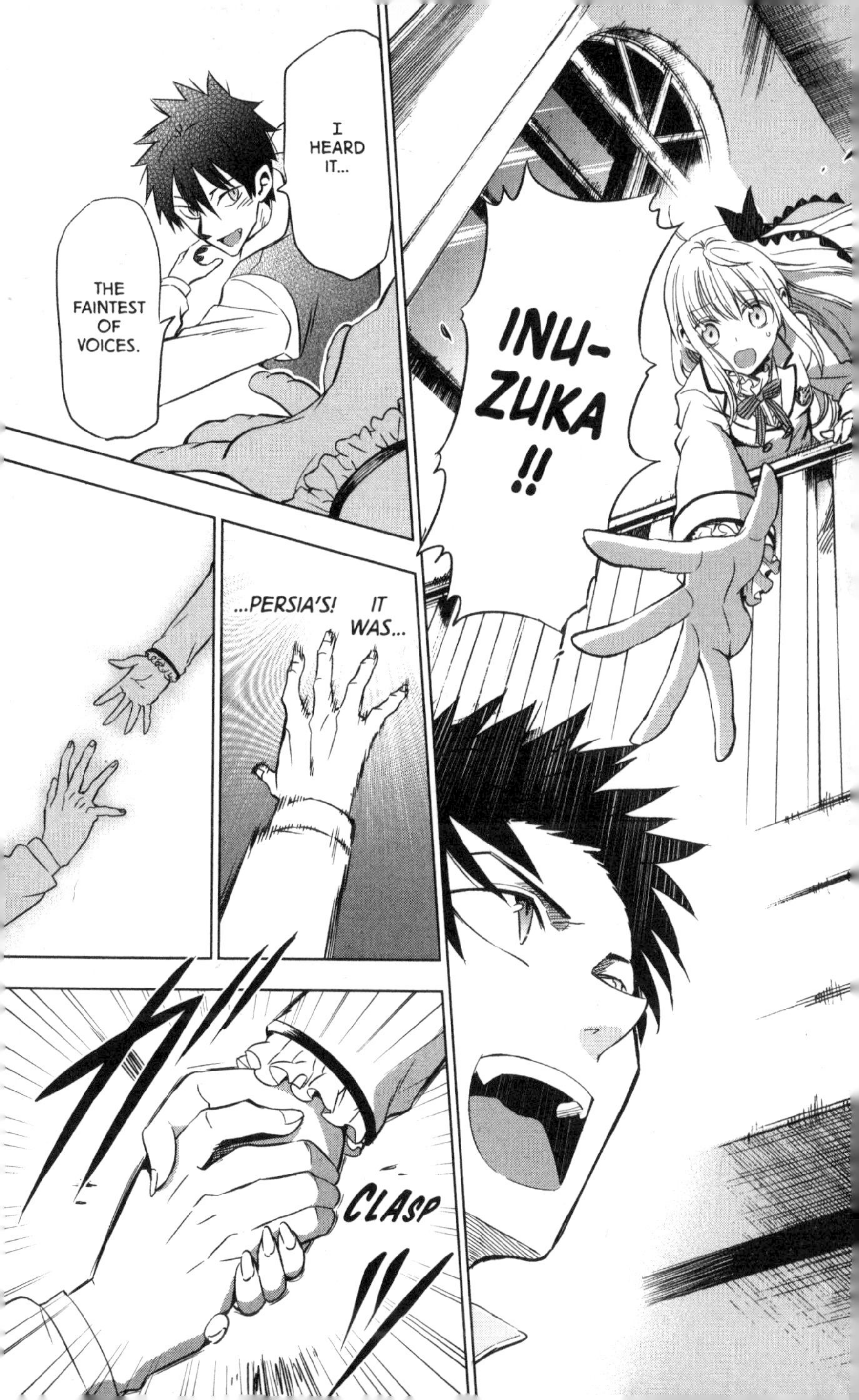
INU-ZUKA!!
I HEARD IT...
THE FAINTEST OF VOICES.
IT WAS...
...PERSIA'S!
CLASP

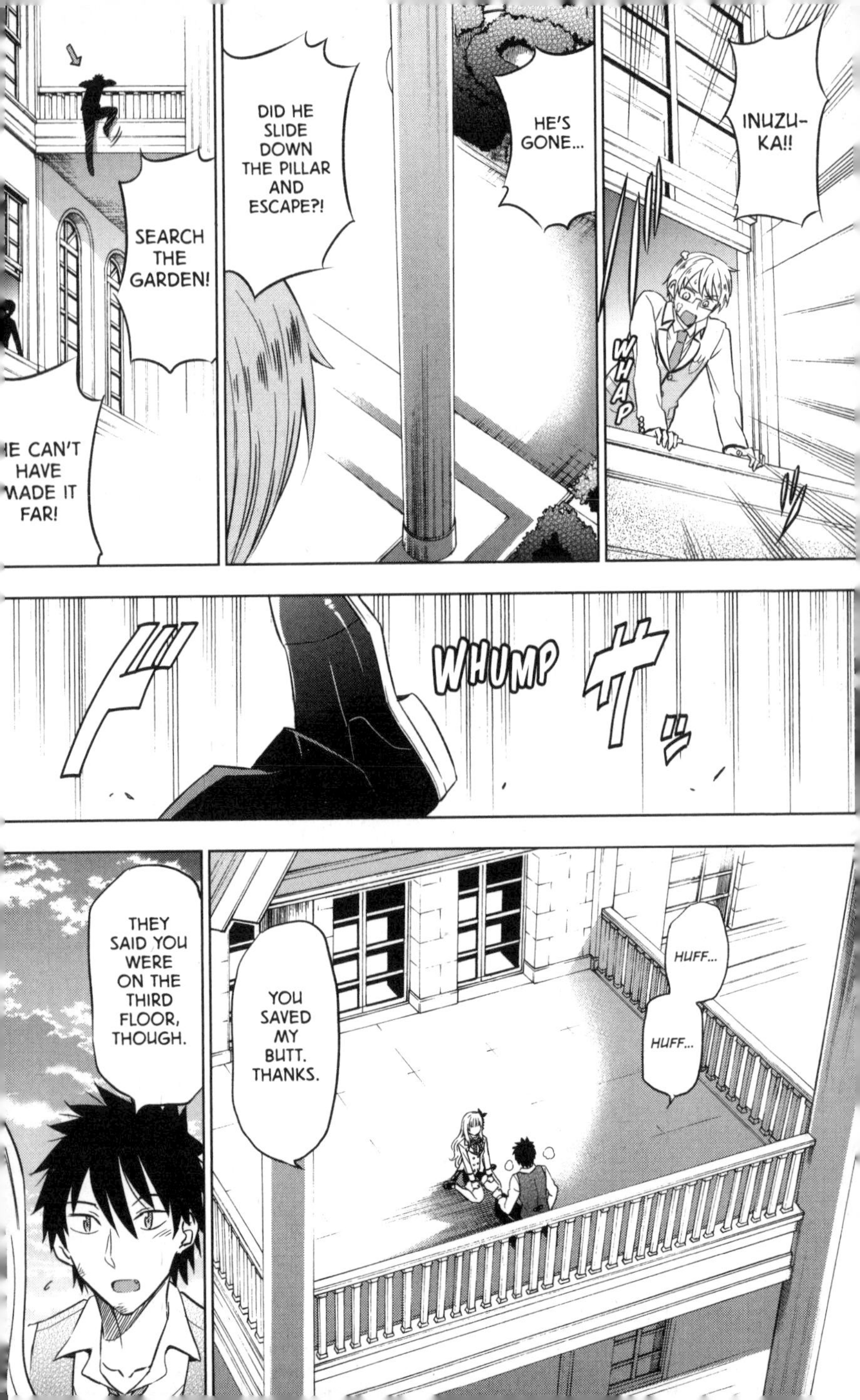

INUZU-KA!!
WHAP
HE'S GONE...
DID HE SLIDE DOWN THE PILLAR AND ESCAPE?!
SEARCH THE GARDEN!
HE CAN'T HAVE MADE IT FAR!
WHUMP
HUFF...
HUFF...
YOU SAVED MY BUTT. THANKS.
THEY SAID YOU WERE ON THE THIRD FLOOR, THOUGH.

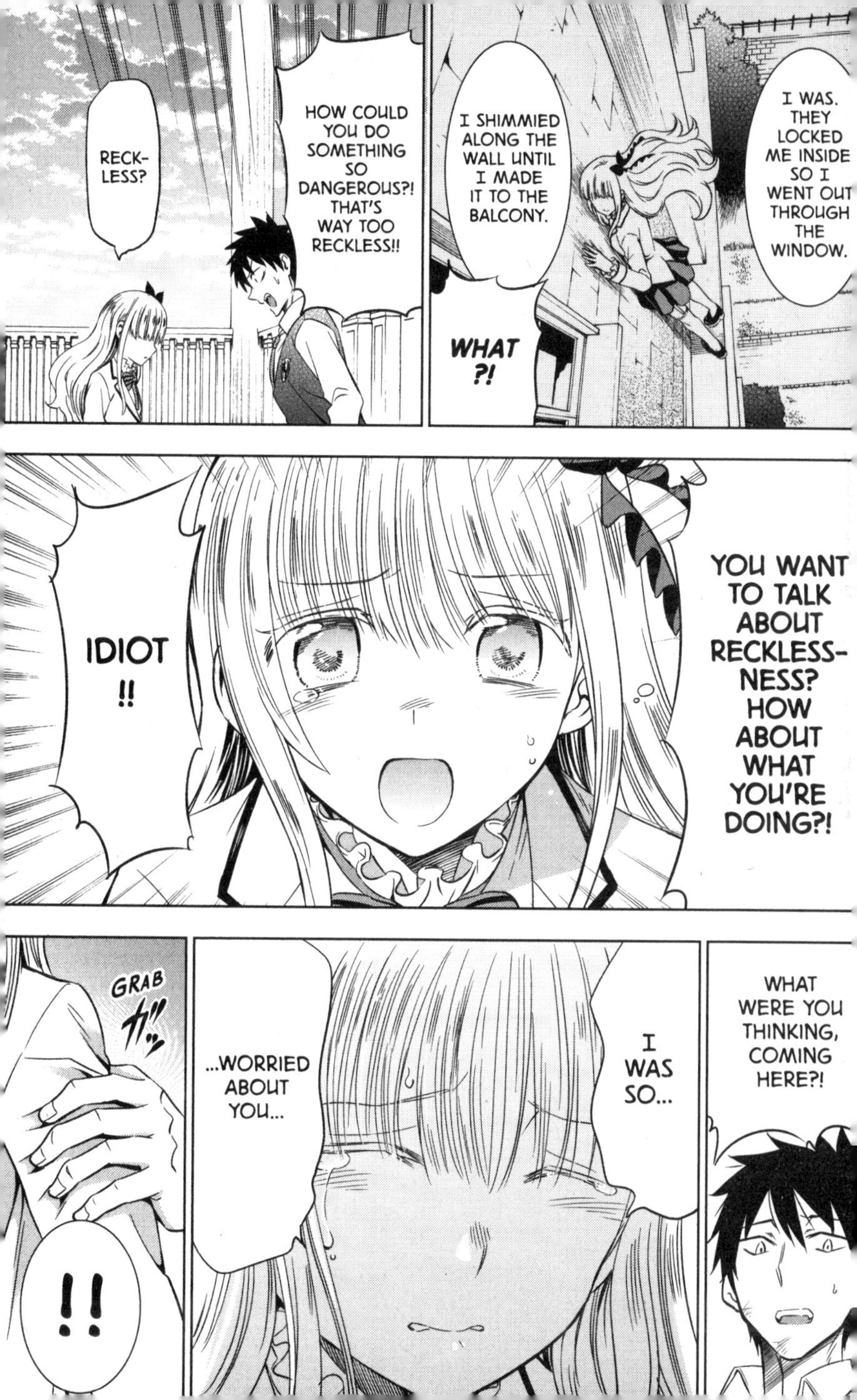
I WAS. THEY LOCKED ME INSIDE SO I WENT OUT THROUGH THE WINDOW.
I SHIMMIED ALONG THE WALL UNTIL I MADE IT TO THE BALCONY.
WHAT ?!
HOW COULD YOU DO SOMETHING SO DANGEROUS?! THAT'S WAY TOO RECKLESS!!
RECK-LESS?
YOU WANT TO TALK ABOUT RECKLESS-NESS? HOW ABOUT WHAT YOU'RE DOING?!
IDIOT !!
WHAT WERE YOU THINKING, COMING HERE?!
I WAS SO...
...WORRIED ABOUT YOU...
GRAB
!!

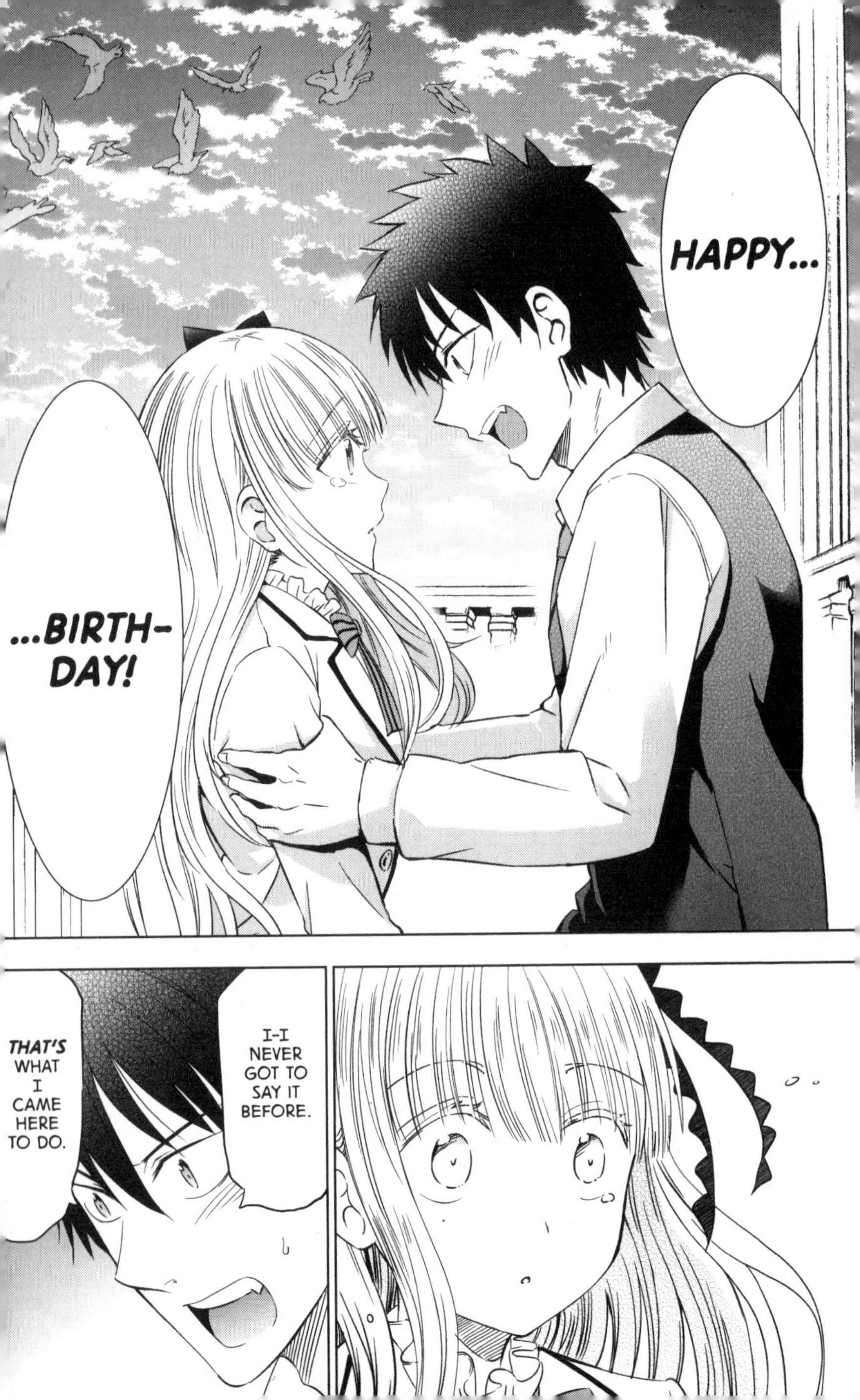
HAPPY...
...BIRTH-DAY!
I-I NEVER GOT TO SAY IT BEFORE.
THAT'S WHAT I CAME HERE TO DO.

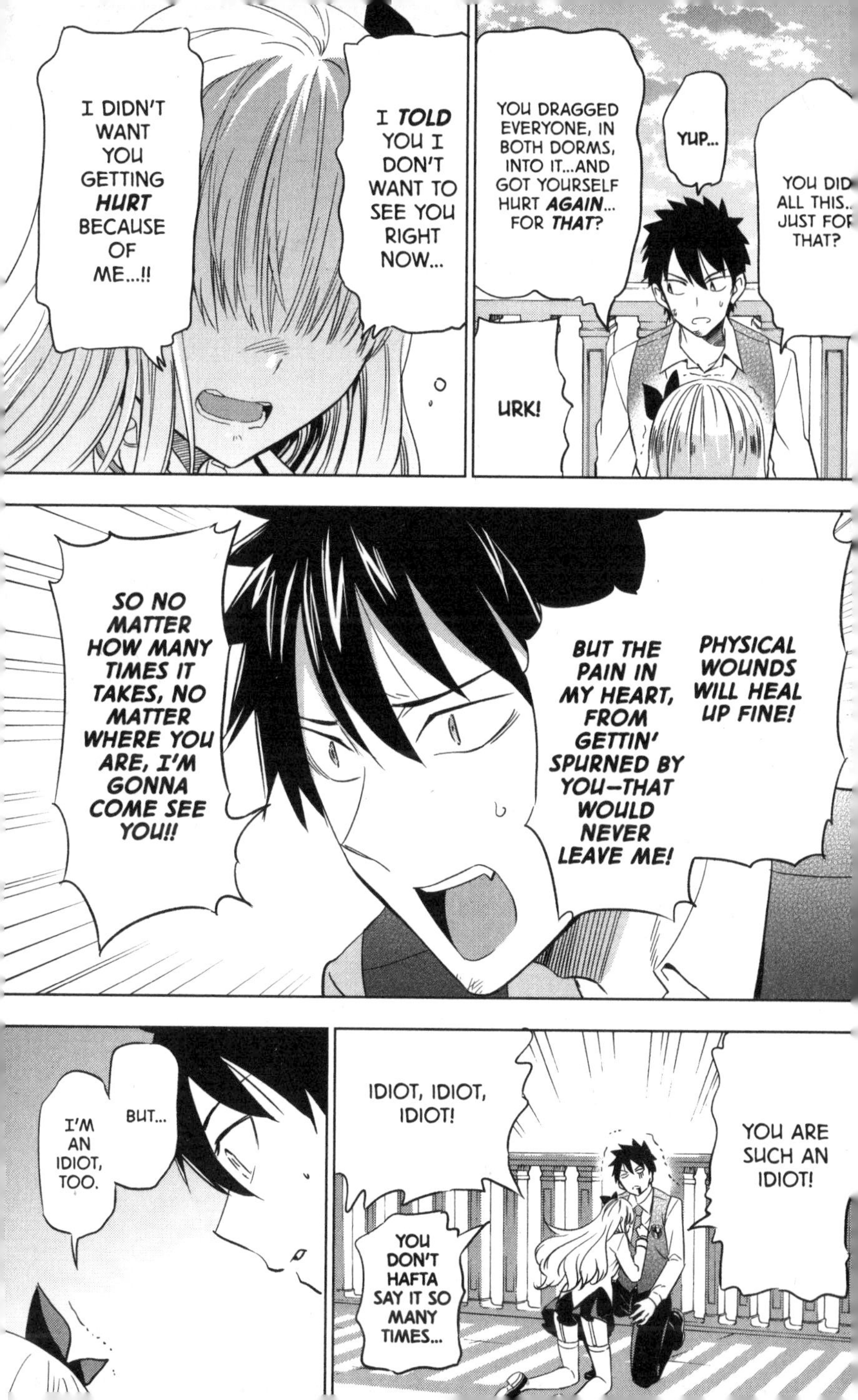
YOU DID ALL THIS... JUST FOR THAT?
YUP...
YOU DRAGGED EVERYONE, IN BOTH DORMS, INTO IT...AND GOT YOURSELF HURT AGAIN... FOR THAT?
URK!
I TOLD YOU I DON'T WANT TO SEE YOU RIGHT NOW...
I DIDN'T WANT YOU GETTING HURT BECAUSE OF ME...!!
PHYSICAL WOUNDS WILL HEAL UP FINE!
BUT THE PAIN IN MY HEART, FROM GETTIN' SPURNED BY YOU—THAT WOULD NEVER LEAVE ME!
SO NO MATTER HOW MANY TIMES IT TAKES, NO MATTER WHERE YOU ARE, I'M GONNA COME SEE YOU!!
YOU ARE SUCH AN IDIOT!
IDIOT, IDIOT, IDIOT!
YOU DON'T HAFTA SAY IT SO MANY TIMES...
BUT...
I'M AN IDIOT, TOO.

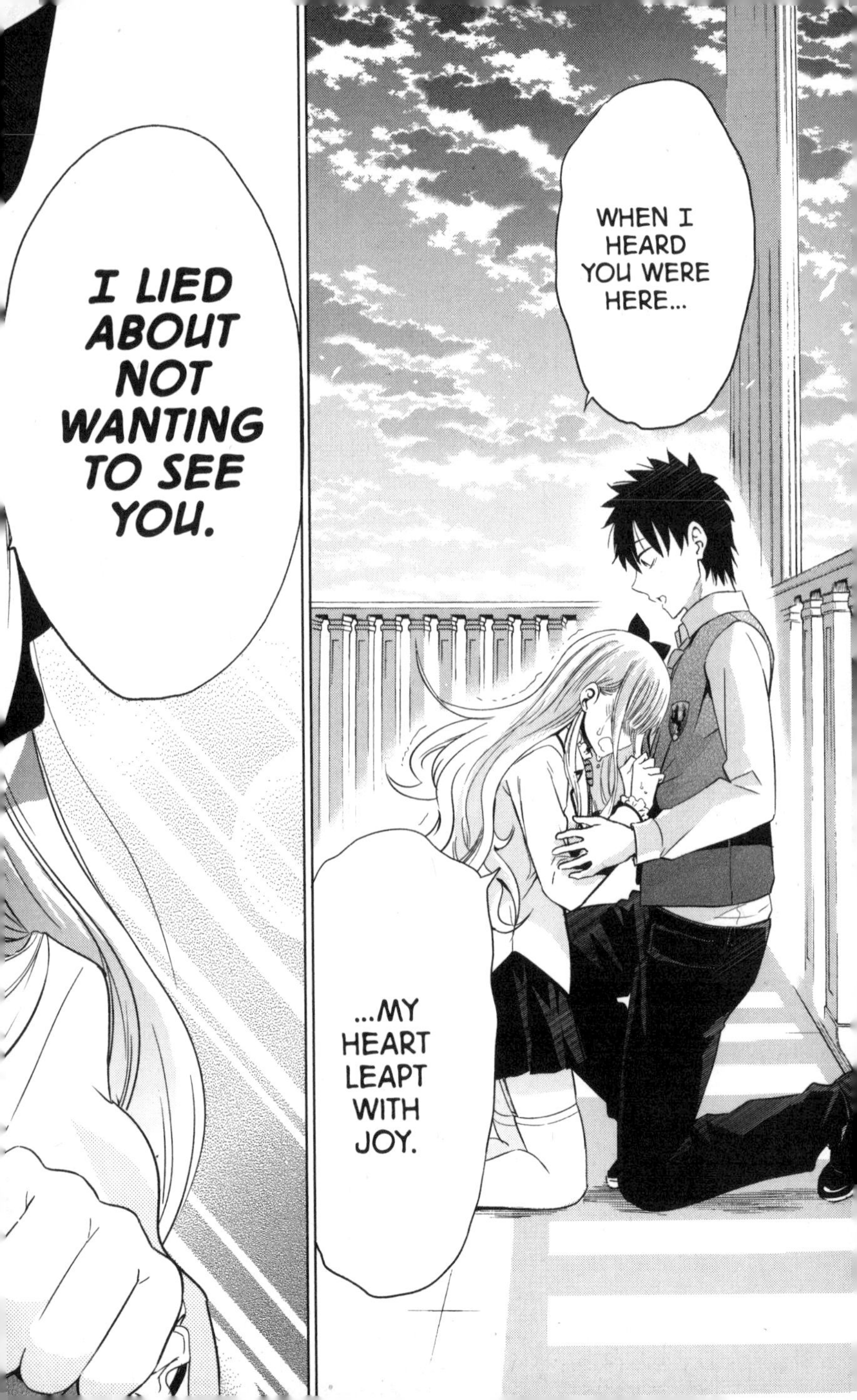
WHEN I HEARD YOU WERE HERE...
...MY HEART LEAPT WITH JOY.
I LIED ABOUT NOT WANTING TO SEE YOU.

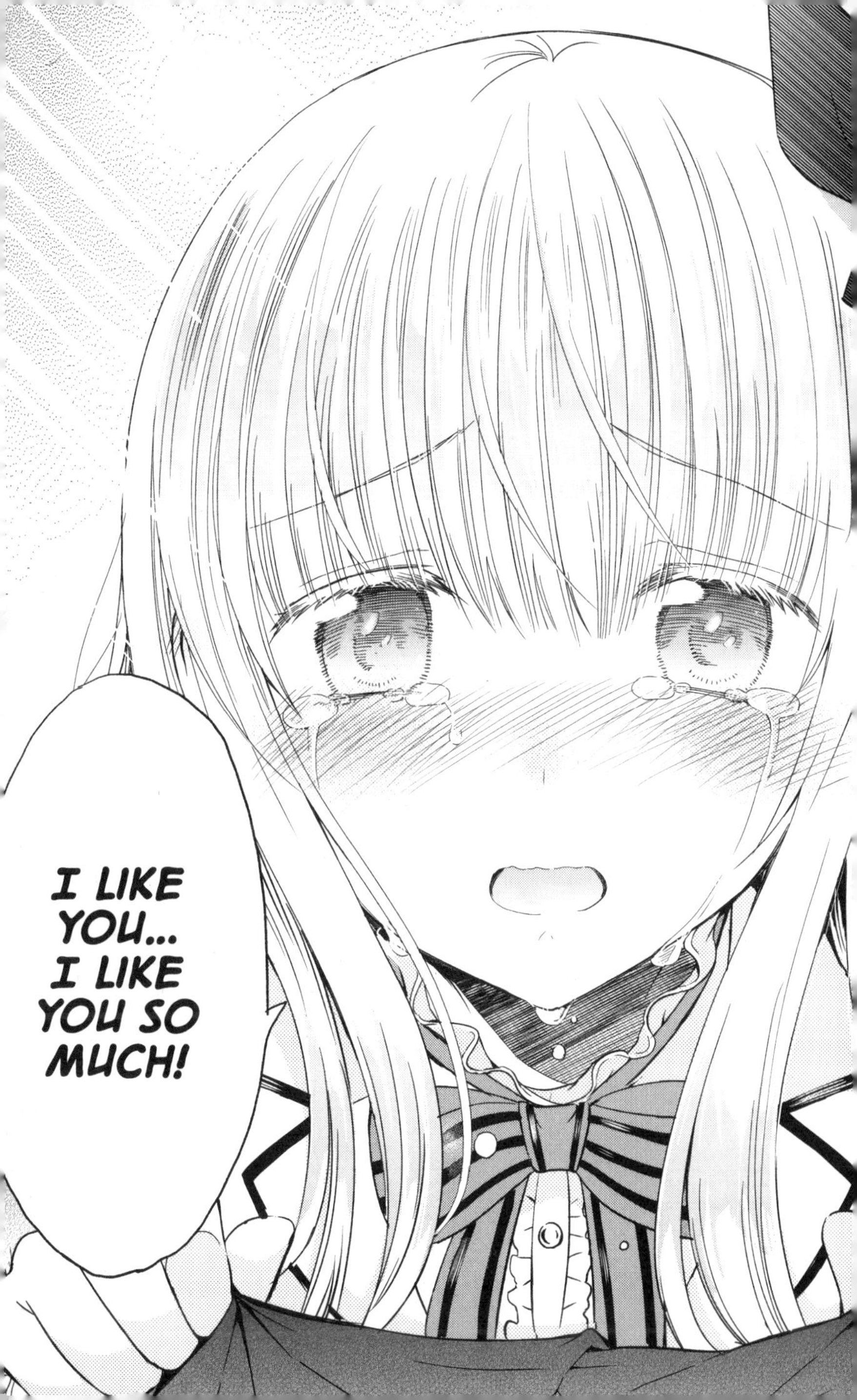
I LIKE YOU... I LIKE YOU SO MUCH!

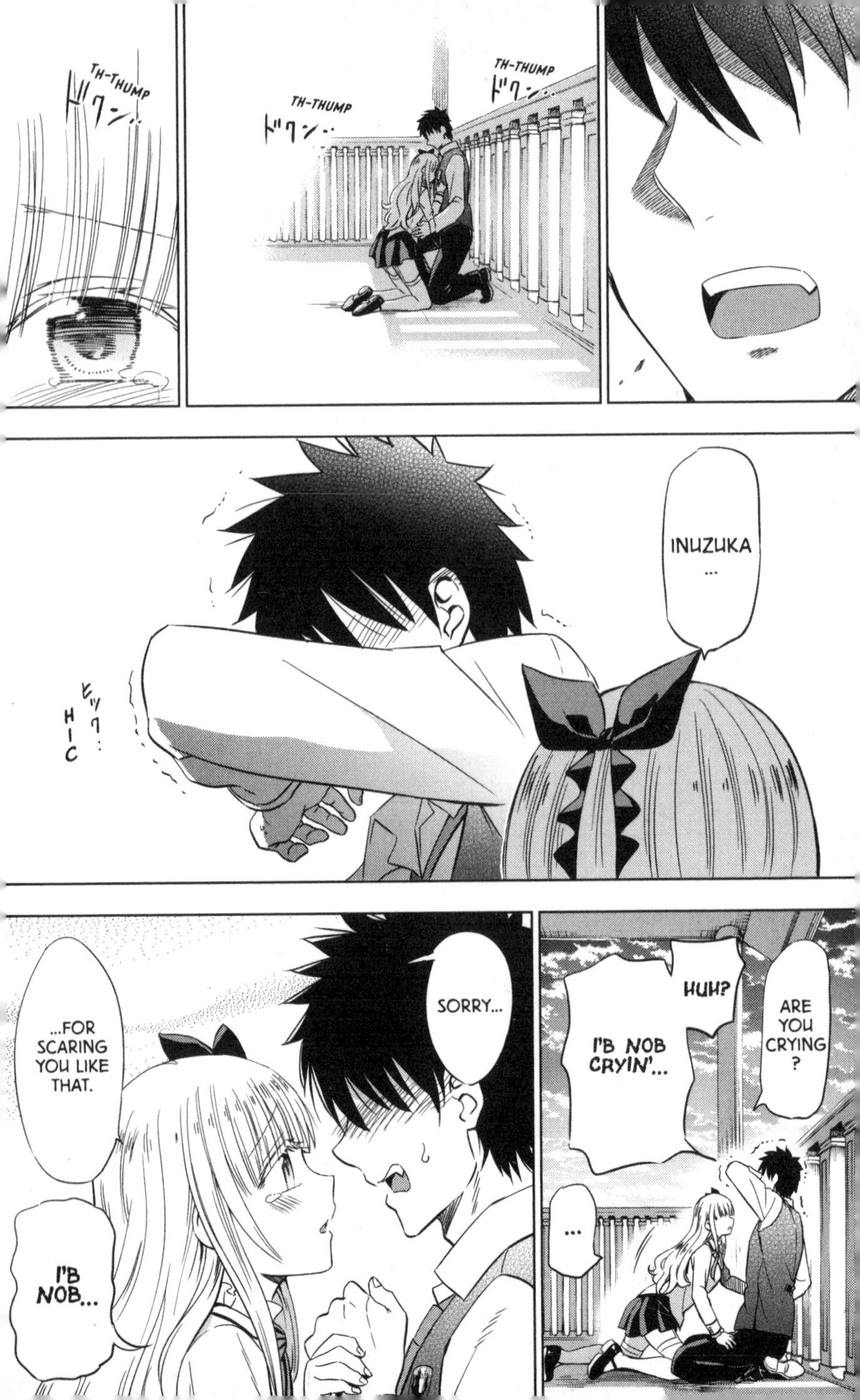
TH-THUMP
TH-THUMP
TH-THUMP
INUZUKA ...
HIC
ARE YOU CRYING?
HUH?
I'B NOB CRYIN'...
...
SORRY...
...FOR SCARING YOU LIKE THAT.
I'B NOB...

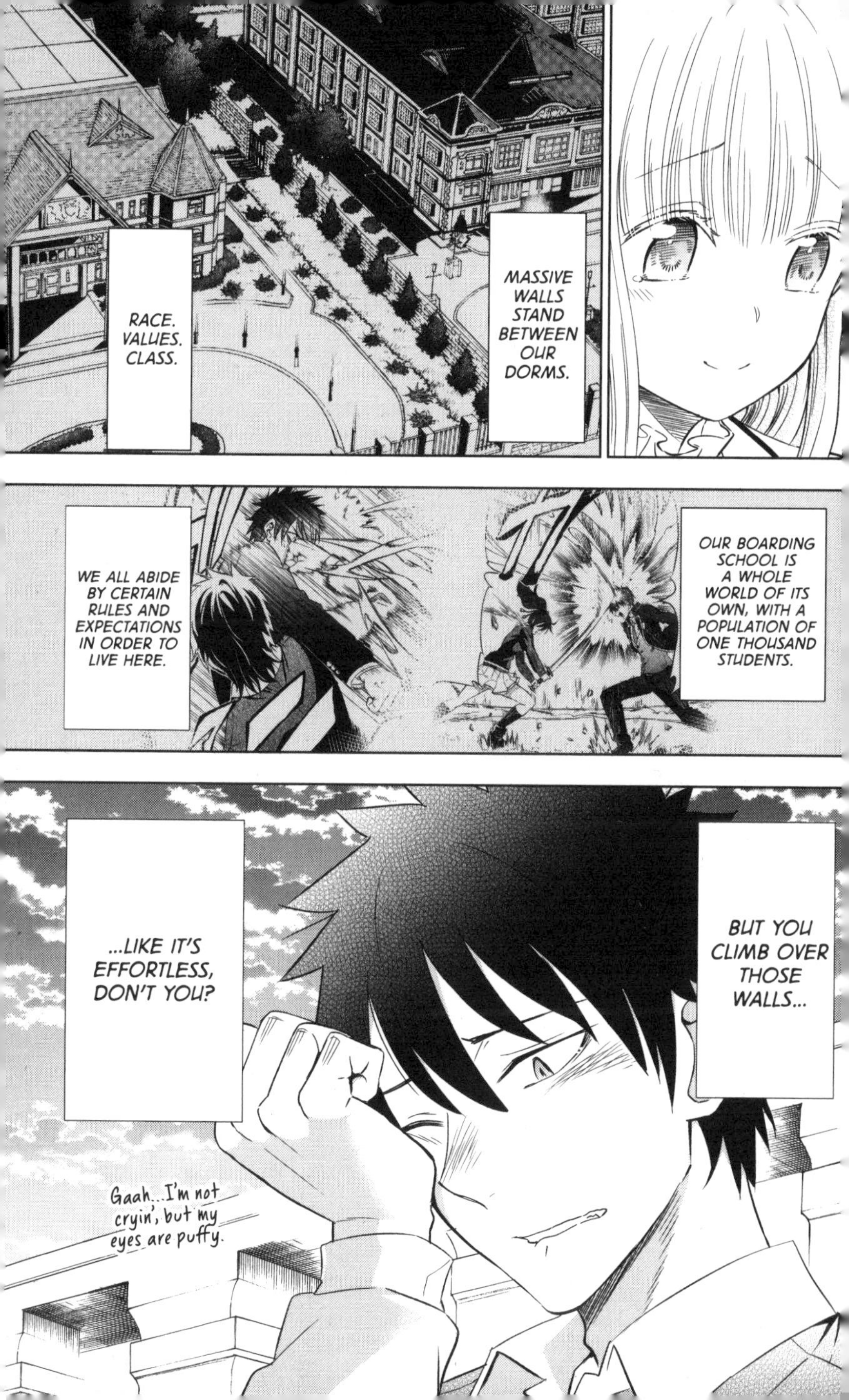
MASSIVE WALLS STAND BETWEEN OUR DORMS.
RACE. VALUES. CLASS.
OUR BOARDING SCHOOL IS A WHOLE WORLD OF ITS OWN, WITH A POPULATION OF ONE THOUSAND STUDENTS.
WE ALL ABIDE BY CERTAIN RULES AND EXPECTATIONS IN ORDER TO LIVE HERE.
BUT YOU CLIMB OVER THOSE WALLS...
...LIKE IT'S EFFORTLESS, DON'T YOU?
Gaah...I'm not cryin', but my eyes are puffy.

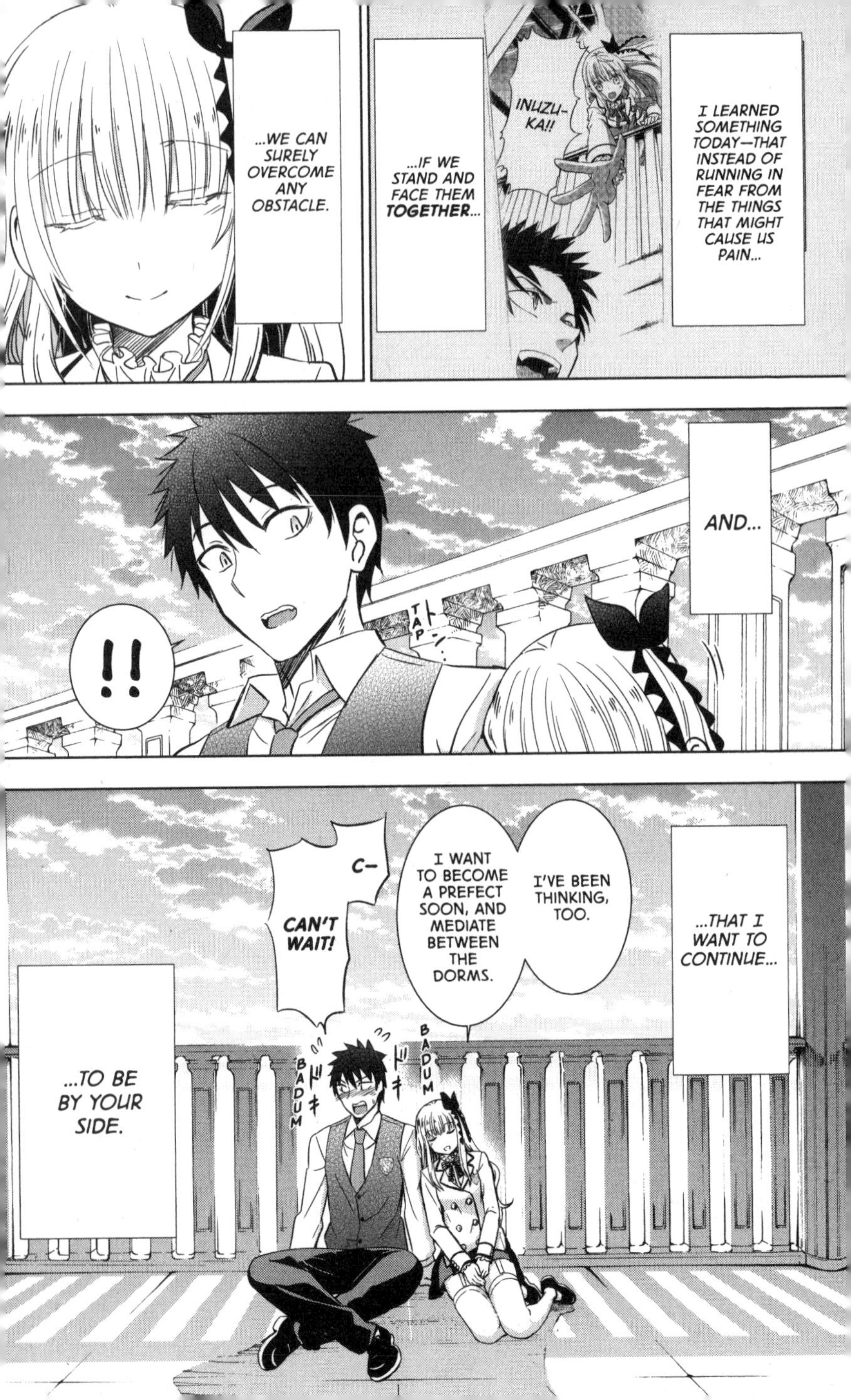
I LEARNED SOMETHING TODAY—THAT INSTEAD OF RUNNING IN FEAR FROM THE THINGS THAT MIGHT CAUSE US PAIN...
INUZUKA!!
...IF WE STAND AND FACE THEM **TOGETHER**...
...WE CAN SURELY OVERCOME ANY OBSTACLE.
AND...
TAP
!!
...THAT I WANT TO CONTINUE...
I'VE BEEN THINKING, TOO.
I WANT TO BECOME A PREFECT SOON, AND MEDIATE BETWEEN THE DORMS.
BADUM
C—
CAN'T WAIT!
BADUM
...TO BE BY YOUR SIDE.

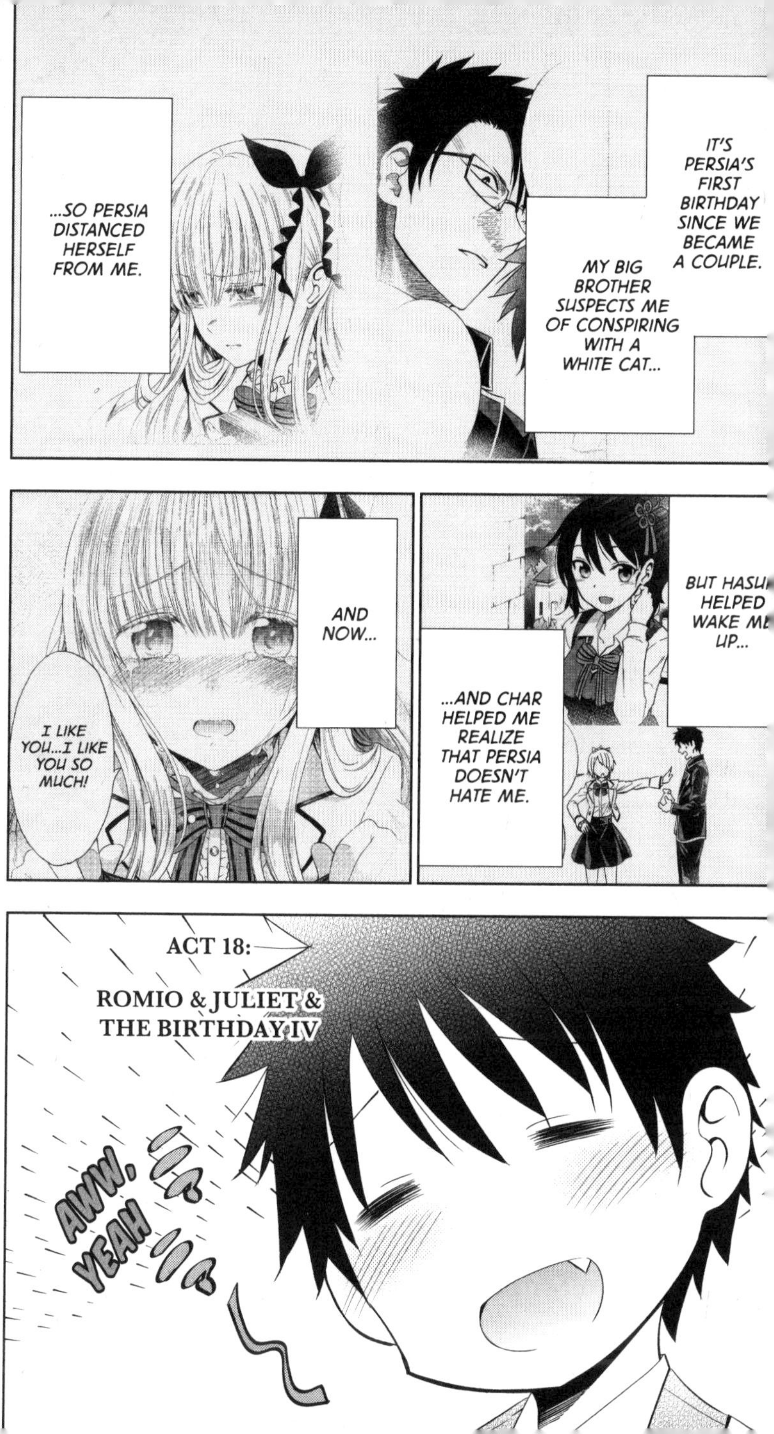
IT'S PERSIA'S FIRST BIRTHDAY SINCE WE BECAME A COUPLE.
MY BIG BROTHER SUSPECTS ME OF CONSPIRING WITH A WHITE CAT...
...SO PERSIA DISTANCED HERSELF FROM ME.
BUT HASU HELPED WAKE ME UP...
...AND CHAR HELPED ME REALIZE THAT PERSIA DOESN'T HATE ME.
AND NOW...
I LIKE YOU...I LIKE YOU SO MUCH!
ACT 18:
ROMIO & JULIET & THE BIRTHDAY IV
AWW, YEAH

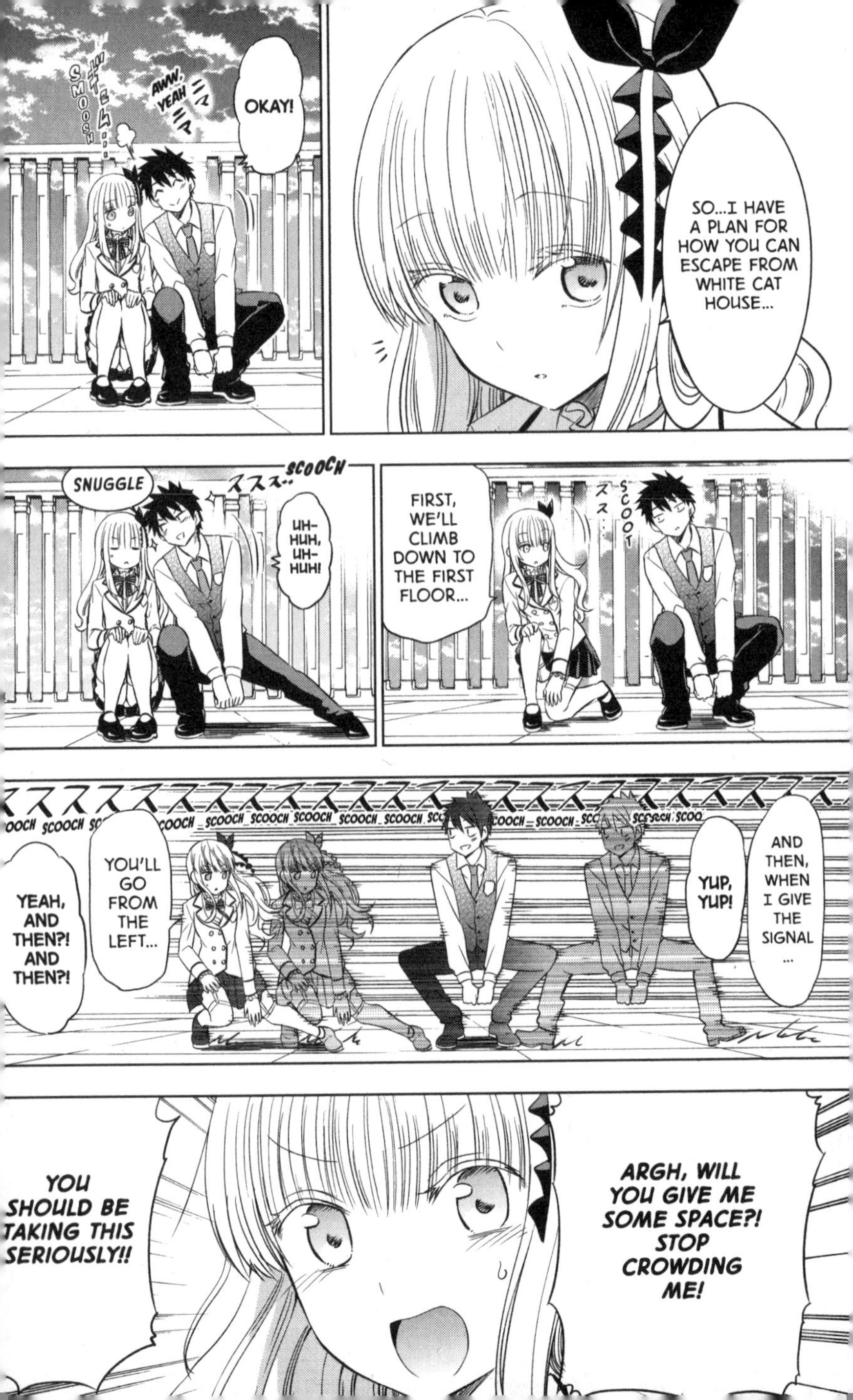

SO...I HAVE A PLAN FOR HOW YOU CAN ESCAPE FROM WHITE CAT HOUSE...
OKAY!
AWW, YEAH
ニマニマ
SMOOSH
FIRST, WE'LL CLIMB DOWN TO THE FIRST FLOOR...
SCOOT
スス...
UH-HUH, UH-HUH!
SCOOCH
ススス..
SNUGGLE
AND THEN, WHEN I GIVE THE SIGNAL...
YUP, YUP!
YOU'LL GO FROM THE LEFT...
YEAH, AND THEN?! AND THEN?!
ARGH, WILL YOU GIVE ME SOME SPACE?! STOP CROWDING ME!
YOU SHOULD BE TAKING THIS SERIOUSLY!!

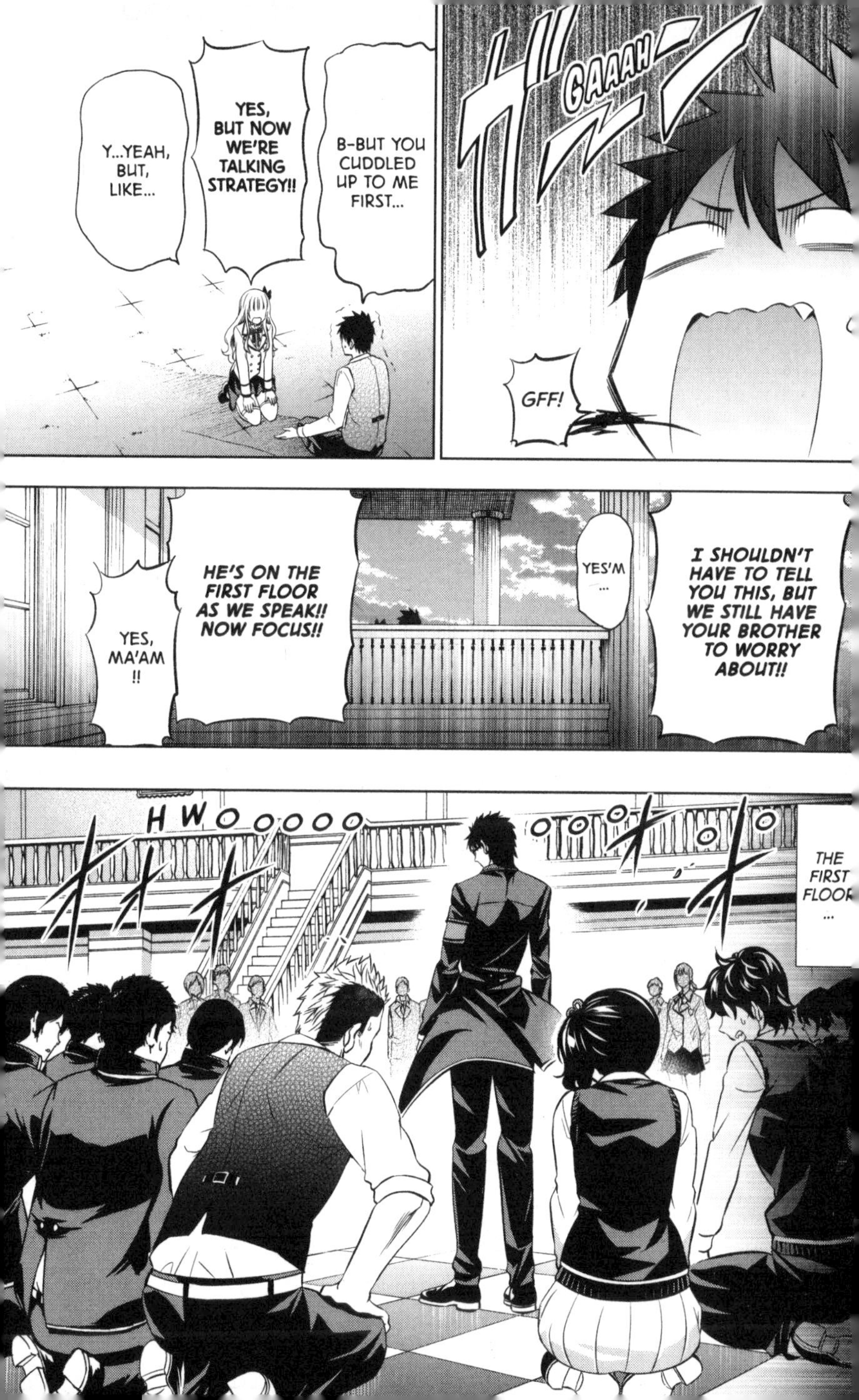
GAAAH
GFF!
B-BUT YOU CUDDLED UP TO ME FIRST...
YES, BUT NOW WE'RE TALKING STRATEGY!!
Y...YEAH, BUT, LIKE...
I SHOULDN'T HAVE TO TELL YOU THIS, BUT WE STILL HAVE YOUR BROTHER TO WORRY ABOUT!!
YES'M...
HE'S ON THE FIRST FLOOR AS WE SPEAK!! NOW FOCUS!!
YES, MA'AM!!
THE FIRST FLOOR...
HWOOOOO
OOOOOO

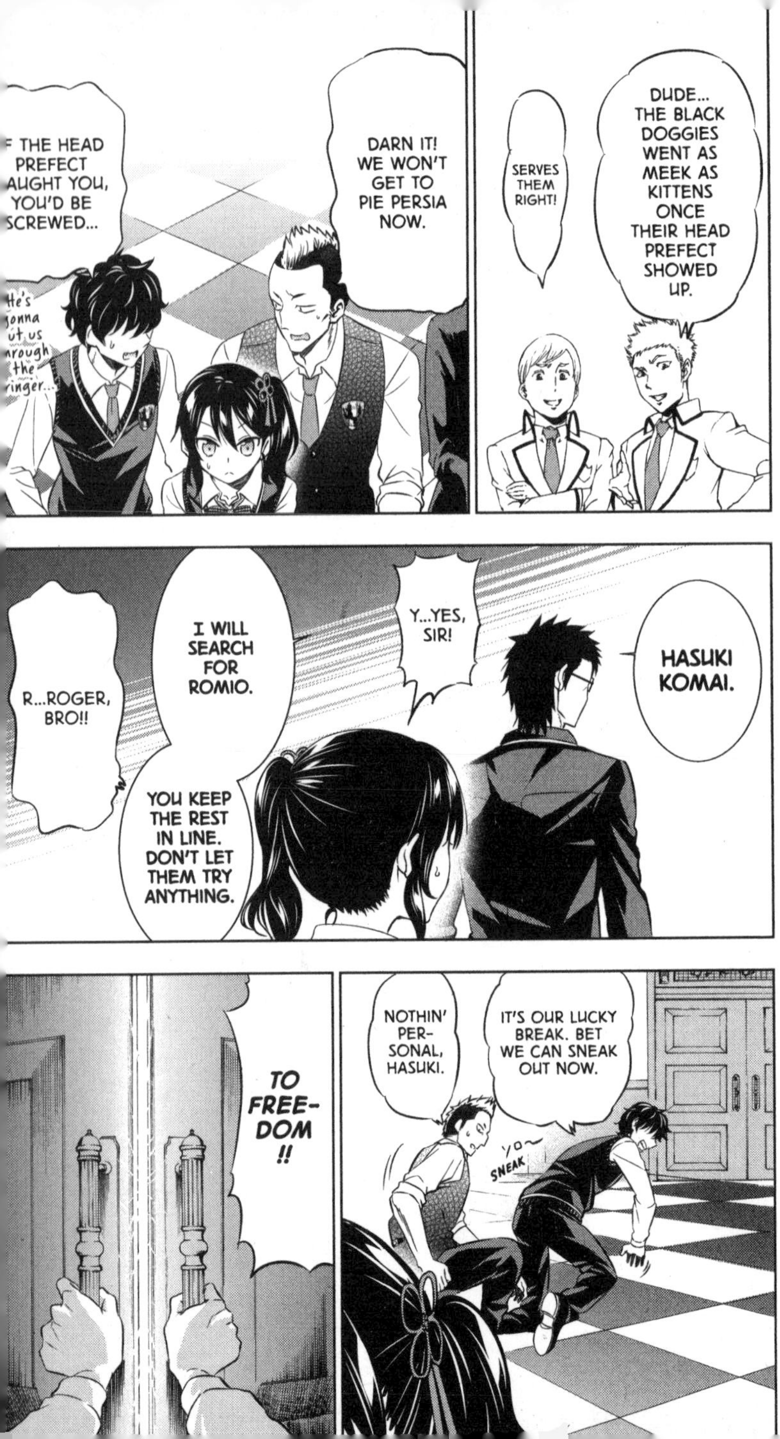
DUDE... THE BLACK DOGGIES WENT AS MEEK AS KITTENS ONCE THEIR HEAD PREFECT SHOWED UP.
SERVES THEM RIGHT!
DARN IT! WE WON'T GET TO PIE PERSIA NOW.
F THE HEAD PREFECT AUGHT YOU, YOU'D BE SCREWED...
He's jonna ut us rough the ringer...
HASUKI KOMAI.
Y...YES, SIR!
I WILL SEARCH FOR ROMIO.
YOU KEEP THE REST IN LINE. DON'T LET THEM TRY ANYTHING.
R...ROGER, BRO!!
IT'S OUR LUCKY BREAK. BET WE CAN SNEAK OUT NOW.
NOTHIN' PER-SONAL, HASUKI.
ソロ〜
SNEAK
TO FREE-DOM !!

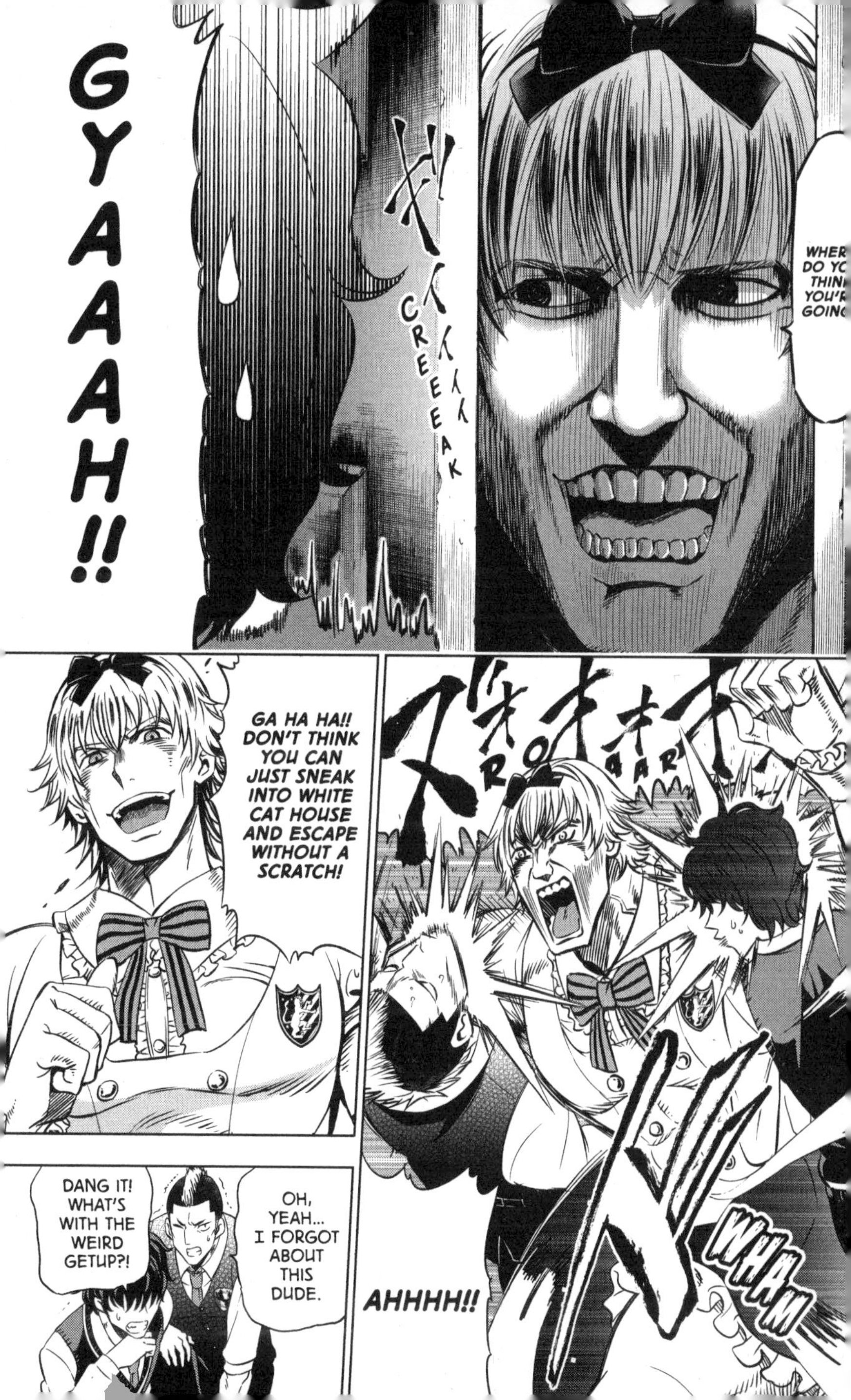

WHER DO YO THIN YOU'R GOING
CREEEAK
GYAAAAH!!
ROAR
WHAM
AHHHH!!
GA HA HA!! DON'T THINK YOU CAN JUST SNEAK INTO WHITE CAT HOUSE AND ESCAPE WITHOUT A SCRATCH!
OH, YEAH... I FORGOT ABOUT THIS DUDE.
DANG IT! WHAT'S WITH THE WEIRD GETUP?!

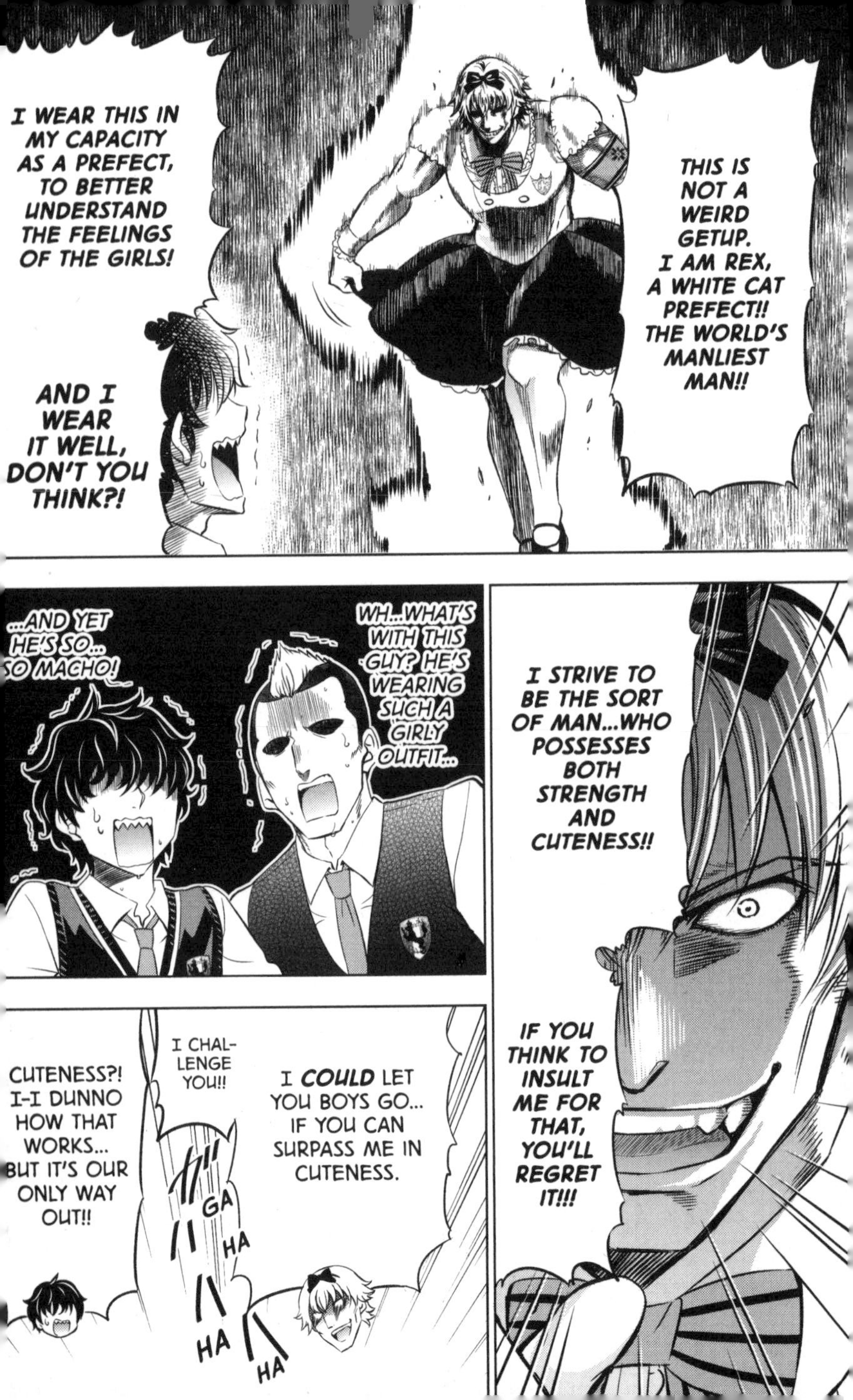
THIS IS NOT A WEIRD GETUP. I AM REX, A WHITE CAT PREFECT!! THE WORLD'S MANLIEST MAN!!
I WEAR THIS IN MY CAPACITY AS A PREFECT, TO BETTER UNDERSTAND THE FEELINGS OF THE GIRLS!
AND I WEAR IT WELL, DON'T YOU THINK?!
I STRIVE TO BE THE SORT OF MAN...WHO POSSESSES BOTH STRENGTH AND CUTENESS!!
IF YOU THINK TO INSULT ME FOR THAT, YOU'LL REGRET IT!!!
WH...WHAT'S WITH THIS GUY? HE'S WEARING SUCH A GIRLY OUTFIT...
...AND YET HE'S SO... SO MACHO!
I COULD LET YOU BOYS GO... IF YOU CAN SURPASS ME IN CUTENESS.
I CHAL-LENGE YOU!!
CUTENESS?! I-I DUNNO HOW THAT WORKS... BUT IT'S OUR ONLY WAY OUT!!
GA HA HA HA HA

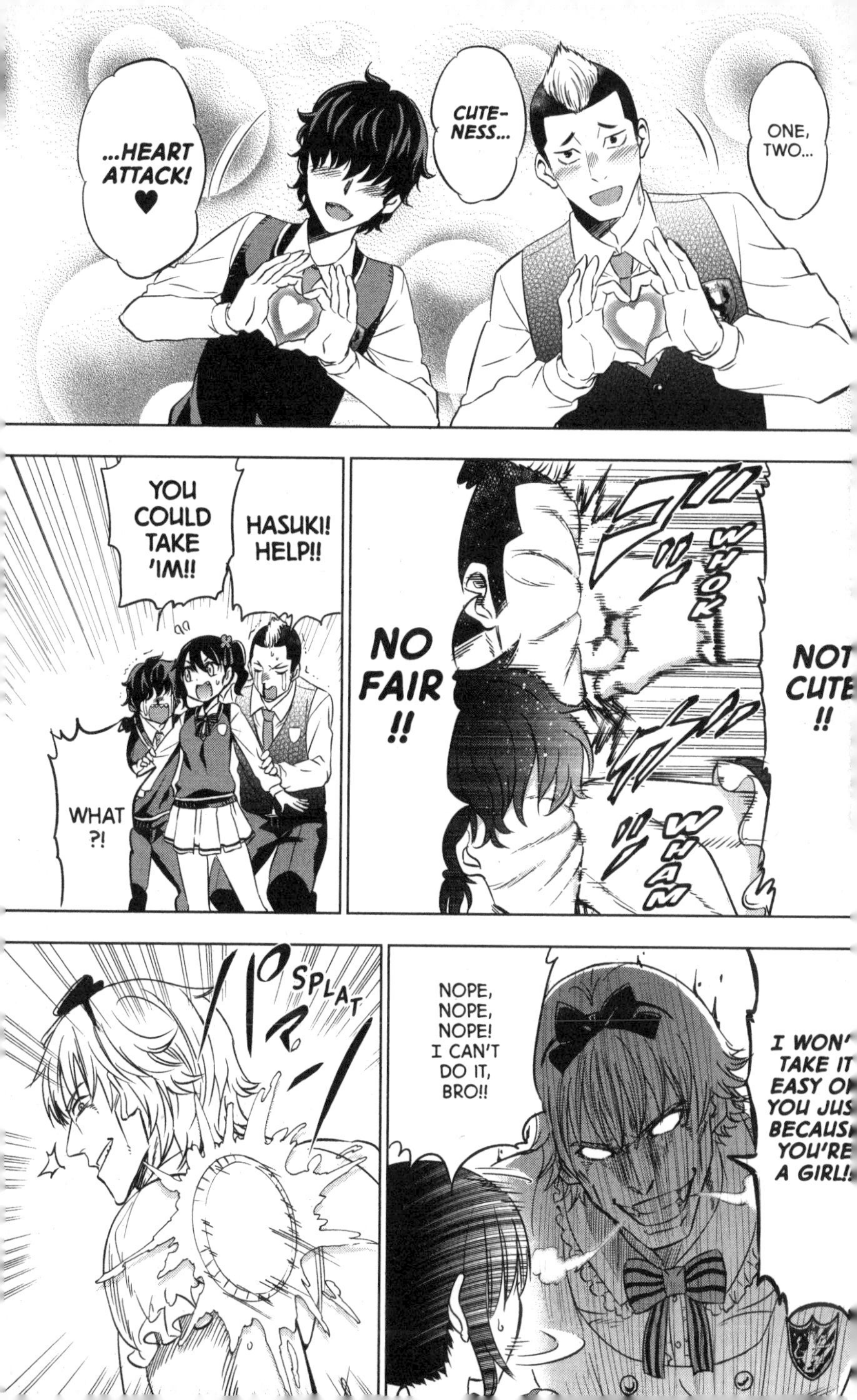
ONE, TWO...
CUTE-NESS...
...HEART ATTACK! ♥
NOT CUTE!!
WHOK
WHAM
NO FAIR!!
HASUKI! HELP!!
YOU COULD TAKE 'IM!!
WHAT?!
I WON' TAKE IT EASY O YOU JUS BECAUS YOU'RE A GIRL!!
NOPE, NOPE, NOPE! I CAN'T DO IT, BRO!!
SPLAT

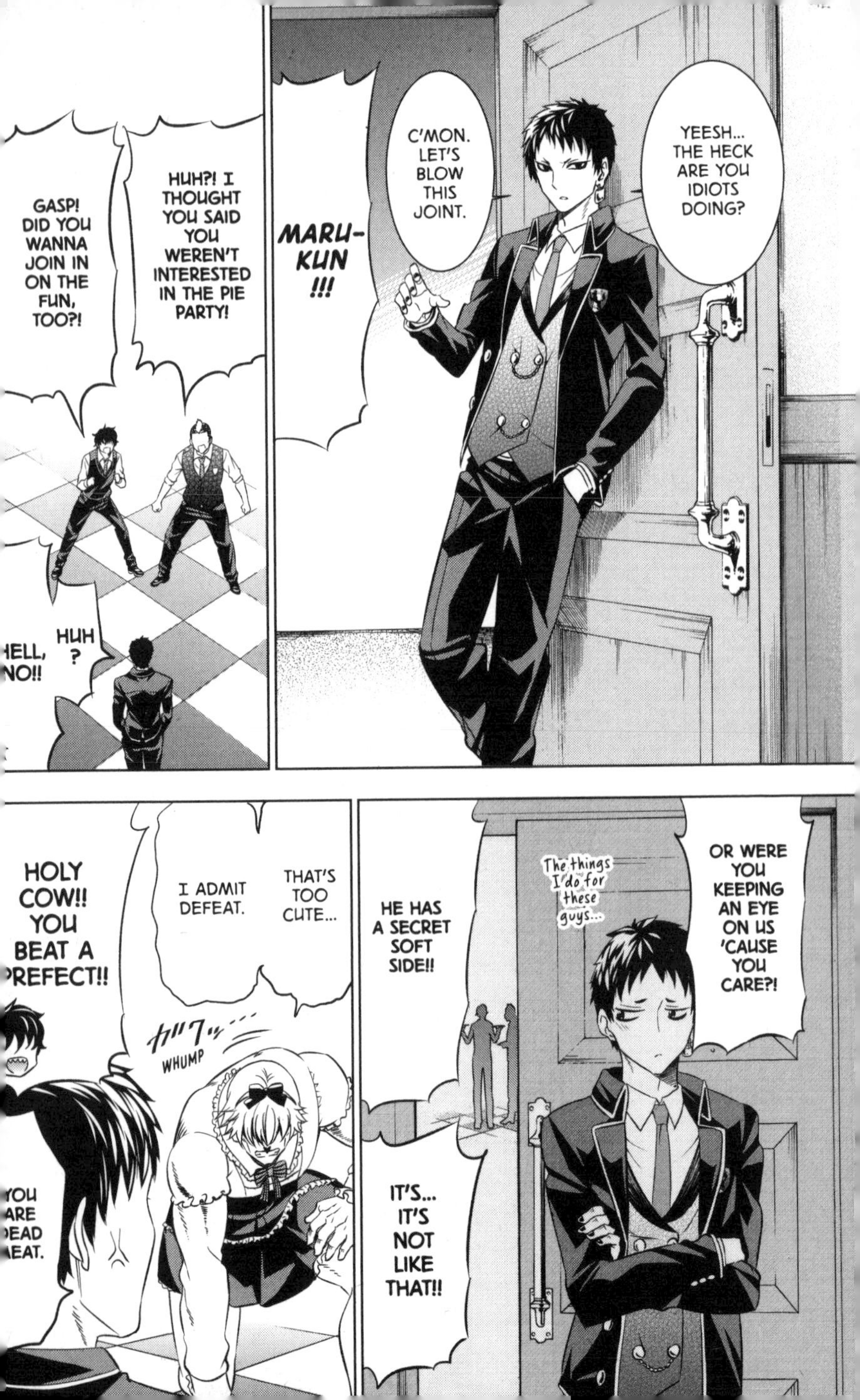
YEESH... THE HECK ARE YOU IDIOTS DOING?
C'MON. LET'S BLOW THIS JOINT.
MARU-KUN!!!
HUH?! I THOUGHT YOU SAID YOU WEREN'T INTERESTED IN THE PIE PARTY!
GASP! DID YOU WANNA JOIN IN ON THE FUN, TOO?!
HUH?
ELL, NO!!
OR WERE YOU KEEPING AN EYE ON US 'CAUSE YOU CARE?!
The things I do for these guys...
HE HAS A SECRET SOFT SIDE!!
IT'S... IT'S NOT LIKE THAT!!
THAT'S TOO CUTE...
I ADMIT DEFEAT.
HOLY COW!! YOU BEAT A REFECT!!
WHUMP
OU ARE EAD EAT.

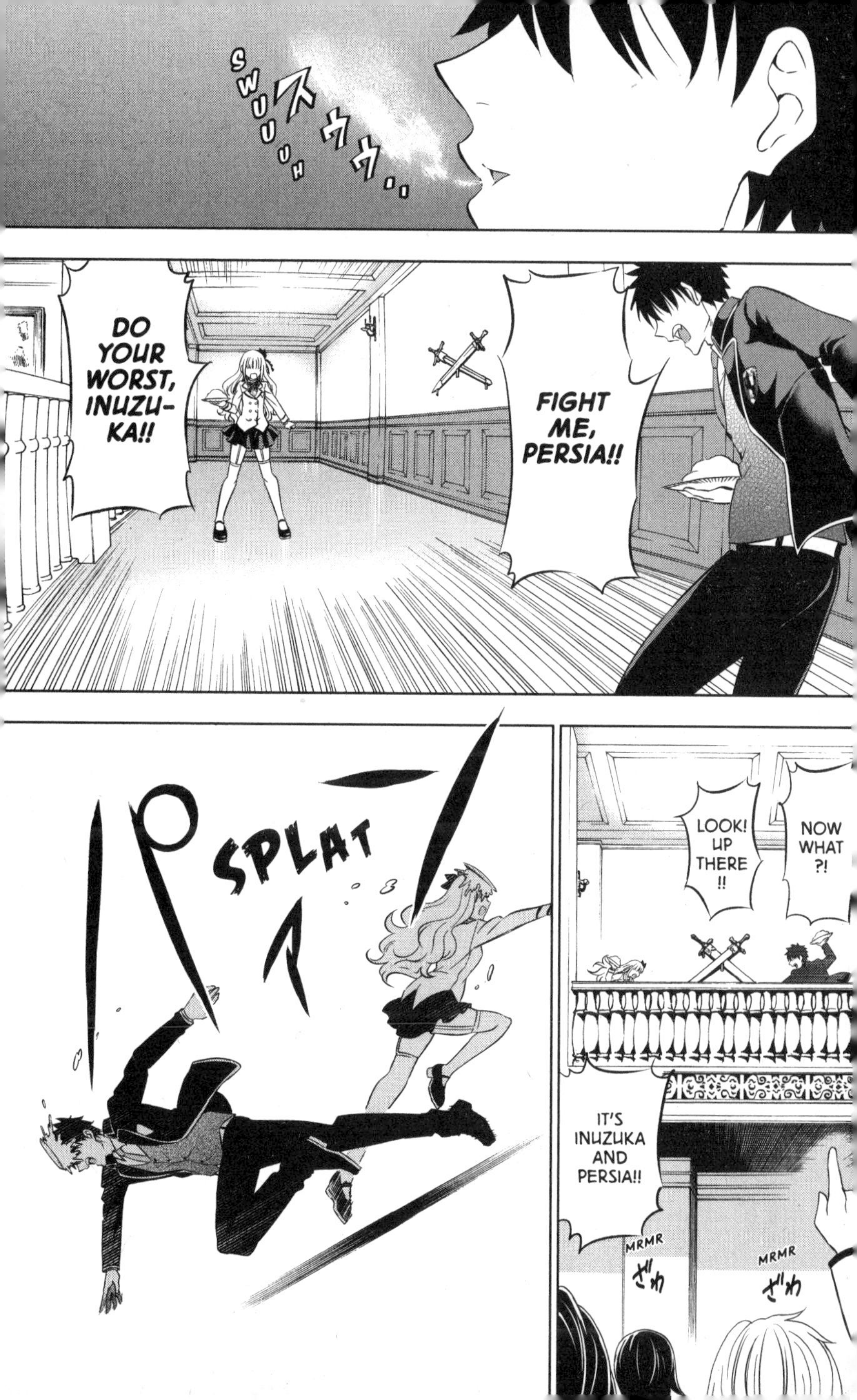

SWUUUH
スウウ‥
FIGHT ME, PERSIA!!
DO YOUR WORST, INUZUKA!!
NOW WHAT ?!
LOOK! UP THERE !!
IT'S INUZUKA AND PERSIA!!
MRMR
ざわ
MRMR
ざわ
SPLAT
パア

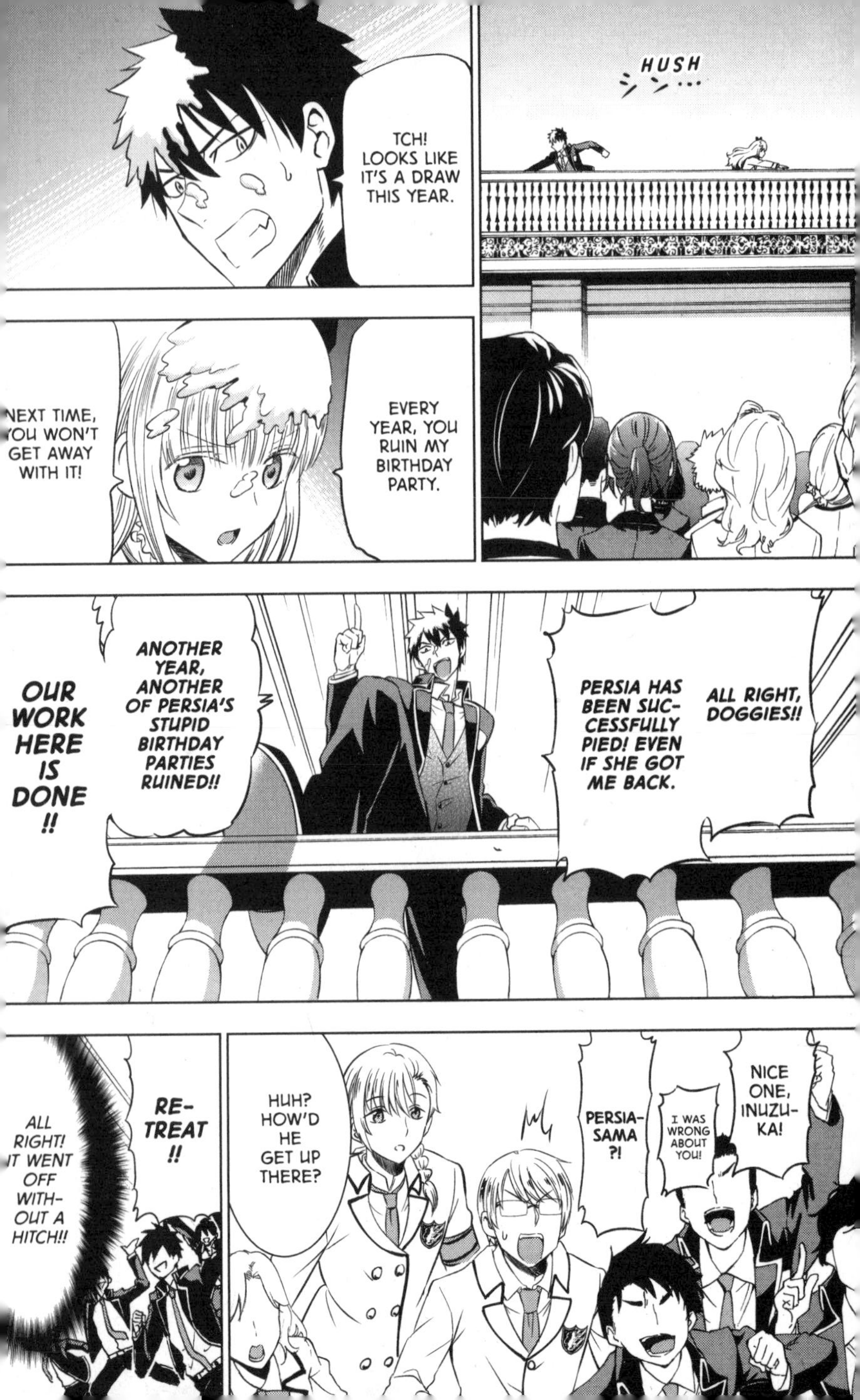
HUSH
TCH! LOOKS LIKE IT'S A DRAW THIS YEAR.
EVERY YEAR, YOU RUIN MY BIRTHDAY PARTY.
NEXT TIME, YOU WON'T GET AWAY WITH IT!
ALL RIGHT, DOGGIES!!
PERSIA HAS BEEN SUC-CESSFULLY PIED! EVEN IF SHE GOT ME BACK.
ANOTHER YEAR, ANOTHER OF PERSIA'S STUPID BIRTHDAY PARTIES RUINED!!
OUR WORK HERE IS DONE!!
NICE ONE, INUZUKA!
I WAS WRONG ABOUT YOU!
PERSIA-SAMA?!
HUH? HOW'D HE GET UP THERE?
RE-TREAT!!
ALL RIGHT! IT WENT OFF WITH-OUT A HITCH!!

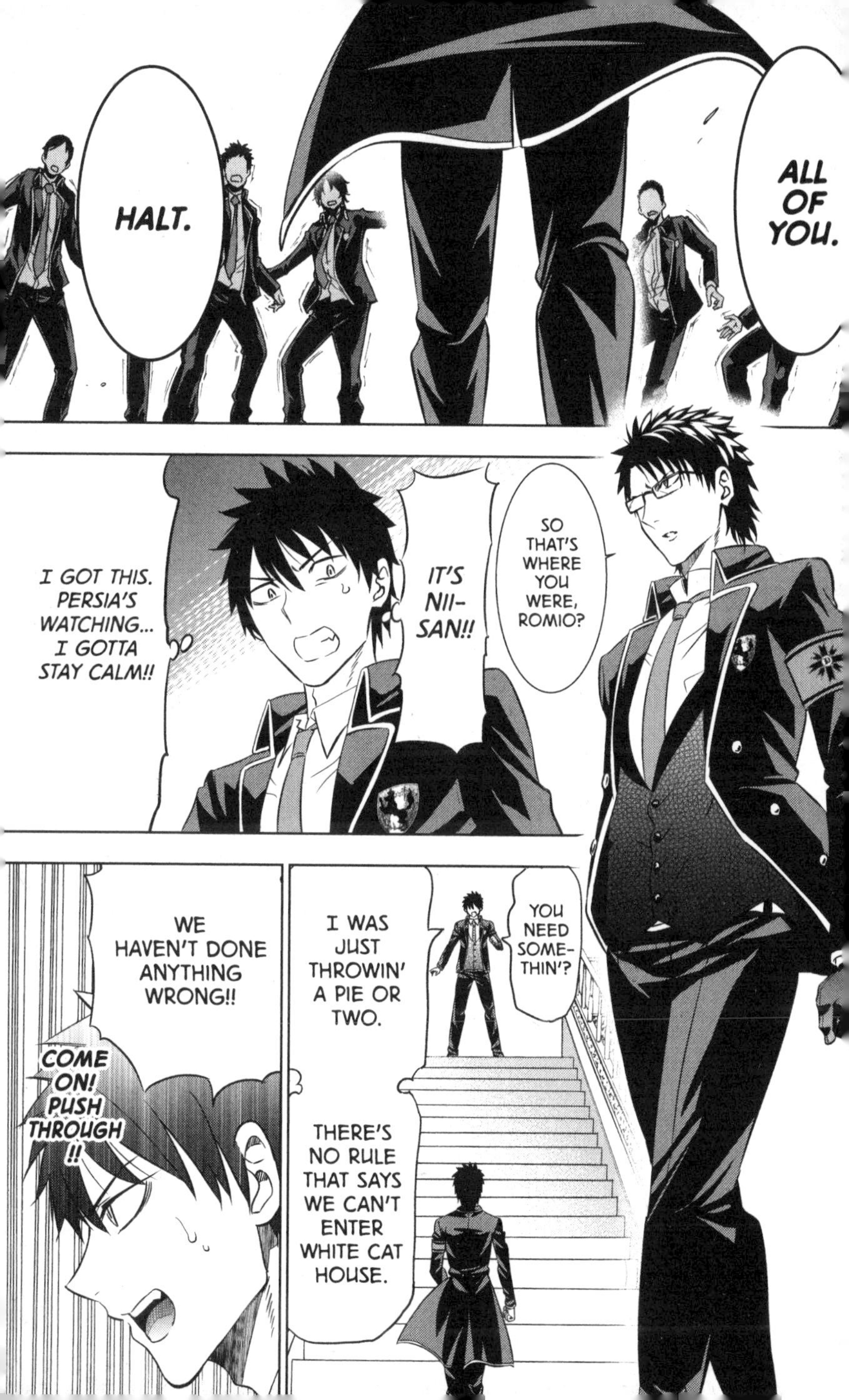
ALL OF YOU.
HALT.
SO THAT'S WHERE YOU WERE, ROMIO?
IT'S NII-SAN!!
I GOT THIS. PERSIA'S WATCHING... I GOTTA STAY CALM!!
YOU NEED SOME-THIN'?
I WAS JUST THROWIN' A PIE OR TWO.
THERE'S NO RULE THAT SAYS WE CAN'T ENTER WHITE CAT HOUSE.
WE HAVEN'T DONE ANYTHING WRONG!!
COME ON! PUSH THROUGH!!

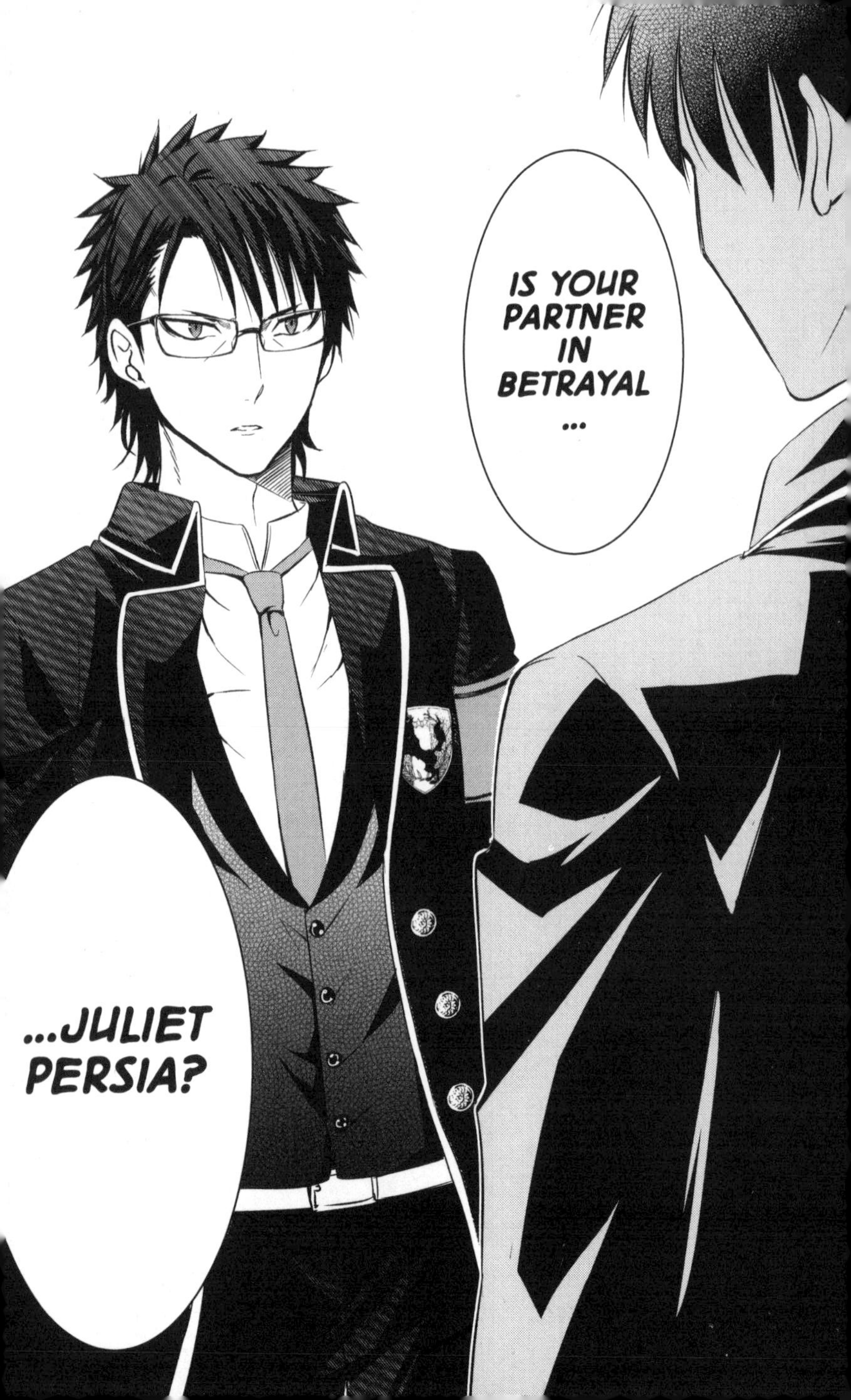
IS YOUR PARTNER IN BETRAYAL ...
...JULIET PERSIA?

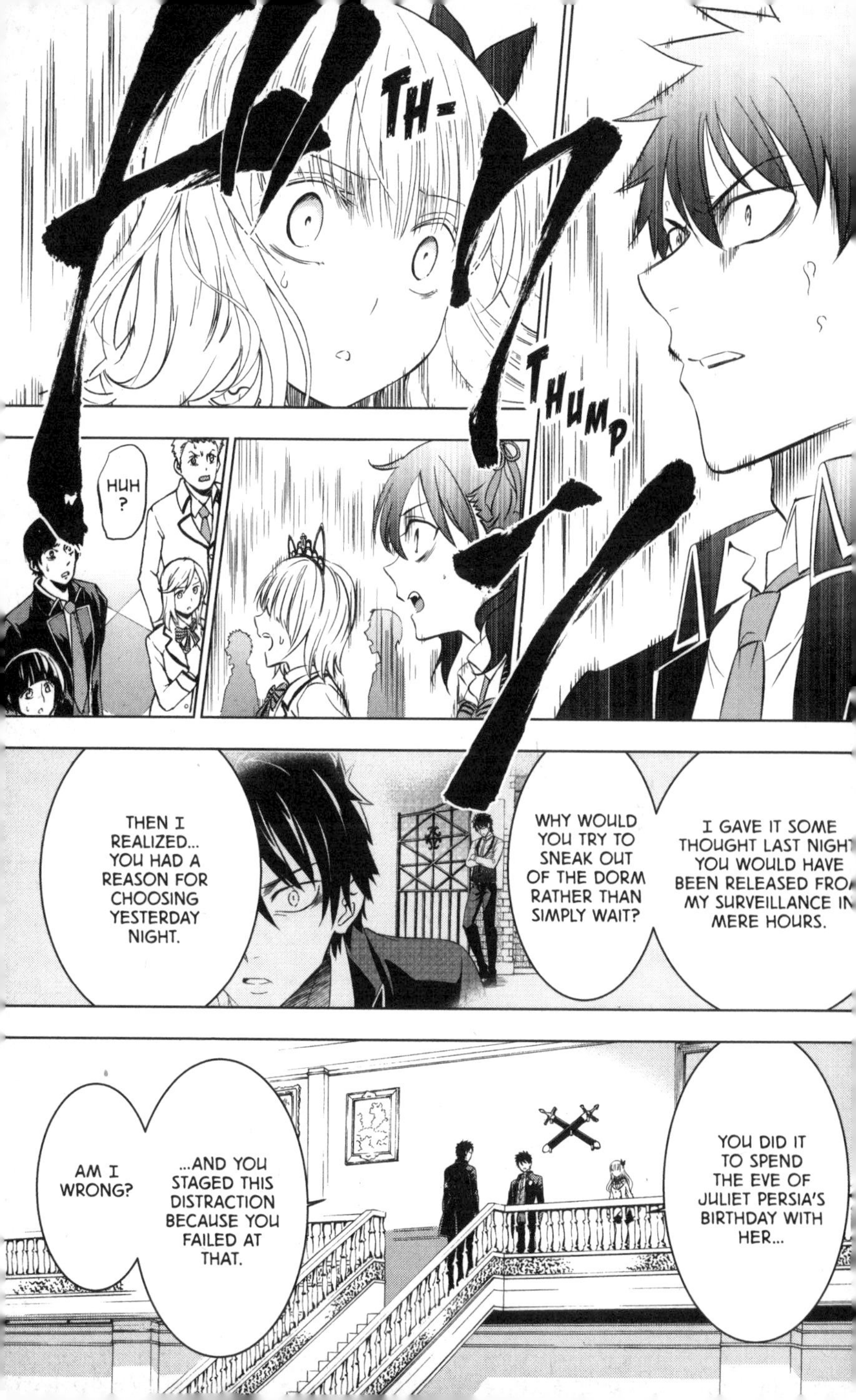
TH-
THUMP
HUH ?
I GAVE IT SOME THOUGHT LAST NIGHT YOU WOULD HAVE BEEN RELEASED FRO MY SURVEILLANCE IN MERE HOURS.
WHY WOULD YOU TRY TO SNEAK OUT OF THE DORM RATHER THAN SIMPLY WAIT?
THEN I REALIZED... YOU HAD A REASON FOR CHOOSING YESTERDAY NIGHT.
YOU DID IT TO SPEND THE EVE OF JULIET PERSIA'S BIRTHDAY WITH HER...
...AND YOU STAGED THIS DISTRACTION BECAUSE YOU FAILED AT THAT.
AM I WRONG?

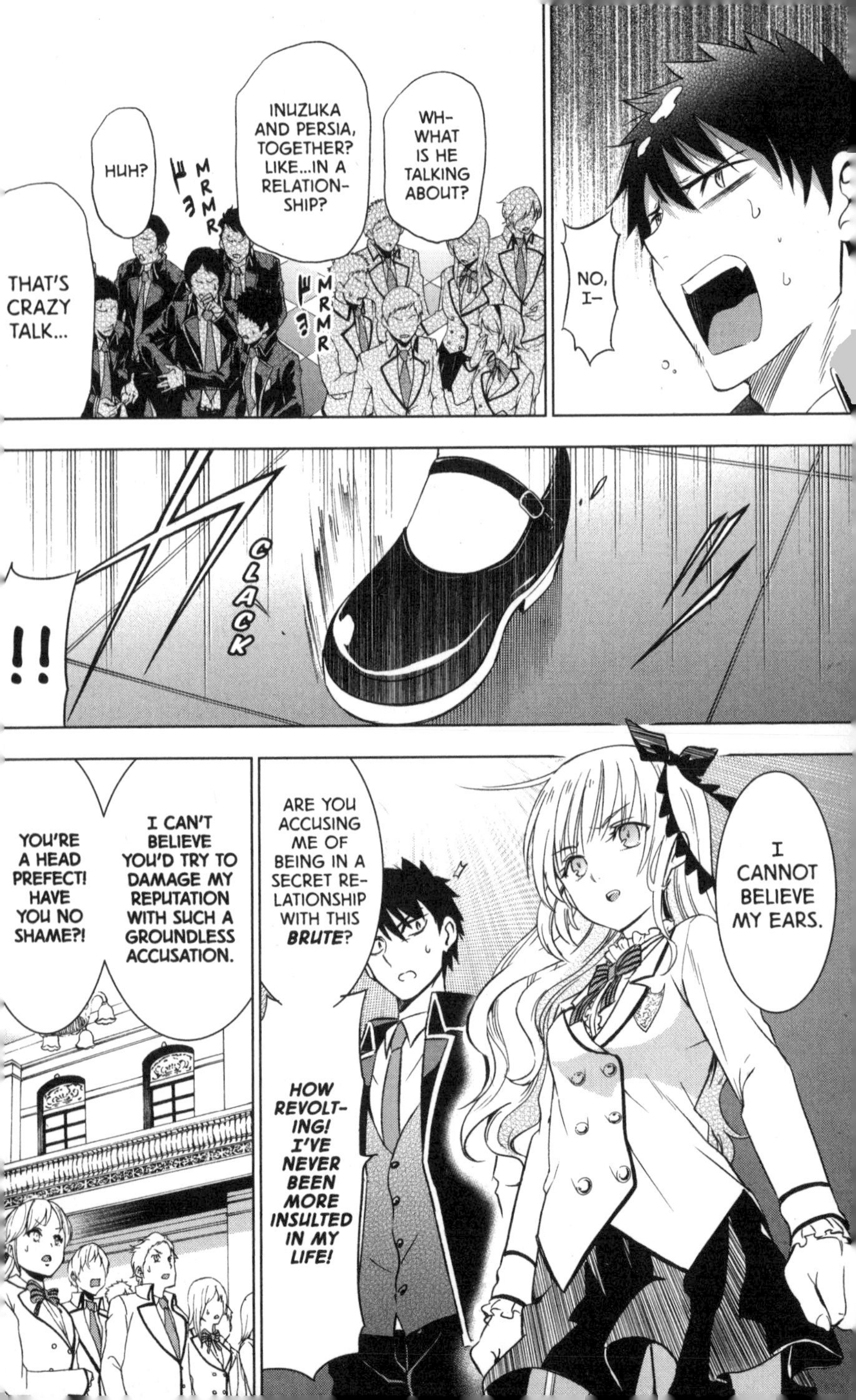
NO, I–
WH- WHAT IS HE TALKING ABOUT?
INUZUKA AND PERSIA, TOGETHER? LIKE...IN A RELATION-SHIP?
MRMR
MRMR
HUH?
THAT'S CRAZY TALK...
CLACK
!!
I CANNOT BELIEVE MY EARS.
ARE YOU ACCUSING ME OF BEING IN A SECRET RE-LATIONSHIP WITH THIS BRUTE?
HOW REVOLT-ING! I'VE NEVER BEEN MORE INSULTED IN MY LIFE!
I CAN'T BELIEVE YOU'D TRY TO DAMAGE MY REPUTATION WITH SUCH A GROUNDLESS ACCUSATION.
YOU'RE A HEAD PREFECT! HAVE YOU NO SHAME?!

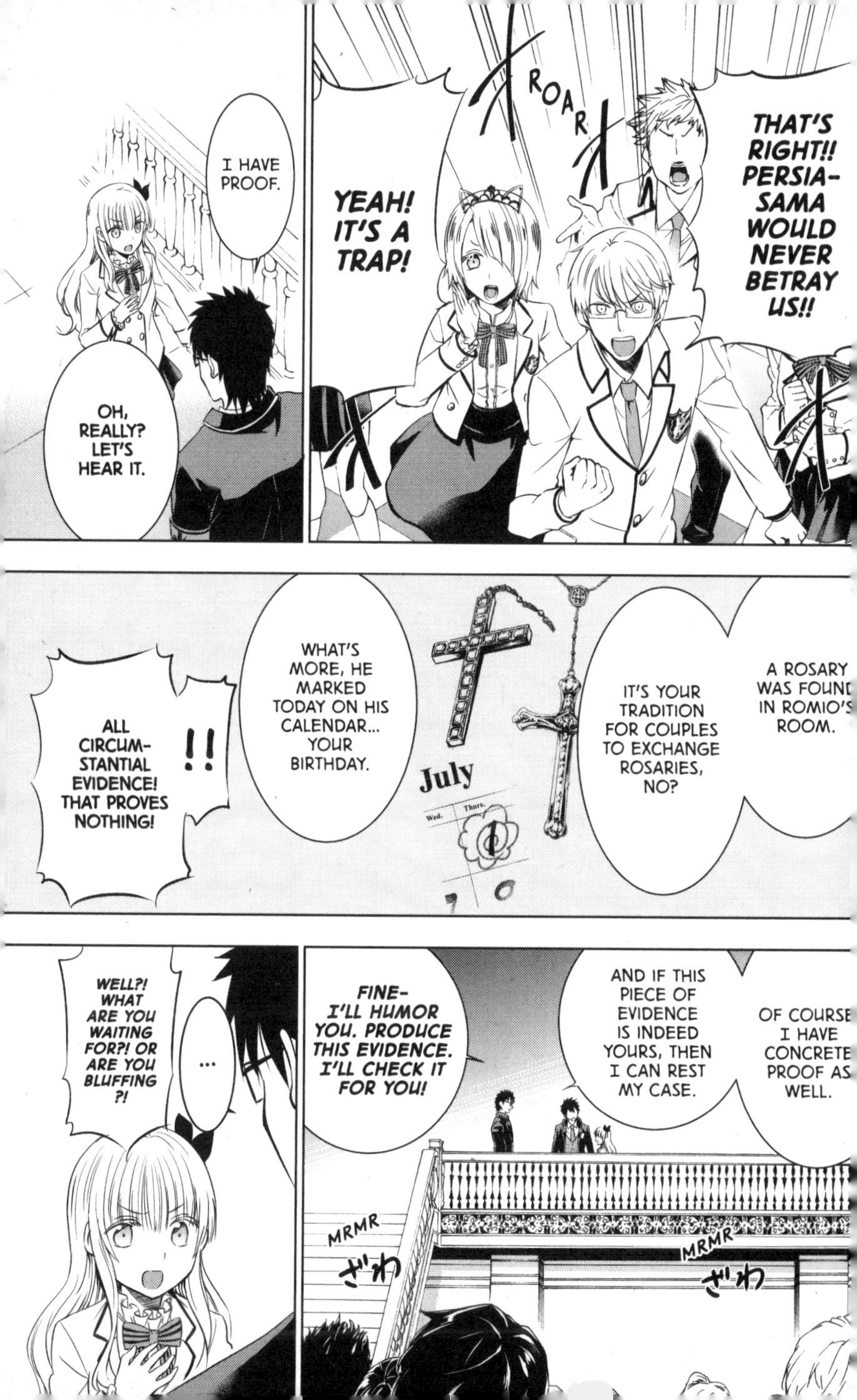
THAT'S RIGHT!! PERSIA-SAMA WOULD NEVER BETRAY US!!
ROAR
YEAH! IT'S A TRAP!
I HAVE PROOF.
OH, REALLY? LET'S HEAR IT.
A ROSARY WAS FOUND IN ROMIO'S ROOM.
IT'S YOUR TRADITION FOR COUPLES TO EXCHANGE ROSARIES, NO?
July
Wed.
Thurs.
WHAT'S MORE, HE MARKED TODAY ON HIS CALENDAR... YOUR BIRTHDAY.
!!
ALL CIRCUM-STANTIAL EVIDENCE! THAT PROVES NOTHING!
OF COURSE I HAVE CONCRETE PROOF AS WELL.
AND IF THIS PIECE OF EVIDENCE IS INDEED YOURS, THEN I CAN REST MY CASE.
FINE- I'LL HUMOR YOU. PRODUCE THIS EVIDENCE. I'LL CHECK IT FOR YOU!
MRMR
ざわ
MRMR
ざわ
WELL?! WHAT ARE YOU WAITING FOR?! OR ARE YOU BLUFFING?!
...

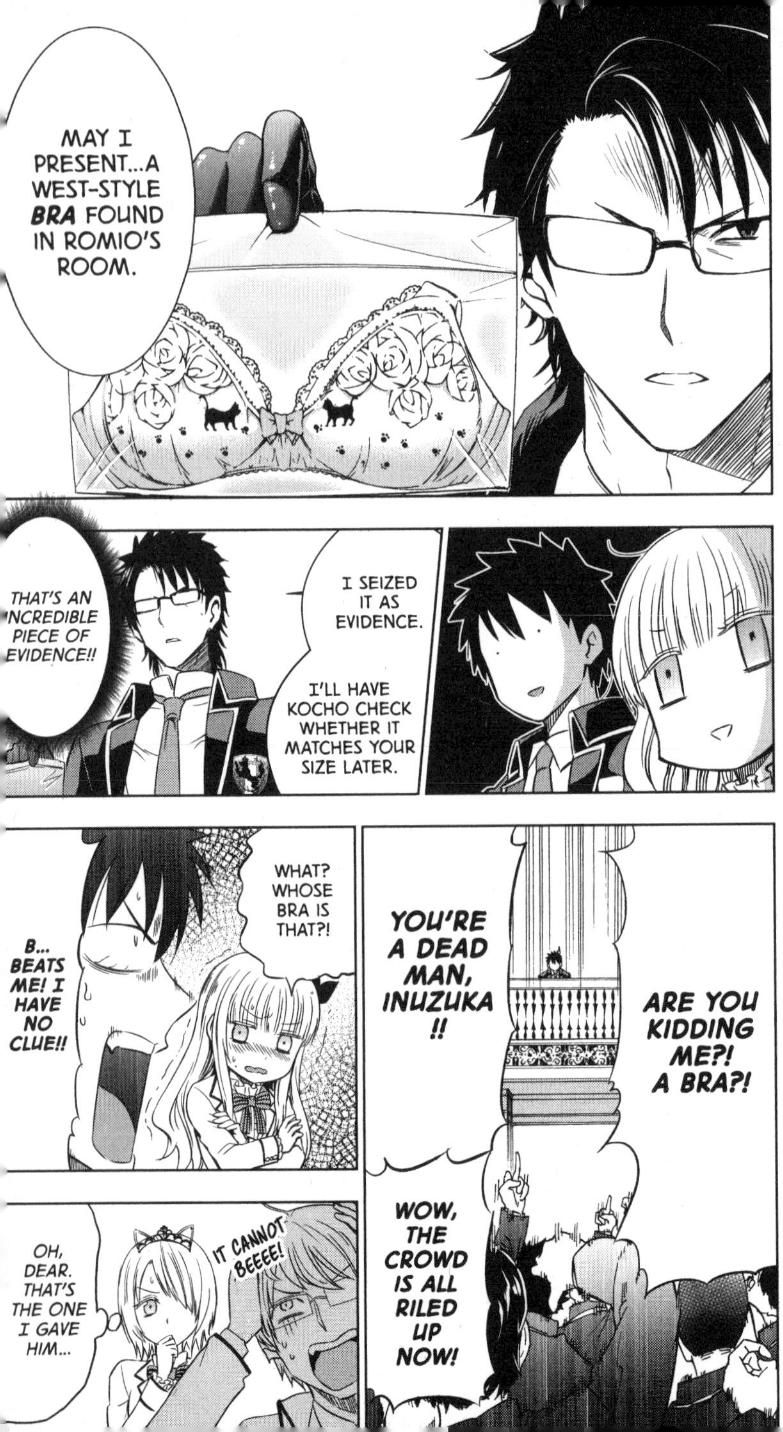
MAY I PRESENT...A WEST-STYLE BRA FOUND IN ROMIO'S ROOM.
I SEIZED IT AS EVIDENCE.
I'LL HAVE KOCHO CHECK WHETHER IT MATCHES YOUR SIZE LATER.
THAT'S AN INCREDIBLE PIECE OF EVIDENCE!!
ARE YOU KIDDING ME?! A BRA?!
YOU'RE A DEAD MAN, INUZUKA!!
WOW, THE CROWD IS ALL RILED UP NOW!
WHAT? WHOSE BRA IS THAT?!
B... BEATS ME! I HAVE NO CLUE!!
IT CANNOT BEEEE!
OH, DEAR. THAT'S THE ONE I GAVE HIM...

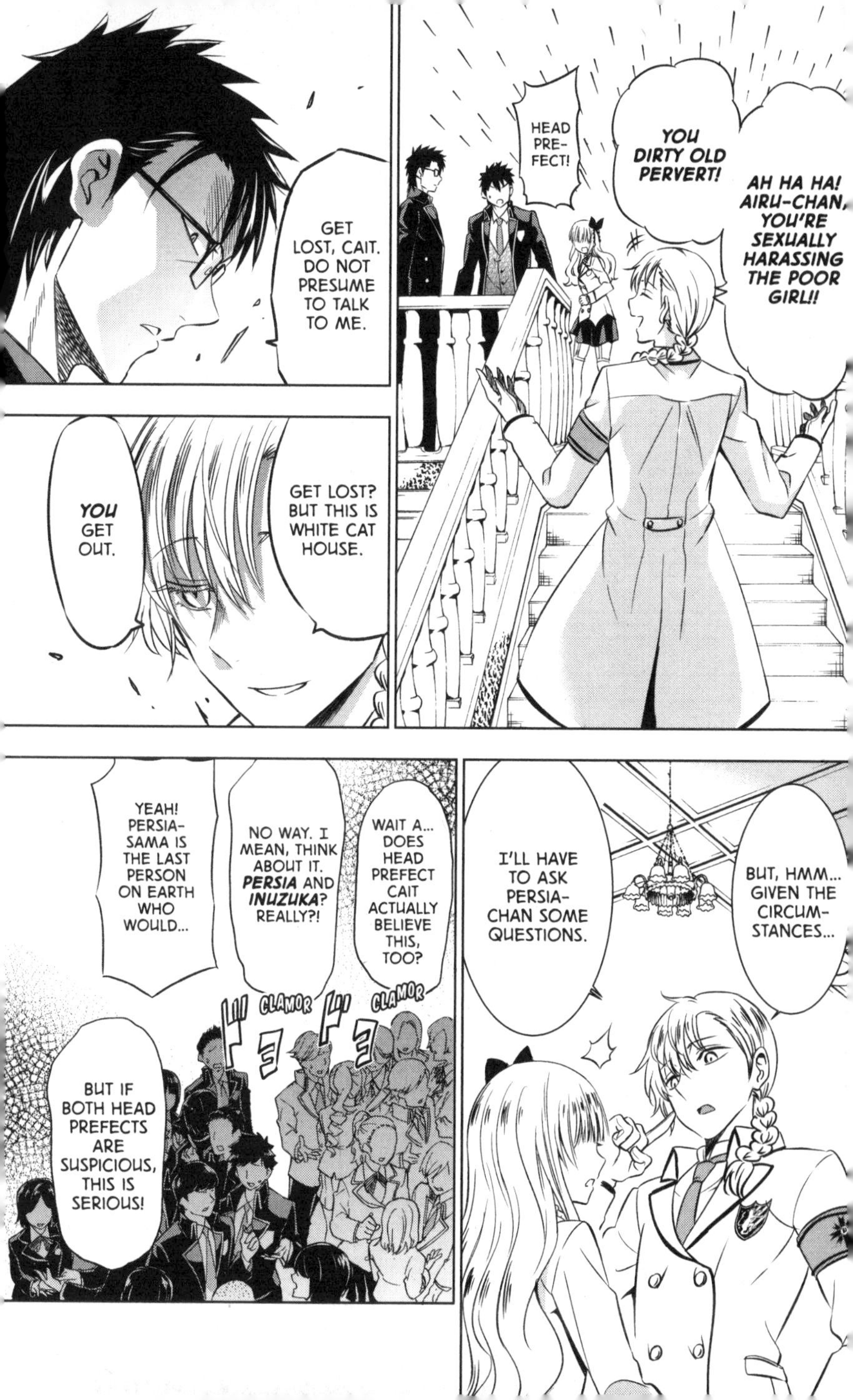
AH HA HA! AIRU-CHAN, YOU'RE SEXUALLY HARASSING THE POOR GIRL!!
YOU DIRTY OLD PERVERT!
HEAD PRE-FECT!
GET LOST, CAIT. DO NOT PRESUME TO TALK TO ME.
GET LOST? BUT THIS IS WHITE CAT HOUSE.
YOU GET OUT.
BUT, HMM... GIVEN THE CIRCUM-STANCES...
I'LL HAVE TO ASK PERSIA-CHAN SOME QUESTIONS.
WAIT A... DOES HEAD PREFECT CAIT ACTUALLY BELIEVE THIS, TOO?
CLAMOR
NO WAY. I MEAN, THINK ABOUT IT. PERSIA AND INUZUKA? REALLY?!
CLAMOR
YEAH! PERSIA-SAMA IS THE LAST PERSON ON EARTH WHO WOULD...
BUT IF BOTH HEAD PREFECTS ARE SUSPICIOUS, THIS IS SERIOUS!

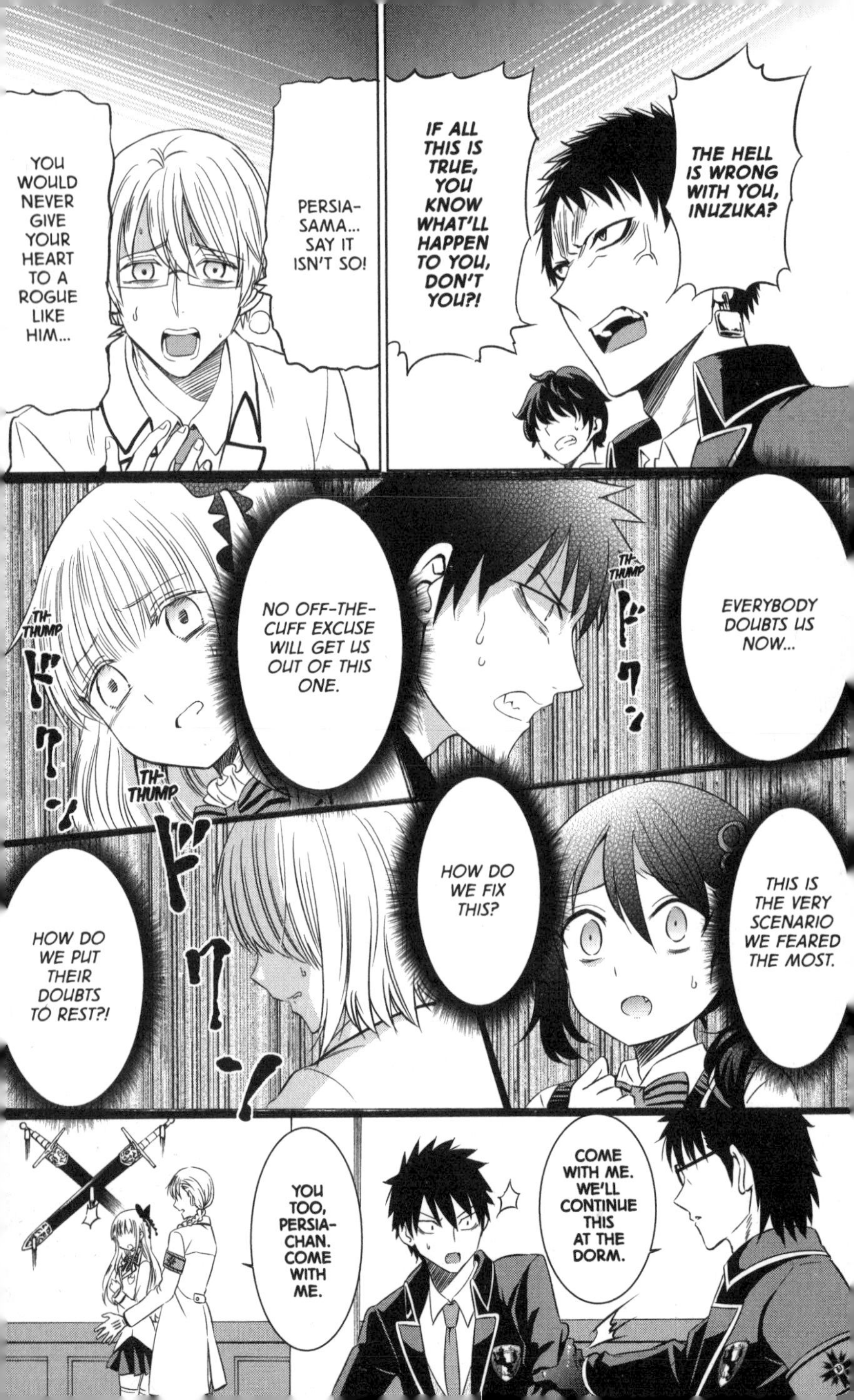
THE HELL IS WRONG WITH YOU, INUZUKA?
IF ALL THIS IS TRUE, YOU KNOW WHAT'LL HAPPEN TO YOU, DON'T YOU?!
PERSIA-SAMA... SAY IT ISN'T SO!
YOU WOULD NEVER GIVE YOUR HEART TO A ROGUE LIKE HIM...
EVERYBODY DOUBTS US NOW...
TH-THUMP
NO OFF-THE-CUFF EXCUSE WILL GET US OUT OF THIS ONE.
TH-THUMP
TH-THUMP
THIS IS THE VERY SCENARIO WE FEARED THE MOST.
HOW DO WE FIX THIS?
HOW DO WE PUT THEIR DOUBTS TO REST?!
COME WITH ME. WE'LL CONTINUE THIS AT THE DORM.
YOU TOO, PERSIA-CHAN. COME WITH ME.

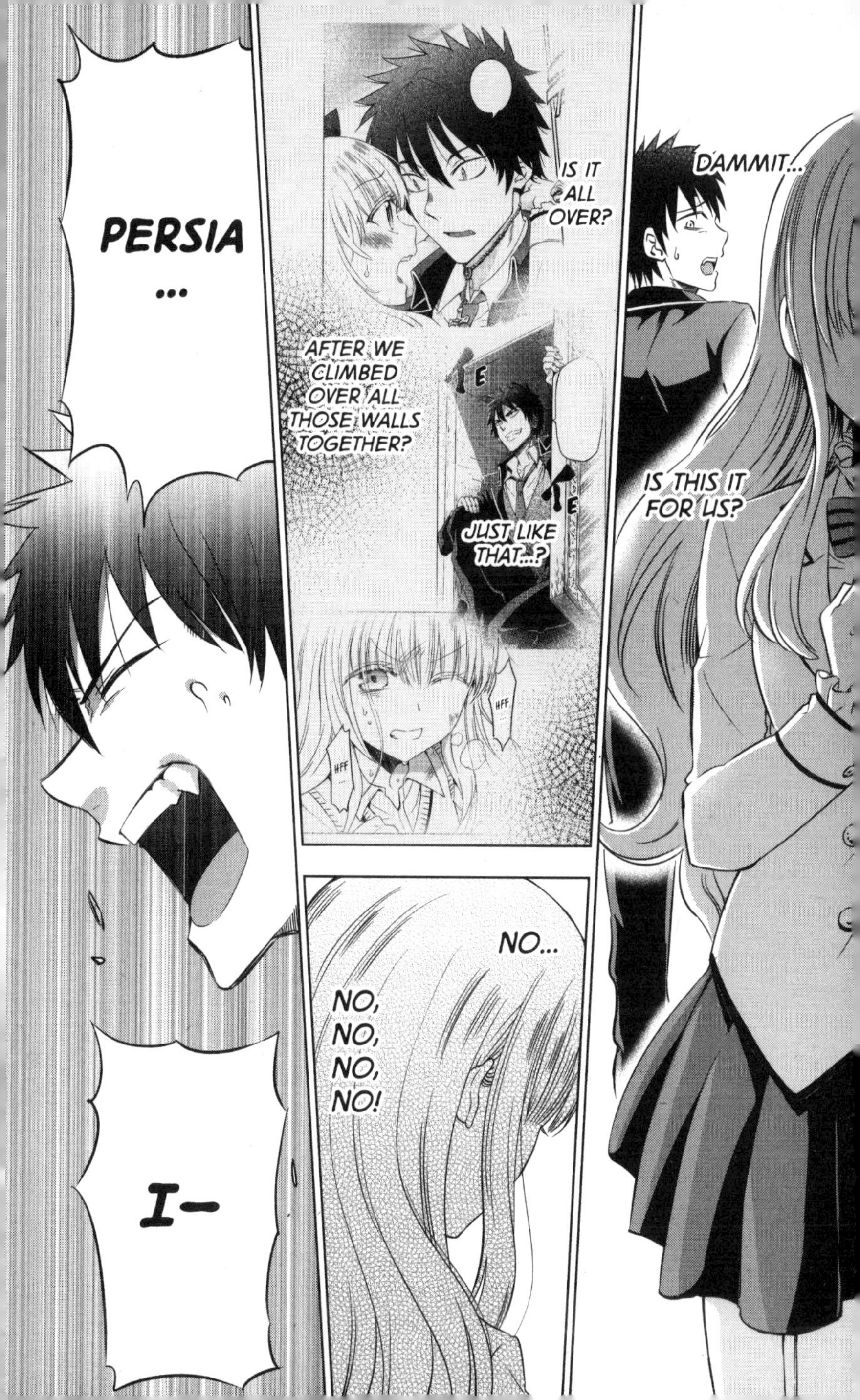

DAMMIT...
IS THIS IT FOR US?
IS IT ALL OVER?
AFTER WE CLIMBED OVER ALL THOSE WALLS TOGETHER?
JUST LIKE THAT...?
HFF
HFF
NO...
NO, NO, NO, NO!
PERSIA ...
I–

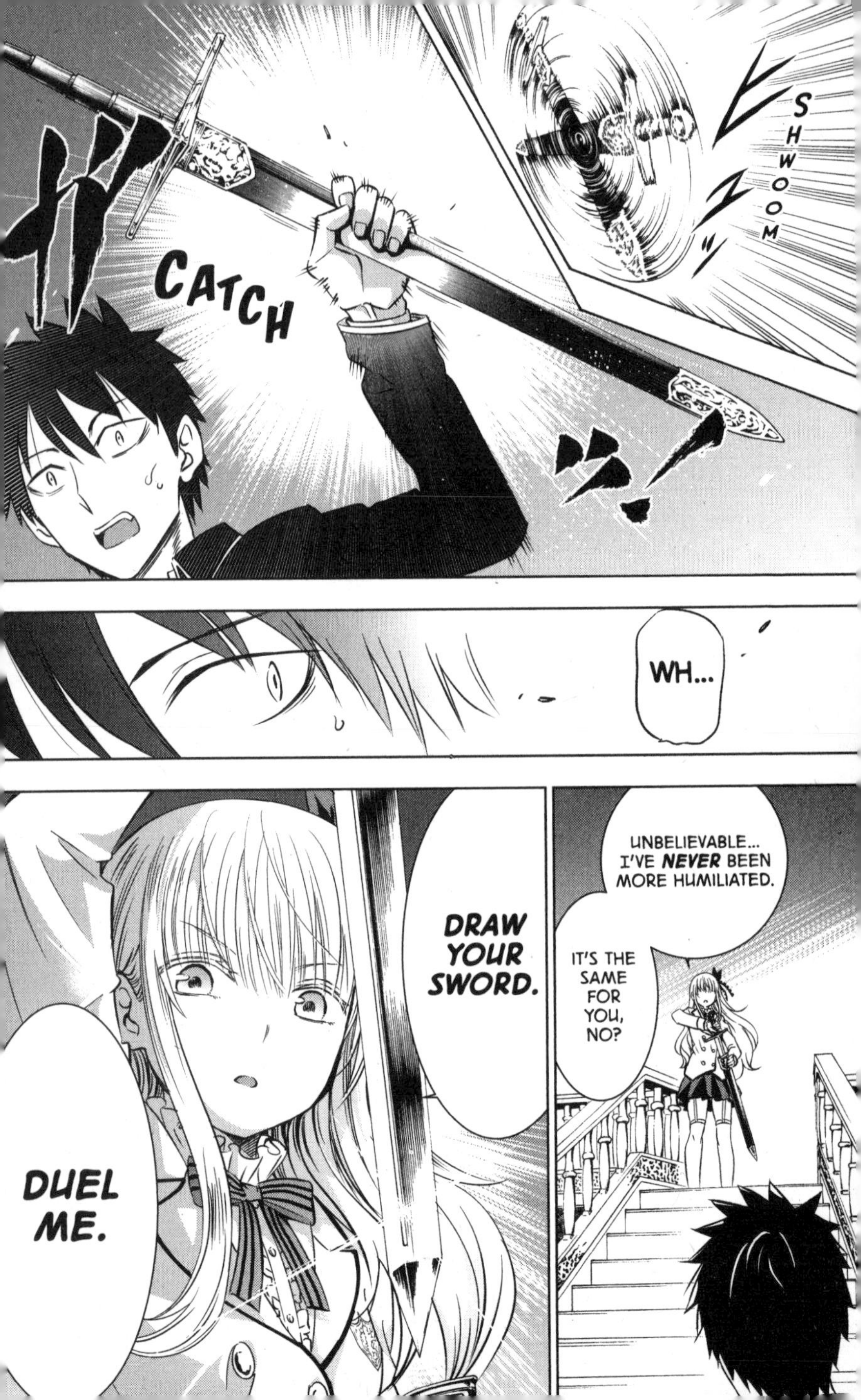
SHWOOM
CATCH
WH...
UNBELIEVABLE... I'VE NEVER BEEN MORE HUMILIATED.
IT'S THE SAME FOR YOU, NO?
DRAW YOUR SWORD.
DUEL ME.

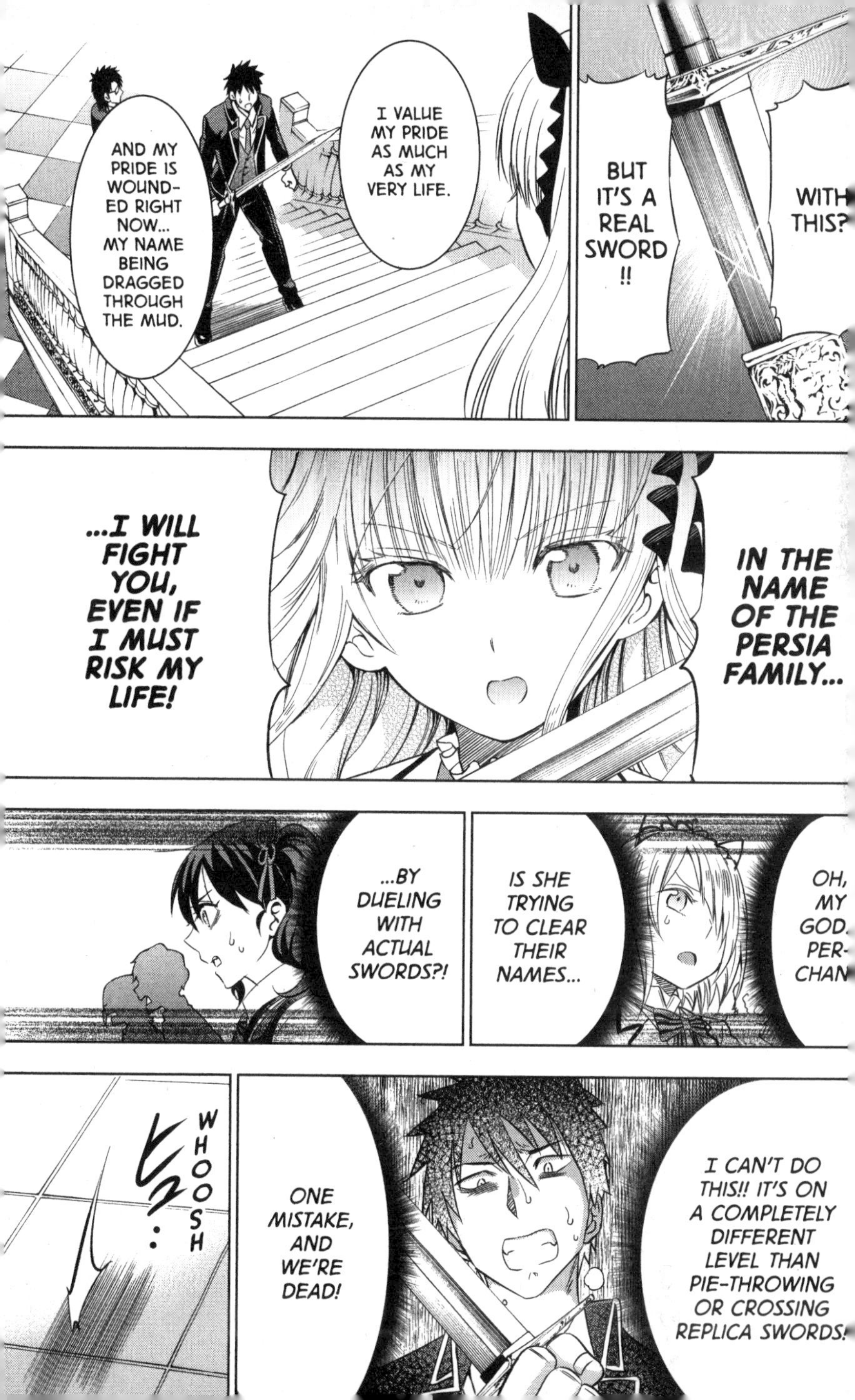
WITH THIS?
BUT IT'S A REAL SWORD!!
I VALUE MY PRIDE AS MUCH AS MY VERY LIFE.
AND MY PRIDE IS WOUND-ED RIGHT NOW... MY NAME BEING DRAGGED THROUGH THE MUD.
IN THE NAME OF THE PERSIA FAMILY...
...I WILL FIGHT YOU, EVEN IF I MUST RISK MY LIFE!
OH, MY GOD. PER-CHAN
IS SHE TRYING TO CLEAR THEIR NAMES...
...BY DUELING WITH ACTUAL SWORDS?!
I CAN'T DO THIS!! IT'S ON A COMPLETELY DIFFERENT LEVEL THAN PIE-THROWING OR CROSSING REPLICA SWORDS!
ONE MISTAKE, AND WE'RE DEAD!
WHOOSH

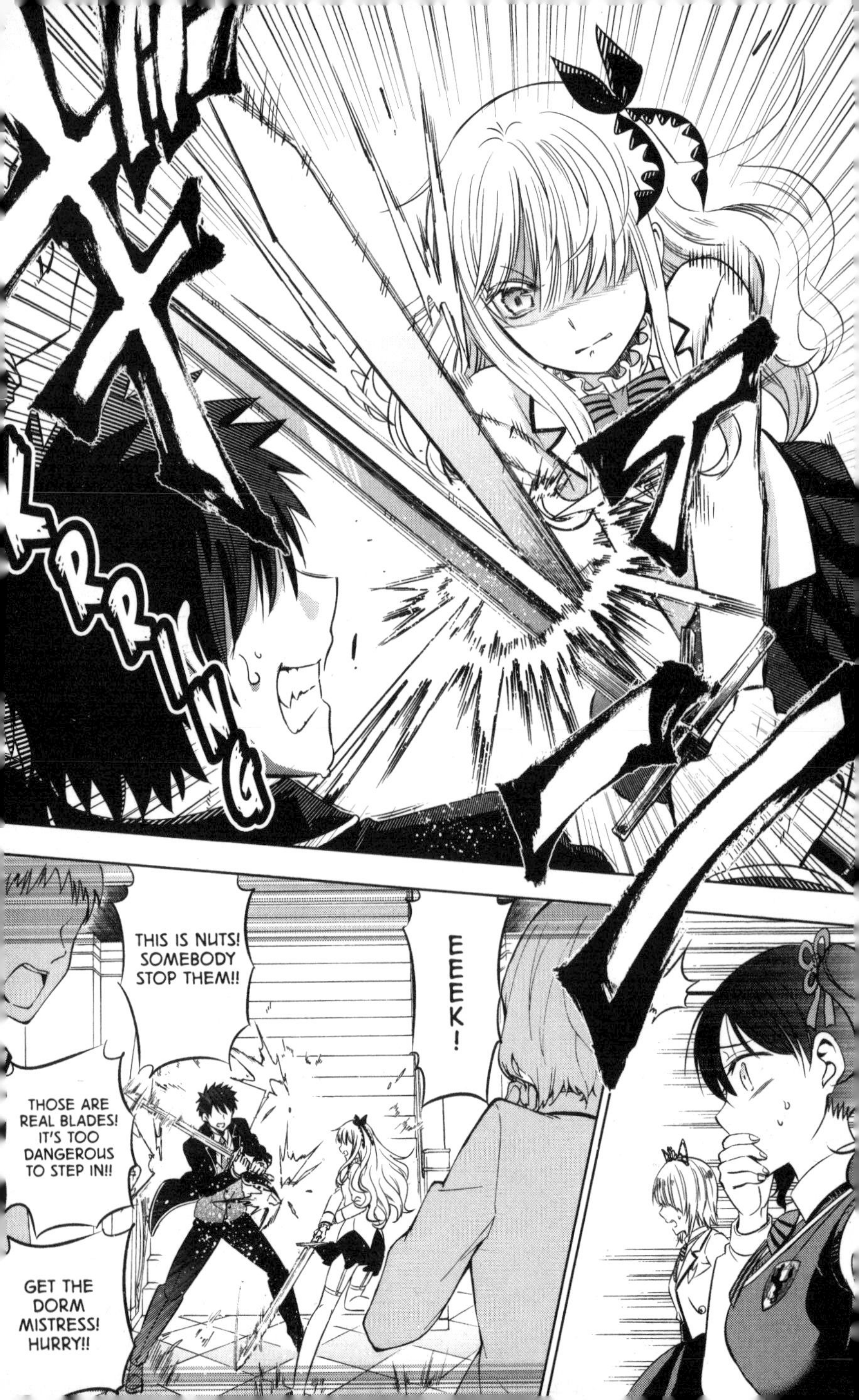
KRRING
EEEK!
THIS IS NUTS! SOMEBODY STOP THEM!!
THOSE ARE REAL BLADES! IT'S TOO DANGEROUS TO STEP IN!!
GET THE DORM MISTRESS! HURRY!!

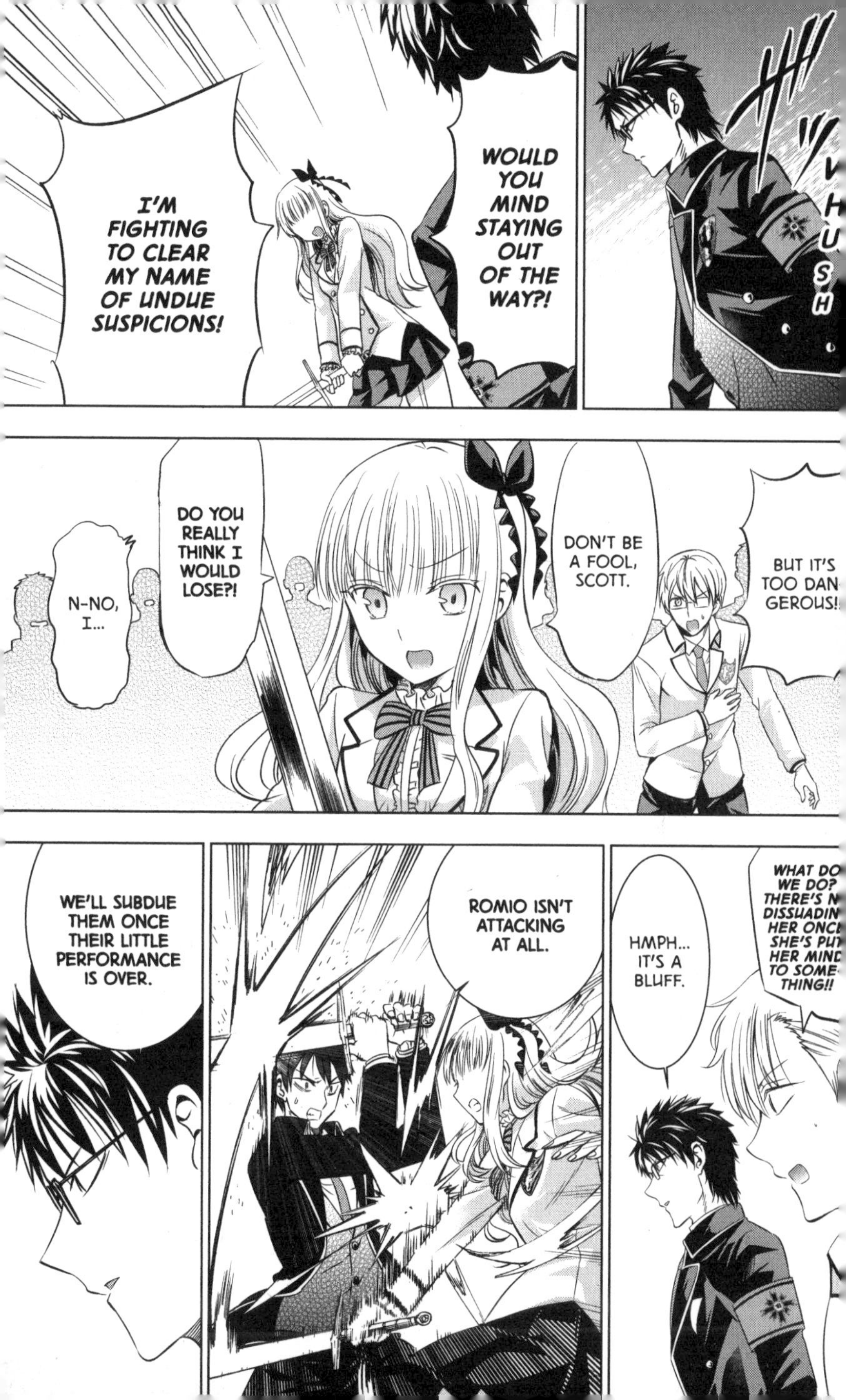
WHUSH
WOULD YOU MIND STAYING OUT OF THE WAY?!
I'M FIGHTING TO CLEAR MY NAME OF UNDUE SUSPICIONS!
BUT IT'S TOO DAN-GEROUS!!
DON'T BE A FOOL, SCOTT.
DO YOU REALLY THINK I WOULD LOSE?!
N-NO, I...
WHAT DO WE DO? THERE'S N DISSUADIN HER ONC SHE'S PU HER MIND TO SOME-THING!!
HMPH... IT'S A BLUFF.
ROMIO ISN'T ATTACKING AT ALL.
WE'LL SUBDUE THEM ONCE THEIR LITTLE PERFORMANCE IS OVER.

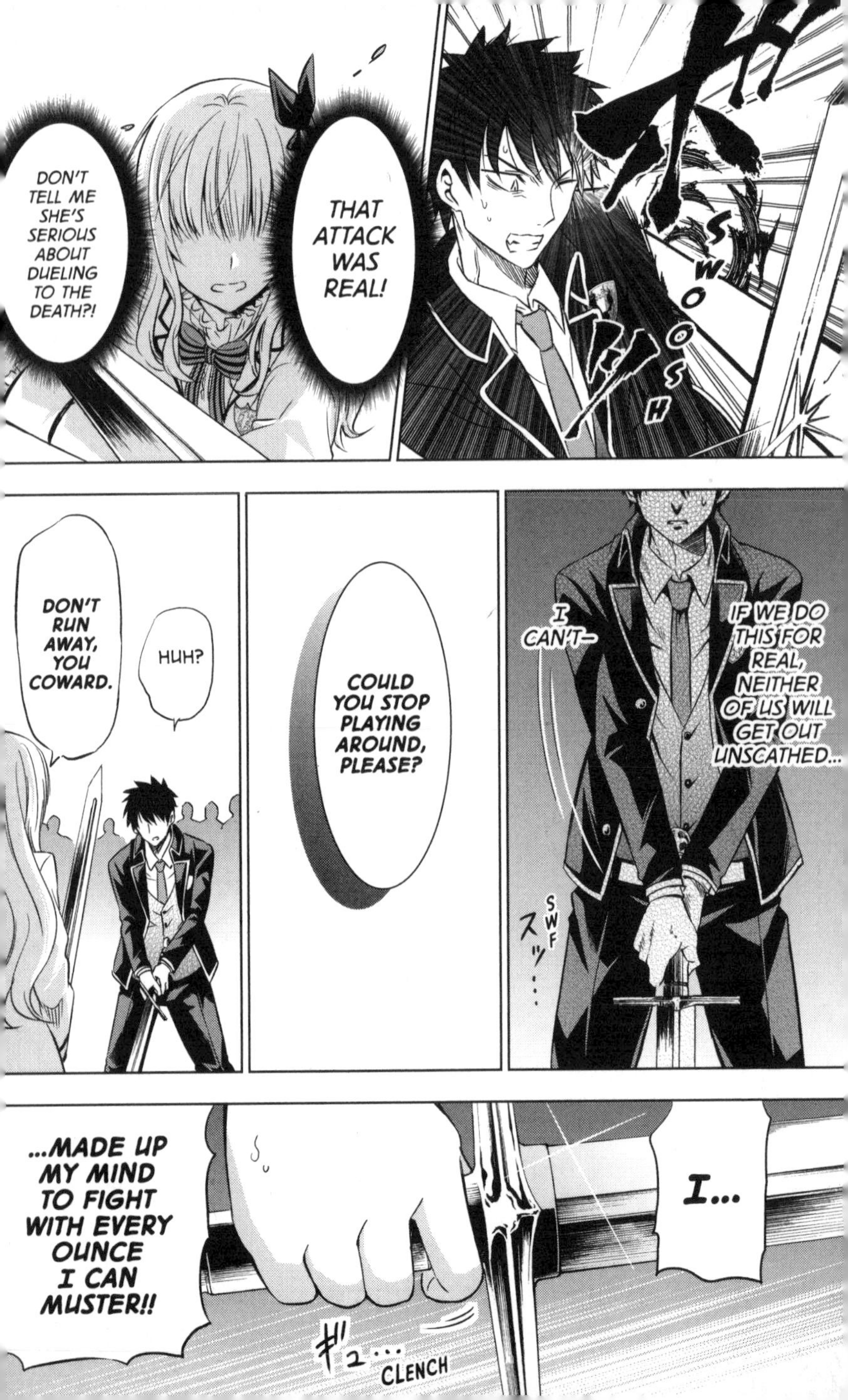
SWOOSH
THAT ATTACK WAS REAL!
DON'T TELL ME SHE'S SERIOUS ABOUT DUELING TO THE DEATH?!
IF WE DO THIS FOR REAL, NEITHER OF US WILL GET OUT UNSCATHED...
I CAN'T—
SWF
COULD YOU STOP PLAYING AROUND, PLEASE?
DON'T RUN AWAY, YOU COWARD.
HUH?
I...
...MADE UP MY MIND TO FIGHT WITH EVERY OUNCE I CAN MUSTER!!
CLENCH

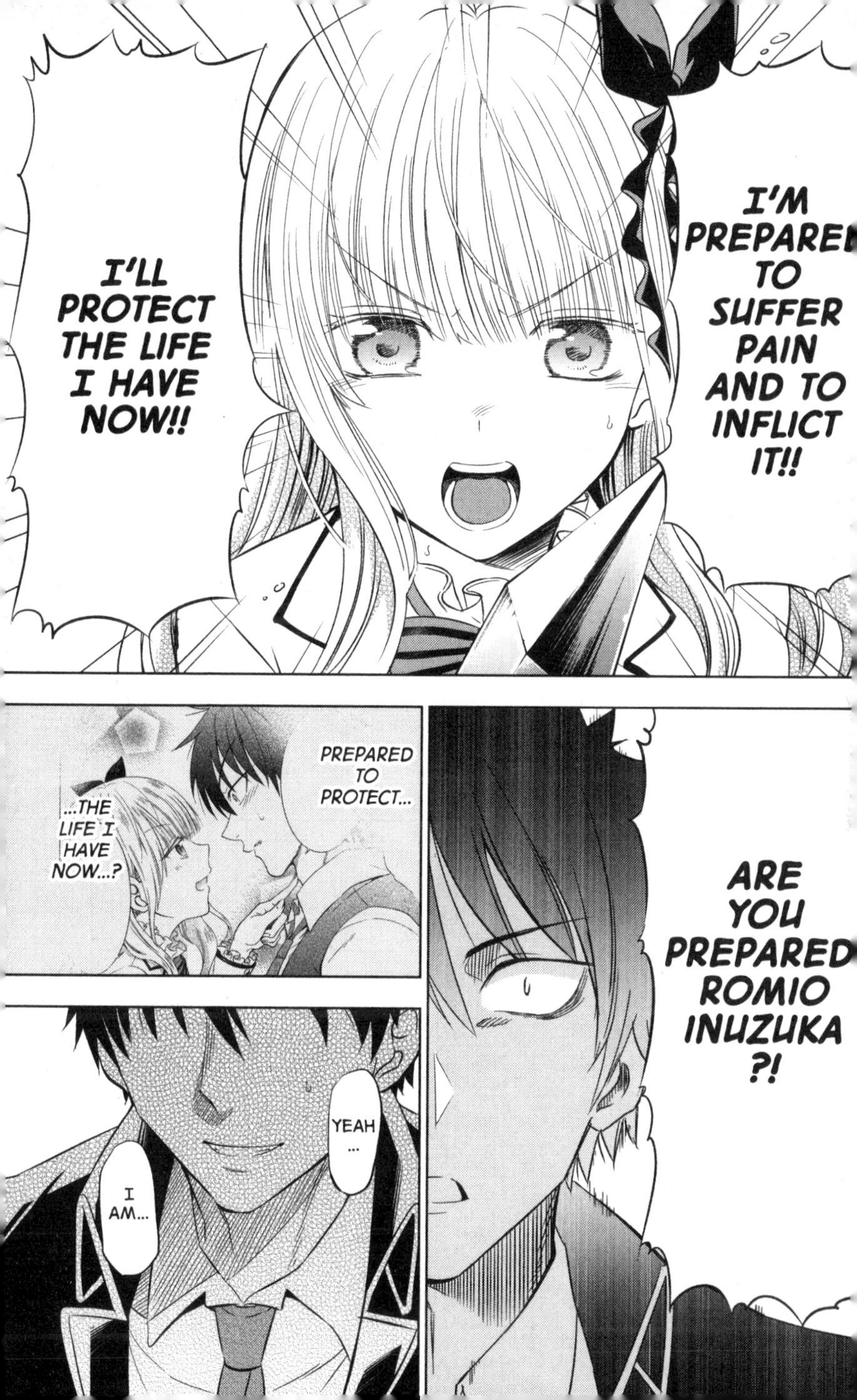
I'M PREPARED TO SUFFER PAIN AND TO INFLICT IT!!
I'LL PROTECT THE LIFE I HAVE NOW!!
ARE YOU PREPARED ROMIO INUZUKA ?!
PREPARED TO PROTECT...
...THE LIFE I HAVE NOW...?
YEAH ...
I AM...

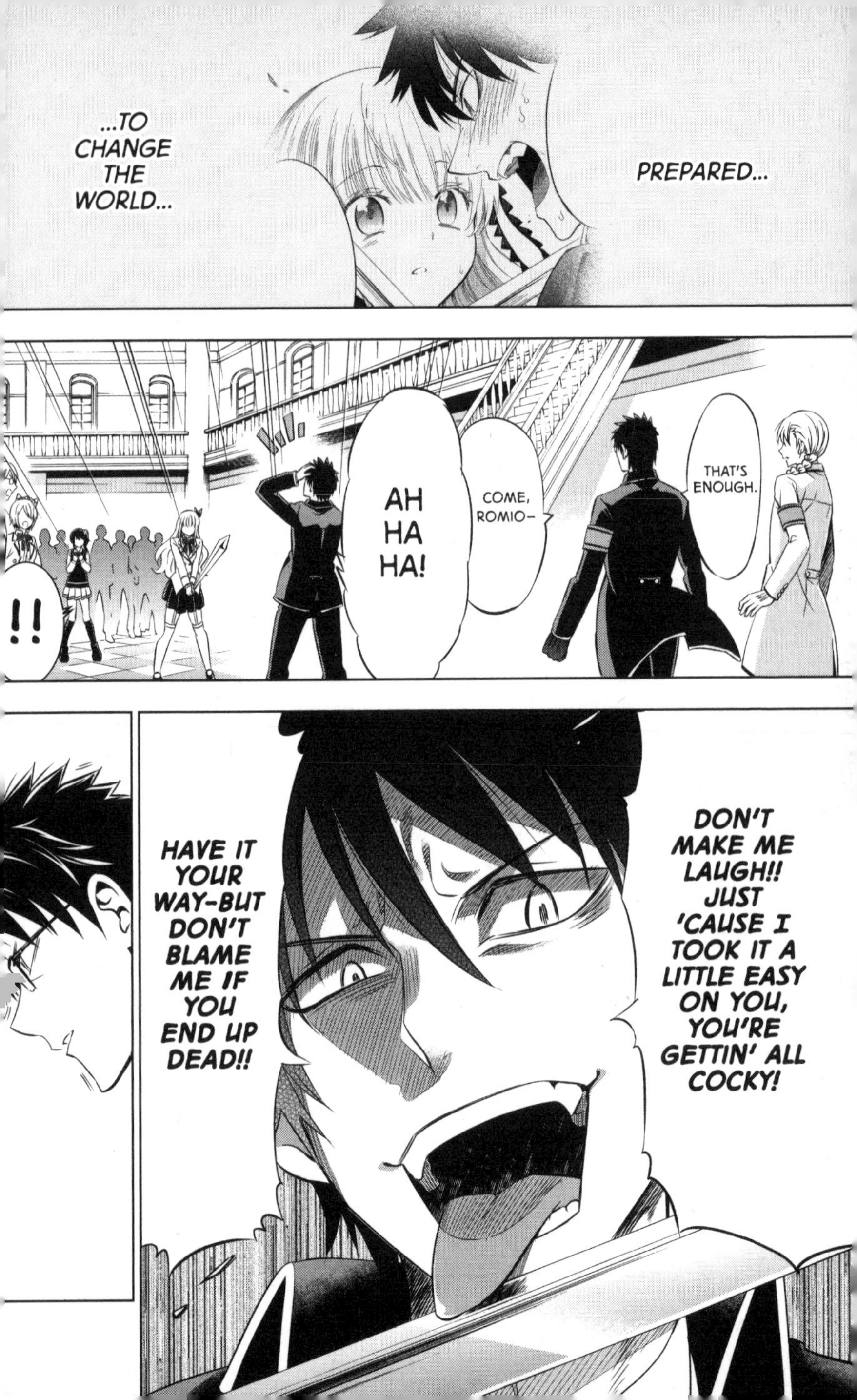
PREPARED...
...TO CHANGE THE WORLD...
THAT'S ENOUGH.
COME, ROMIO–
AH HA HA!
!!
DON'T MAKE ME LAUGH!! JUST 'CAUSE I TOOK IT A LITTLE EASY ON YOU, YOU'RE GETTIN' ALL COCKY!
HAVE IT YOUR WAY–BUT DON'T BLAME ME IF YOU END UP DEAD!!

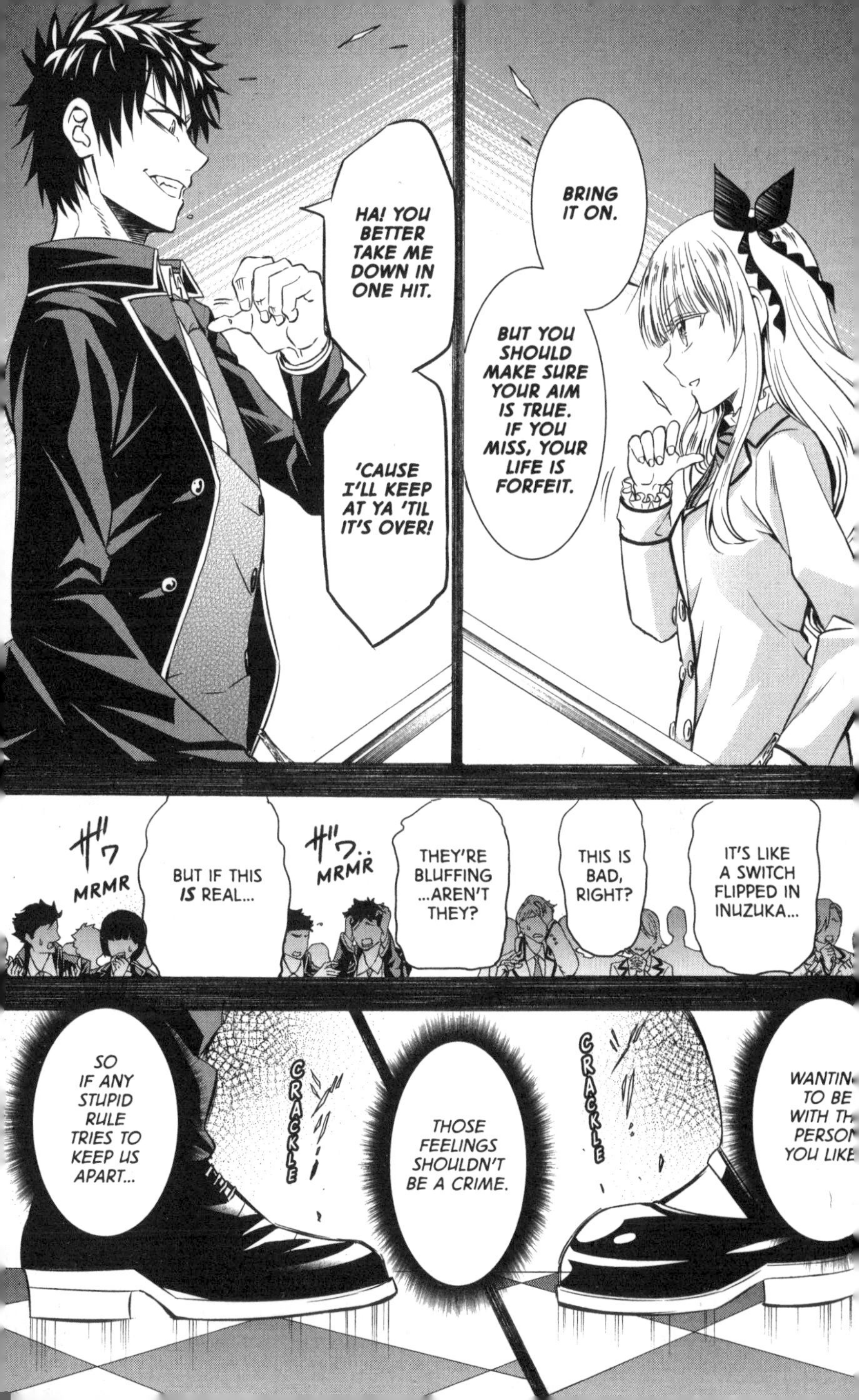
BRING IT ON.
BUT YOU SHOULD MAKE SURE YOUR AIM IS TRUE. IF YOU MISS, YOUR LIFE IS FORFEIT.
HA! YOU BETTER TAKE ME DOWN IN ONE HIT.
'CAUSE I'LL KEEP AT YA 'TIL IT'S OVER!
IT'S LIKE A SWITCH FLIPPED IN INUZUKA...
THIS IS BAD, RIGHT?
THEY'RE BLUFFING ...AREN'T THEY?
ザワ..
MRMR
BUT IF THIS *IS* REAL...
ザワ
MRMR
WANTIN TO BE WITH TH PERSON YOU LIKE
CRACKLE
THOSE FEELINGS SHOULDN'T BE A CRIME.
CRACKLE
SO IF ANY STUPID RULE TRIES TO KEEP US APART...

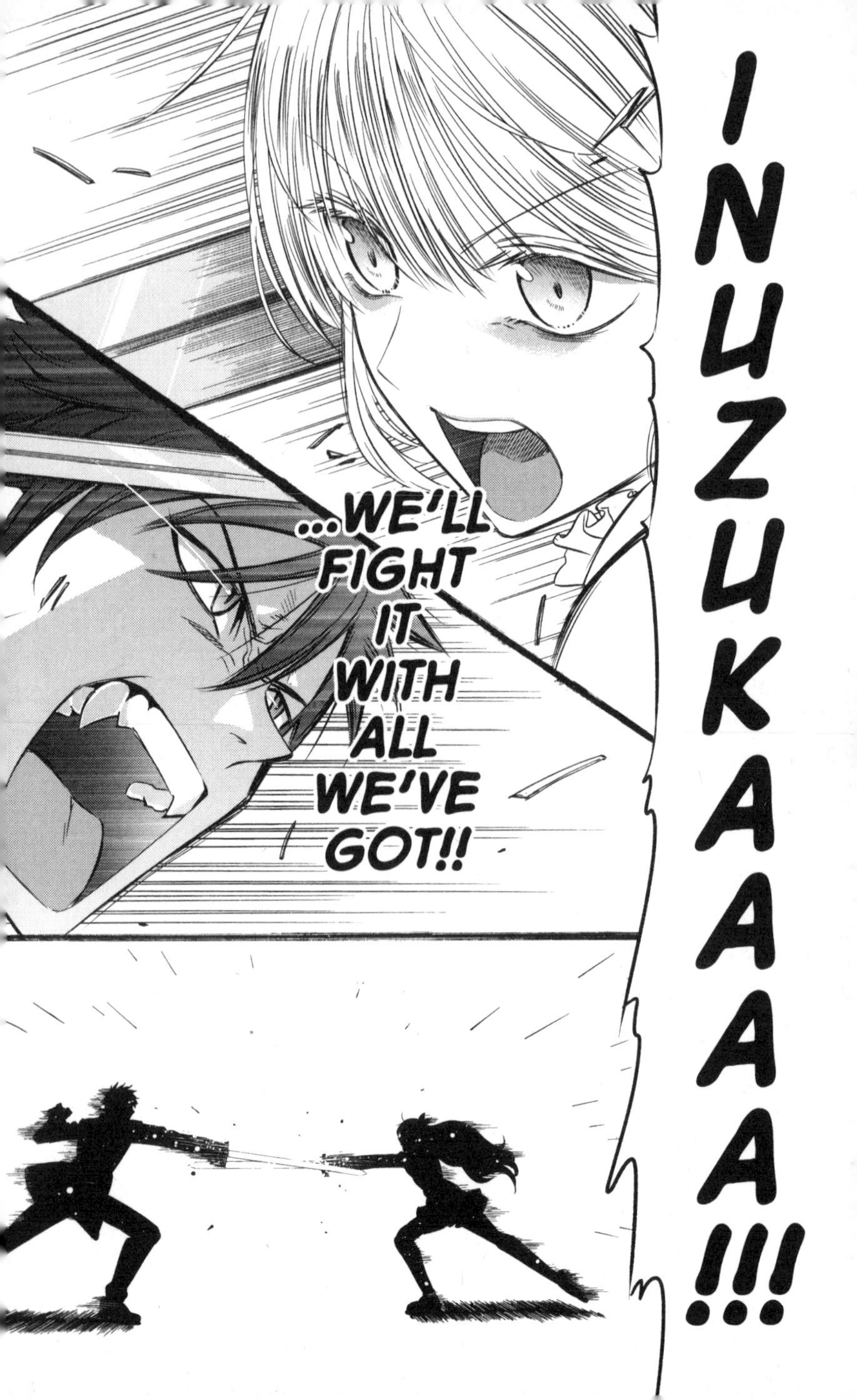
INUZUKAAAA!!!
...WE'LL FIGHT IT WITH ALL WE'VE GOT!!

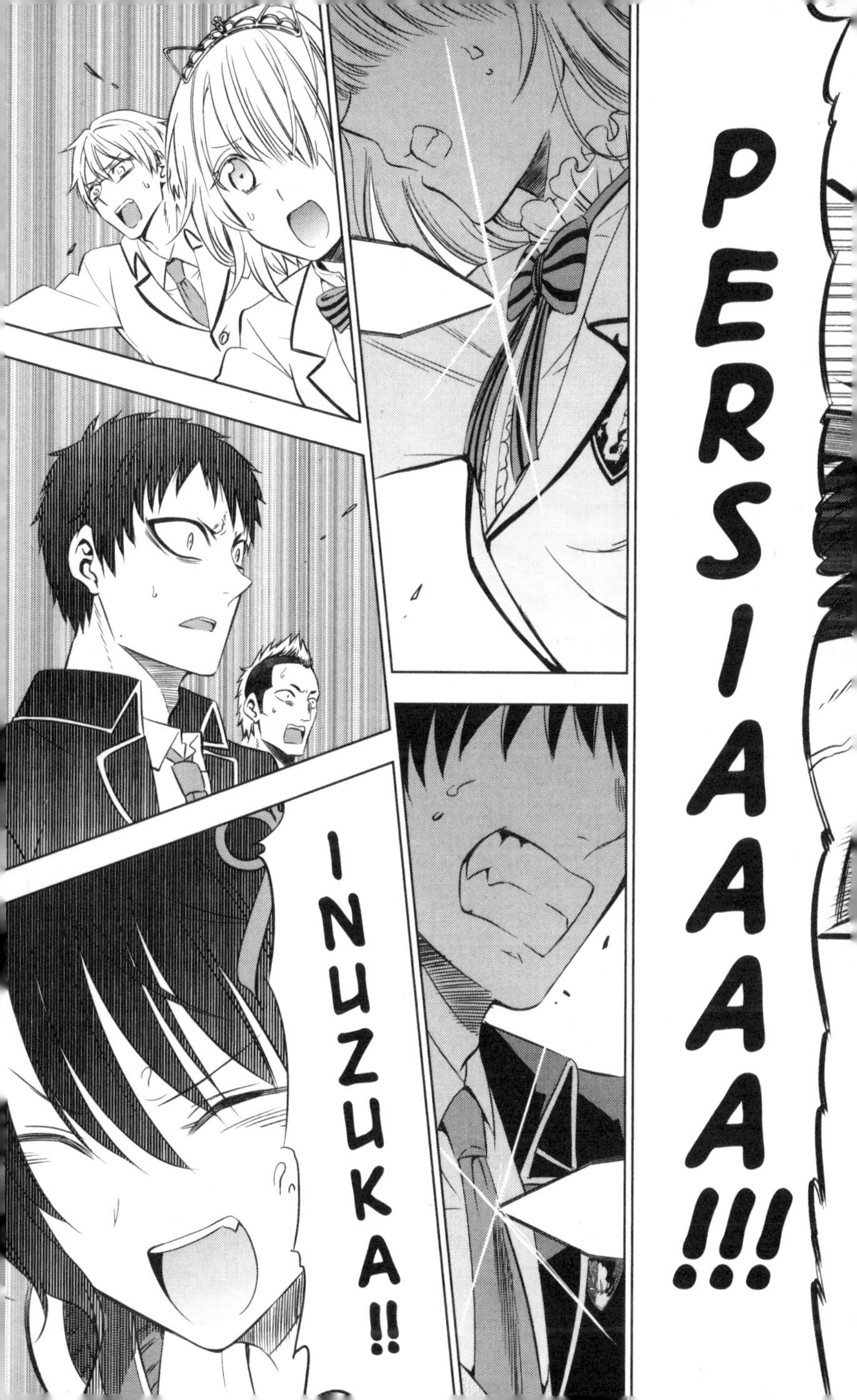
PERSIAAAAA!!!
INUZUKA!!

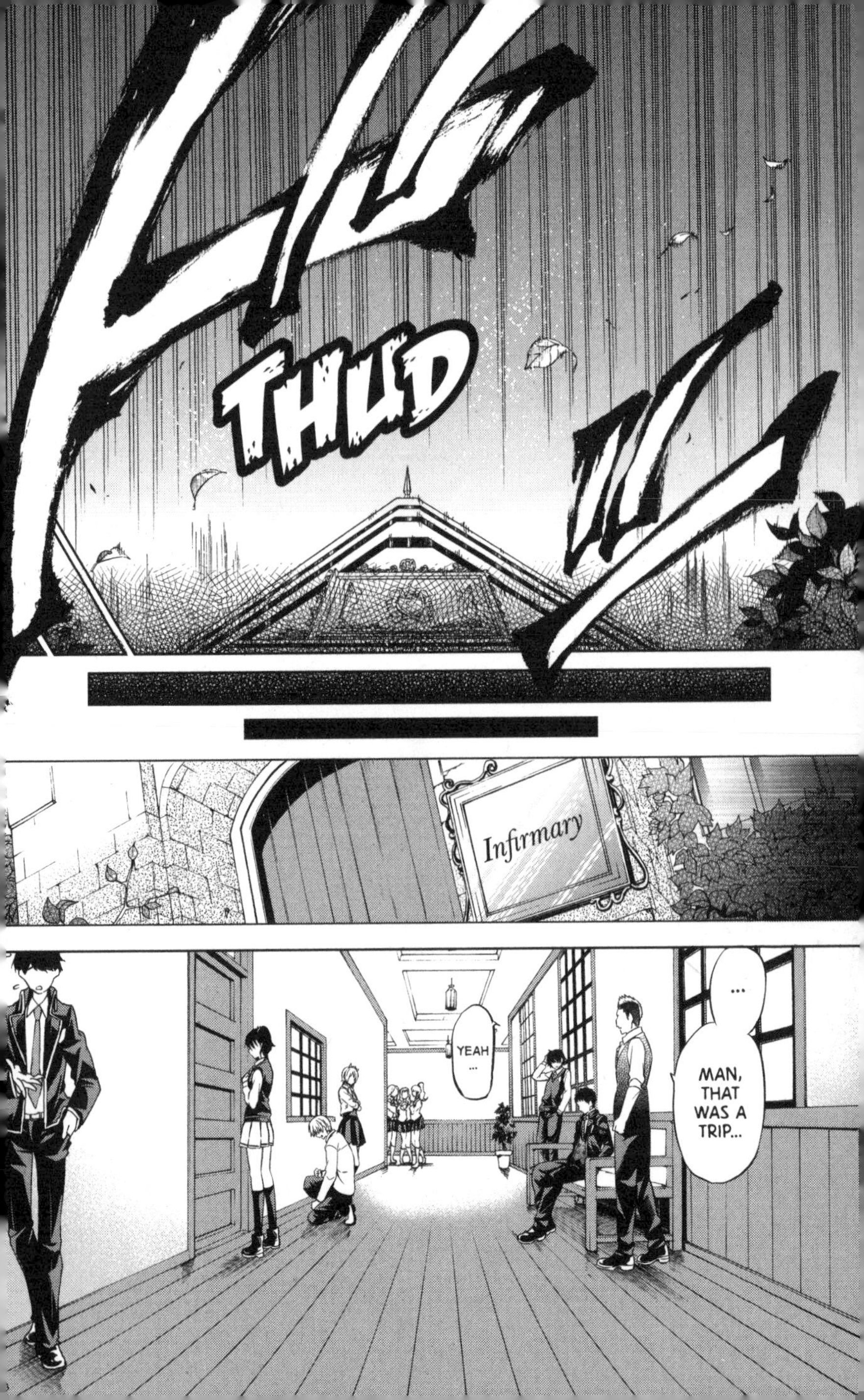
THUD
Infirmary
...
MAN, THAT WAS A TRIP...
YEAH ...

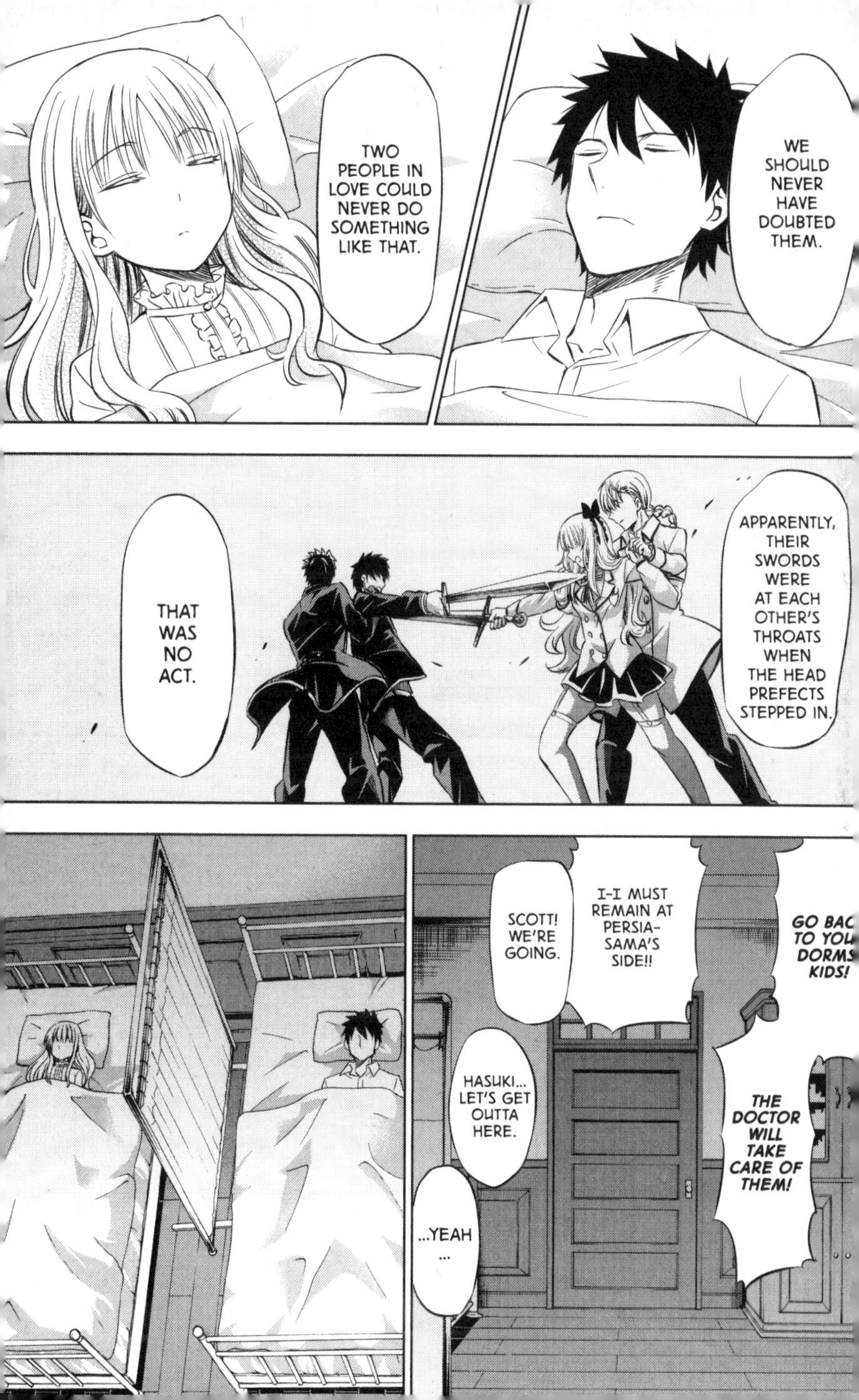
WE SHOULD NEVER HAVE DOUBTED THEM.
TWO PEOPLE IN LOVE COULD NEVER DO SOMETHING LIKE THAT.
APPARENTLY, THEIR SWORDS WERE AT EACH OTHER'S THROATS WHEN THE HEAD PREFECTS STEPPED IN.
THAT WAS NO ACT.
GO BAC TO YOU DORMS KIDS!
THE DOCTOR WILL TAKE CARE OF THEM!
I-I MUST REMAIN AT PERSIA-SAMA'S SIDE!!
SCOTT! WE'RE GOING.
HASUKI... LET'S GET OUTTA HERE.
...YEAH ...

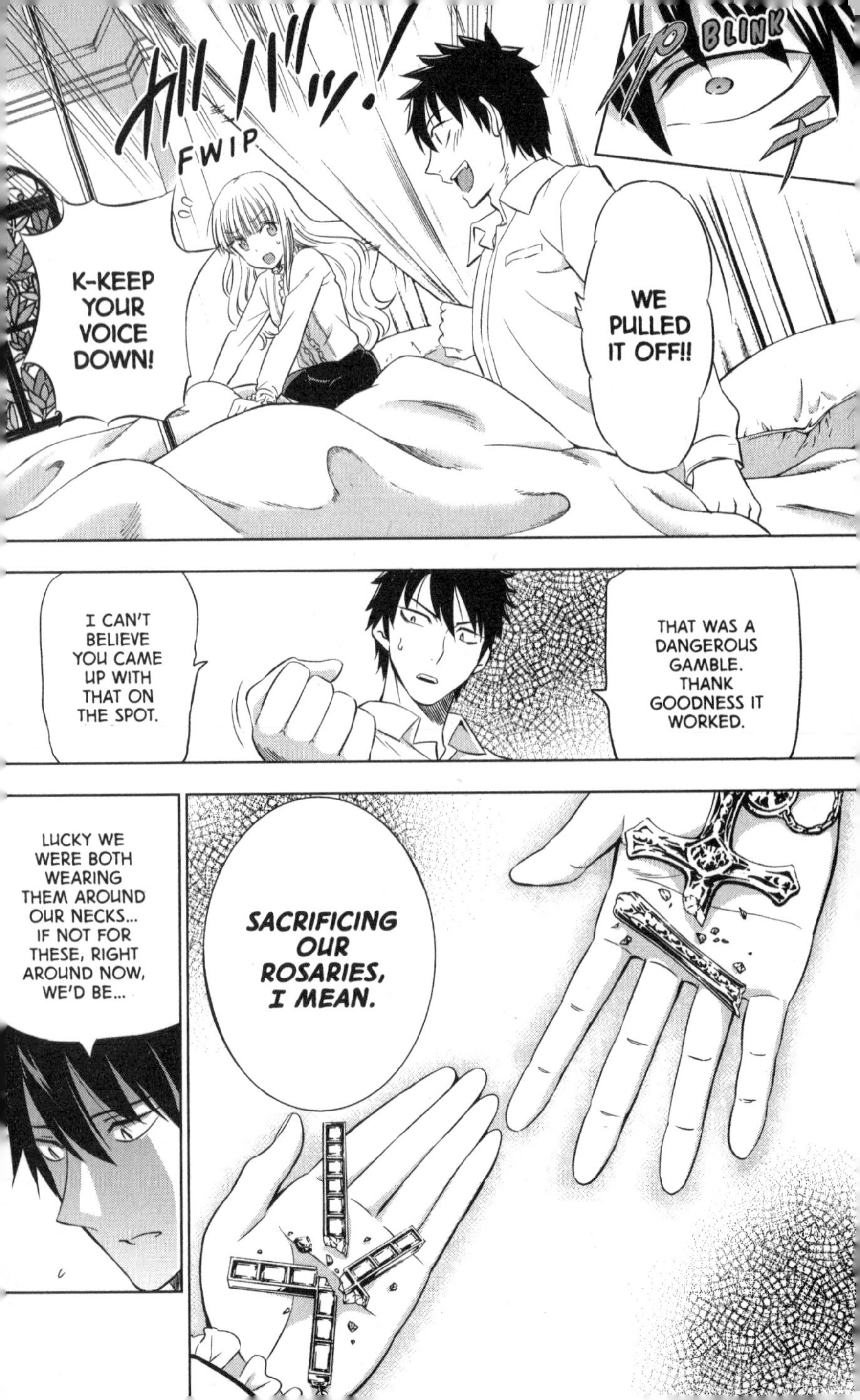
BLINK
FWIP
WE PULLED IT OFF!!
K-KEEP YOUR VOICE DOWN!
THAT WAS A DANGEROUS GAMBLE. THANK GOODNESS IT WORKED.
I CAN'T BELIEVE YOU CAME UP WITH THAT ON THE SPOT.
SACRIFICING OUR ROSARIES, I MEAN.
LUCKY WE WERE BOTH WEARING THEM AROUND OUR NECKS... IF NOT FOR THESE, RIGHT AROUND NOW, WE'D BE...

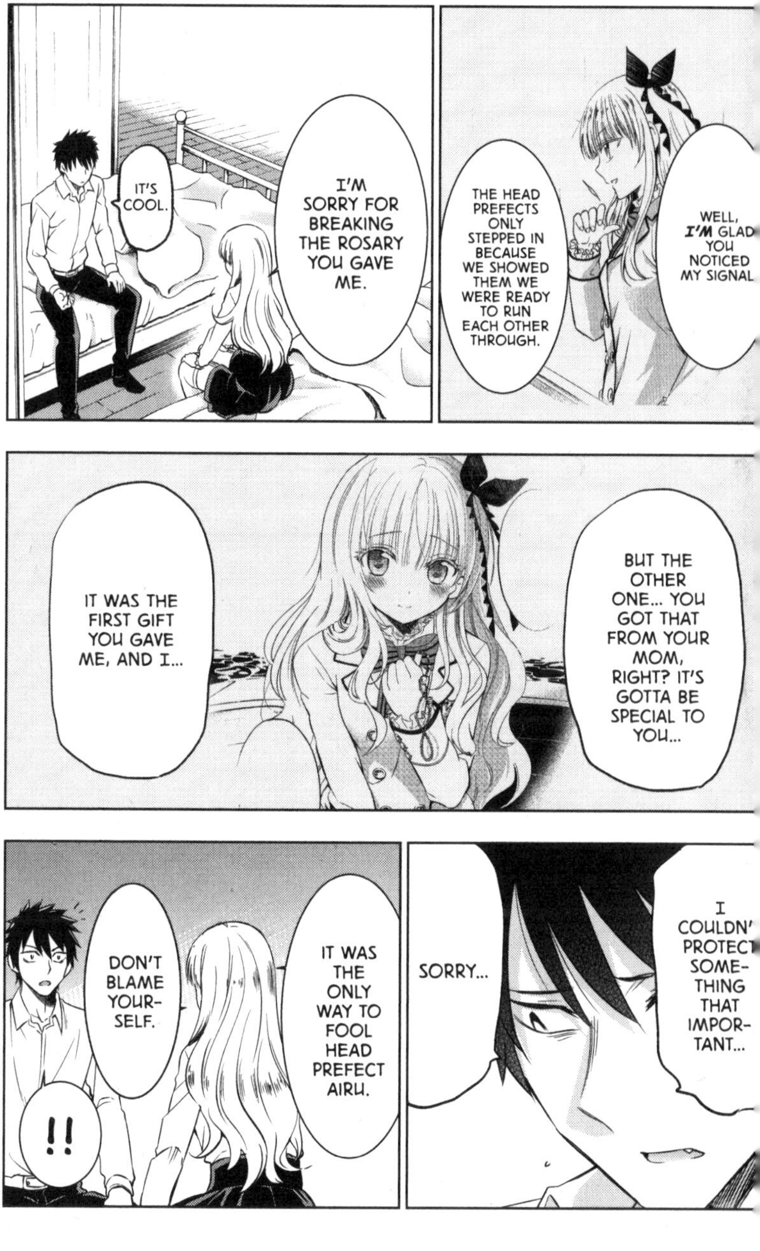
WELL, *I'M* GLAD YOU NOTICED MY SIGNAL
THE HEAD PREFECTS ONLY STEPPED IN BECAUSE WE SHOWED THEM WE WERE READY TO RUN EACH OTHER THROUGH.
I'M SORRY FOR BREAKING THE ROSARY YOU GAVE ME.
IT'S COOL.
BUT THE OTHER ONE... YOU GOT THAT FROM YOUR MOM, RIGHT? IT'S GOTTA BE SPECIAL TO YOU...
IT WAS THE FIRST GIFT YOU GAVE ME, AND I...
I COULDN' PROTECT SOMETHING THAT IMPORTANT...
SORRY...
IT WAS THE ONLY WAY TO FOOL HEAD PREFECT AIRU.
DON'T BLAME YOURSELF.
!!

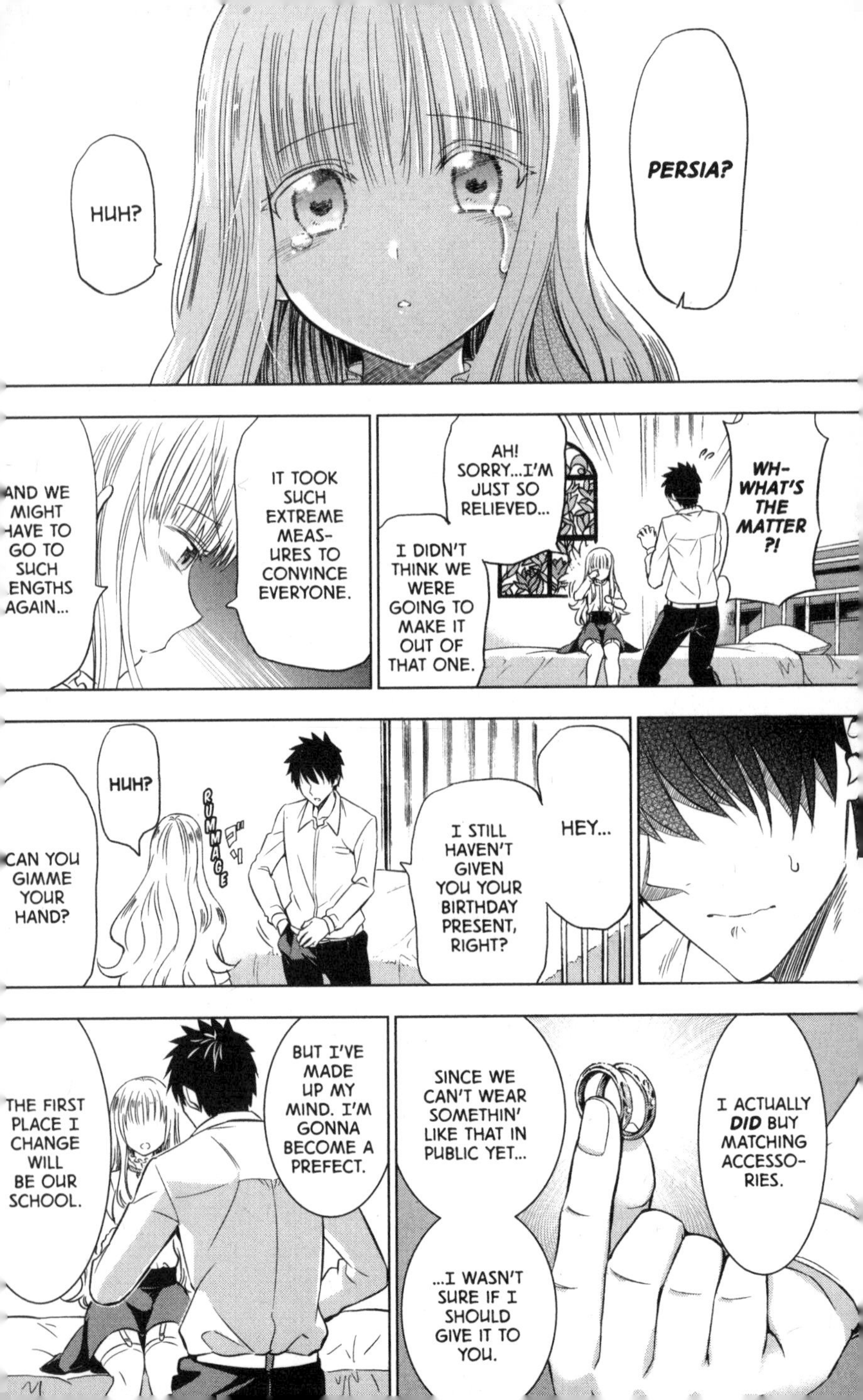
PERSIA?
HUH?
WH-WHAT'S THE MATTER?!
AH! SORRY...I'M JUST SO RELIEVED...
I DIDN'T THINK WE WERE GOING TO MAKE IT OUT OF THAT ONE.
IT TOOK SUCH EXTREME MEAS-URES TO CONVINCE EVERYONE.
AND WE MIGHT HAVE TO GO TO SUCH ENGTHS AGAIN...
HEY...
I STILL HAVEN'T GIVEN YOU YOUR BIRTHDAY PRESENT, RIGHT?
RUMMAGE
HUH?
CAN YOU GIMME YOUR HAND?
I ACTUALLY DID BUY MATCHING ACCESSO-RIES.
SINCE WE CAN'T WEAR SOMETHIN' LIKE THAT IN PUBLIC YET...
...I WASN'T SURE IF I SHOULD GIVE IT TO YOU.
BUT I'VE MADE UP MY MIND. I'M GONNA BECOME A PREFECT.
THE FIRST PLACE I CHANGE WILL BE OUR SCHOOL.

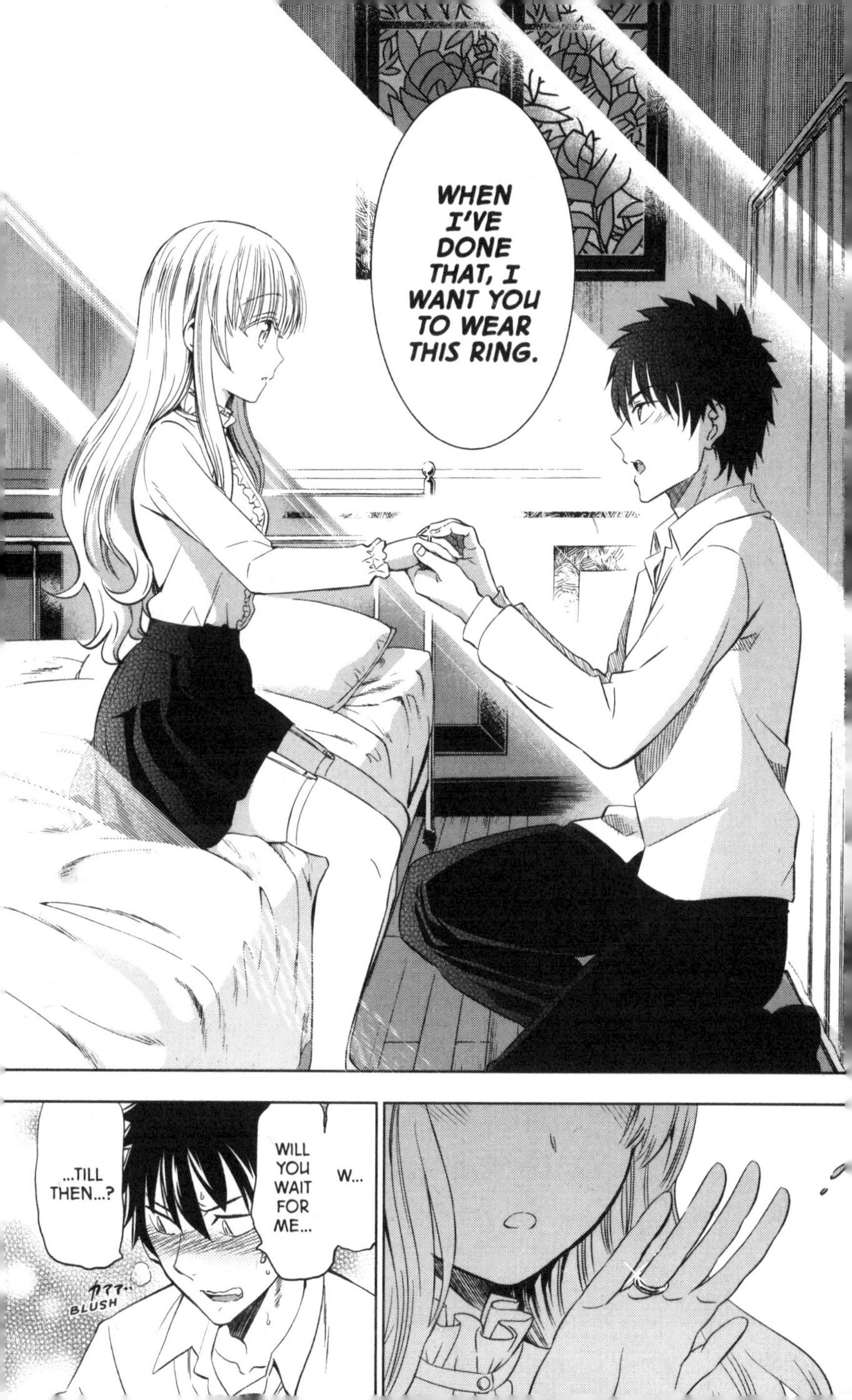
WHEN I'VE DONE THAT, I WANT YOU TO WEAR THIS RING.
W...
WILL YOU WAIT FOR ME...
...TILL THEN...?
BLUSH

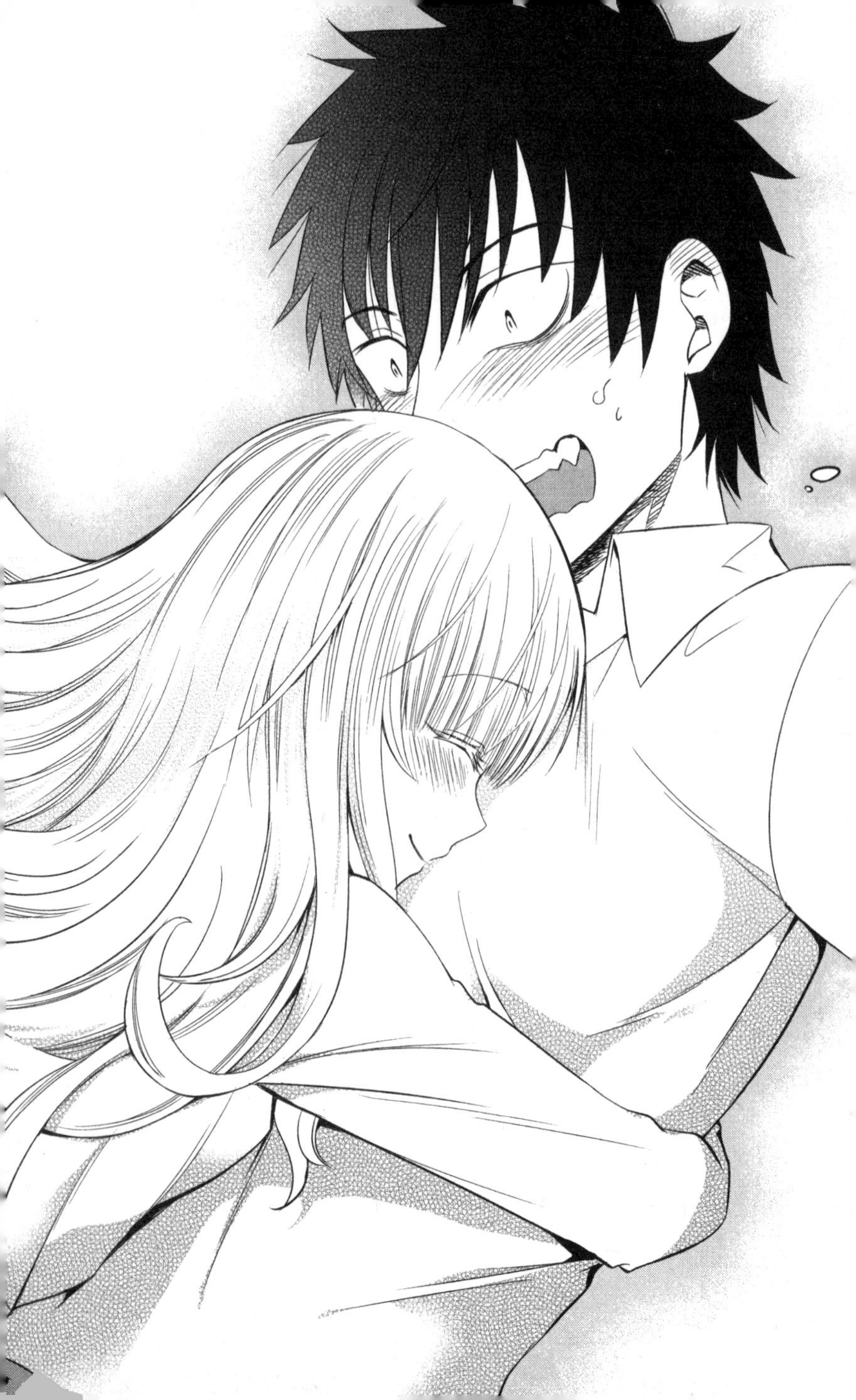

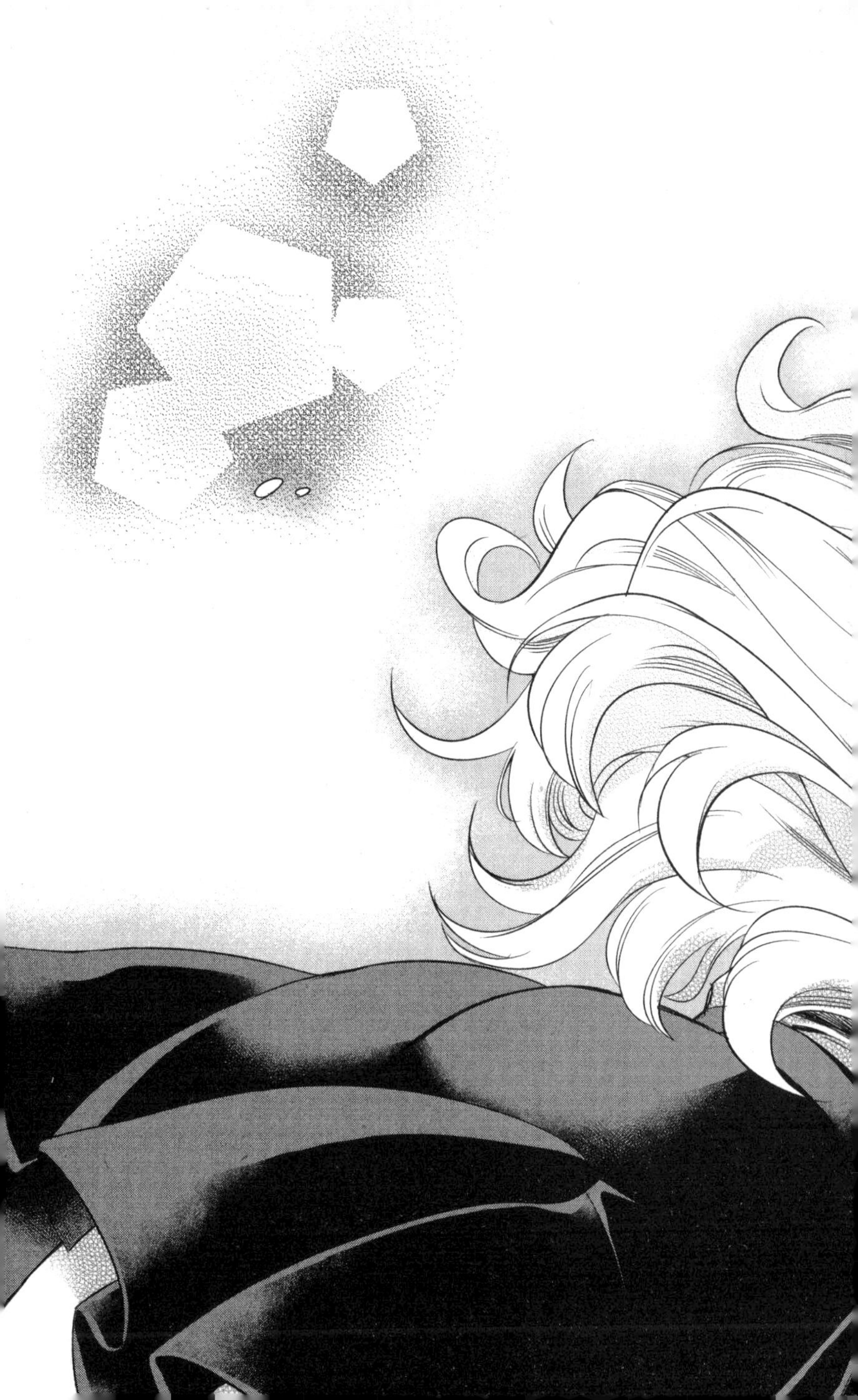

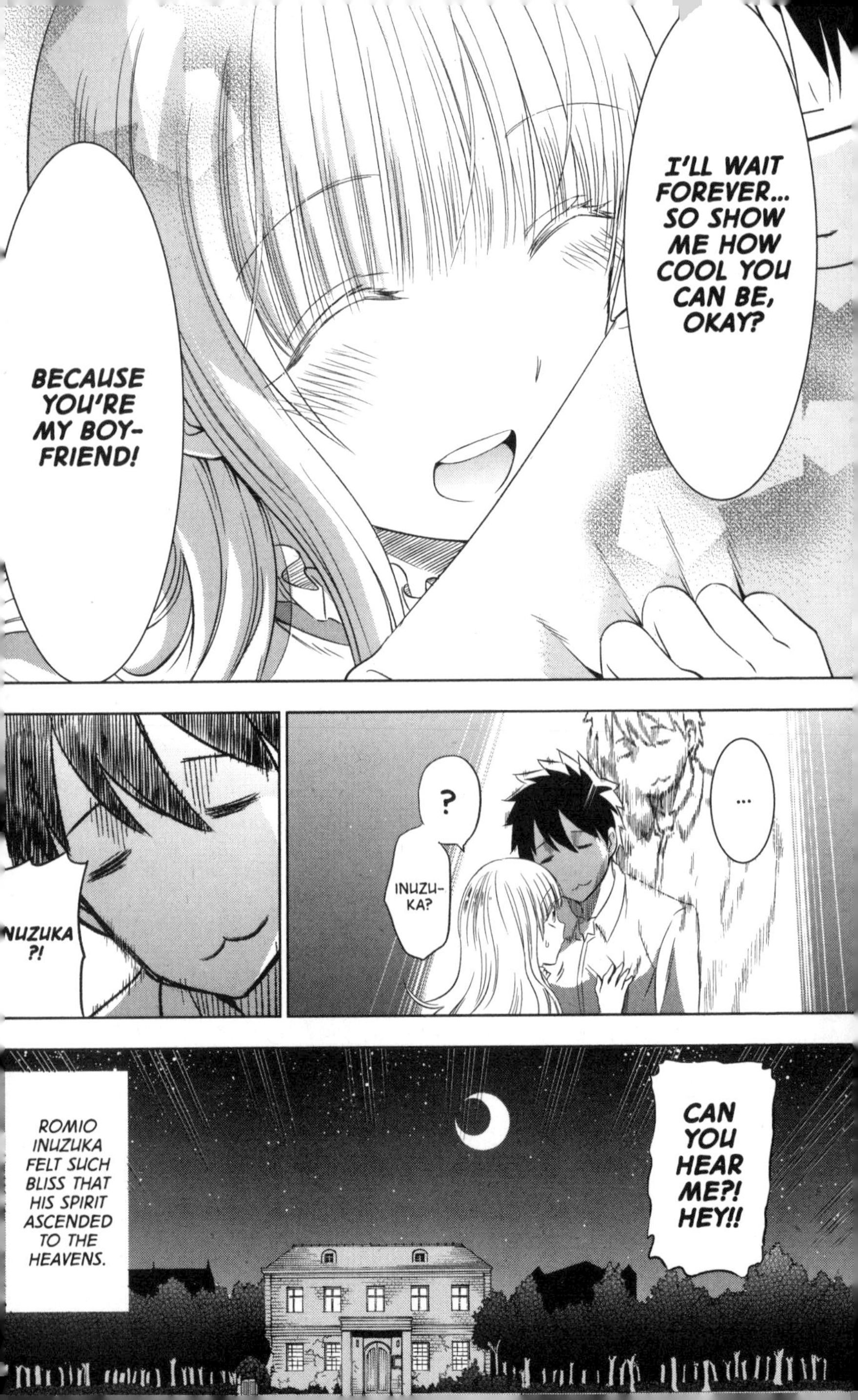
I'LL WAIT FOREVER... SO SHOW ME HOW COOL YOU CAN BE, OKAY?
BECAUSE YOU'RE MY BOY-FRIEND!
...
?
INUZUKA?
NUZUKA?!
CAN YOU HEAR ME?! HEY!!
ROMIO INUZUKA FELT SUCH BLISS THAT HIS SPIRIT ASCENDED TO THE HEAVENS.

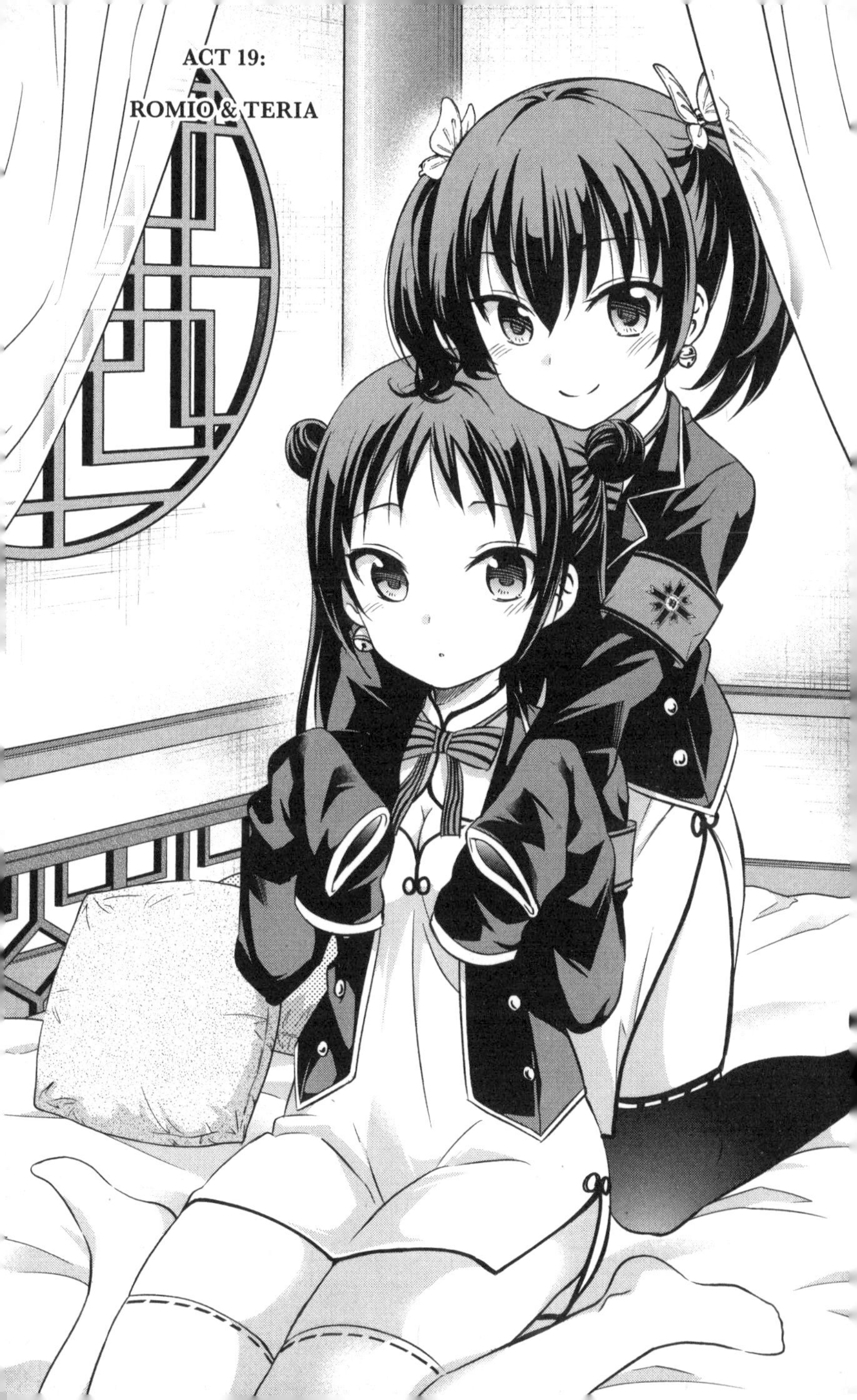
ACT 19:
ROMIO & TERIA

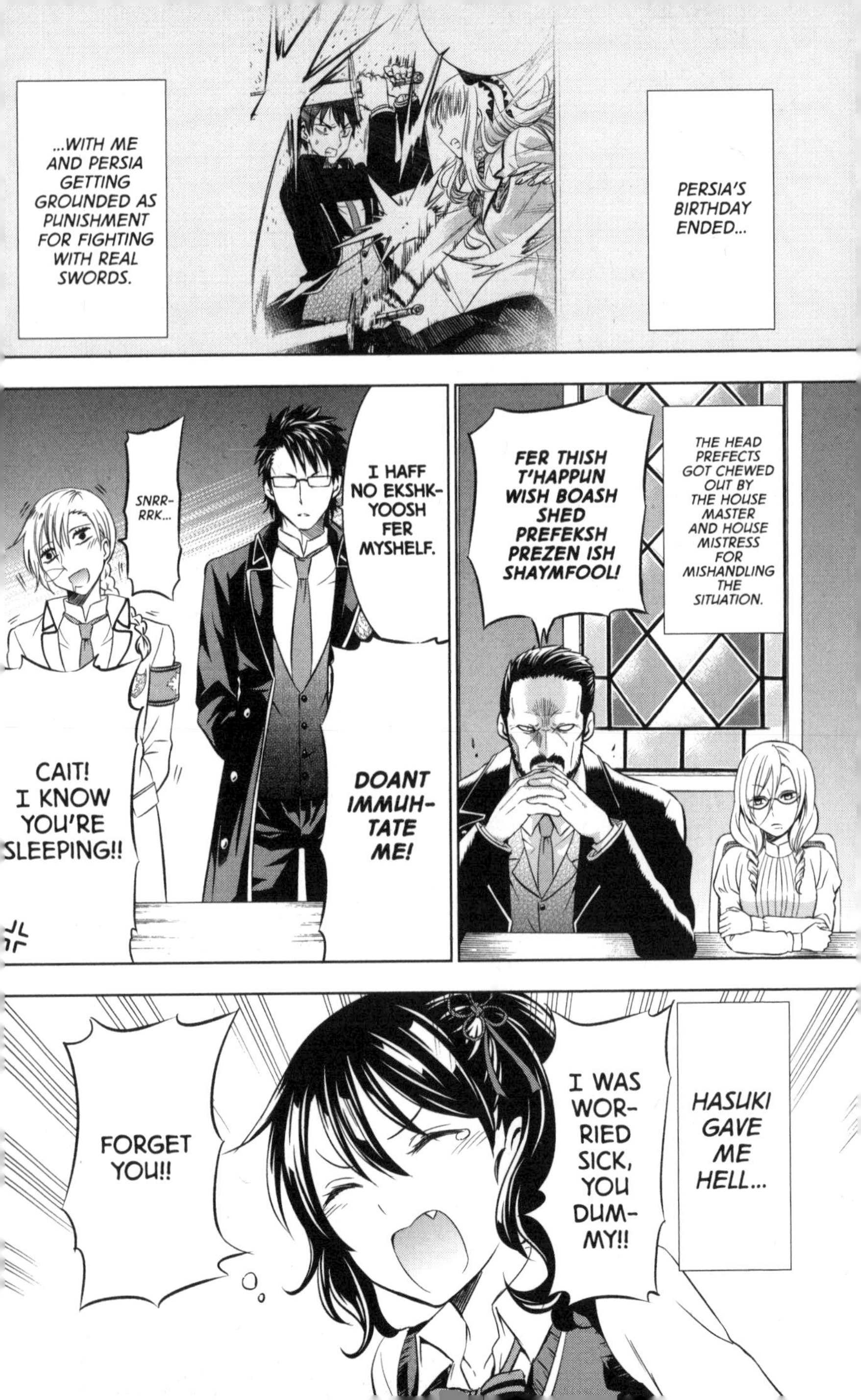
PERSIA'S BIRTHDAY ENDED...
...WITH ME AND PERSIA GETTING GROUNDED AS PUNISHMENT FOR FIGHTING WITH REAL SWORDS.
THE HEAD PREFECTS GOT CHEWED OUT BY THE HOUSE MASTER AND HOUSE MISTRESS FOR MISHANDLING THE SITUATION.
FER THISH T'HAPPUN WISH BOASH SHED PREFEKSH PREZEN ISH SHAYMFOOL!
I HAFF NO EKSHK-YOOSH FER MYSHELF.
SNRR-RRK...
DOANT IMMUH-TATE ME!
CAIT! I KNOW YOU'RE SLEEPING!!
HASUKI GAVE ME HELL...
I WAS WOR-RIED SICK, YOU DUM-MY!!
FORGET YOU!!

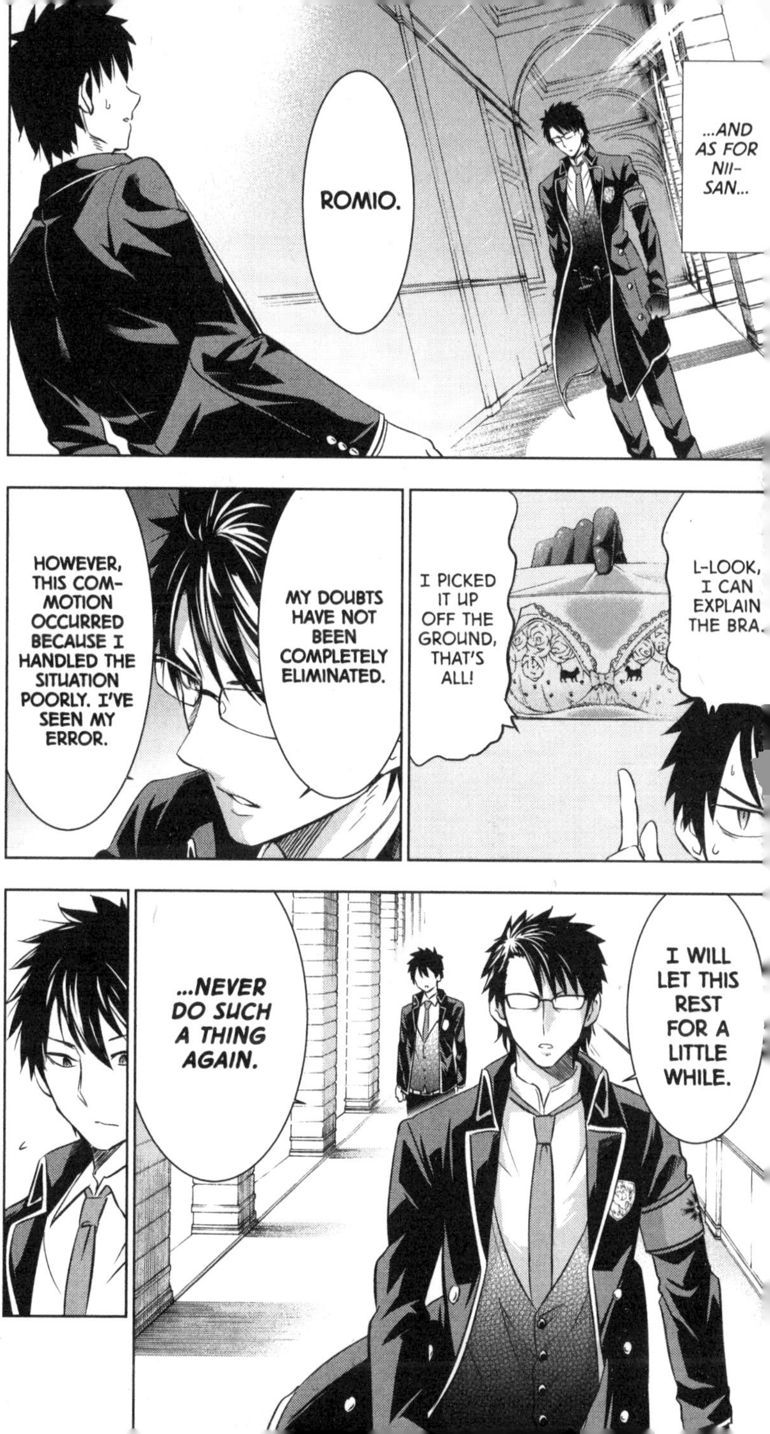
...AND AS FOR NII-SAN...
ROMIO.
L-LOOK, I CAN EXPLAIN THE BRA.
I PICKED IT UP OFF THE GROUND, THAT'S ALL!
MY DOUBTS HAVE NOT BEEN COMPLETELY ELIMINATED.
HOWEVER, THIS COMMOTION OCCURRED BECAUSE I HANDLED THE SITUATION POORLY. I'VE SEEN MY ERROR.
I WILL LET THIS REST FOR A LITTLE WHILE.
...NEVER DO SUCH A THING AGAIN.

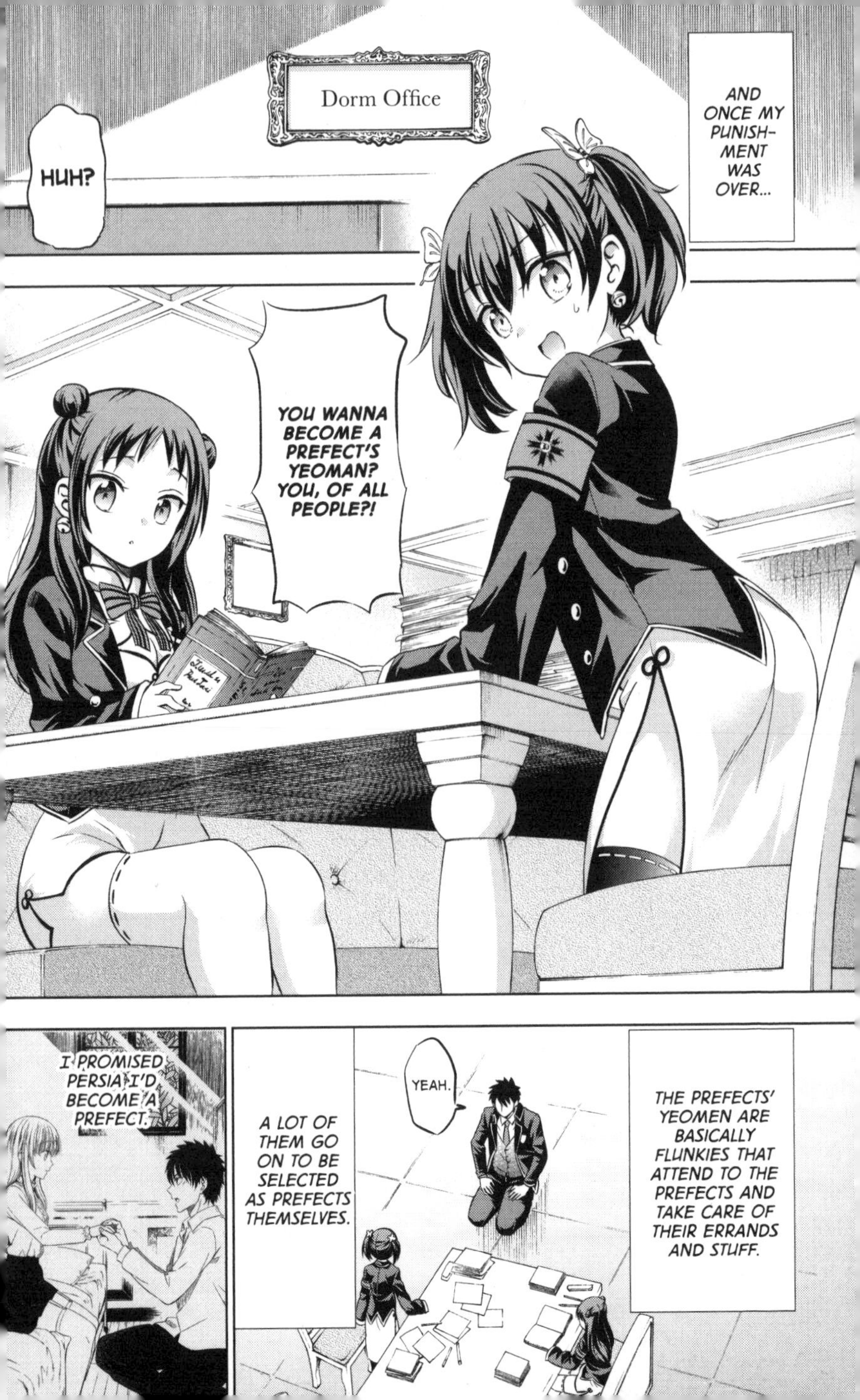
AND ONCE MY PUNISHMENT WAS OVER...
Dorm Office
HUH?
YOU WANNA BECOME A PREFECT'S YEOMAN? YOU, OF ALL PEOPLE?!
THE PREFECTS' YEOMEN ARE BASICALLY FLUNKIES THAT ATTEND TO THE PREFECTS AND TAKE CARE OF THEIR ERRANDS AND STUFF.
YEAH.
A LOT OF THEM GO ON TO BE SELECTED AS PREFECTS THEMSELVES.
I PROMISED PERSIA I'D BECOME A PREFECT.

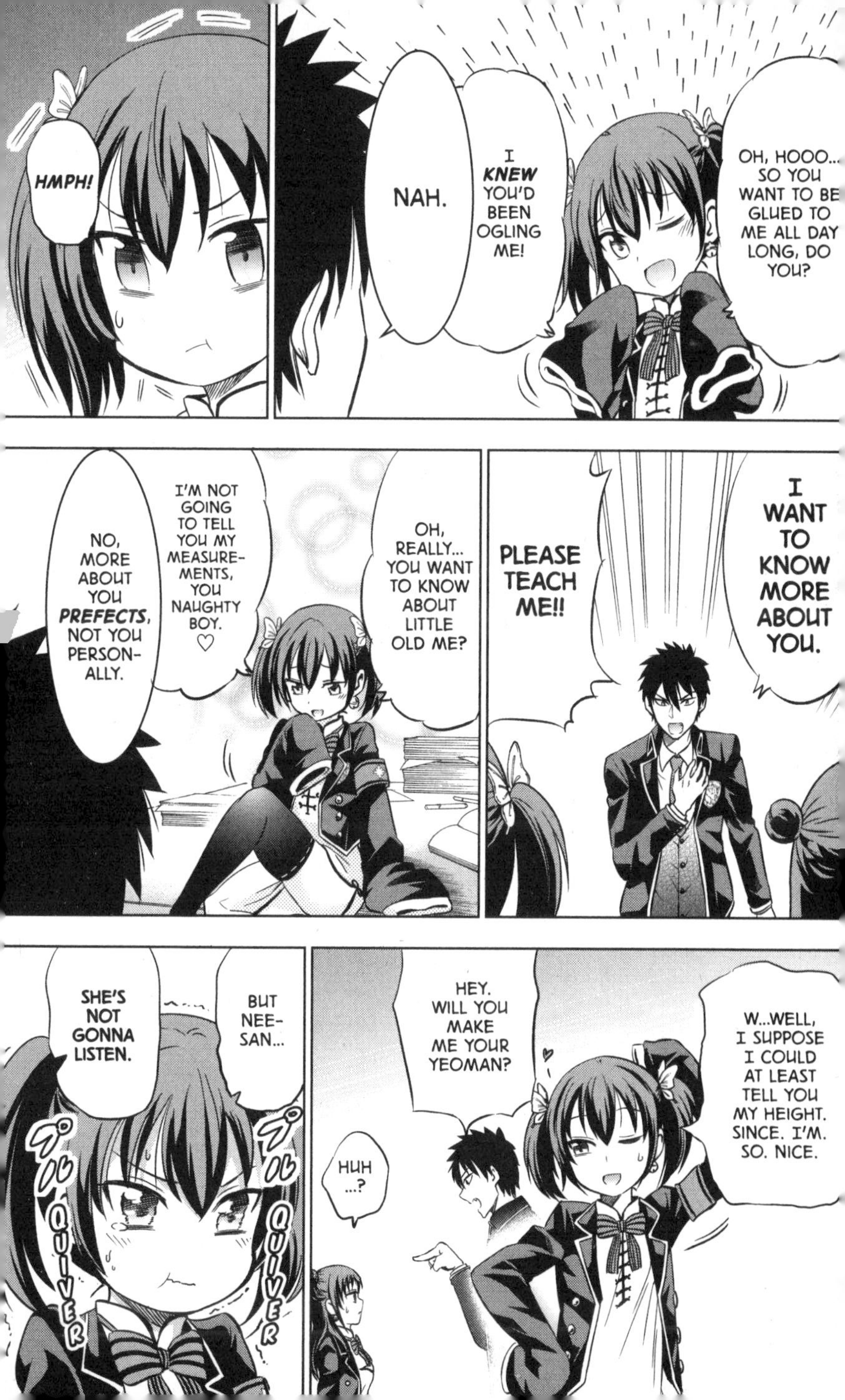
OH, HOOO... SO YOU WANT TO BE GLUED TO ME ALL DAY LONG, DO YOU?
I *KNEW* YOU'D BEEN OGLING ME!
NAH.
HMPH!
I WANT TO KNOW MORE ABOUT YOU.
PLEASE TEACH ME!!
OH, REALLY... YOU WANT TO KNOW ABOUT LITTLE OLD ME?
I'M NOT GOING TO TELL YOU MY MEASUREMENTS, YOU NAUGHTY BOY. ♡
NO, MORE ABOUT YOU *PREFECTS*, NOT YOU PERSONALLY.
W...WELL, I SUPPOSE I COULD AT LEAST TELL YOU MY HEIGHT. SINCE. I'M. SO. NICE.
HEY. WILL YOU MAKE ME YOUR YEOMAN?
HUH ...?
BUT NEE-SAN...
SHE'S NOT GONNA LISTEN.
QUIVER
QUIVER

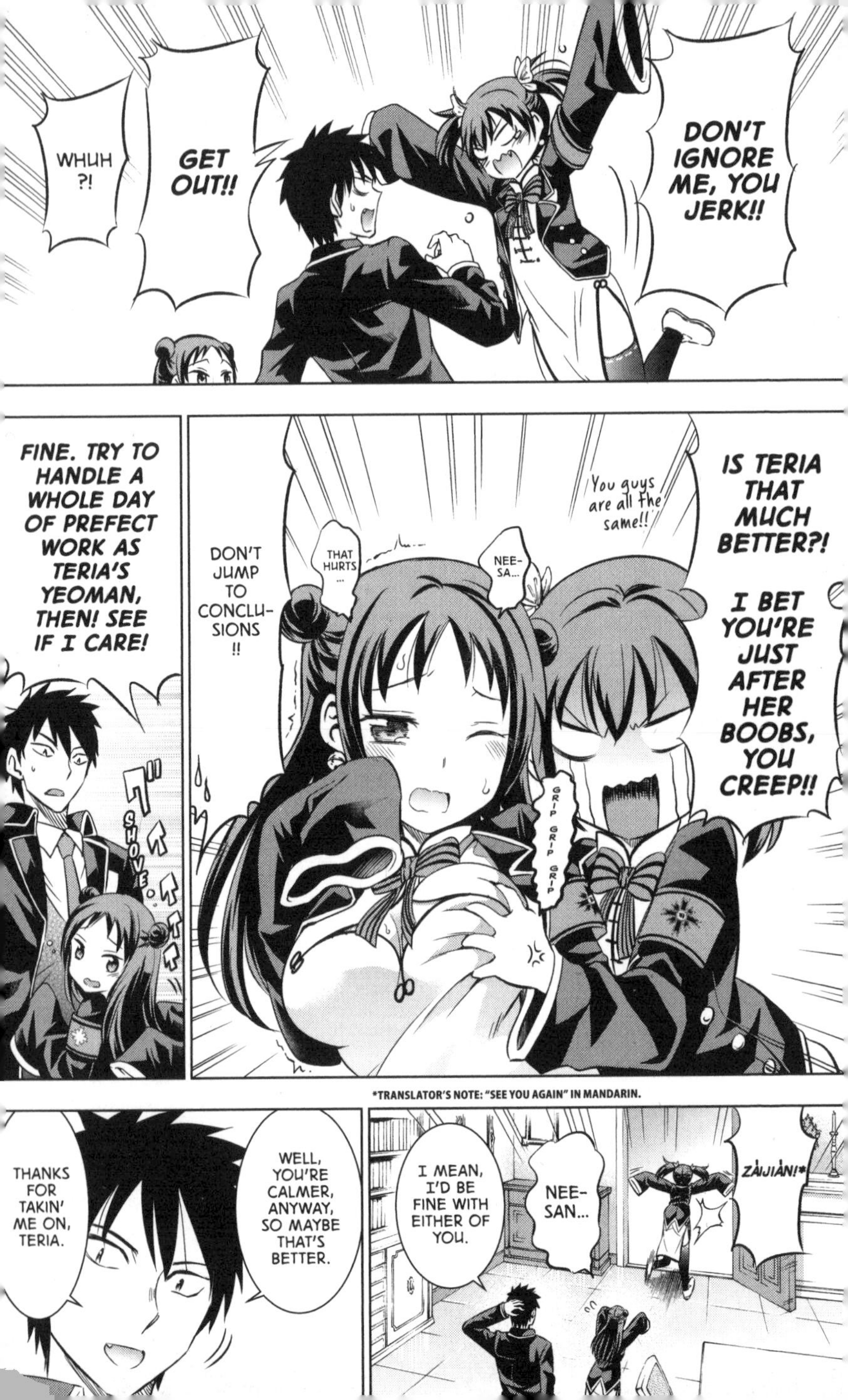
DON'T IGNORE ME, YOU JERK!!
GET OUT!!
WHUH ?!
IS TERIA THAT MUCH BETTER?!
I BET YOU'RE JUST AFTER HER BOOBS, YOU CREEP!!
You guys are all the same!!
NEE-SA...
THAT HURTS...
DON'T JUMP TO CONCLUSIONS!!
GRIP GRIP GRIP
FINE. TRY TO HANDLE A WHOLE DAY OF PREFECT WORK AS TERIA'S YEOMAN, THEN! SEE IF I CARE!
SHOVE
*TRANSLATOR'S NOTE: "SEE YOU AGAIN" IN MANDARIN.
ZÀIJIÀN!*
NEE-SAN...
I MEAN, I'D BE FINE WITH EITHER OF YOU.
WELL, YOU'RE CALMER, ANYWAY, SO MAYBE THAT'S BETTER.
THANKS FOR TAKIN' ME ON, TERIA.

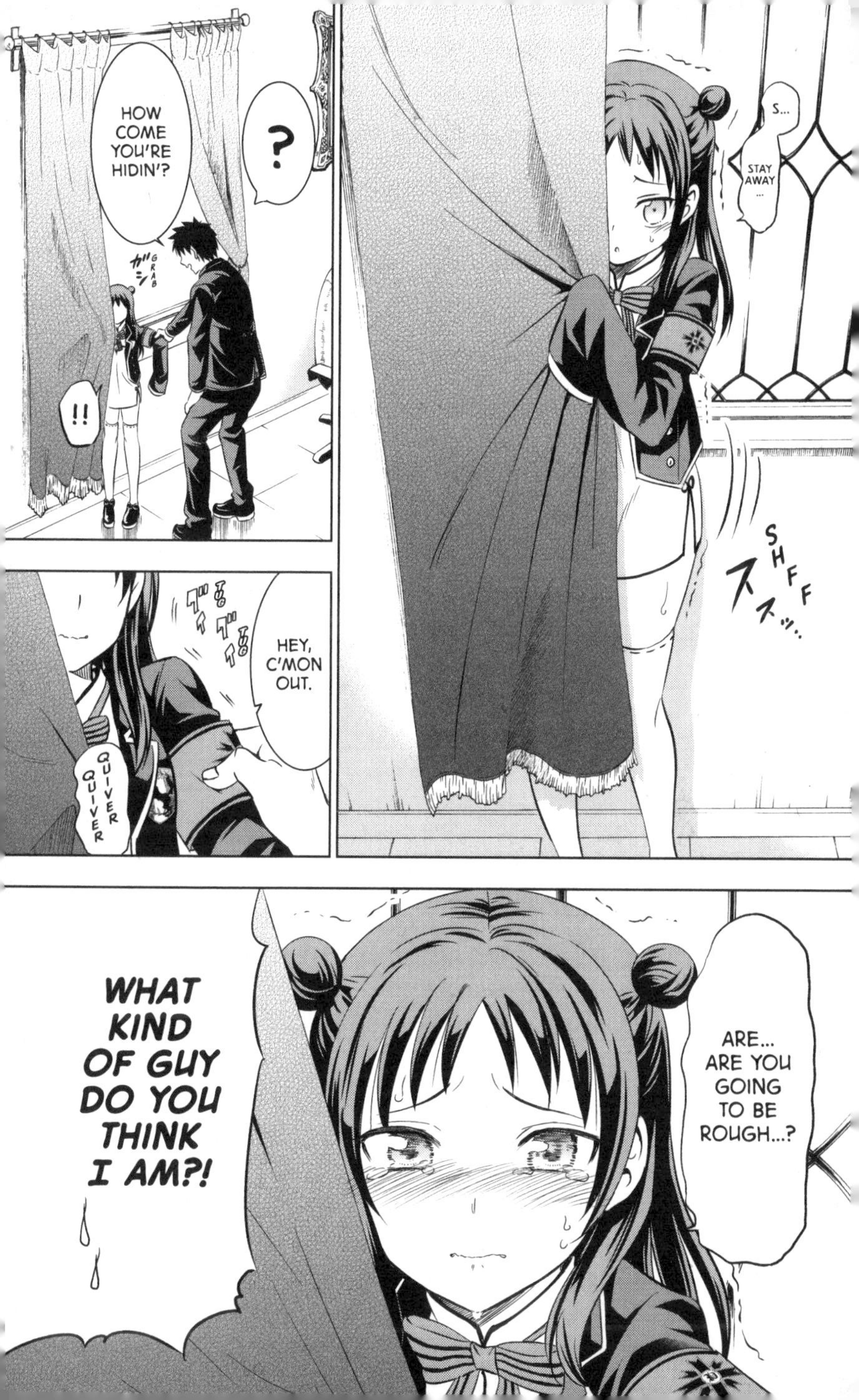

S...
STAY AWAY...
SHFF
?
HOW COME YOU'RE HIDIN'?
GRAB
!!
HEY, C'MON OUT.
TUG
TUG
QUIVER QUIVER
ARE... ARE YOU GOING TO BE ROUGH...?
WHAT KIND OF GUY DO YOU THINK I AM?!

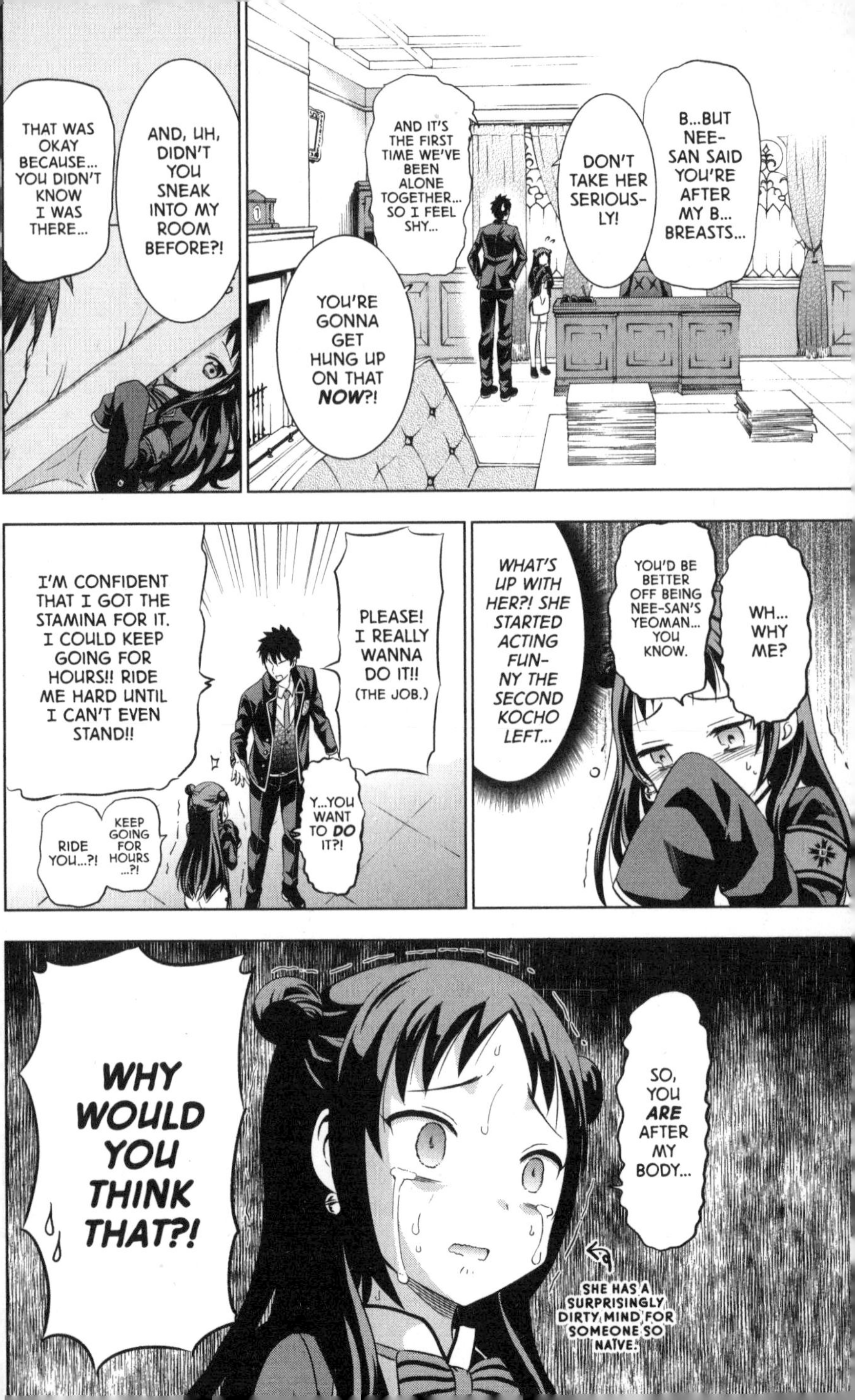
B...BUT NEE-SAN SAID YOU'RE AFTER MY B... BREASTS...
DON'T TAKE HER SERIOUS-LY!
AND IT'S THE FIRST TIME WE'VE BEEN ALONE TOGETHER... SO I FEEL SHY...
YOU'RE GONNA GET HUNG UP ON THAT *NOW*?!
AND, UH, DIDN'T YOU SNEAK INTO MY ROOM BEFORE?!
THAT WAS OKAY BECAUSE... YOU DIDN'T KNOW I WAS THERE...
WH... WHY ME?
YOU'D BE BETTER OFF BEING NEE-SAN'S YEOMAN... YOU KNOW.
WHAT'S UP WITH HER?! SHE STARTED ACTING FUN-NY THE SECOND KOCHO LEFT...
PLEASE! I REALLY WANNA DO IT!! (THE JOB.)
I'M CONFIDENT THAT I GOT THE STAMINA FOR IT. I COULD KEEP GOING FOR HOURS!! RIDE ME HARD UNTIL I CAN'T EVEN STAND!!
Y...YOU WANT TO *DO* IT?!
KEEP GOING FOR HOURS ...?!
RIDE YOU...?!
SO, YOU *ARE* AFTER MY BODY...
WHY WOULD YOU THINK THAT?!
SHE HAS A SURPRISINGLY DIRTY MIND FOR SOMEONE SO NAIVE.

SHE TURNS INTO A MESS WITHOUT ME.

TERIA'S *EXTREMELY* SHY...

NO FUNNY STUFF PLEAS... JUST TEAC... ME YO... JOB.

O-OKAY... COME WITH ME...

BUT THIS IS THE PERFECT OPPORTUNITY FOR YOU TO TRY SPREADING YOUR WINGS... GOOD LUCK, TERIA.

MINE IS THE GENERAL AFFAIRS AND TREASURER ROLE.

THERE ARE FOUR BASIC ROLES A PREFECT CAN HAVE.

Secretary	General Affairs/ Treasurer	Deputy	Head Prefec...
Prepares agendas Takes meeting minutes Writes reports	Patrols campus Handles volunteer work Manages payments Adjusts club budgets	Assists the Head Prefect Manages events Responds to the suggestion box	Executi... authority Convene... assemblie... and counci... meetings Oversees dorm students
Kocho	Teria	Kocho	Airu
Siber	Siber	Rex	Cait

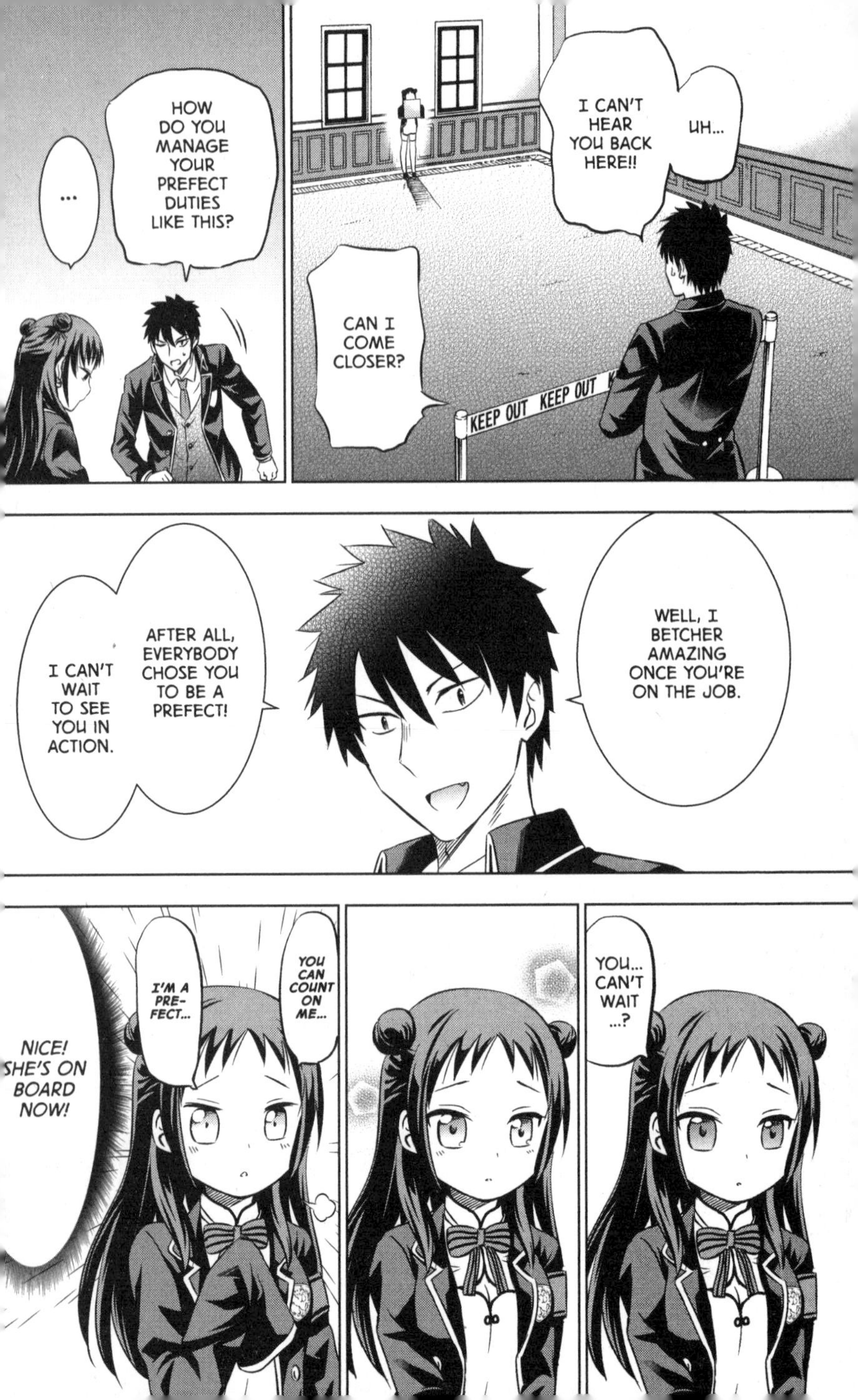
UH...
I CAN'T HEAR YOU BACK HERE!!
KEEP OUT KEEP OUT
CAN I COME CLOSER?
HOW DO YOU MANAGE YOUR PREFECT DUTIES LIKE THIS?
...
WELL, I BETCHER AMAZING ONCE YOU'RE ON THE JOB.
AFTER ALL, EVERYBODY CHOSE YOU TO BE A PREFECT!
I CAN'T WAIT TO SEE YOU IN ACTION.
YOU... CAN'T WAIT ...?
YOU CAN COUNT ON ME...
I'M A PRE-FECT...
NICE! SHE'S ON BOARD NOW!

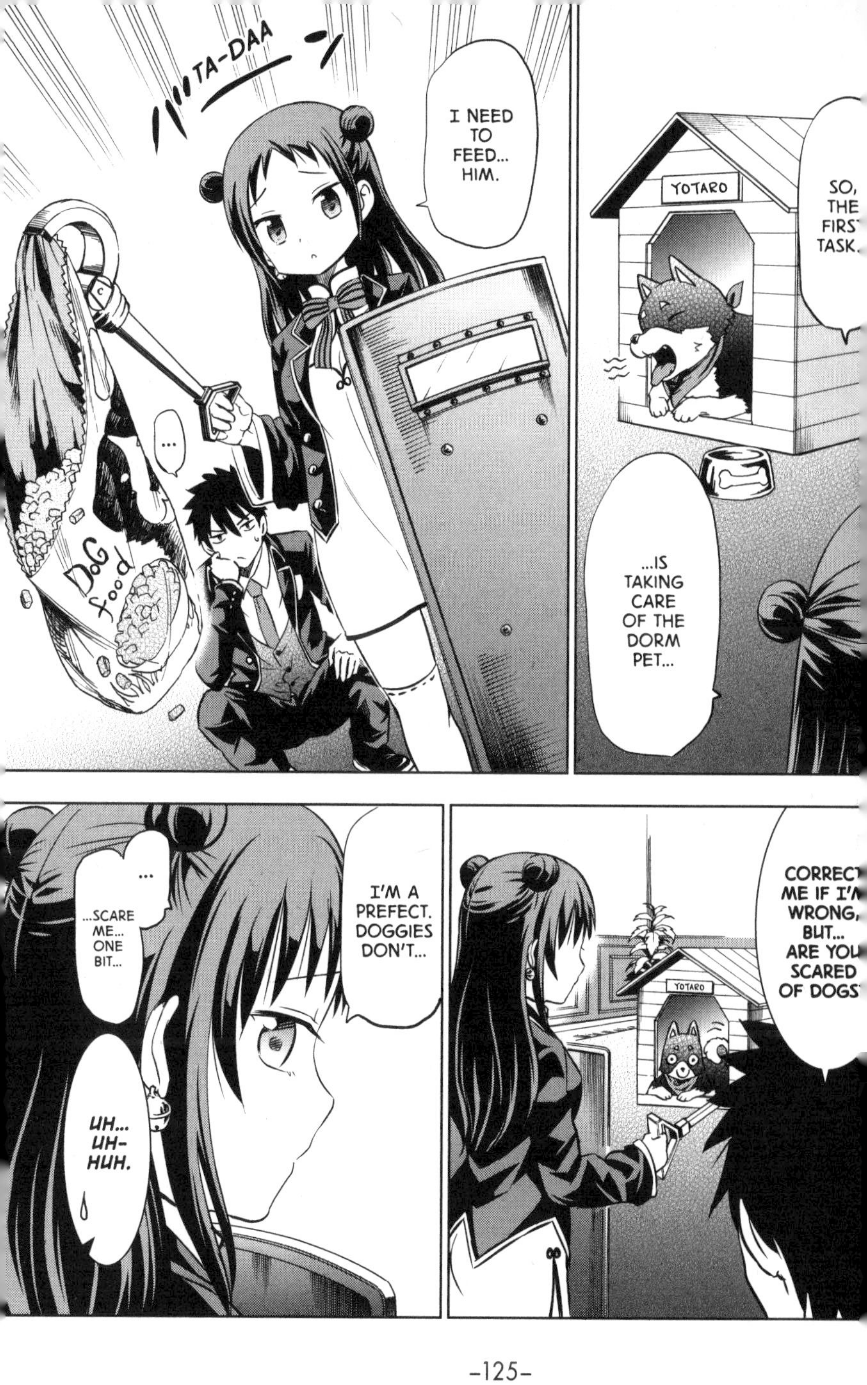
SO, THE FIRST TASK.
YOTARO
...IS TAKING CARE OF THE DORM PET...
TA-DAA
I NEED TO FEED... HIM.
...
DoG food
CORRECT ME IF I'M WRONG, BUT... ARE YOU SCARED OF DOGS
YOTARO
I'M A PREFECT. DOGGIES DON'T...
...
...SCARE ME... ONE BIT...
UH... UH-HUH.

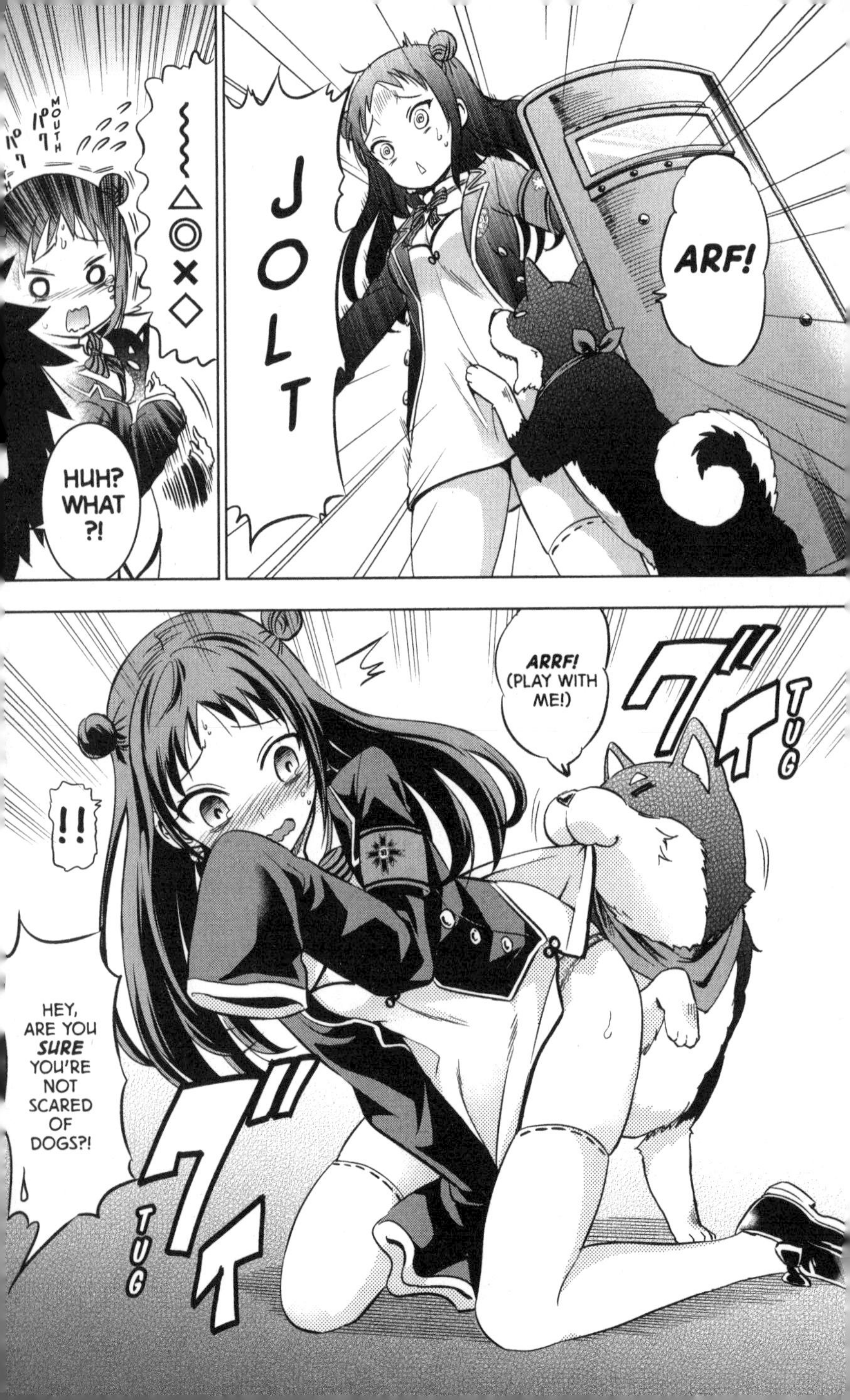
ARF!
JOLT
~△◎×◇
MOUTH
HUH? WHAT ?!
ARRF! (PLAY WITH ME!)
TUG
!!
HEY, ARE YOU SURE YOU'RE NOT SCARED OF DOGS?!
TUG

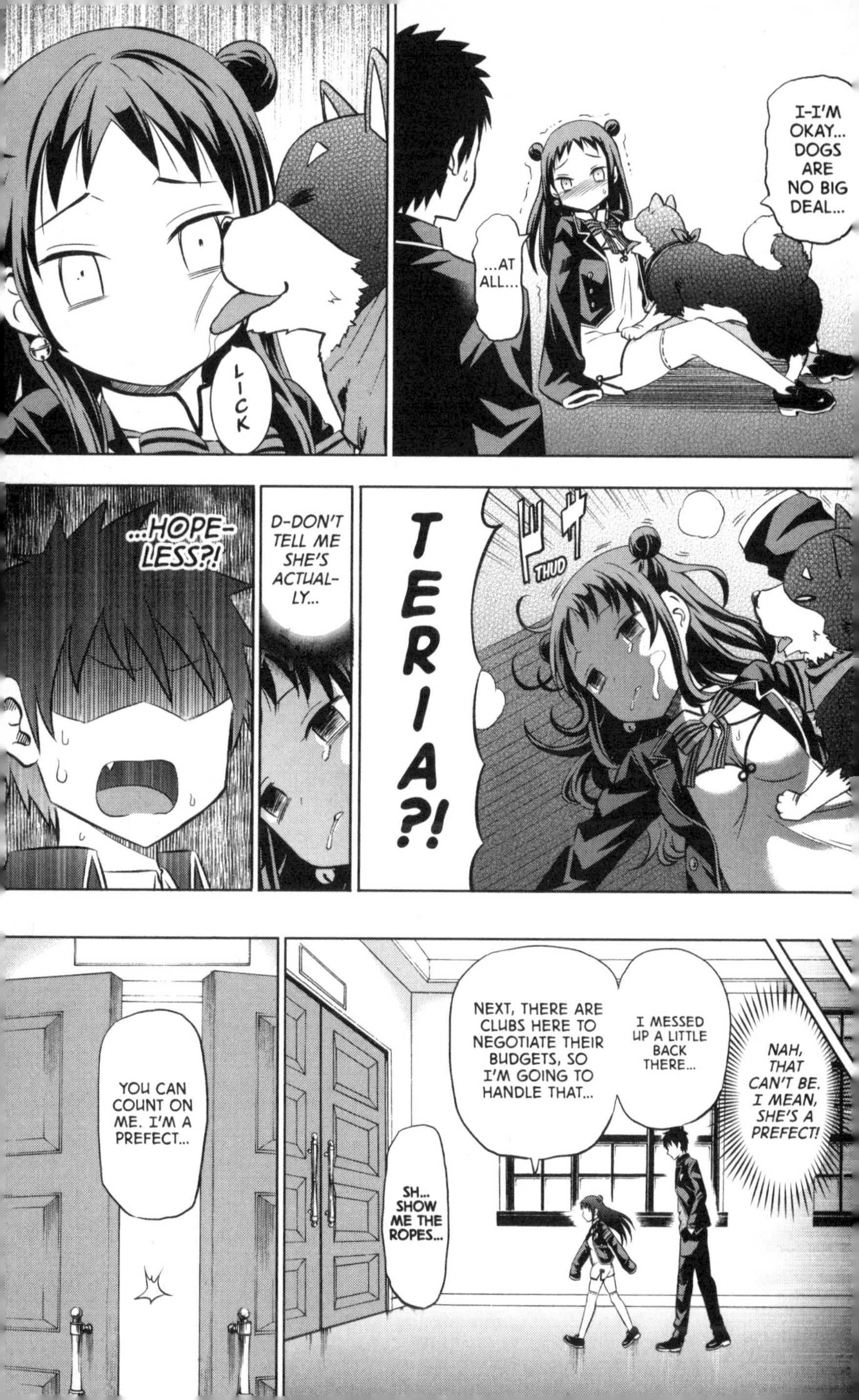
I-I'M OKAY... DOGS ARE NO BIG DEAL...
...AT ALL...
LICK
THUD
TERIA?!
D-DON'T TELL ME SHE'S ACTUAL-LY...
...HOPE-LESS?!
NAH, THAT CAN'T BE. I MEAN, SHE'S A PREFECT!
I MESSED UP A LITTLE BACK THERE...
NEXT, THERE ARE CLUBS HERE TO NEGOTIATE THEIR BUDGETS, SO I'M GOING TO HANDLE THAT...
SH... SHOW ME THE ROPES...
YOU CAN COUNT ON ME. I'M A PREFECT...

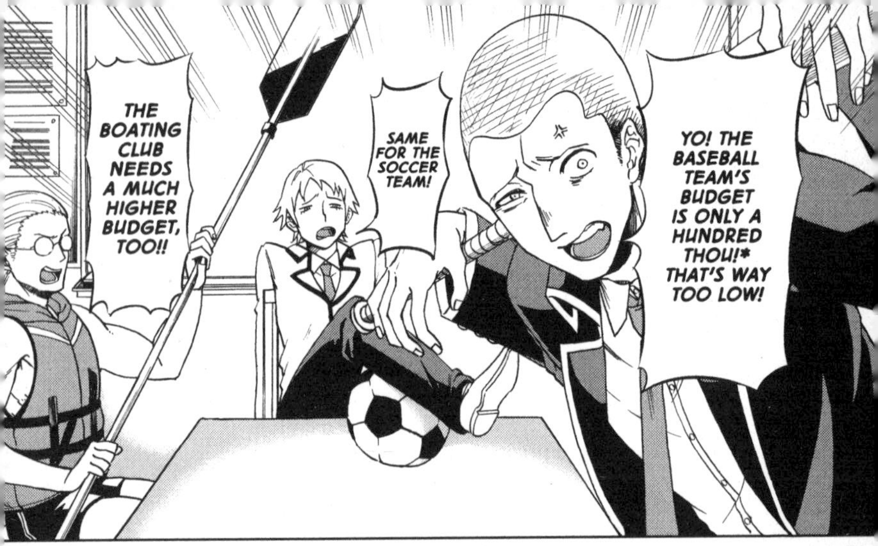
YO! THE BASEBALL TEAM'S BUDGET IS ONLY A HUNDRED THOU!* THAT'S WAY TOO LOW!
SAME FOR THE SOCCER TEAM!
THE BOATING CLUB NEEDS A MUCH HIGHER BUDGET, TOO!!

*TRANSLATOR'S NOTE: 100,000 YEN IS AROUND $1,000 US.

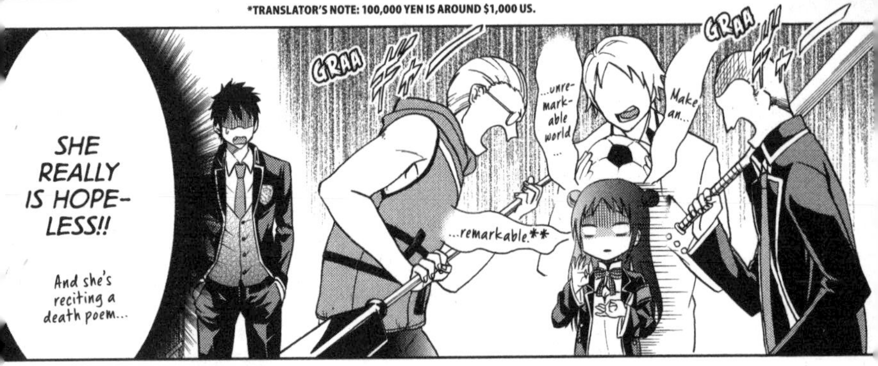
GRAA
Make an...
...unremarkable world...
...remarkable.**
GRAA
SHE REALLY IS HOPELESS!!
And she's reciting a death poem...

**TRANSLATOR'S NOTE: A DEATH POEM BY SHINSAKU TAKASUGI.

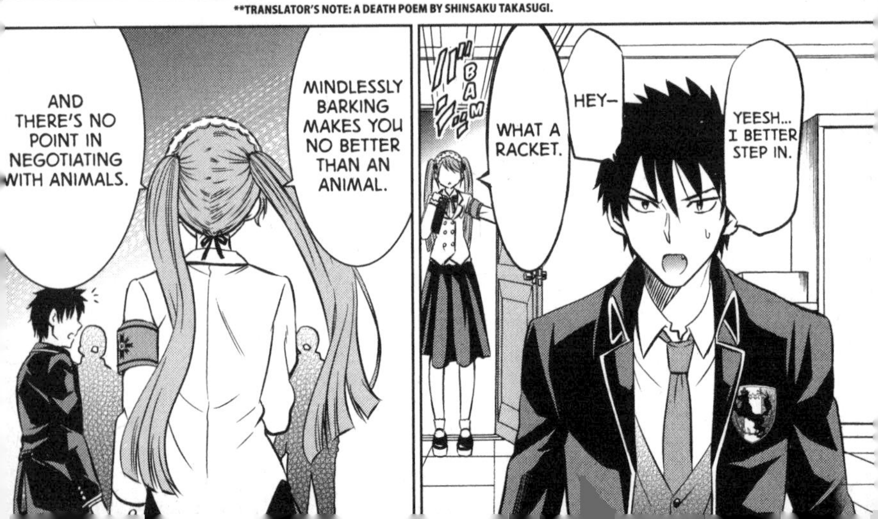
YEESH... I BETTER STEP IN.
HEY—
WHAT A RACKET.
BAM
MINDLESSLY BARKING MAKES YOU NO BETTER THAN AN ANIMAL.
AND THERE'S NO POINT IN NEGOTIATING WITH ANIMALS.

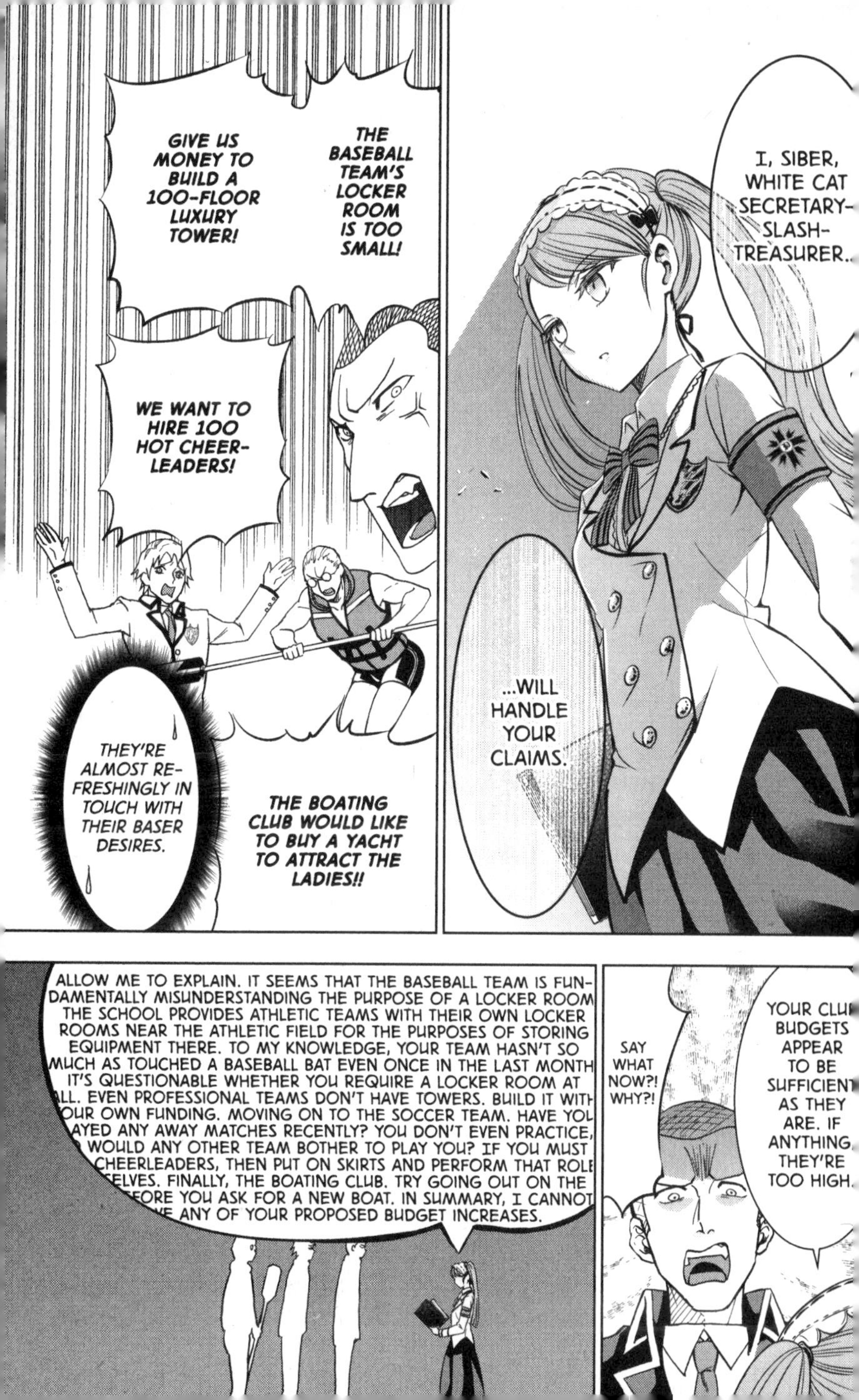
I, SIBER, WHITE CAT SECRETARY-SLASH-TREASURER...
...WILL HANDLE YOUR CLAIMS.
THE BASEBALL TEAM'S LOCKER ROOM IS TOO SMALL!
GIVE US MONEY TO BUILD A 100-FLOOR LUXURY TOWER!
WE WANT TO HIRE 100 HOT CHEER-LEADERS!
THE BOATING CLUB WOULD LIKE TO BUY A YACHT TO ATTRACT THE LADIES!!
THEY'RE ALMOST RE-FRESHINGLY IN TOUCH WITH THEIR BASER DESIRES.
YOUR CLUB BUDGETS APPEAR TO BE SUFFICIENT AS THEY ARE. IF ANYTHING, THEY'RE TOO HIGH.
SAY WHAT NOW?! WHY?!
ALLOW ME TO EXPLAIN. IT SEEMS THAT THE BASEBALL TEAM IS FUNDAMENTALLY MISUNDERSTANDING THE PURPOSE OF A LOCKER ROOM THE SCHOOL PROVIDES ATHLETIC TEAMS WITH THEIR OWN LOCKER ROOMS NEAR THE ATHLETIC FIELD FOR THE PURPOSES OF STORING EQUIPMENT THERE. TO MY KNOWLEDGE, YOUR TEAM HASN'T SO MUCH AS TOUCHED A BASEBALL BAT EVEN ONCE IN THE LAST MONTH IT'S QUESTIONABLE WHETHER YOU REQUIRE A LOCKER ROOM AT LL. EVEN PROFESSIONAL TEAMS DON'T HAVE TOWERS. BUILD IT WITH OUR OWN FUNDING. MOVING ON TO THE SOCCER TEAM. HAVE YOU AYED ANY AWAY MATCHES RECENTLY? YOU DON'T EVEN PRACTICE, WOULD ANY OTHER TEAM BOTHER TO PLAY YOU? IF YOU MUST CHEERLEADERS, THEN PUT ON SKIRTS AND PERFORM THAT ROLE ELVES. FINALLY, THE BOATING CLUB. TRY GOING OUT ON THE EFORE YOU ASK FOR A NEW BOAT. IN SUMMARY, I CANNOT E ANY OF YOUR PROPOSED BUDGET INCREASES.

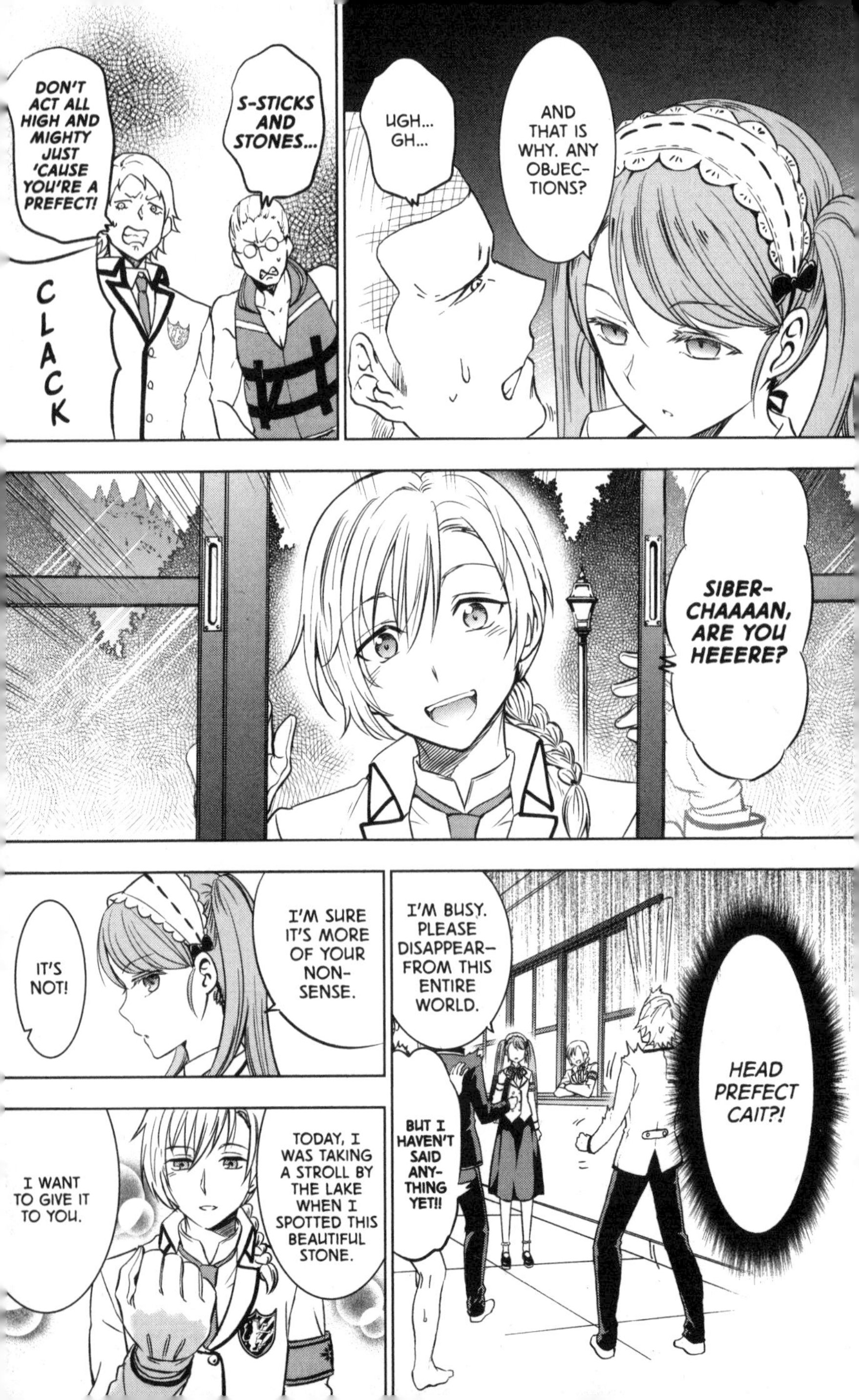
AND THAT IS WHY. ANY OBJECTIONS?
UGH... GH...
S-STICKS AND STONES...
DON'T ACT ALL HIGH AND MIGHTY JUST 'CAUSE YOU'RE A PREFECT!
CLACK
SIBER-CHAAAAN, ARE YOU HEEERE?
HEAD PREFECT CAIT?!
I'M BUSY. PLEASE DISAPPEAR—FROM THIS ENTIRE WORLD.
BUT I HAVEN'T SAID ANYTHING YET!!
I'M SURE IT'S MORE OF YOUR NONSENSE.
IT'S NOT!
TODAY, I WAS TAKING A STROLL BY THE LAKE WHEN I SPOTTED THIS BEAUTIFUL STONE.
I WANT TO GIVE IT TO YOU.

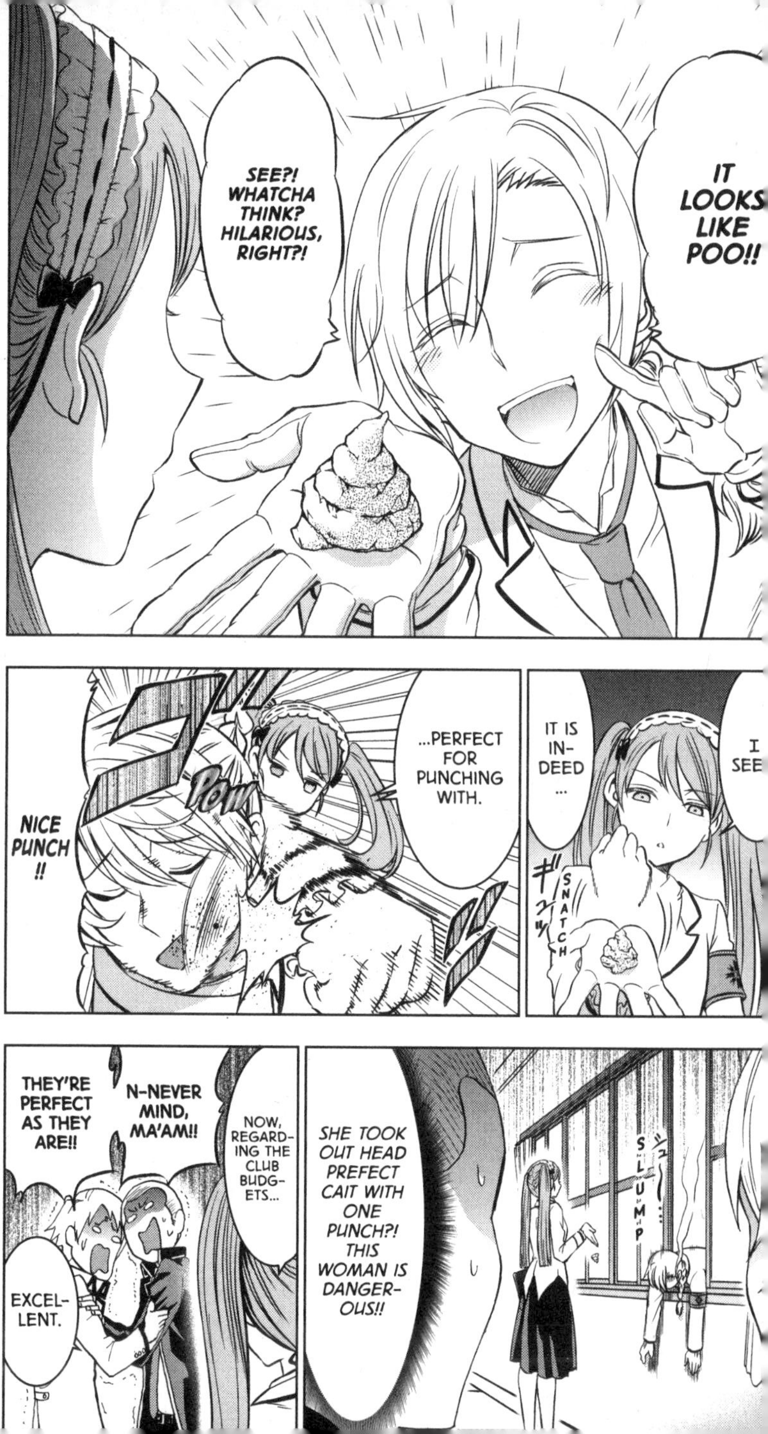
IT LOOKS LIKE POO!!
SEE?! WHATCHA THINK? HILARIOUS, RIGHT?!
I SEE
IT IS IN-DEED ...
SNATCH
...PERFECT FOR PUNCHING WITH.
POW
NICE PUNCH!!
SLUMP
SHE TOOK OUT HEAD PREFECT CAIT WITH ONE PUNCH?! THIS WOMAN IS DANGER-OUS!!
NOW, REGARD-ING THE CLUB BUDG-ETS...
N-NEVER MIND, MA'AM!!
THEY'RE PERFECT AS THEY ARE!!
EXCEL-LENT.

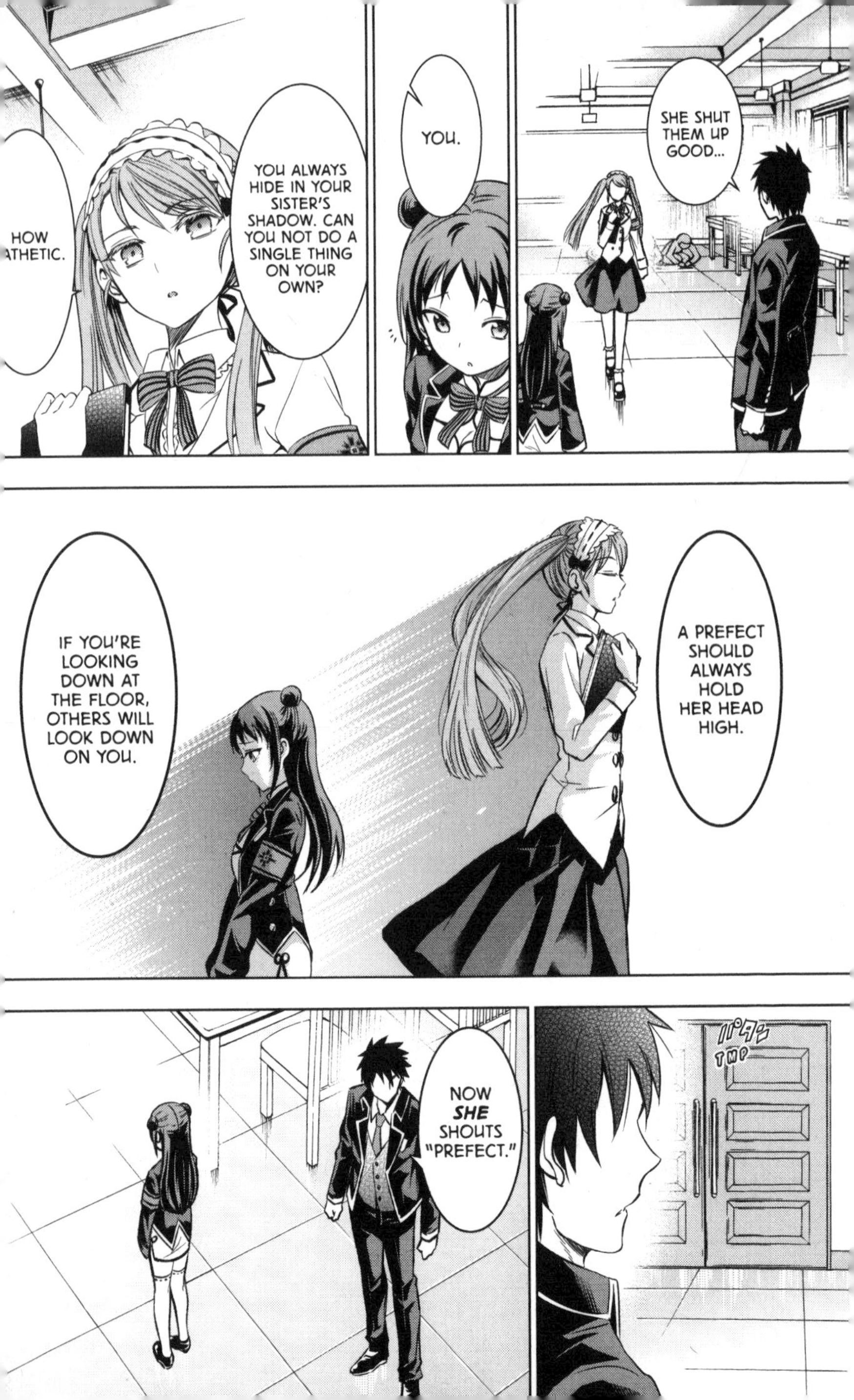
SHE SHUT THEM UP GOOD...
YOU.
YOU ALWAYS HIDE IN YOUR SISTER'S SHADOW. CAN YOU NOT DO A SINGLE THING ON YOUR OWN?
HOW ATHETIC.
A PREFECT SHOULD ALWAYS HOLD HER HEAD HIGH.
IF YOU'RE LOOKING DOWN AT THE FLOOR, OTHERS WILL LOOK DOWN ON YOU.
パタン
TMP
NOW ***SHE*** SHOUTS "PREFECT."

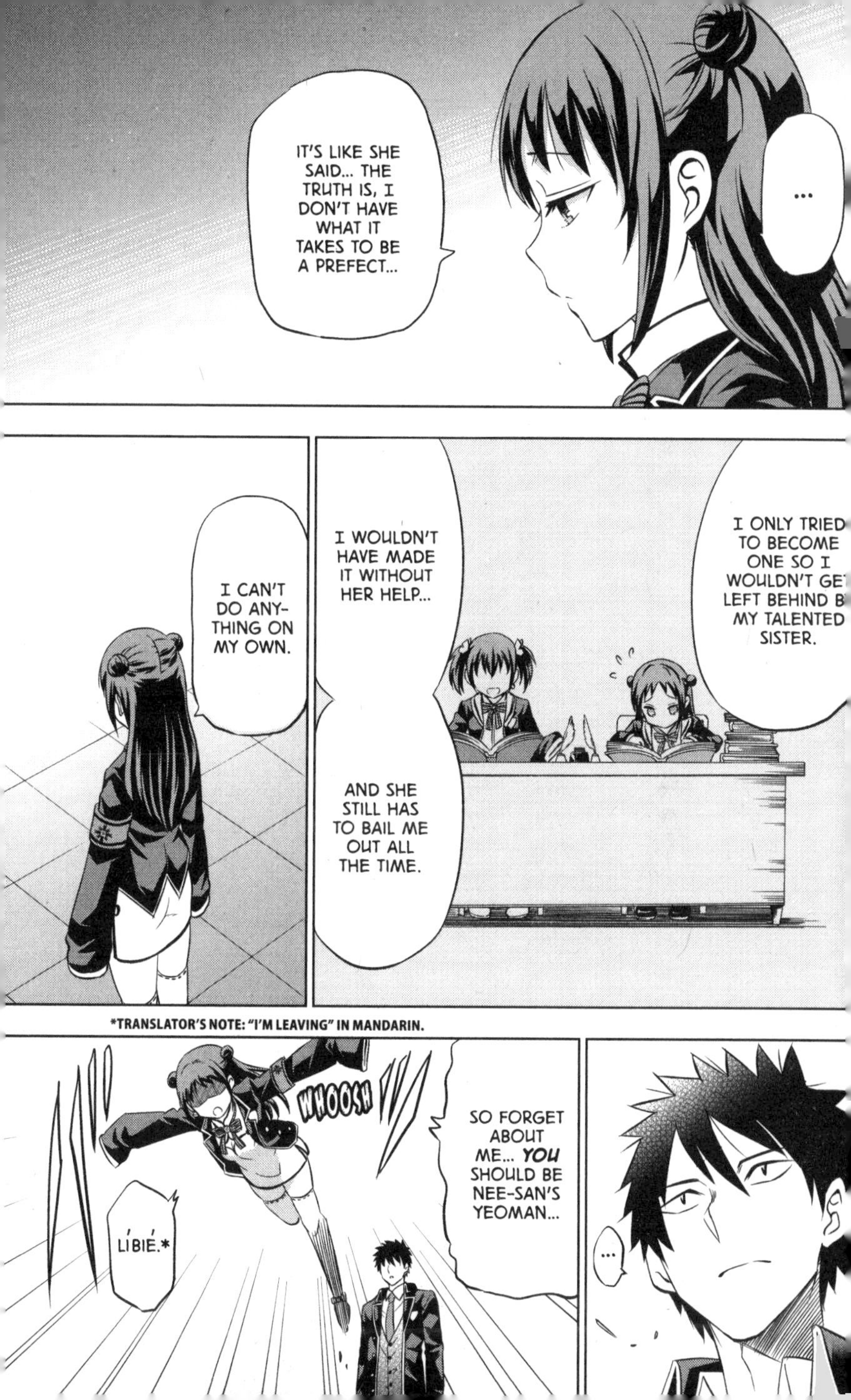
...
IT'S LIKE SHE SAID... THE TRUTH IS, I DON'T HAVE WHAT IT TAKES TO BE A PREFECT...
I ONLY TRIED TO BECOME ONE SO I WOULDN'T GET LEFT BEHIND BY MY TALENTED SISTER.
I WOULDN'T HAVE MADE IT WITHOUT HER HELP...
AND SHE STILL HAS TO BAIL ME OUT ALL THE TIME.
I CAN'T DO ANYTHING ON MY OWN.
...
SO FORGET ABOUT ME... ***YOU*** SHOULD BE NEE-SAN'S YEOMAN...
WHOOSH
LÍBIÉ.*

*TRANSLATOR'S NOTE: "I'M LEAVING" IN MANDARIN.

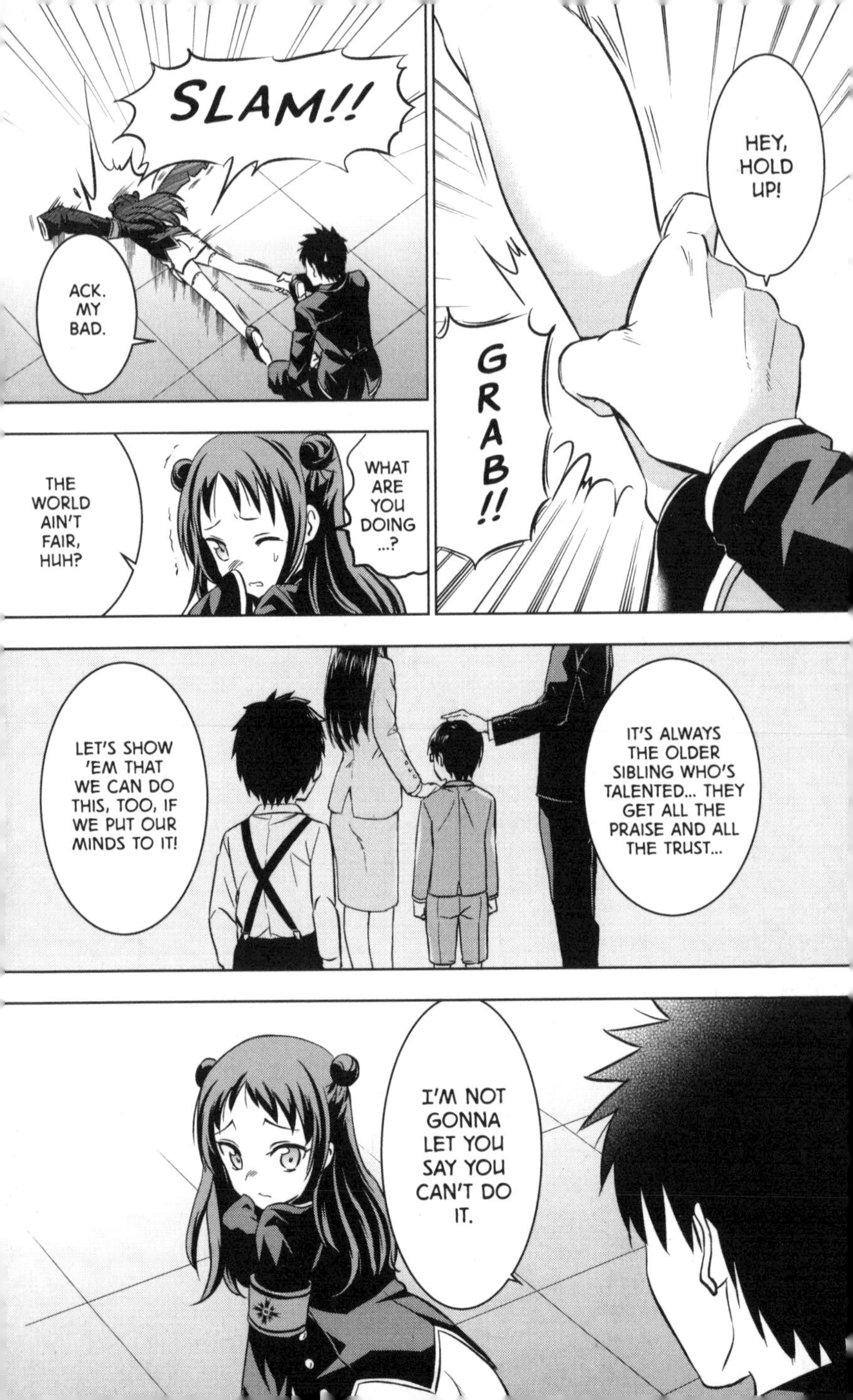
HEY, HOLD UP!
GRAB!!
SLAM!!
ACK. MY BAD.
WHAT ARE YOU DOING ...?
THE WORLD AIN'T FAIR, HUH?
IT'S ALWAYS THE OLDER SIBLING WHO'S TALENTED... THEY GET ALL THE PRAISE AND ALL THE TRUST...
LET'S SHOW 'EM THAT WE CAN DO THIS, TOO, IF WE PUT OUR MINDS TO IT!
I'M NOT GONNA LET YOU SAY YOU CAN'T DO IT.

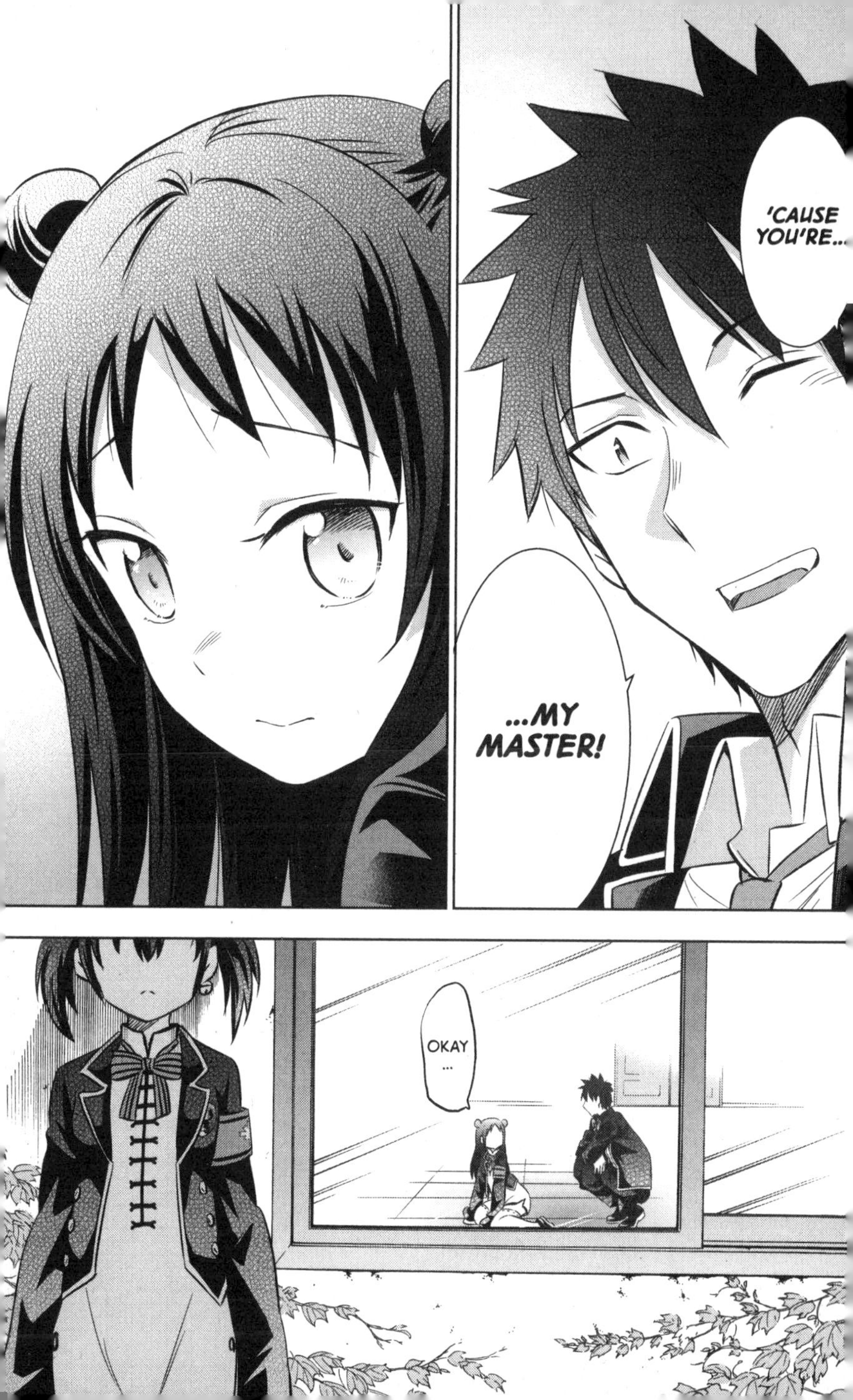
'CAUSE YOU'RE...
...MY MASTER!
OKAY ...

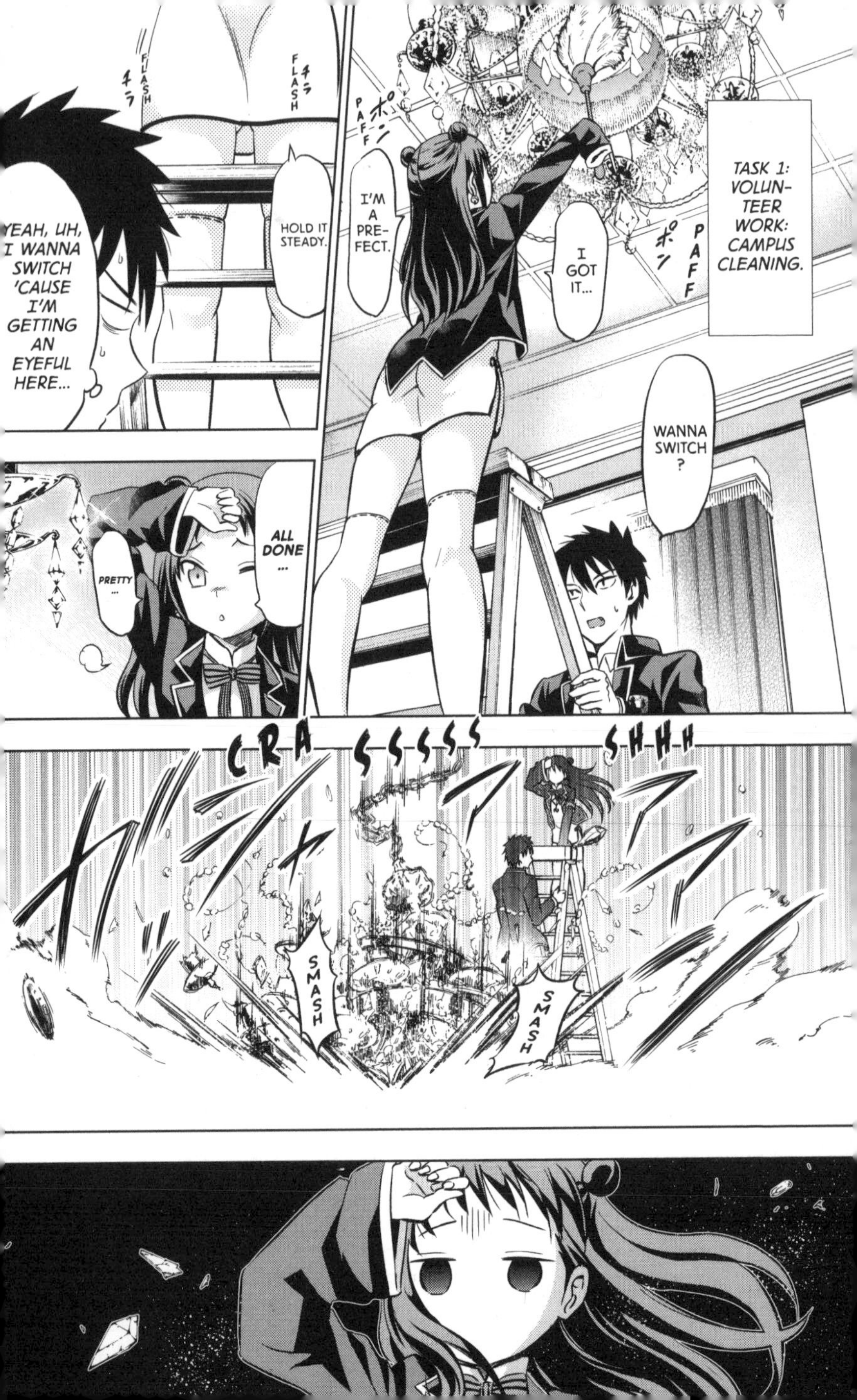
TASK 1: VOLUNTEER WORK: CAMPUS CLEANING.
PAFF
I GOT IT...
PAFF
I'M A PREFECT.
WANNA SWITCH?
HOLD IT STEADY.
FLASH
FLASH
YEAH, UH, I WANNA SWITCH 'CAUSE I'M GETTING AN EYEFUL HERE...
ALL DONE...
PRETTY...
CRASSSSSS
SHHH
SMASH
SMASH

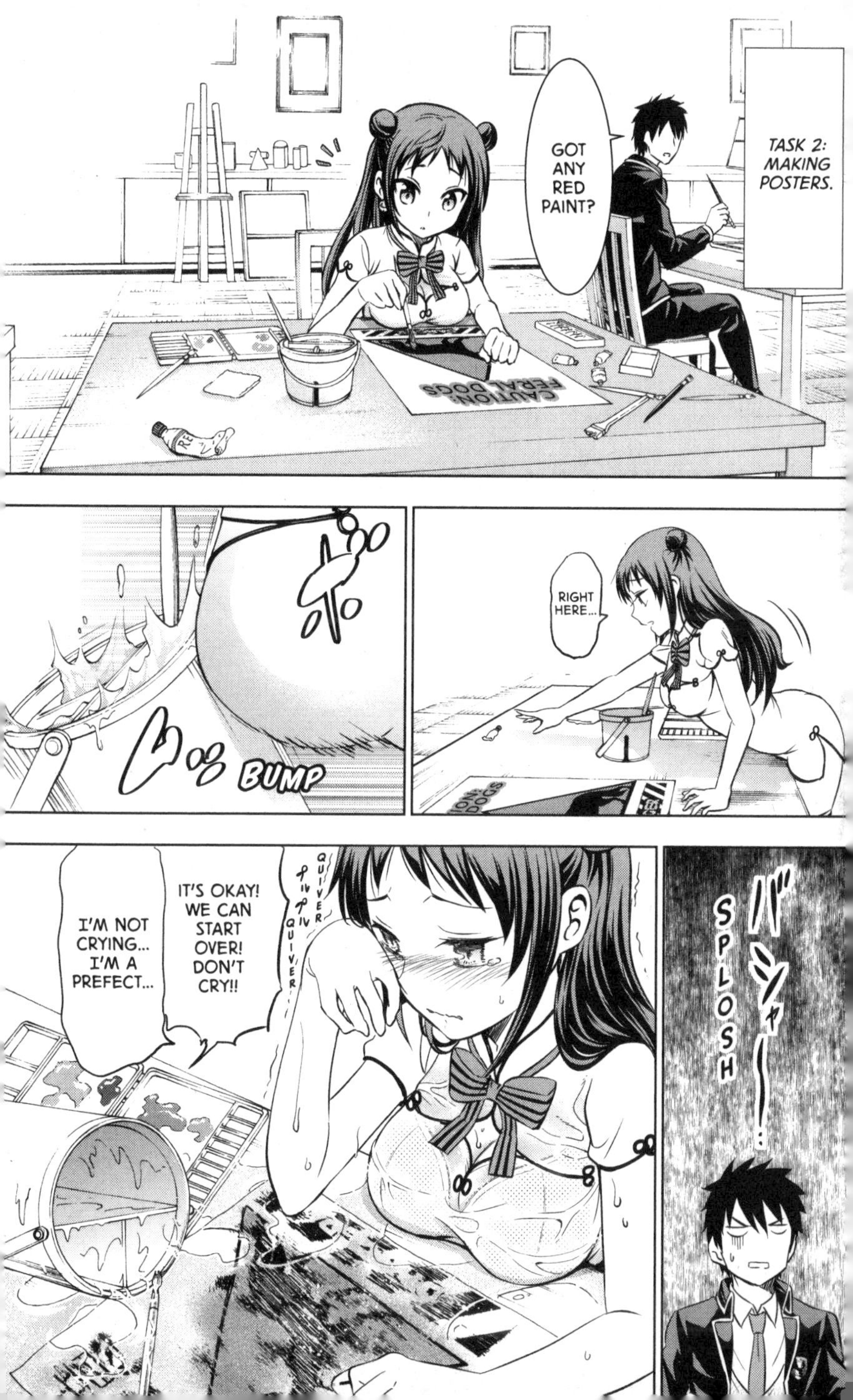
TASK 2: MAKING POSTERS.
GOT ANY RED PAINT?
CAUTION: FERAL DOGS
RIGHT HERE...
BUMP
SPLOSH
IT'S OKAY! WE CAN START OVER! DON'T CRY!!
QUIVER QUIVER
I'M NOT CRYING... I'M A PREFECT...

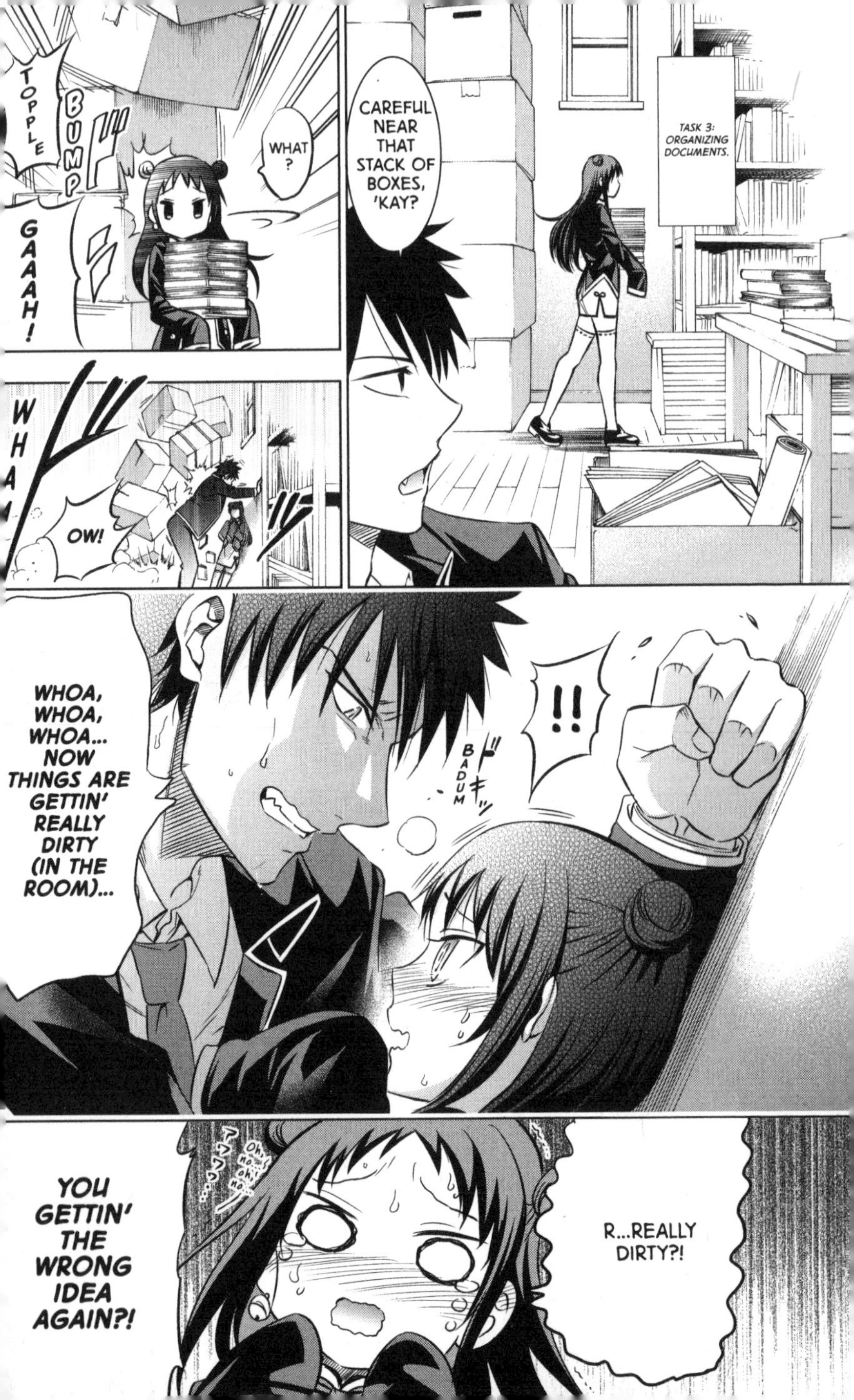
TASK 3: ORGANIZING DOCUMENTS.
CAREFUL NEAR THAT STACK OF BOXES, 'KAY?
WHAT?
TOPPLE
BUMP
GAAAAH!
WHA
OW!
!!
BADUM
WHOA, WHOA, WHOA... NOW THINGS ARE GETTIN' REALLY DIRTY (IN THE ROOM)...
R...REALLY DIRTY?!
Oh, no... oh, no...
YOU GETTIN' THE WRONG IDEA AGAIN?!

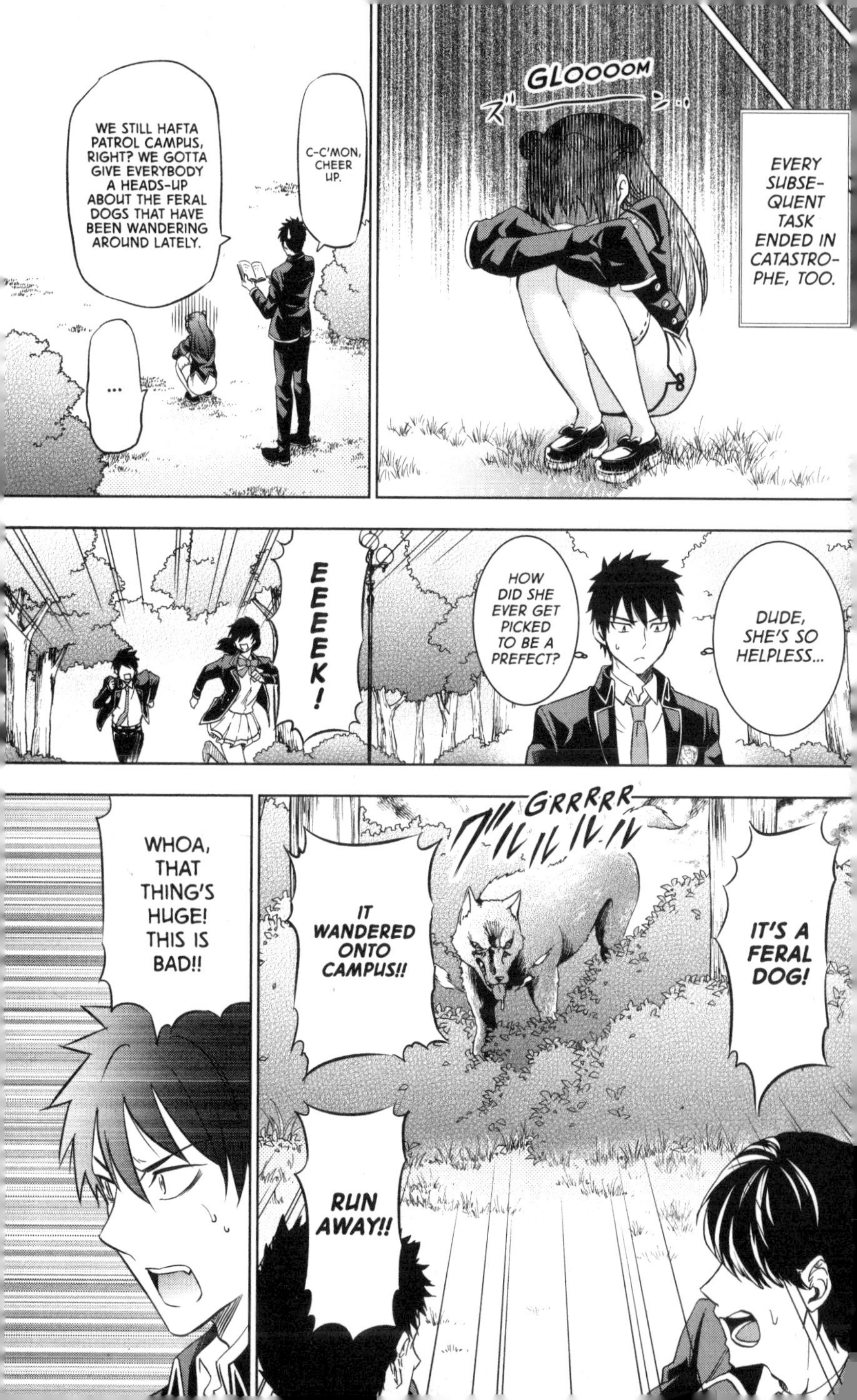
GLOOOOM
EVERY SUBSEQUENT TASK ENDED IN CATASTROPHE, TOO.
C-C'MON, CHEER UP.
WE STILL HAFTA PATROL CAMPUS, RIGHT? WE GOTTA GIVE EVERYBODY A HEADS-UP ABOUT THE FERAL DOGS THAT HAVE BEEN WANDERING AROUND LATELY.
...
DUDE, SHE'S SO HELPLESS...
HOW DID SHE EVER GET PICKED TO BE A PREFECT?
EEEEEK!
GRRRRR
IT'S A FERAL DOG!
IT WANDERED ONTO CAMPUS!!
RUN AWAY!!
WHOA, THAT THING'S HUGE! THIS IS BAD!!

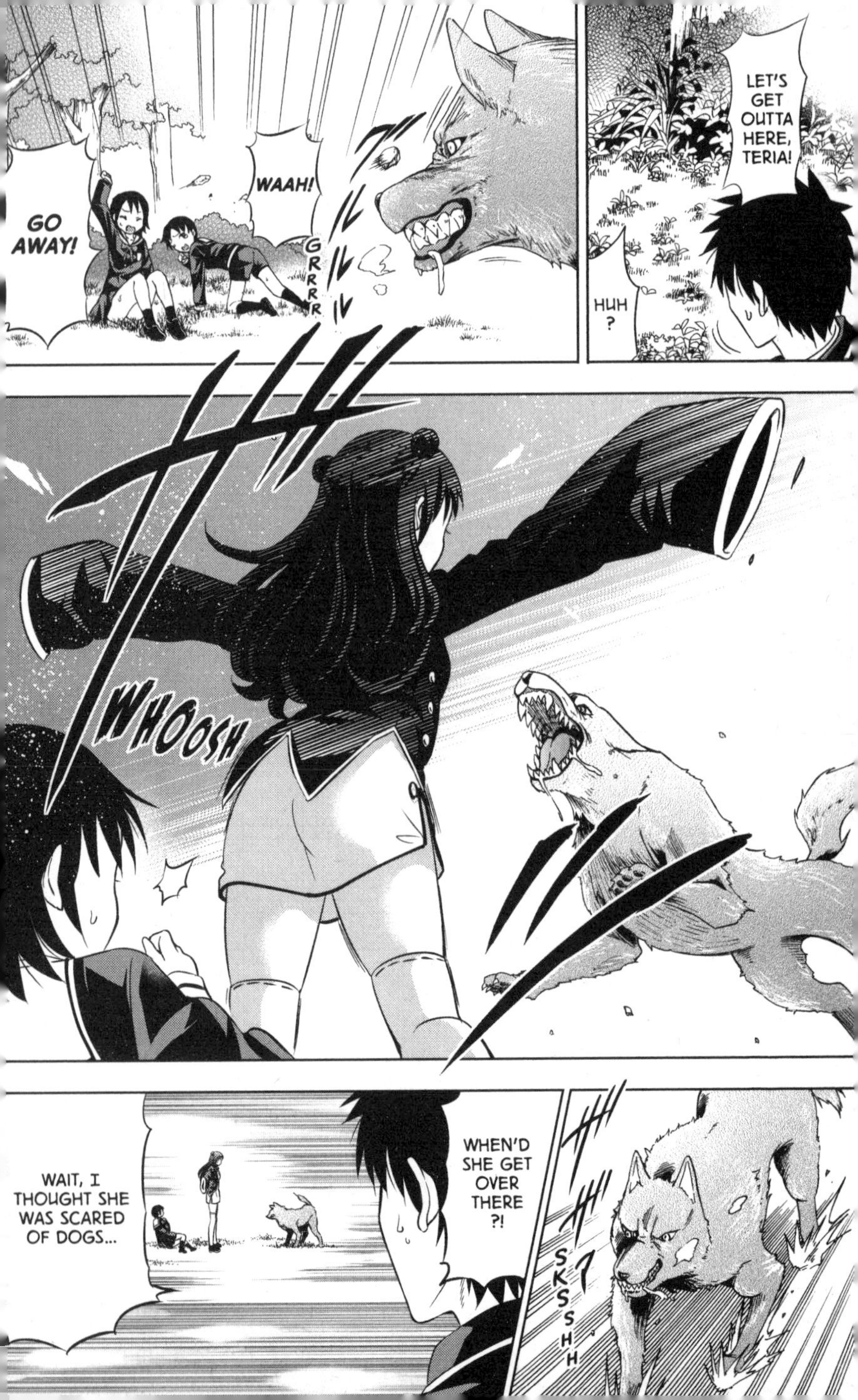
LET'S GET OUTTA HERE, TERIA!
HUH?
WAAH!
GRRRR
GO AWAY!
WHOOSH
SKSSHH
WHEN'D SHE GET OVER THERE?!
WAIT, I THOUGHT SHE WAS SCARED OF DOGS...

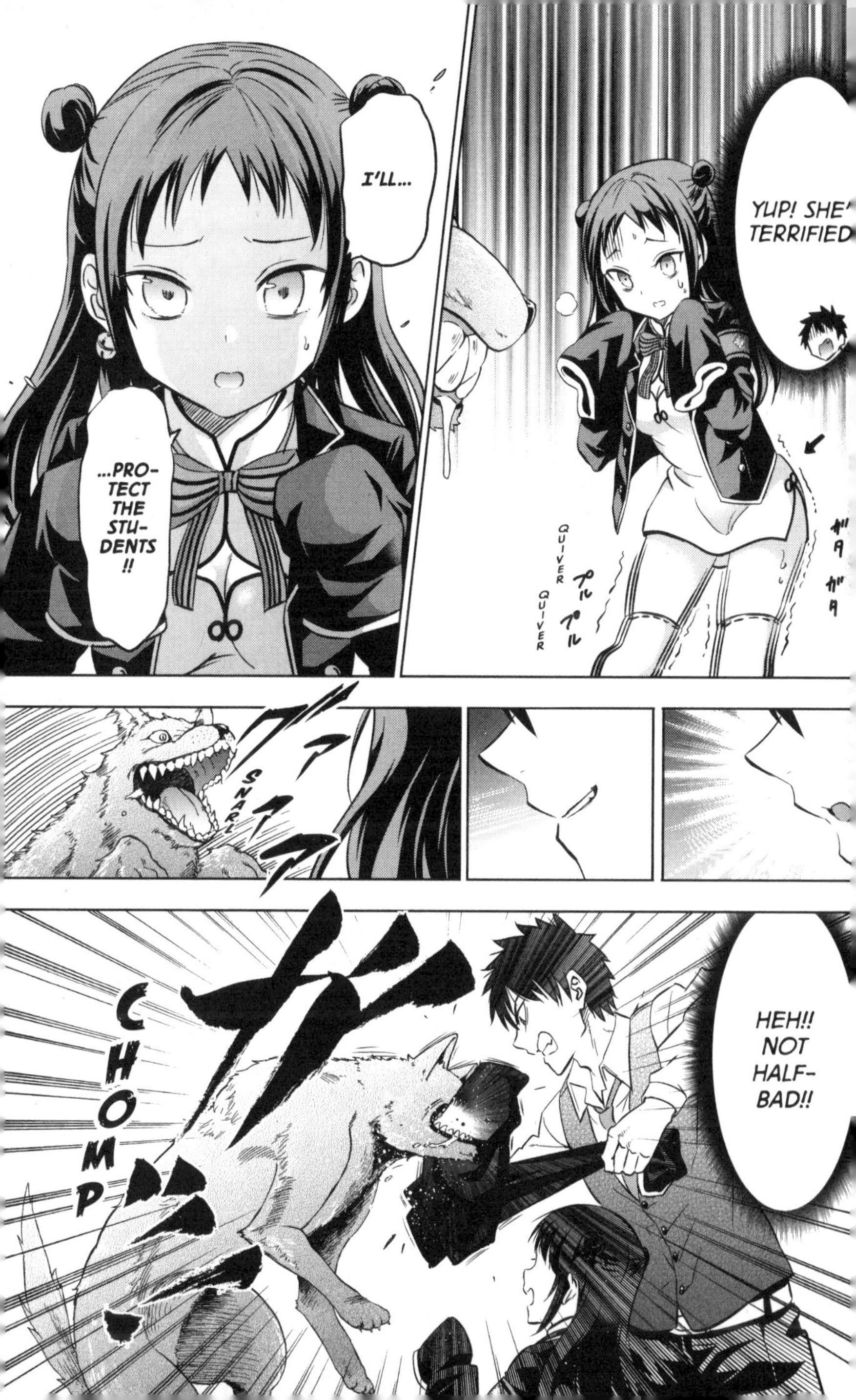
YUP! SHE' TERRIFIED
QUIVER QUIVER
プルプル
ガタガタ
I'LL...
...PRO-TECT THE STU-DENTS!!
SNARL
HEH!! NOT HALF-BAD!!
CHOMP

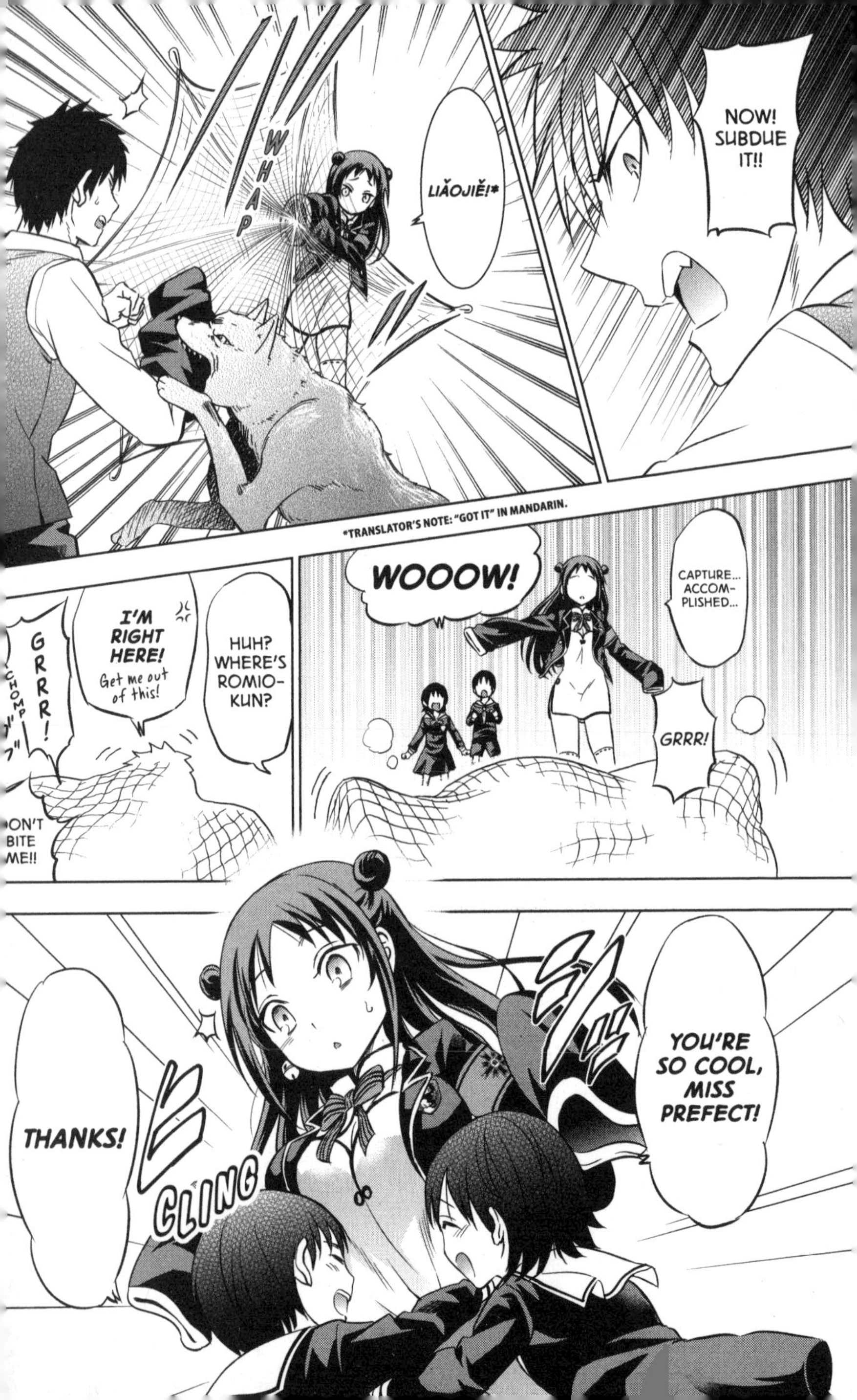
NOW! SUBDUE IT!!
LIǍOJIĚ!*
WHAP
*TRANSLATOR'S NOTE: "GOT IT" IN MANDARIN.
CAPTURE... ACCOMPLISHED...
WOOOW!
GRRR!
HUH? WHERE'S ROMIO-KUN?
I'M RIGHT HERE! Get me out of this!
GRRR!
CHOMP
ON'T BITE ME!!
YOU'RE SO COOL, MISS PREFECT!
THANKS!
CLING

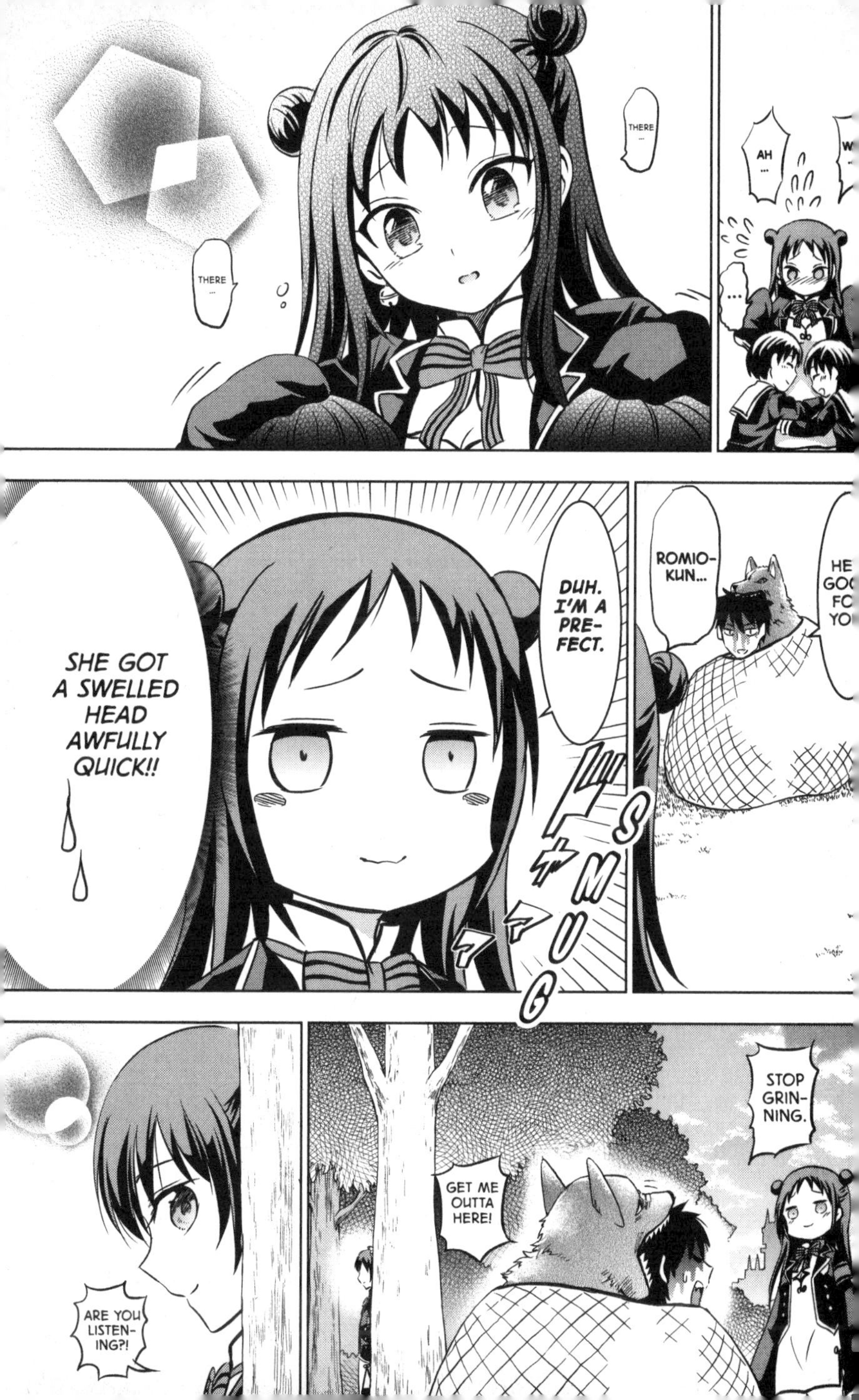
AH ...
...
THERE ...
THERE ...
ROMIO-KUN...
DUH. I'M A PRE-FECT.
SMUG
SHE GOT A SWELLED HEAD AWFULLY QUICK!!
STOP GRIN-NING.
GET ME OUTTA HERE!
ARE YOU LISTEN-ING?!

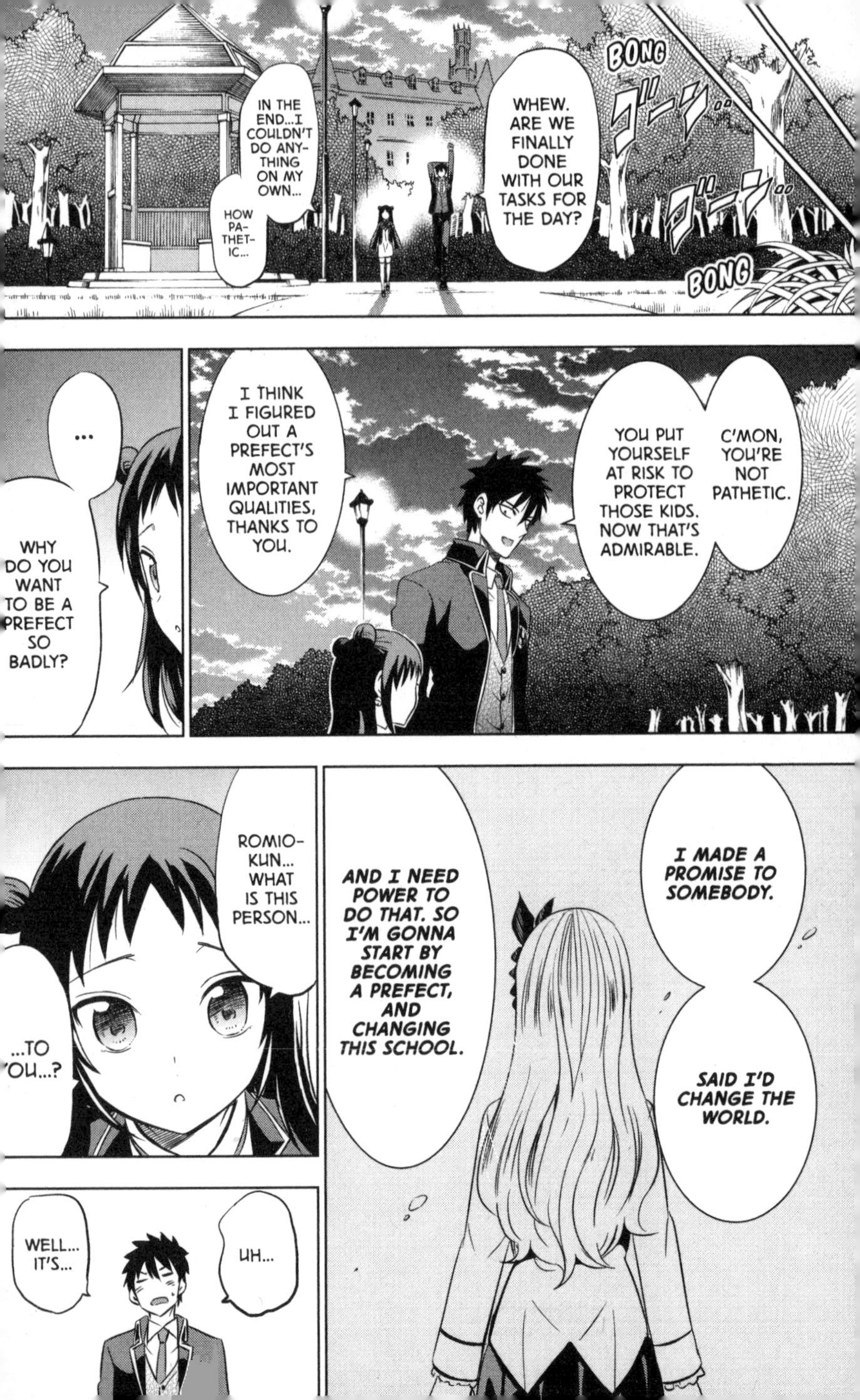
BONG
BONG
WHEW. ARE WE FINALLY DONE WITH OUR TASKS FOR THE DAY?
IN THE END...I COULDN'T DO ANY-THING ON MY OWN...
HOW PA-THET-IC...
C'MON, YOU'RE NOT PATHETIC.
YOU PUT YOURSELF AT RISK TO PROTECT THOSE KIDS. NOW THAT'S ADMIRABLE.
I THINK I FIGURED OUT A PREFECT'S MOST IMPORTANT QUALITIES, THANKS TO YOU.
...
WHY DO YOU WANT TO BE A PREFECT SO BADLY?
I MADE A PROMISE TO SOMEBODY.
SAID I'D CHANGE THE WORLD.
AND I NEED POWER TO DO THAT. SO I'M GONNA START BY BECOMING A PREFECT, AND CHANGING THIS SCHOOL.
ROMIO-KUN... WHAT IS THIS PERSON...
...TO YOU...?
UH...
WELL... IT'S...

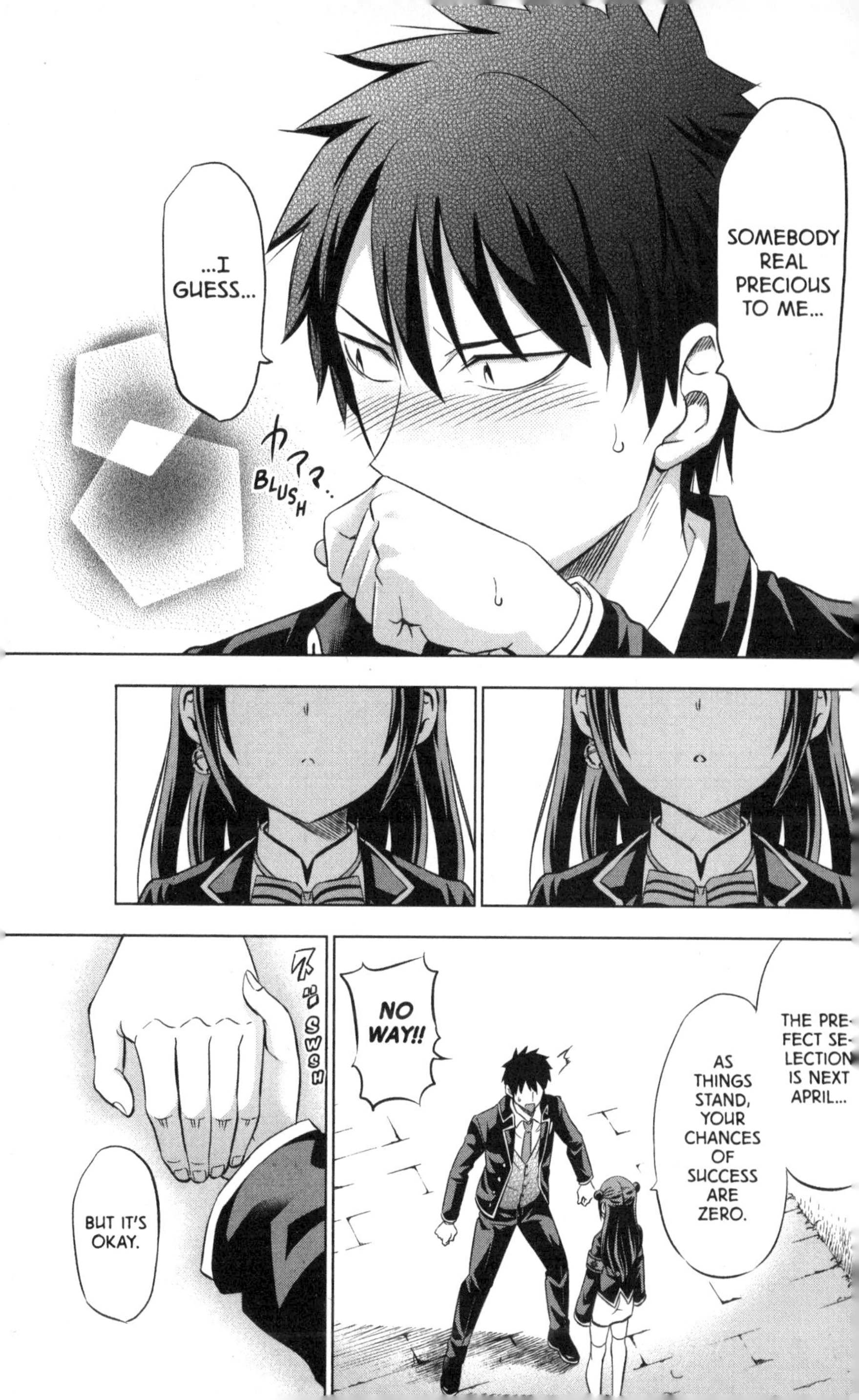
SOMEBODY REAL PRECIOUS TO ME...
...I GUESS...
BLUSH
THE PRE-FECT SE-LECTION IS NEXT APRIL...
AS THINGS STAND, YOUR CHANCES OF SUCCESS ARE ZERO.
NO WAY!!
SWSH
BUT IT'S OKAY.

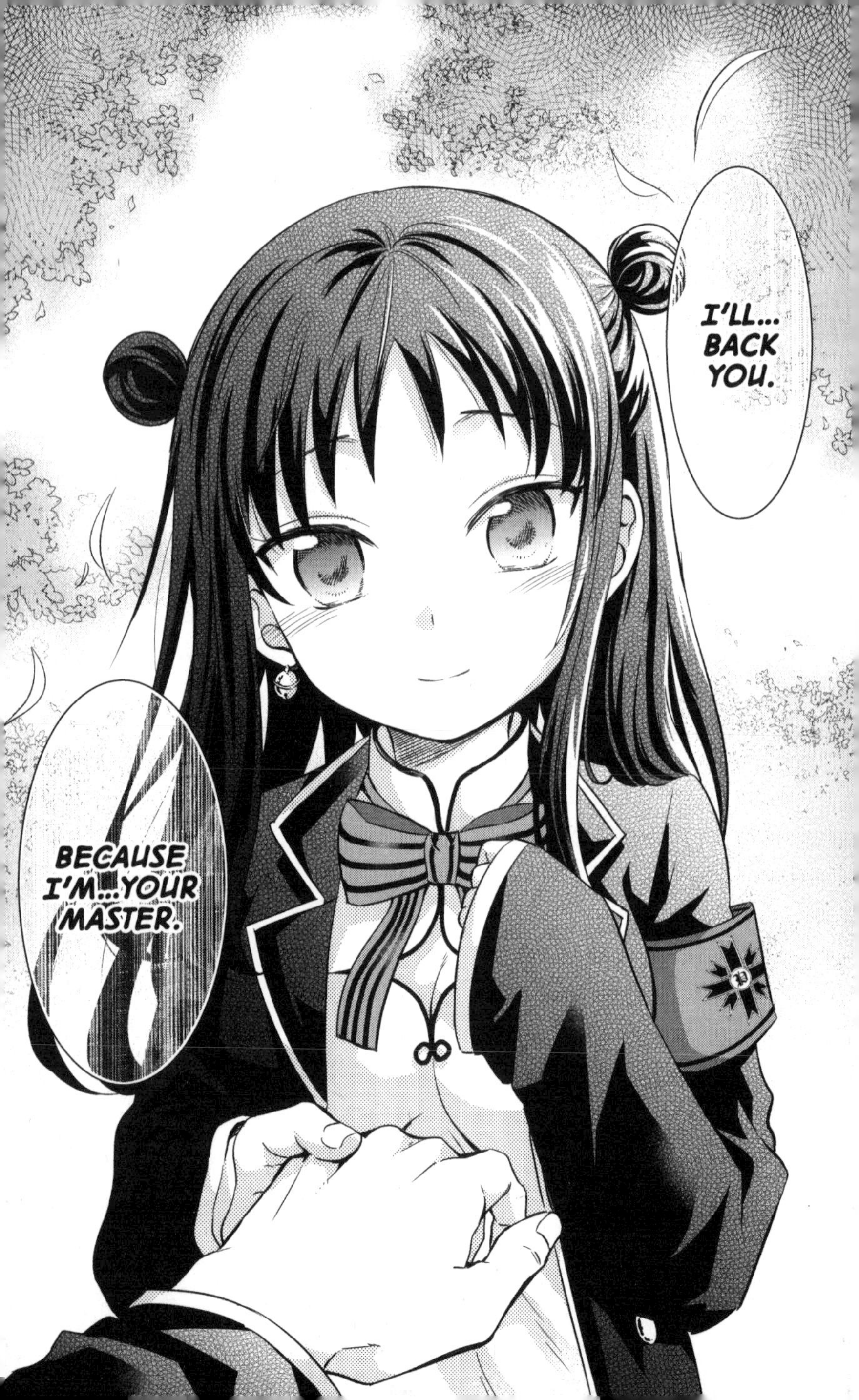
I'LL... BACK YOU.
BECAUSE I'M...YOUR MASTER.

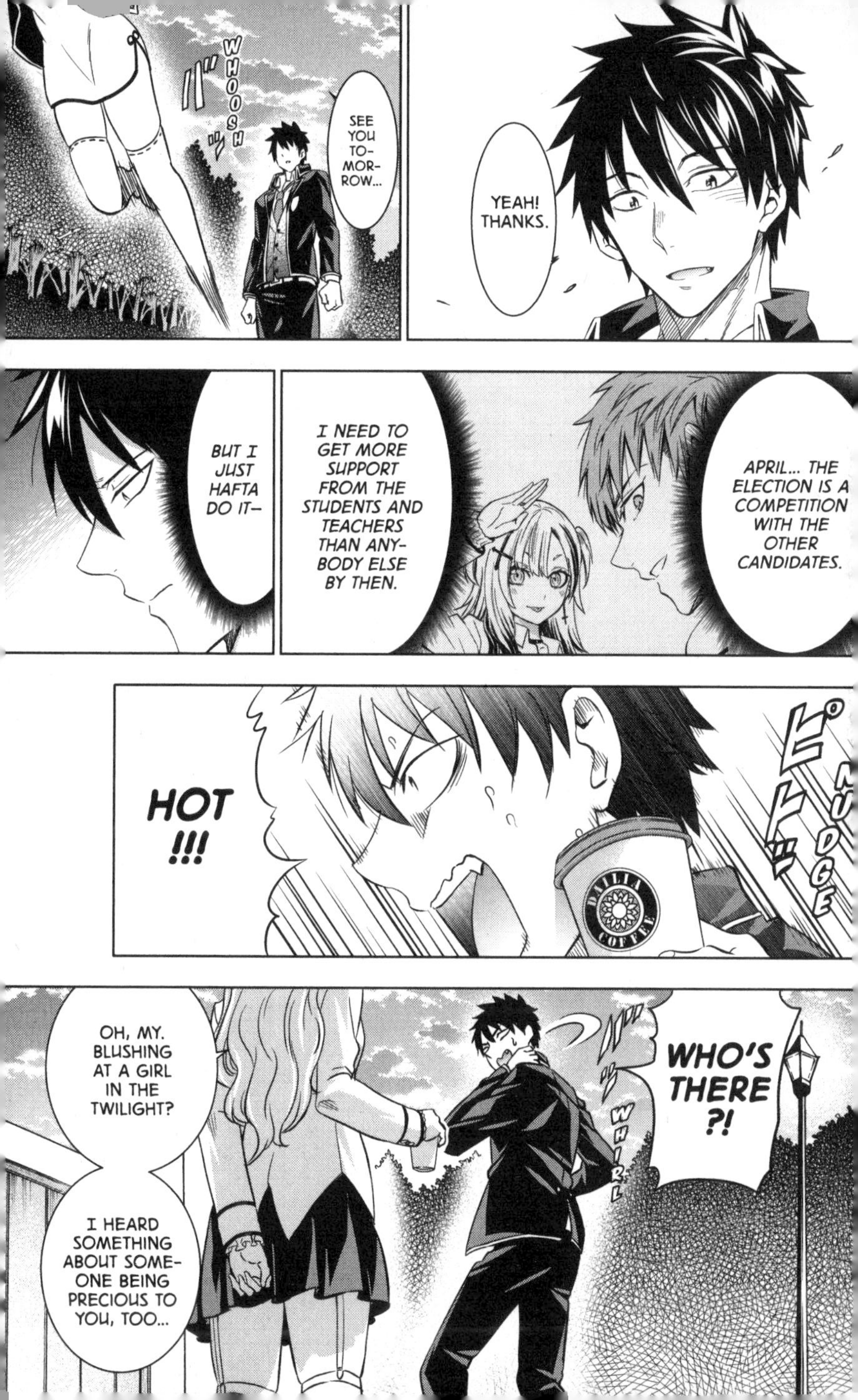
YEAH! THANKS.
WHOOSH
SEE YOU TO-MOR-ROW...
APRIL... THE ELECTION IS A COMPETITION WITH THE OTHER CANDIDATES.
I NEED TO GET MORE SUPPORT FROM THE STUDENTS AND TEACHERS THAN ANY-BODY ELSE BY THEN.
BUT I JUST HAFTA DO IT—
NUDGE
HOT!!!
WHO'S THERE?!
WHIRL
OH, MY. BLUSHING AT A GIRL IN THE TWILIGHT?
I HEARD SOMETHING ABOUT SOME-ONE BEING PRECIOUS TO YOU, TOO...

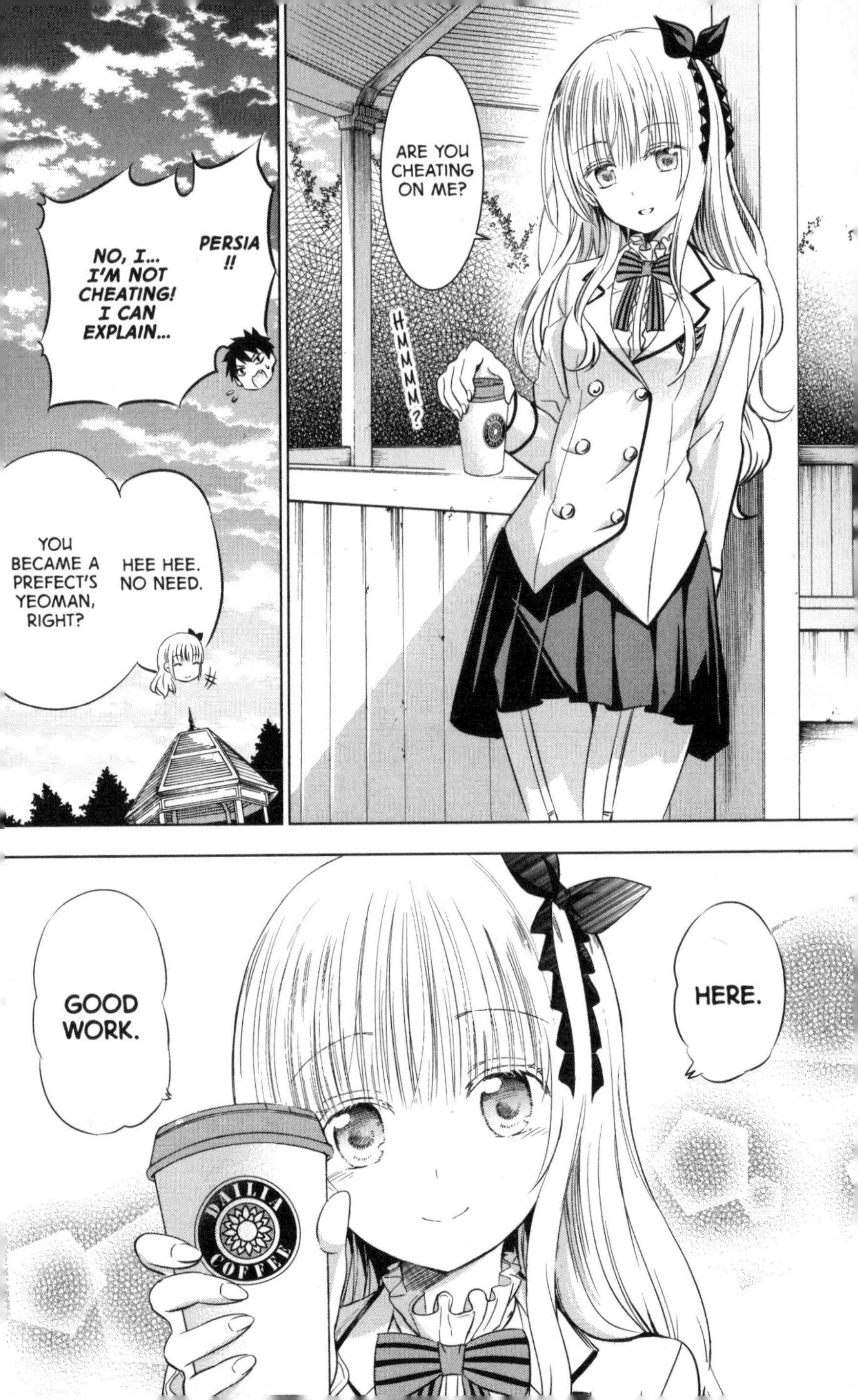
ARE YOU CHEATING ON ME?
HMMMM?
PERSIA !!
NO, I... I'M NOT CHEATING! I CAN EXPLAIN...
HEE HEE. NO NEED.
YOU BECAME A PREFECT'S YEOMAN, RIGHT?
HERE.
GOOD WORK.
DAHLIA COFFEE

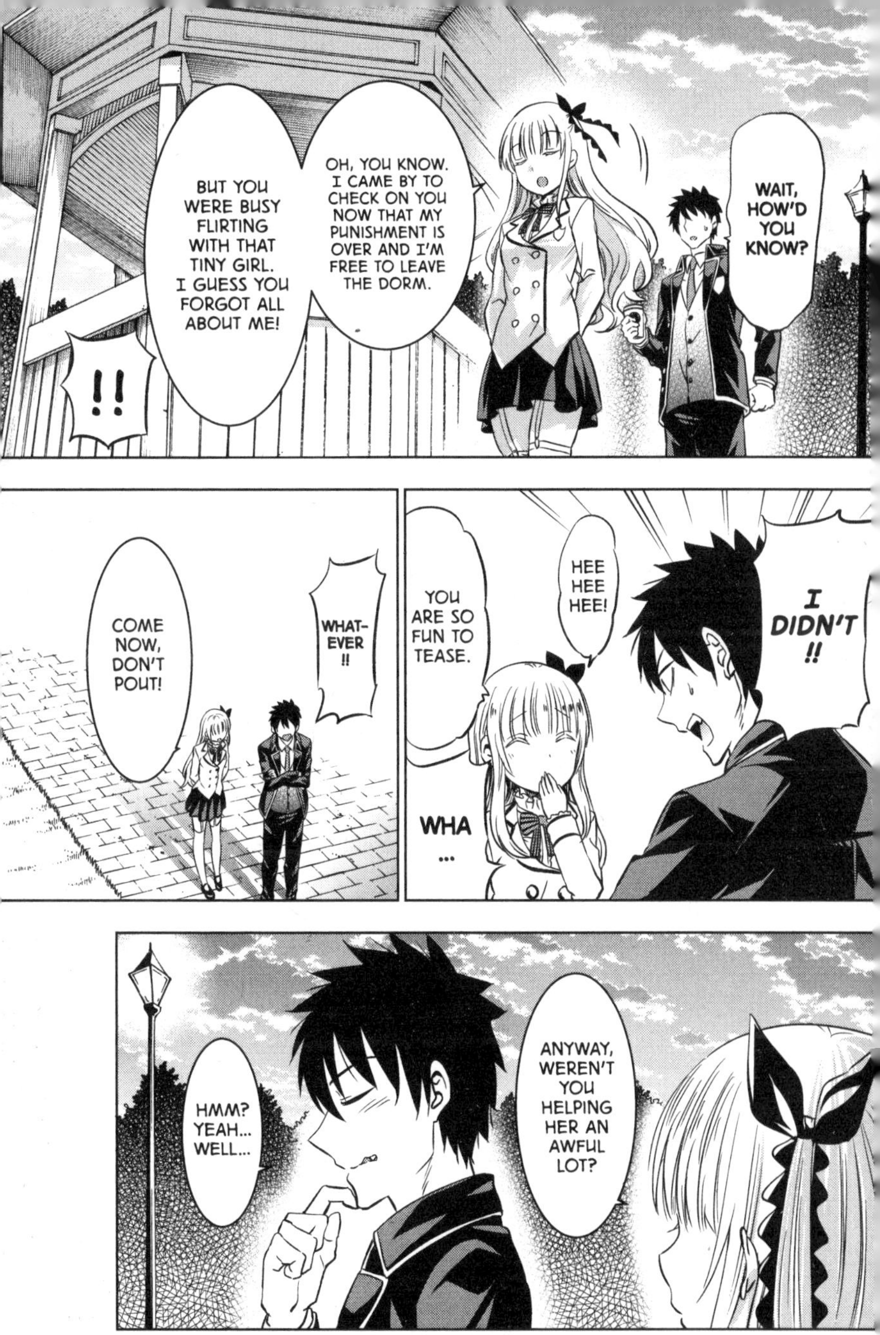
WAIT, HOW'D YOU KNOW?
OH, YOU KNOW. I CAME BY TO CHECK ON YOU NOW THAT MY PUNISHMENT IS OVER AND I'M FREE TO LEAVE THE DORM.
BUT YOU WERE BUSY FLIRTING WITH THAT TINY GIRL. I GUESS YOU FORGOT ALL ABOUT ME!
!!
I DIDN'T !!
HEE HEE HEE!
YOU ARE SO FUN TO TEASE.
WHA ...
WHAT-EVER !!
COME NOW, DON'T POUT!
ANYWAY, WEREN'T YOU HELPING HER AN AWFUL LOT?
HMM? YEAH... WELL...

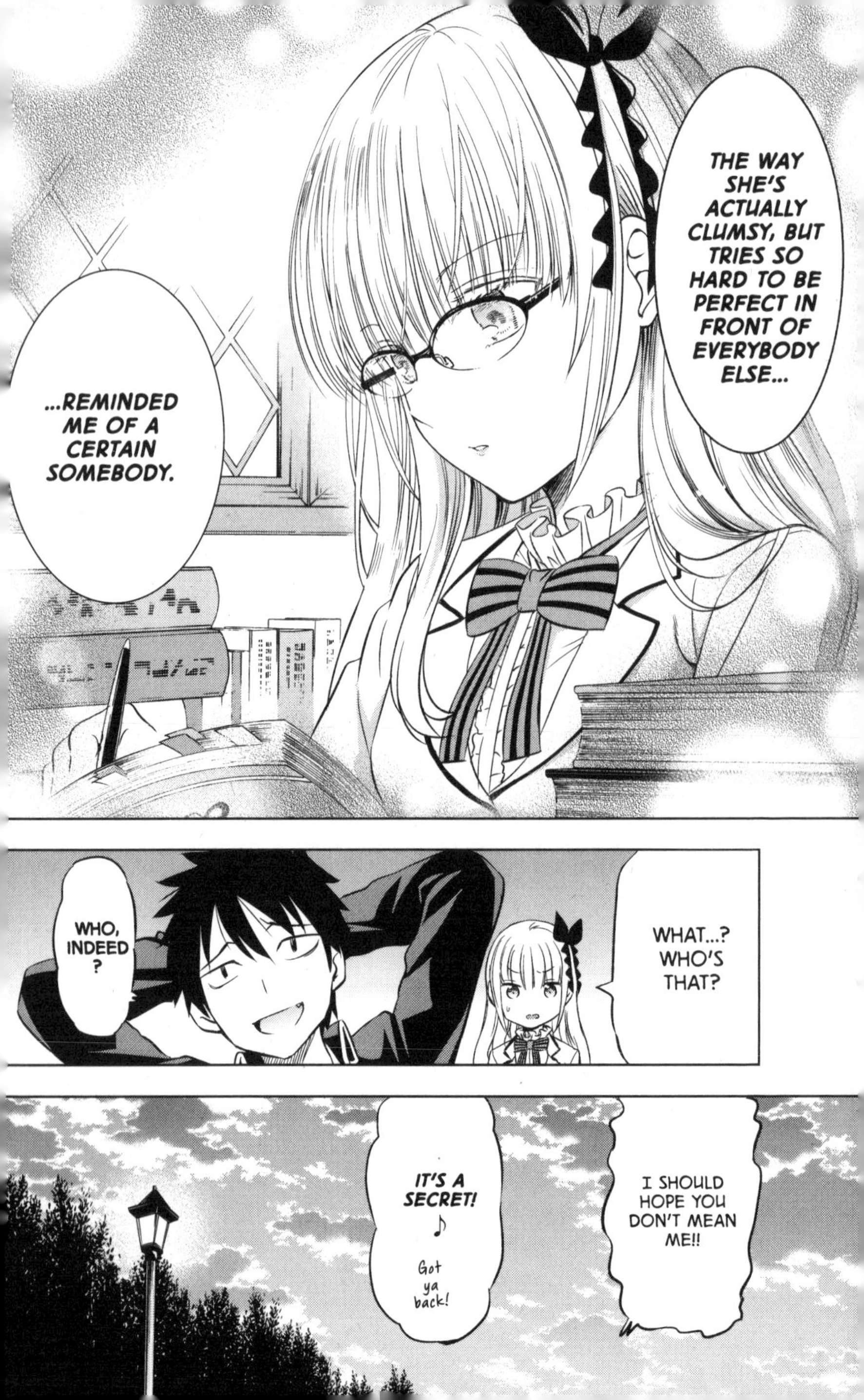
THE WAY SHE'S ACTUALLY CLUMSY, BUT TRIES SO HARD TO BE PERFECT IN FRONT OF EVERYBODY ELSE...
...REMINDED ME OF A CERTAIN SOMEBODY.
WHAT...? WHO'S THAT?
WHO, INDEED ?
I SHOULD HOPE YOU DON'T MEAN ME!!
IT'S A SECRET! ♪
Got ya back!

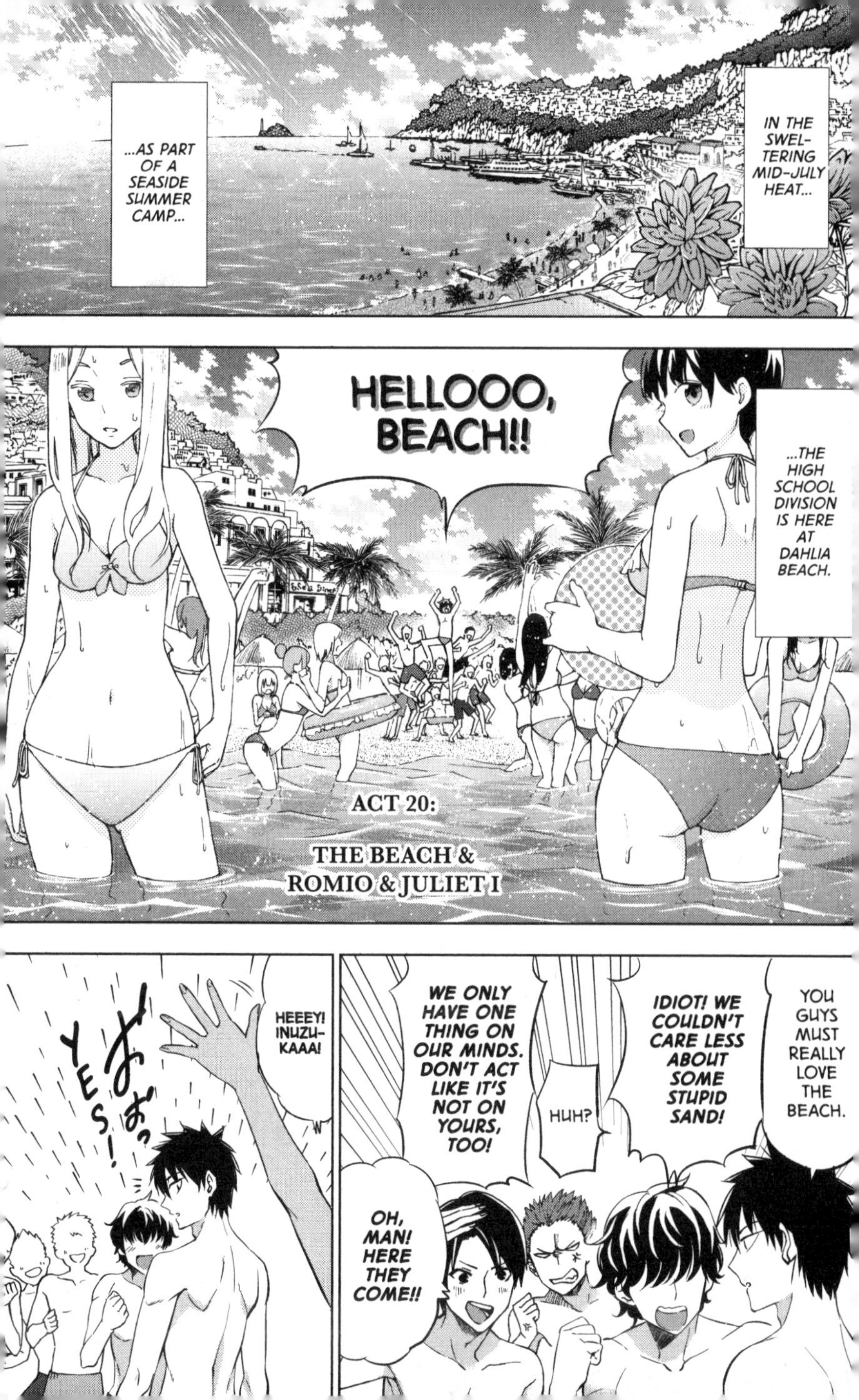
IN THE SWELTERING MID-JULY HEAT...
...AS PART OF A SEASIDE SUMMER CAMP...
...THE HIGH SCHOOL DIVISION IS HERE AT DAHLIA BEACH.
HELLOOO, BEACH!!
ACT 20:
THE BEACH & ROMIO & JULIET I
YOU GUYS MUST REALLY LOVE THE BEACH.
IDIOT! WE COULDN'T CARE LESS ABOUT SOME STUPID SAND!
HUH?
WE ONLY HAVE ONE THING ON OUR MINDS. DON'T ACT LIKE IT'S NOT ON YOURS, TOO!
OH, MAN! HERE THEY COME!!
HEEEY! INUZUKAAA!
YES!

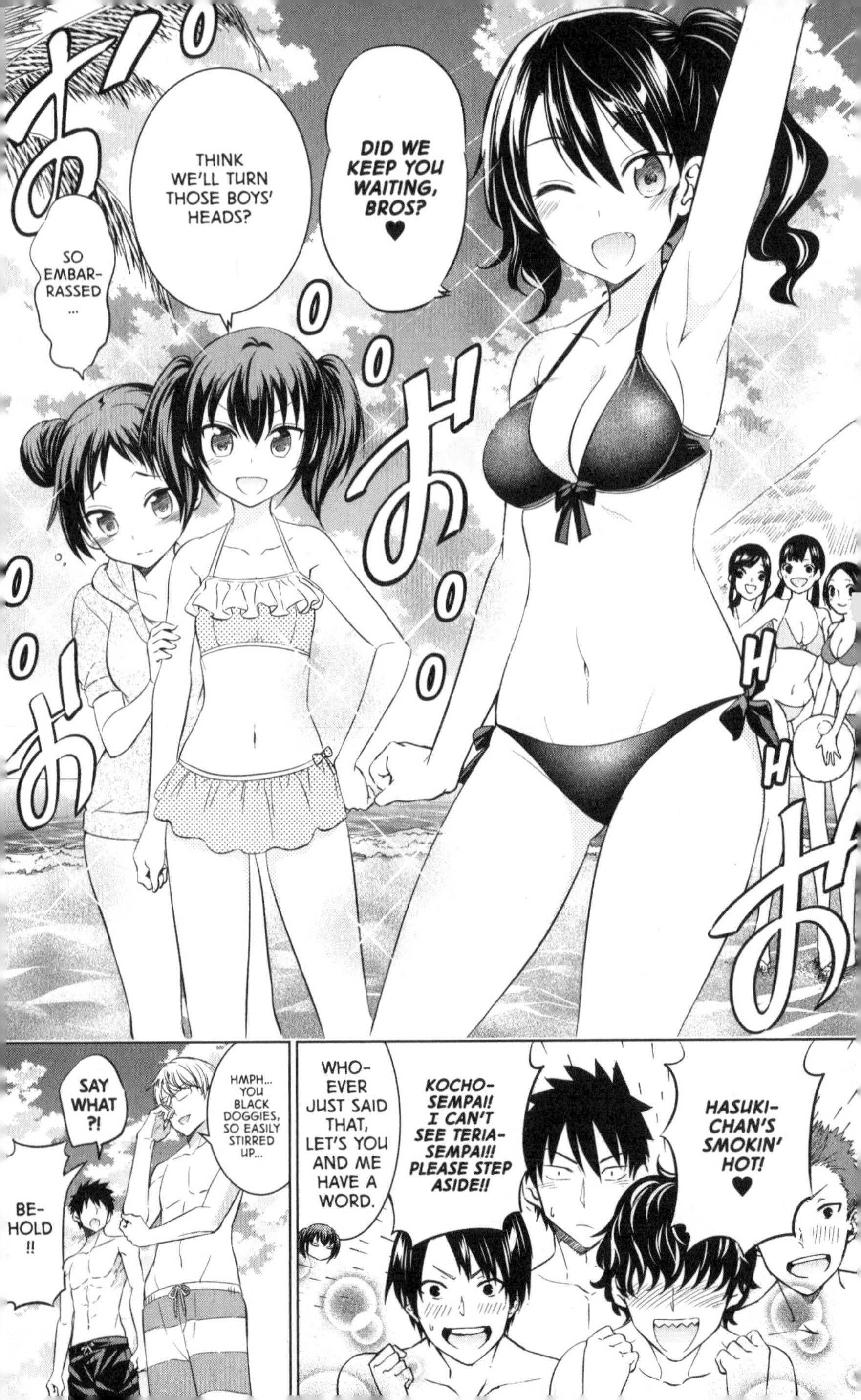
DID WE KEEP YOU WAITING, BROS? ♥
THINK WE'LL TURN THOSE BOYS' HEADS?
SO EMBARRASSED...
HASUKI-CHAN'S SMOKIN' HOT! ♥
KOCHO-SEMPAI!! I CAN'T SEE TERIA-SEMPAI!! PLEASE STEP ASIDE!!
WHOEVER JUST SAID THAT, LET'S YOU AND ME HAVE A WORD.
HMPH... YOU BLACK DOGGIES, SO EASILY STIRRED UP...
SAY WHAT?!
BEHOLD!!

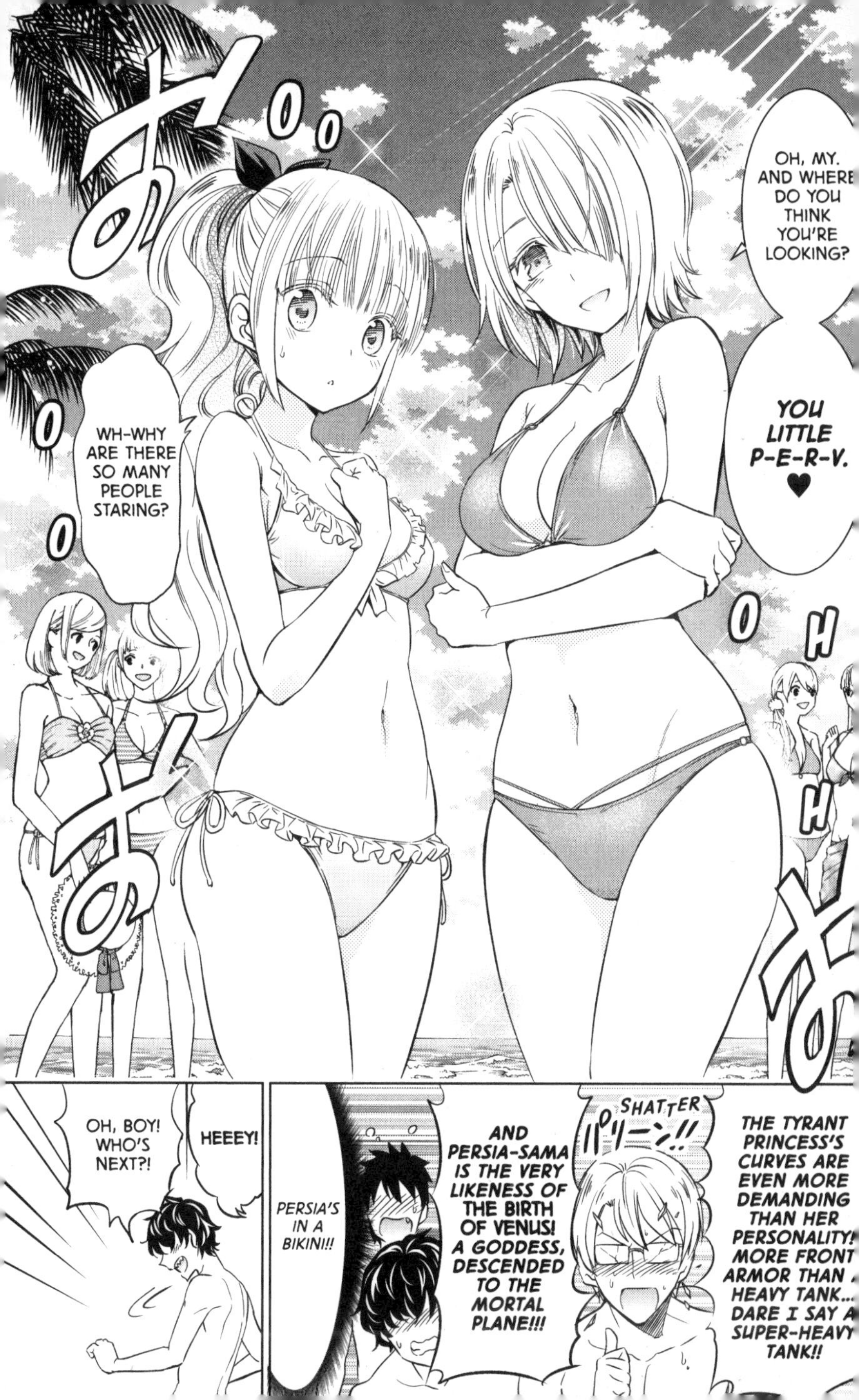
OH, MY. AND WHERE DO YOU THINK YOU'RE LOOKING?
YOU LITTLE P-E-R-V. ♥
OHH
WH-WHY ARE THERE SO MANY PEOPLE STARING?
THE TYRANT PRINCESS'S CURVES ARE EVEN MORE DEMANDING THAN HER PERSONALITY! MORE FRONT ARMOR THAN HEAVY TANK... DARE I SAY A SUPER-HEAVY TANK!!
SHATTER
パリーン!!
AND PERSIA-SAMA IS THE VERY LIKENESS OF THE BIRTH OF VENUS! A GODDESS, DESCENDED TO THE MORTAL PLANE!!!
PERSIA'S IN A BIKINI!!
HEEEY!
OH, BOY! WHO'S NEXT?!

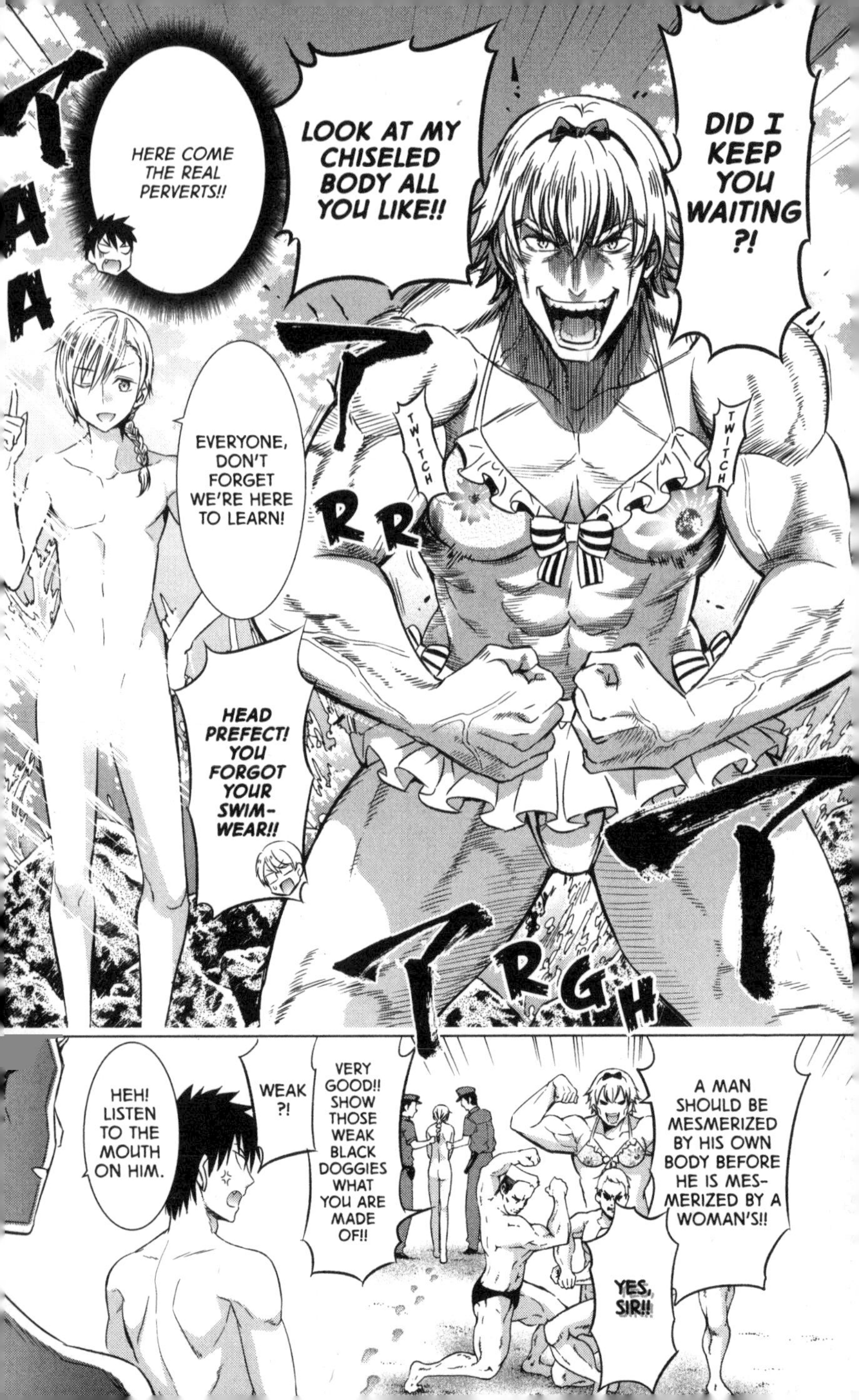
DID I KEEP YOU WAITING?!
LOOK AT MY CHISELED BODY ALL YOU LIKE!!
HERE COME THE REAL PERVERTS!!
AA
TWITCH
TWITCH
RR
EVERYONE, DON'T FORGET WE'RE HERE TO LEARN!
HEAD PREFECT! YOU FORGOT YOUR SWIM-WEAR!!
RGH
A MAN SHOULD BE MESMERIZED BY HIS OWN BODY BEFORE HE IS MES-MERIZED BY A WOMAN'S!!
YES, SIR!!
VERY GOOD!! SHOW THOSE WEAK BLACK DOGGIES WHAT YOU ARE MADE OF!!
WEAK?!
HEH! LISTEN TO THE MOUTH ON HIM.

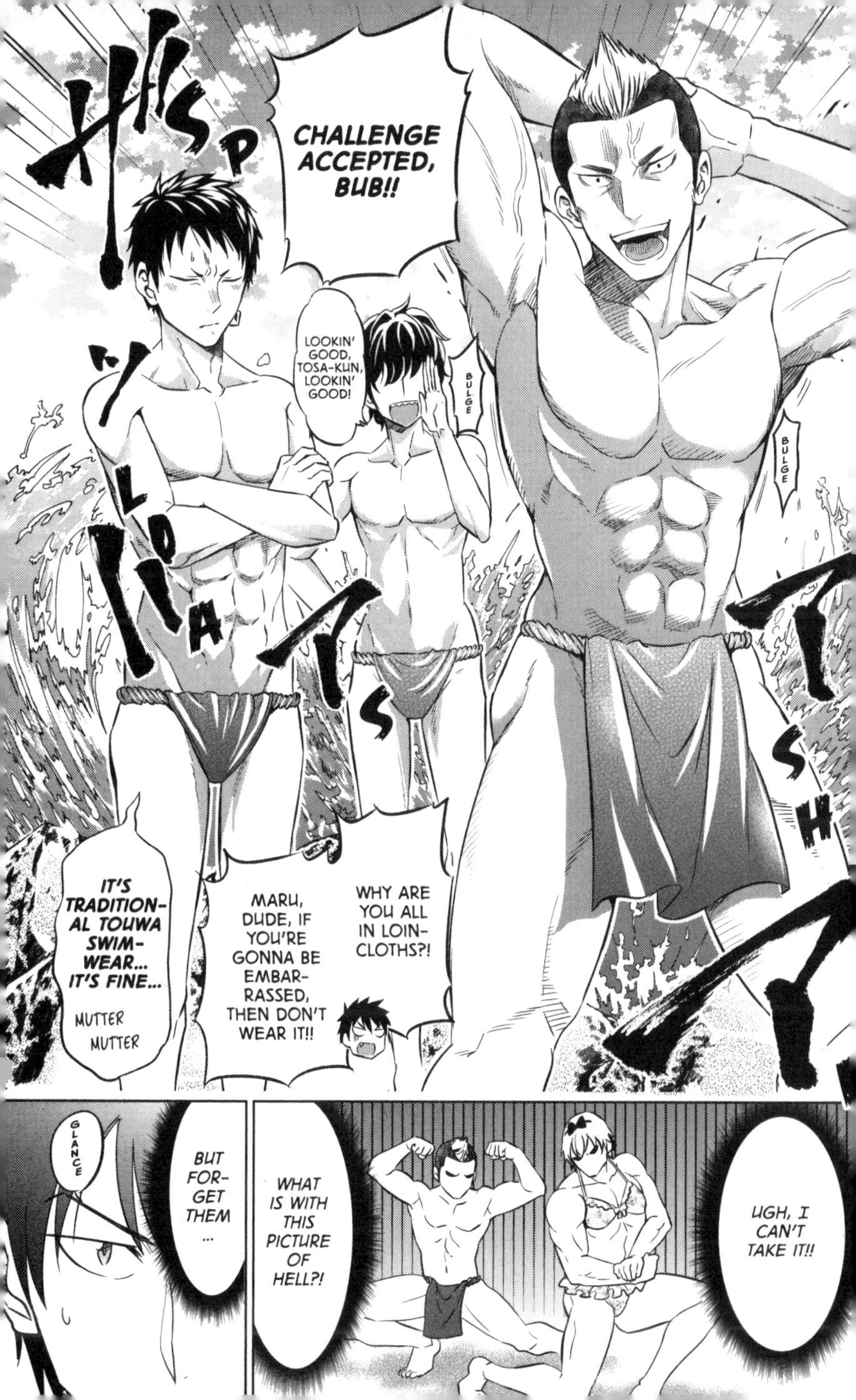
CHALLENGE ACCEPTED, BUB!!
BULGE
BULGE
LOOKIN' GOOD, TOSA-KUN, LOOKIN' GOOD!
WHY ARE YOU ALL IN LOIN-CLOTHS?!
MARU, DUDE, IF YOU'RE GONNA BE EMBAR-RASSED, THEN DON'T WEAR IT!!
IT'S TRADITION-AL TOUWA SWIM-WEAR... IT'S FINE...
MUTTER MUTTER
UGH, I CAN'T TAKE IT!!
WHAT IS WITH THIS PICTURE OF HELL?!
BUT FOR-GET THEM ...
GLANCE

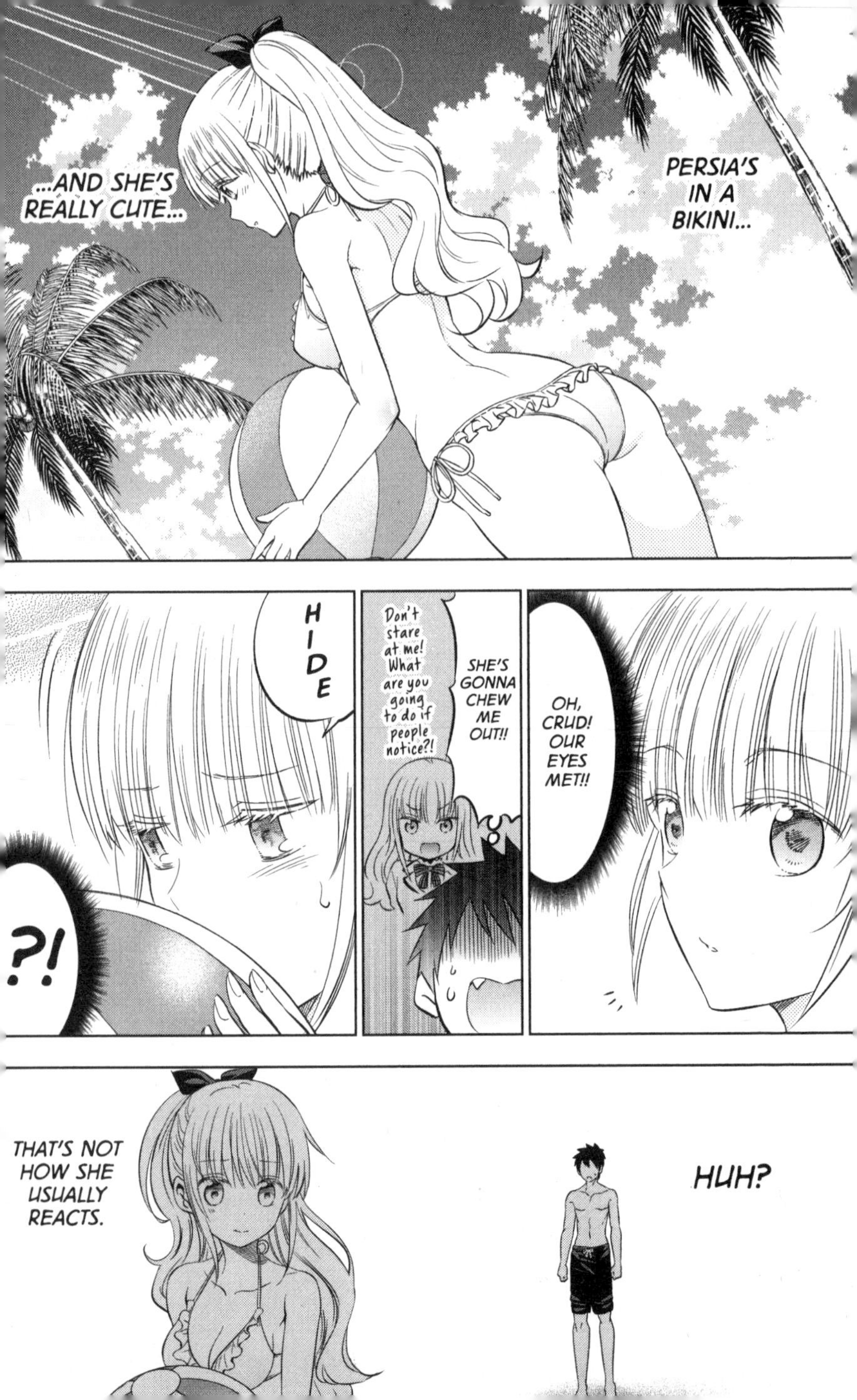
PERSIA'S IN A BIKINI...
...AND SHE'S REALLY CUTE...
OH, CRUD! OUR EYES MET!!
SHE'S GONNA CHEW ME OUT!!
Don't stare at me! What are you going to do if people notice?!
HIDE
?!
HUH?
THAT'S NOT HOW SHE USUALLY REACTS.

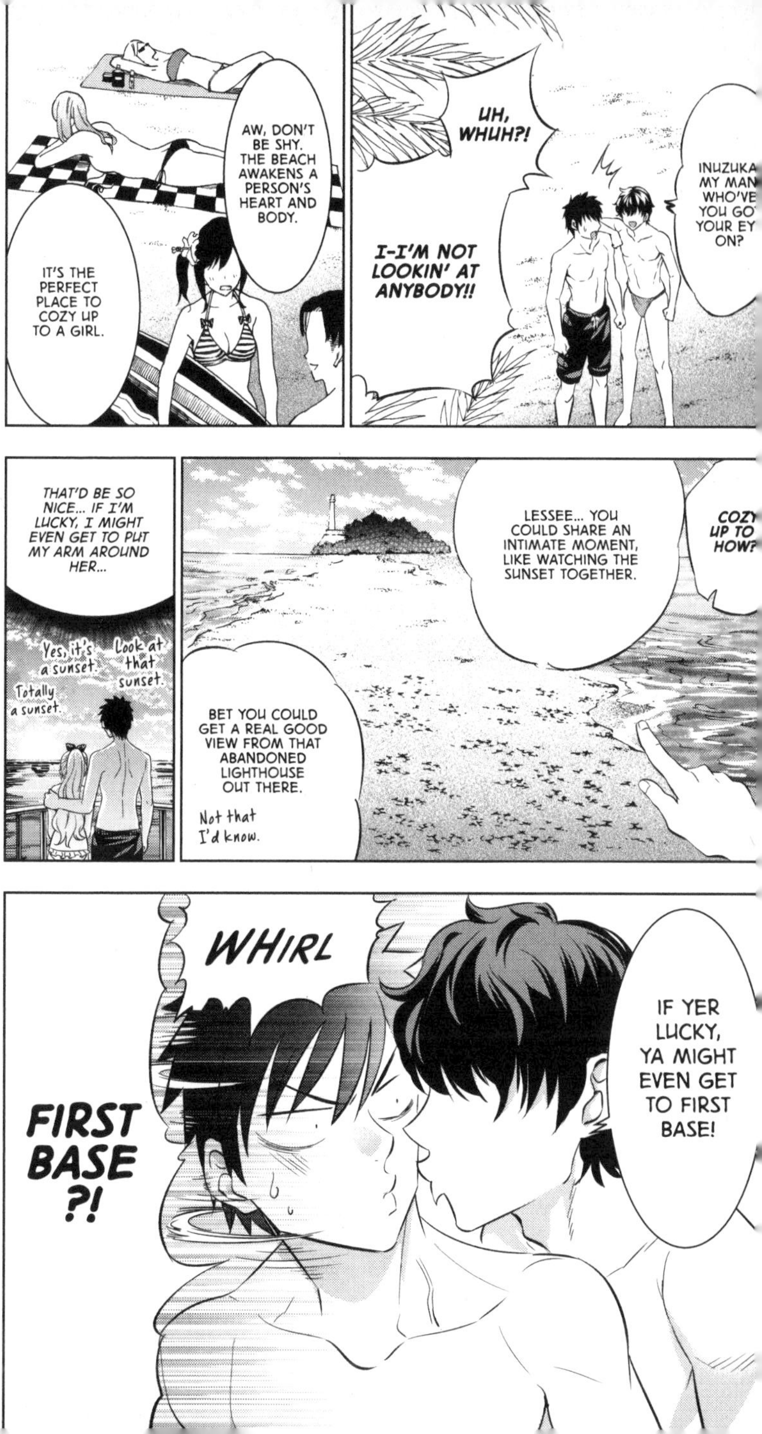
INUZUKA MY MAN WHO'VE YOU GO YOUR EY ON?
UH, WHUH?!
I-I'M NOT LOOKIN' AT ANYBODY!!
AW, DON'T BE SHY. THE BEACH AWAKENS A PERSON'S HEART AND BODY.
IT'S THE PERFECT PLACE TO COZY UP TO A GIRL.
COZY UP TO HOW?
LESSEE... YOU COULD SHARE AN INTIMATE MOMENT, LIKE WATCHING THE SUNSET TOGETHER.
BET YOU COULD GET A REAL GOOD VIEW FROM THAT ABANDONED LIGHTHOUSE OUT THERE.
Not that I'd know.
THAT'D BE SO NICE... IF I'M LUCKY, I MIGHT EVEN GET TO PUT MY ARM AROUND HER...
Look at that sunset.
Yes, it's a sunset.
Totally a sunset.
WHIRL
IF YER LUCKY, YA MIGHT EVEN GET TO FIRST BASE!
FIRST BASE?!

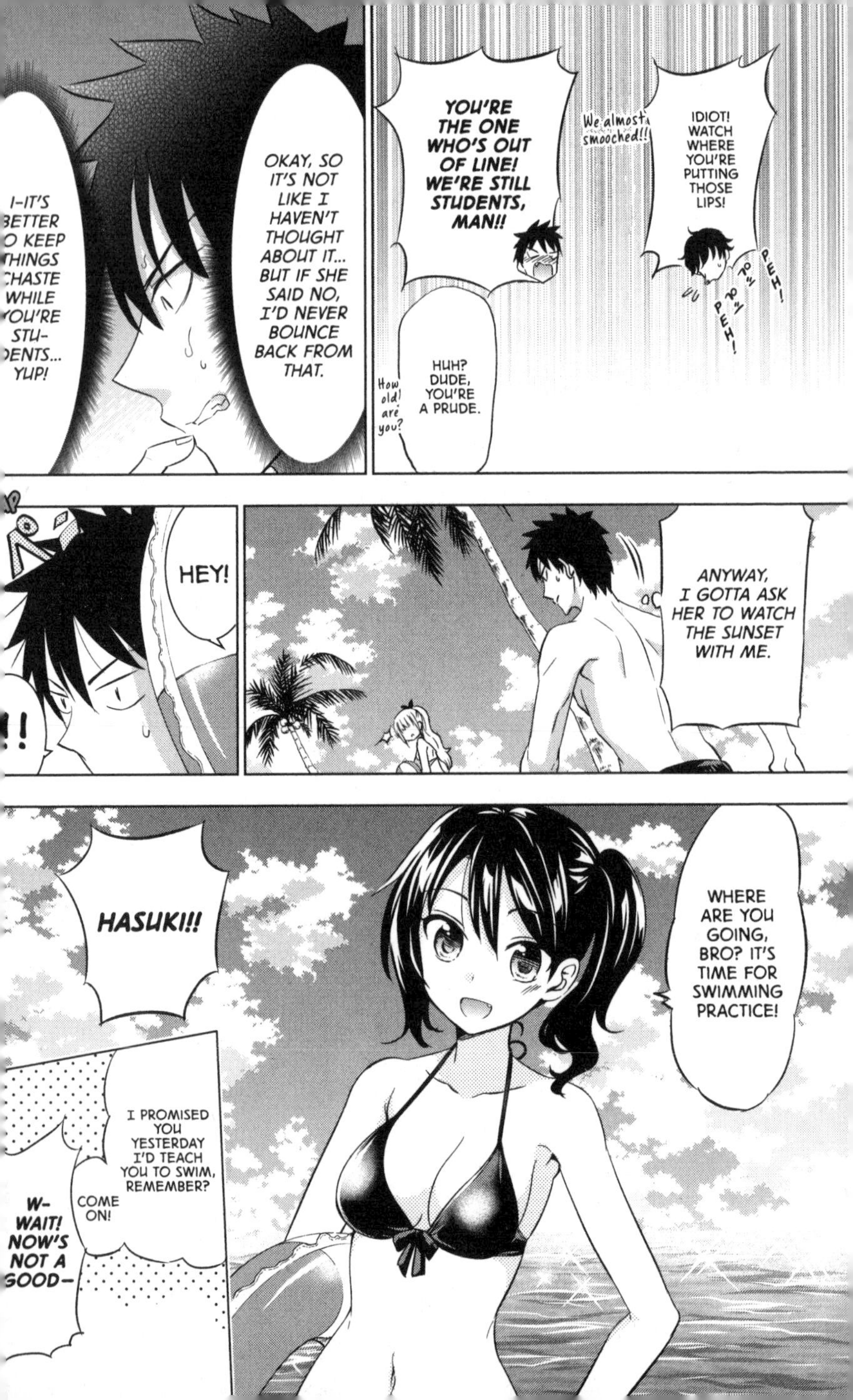
IDIOT! WATCH WHERE YOU'RE PUTTING THOSE LIPS!
We almost smooched!!
YOU'RE THE ONE WHO'S OUT OF LINE! WE'RE STILL STUDENTS, MAN!!
PEH! PEH!
HUH? DUDE, YOU'RE A PRUDE.
How old are you?
OKAY, SO IT'S NOT LIKE I HAVEN'T THOUGHT ABOUT IT... BUT IF SHE SAID NO, I'D NEVER BOUNCE BACK FROM THAT.
I-IT'S BETTER O KEEP THINGS CHASTE WHILE OU'RE STU- DENTS... YUP!
ANYWAY, I GOTTA ASK HER TO WATCH THE SUNSET WITH ME.
HEY!
!!
WHERE ARE YOU GOING, BRO? IT'S TIME FOR SWIMMING PRACTICE!
HASUKI!!!
I PROMISED YOU YESTERDAY I'D TEACH YOU TO SWIM, REMEMBER?
COME ON!
W-WAIT! NOW'S NOT A GOOD—

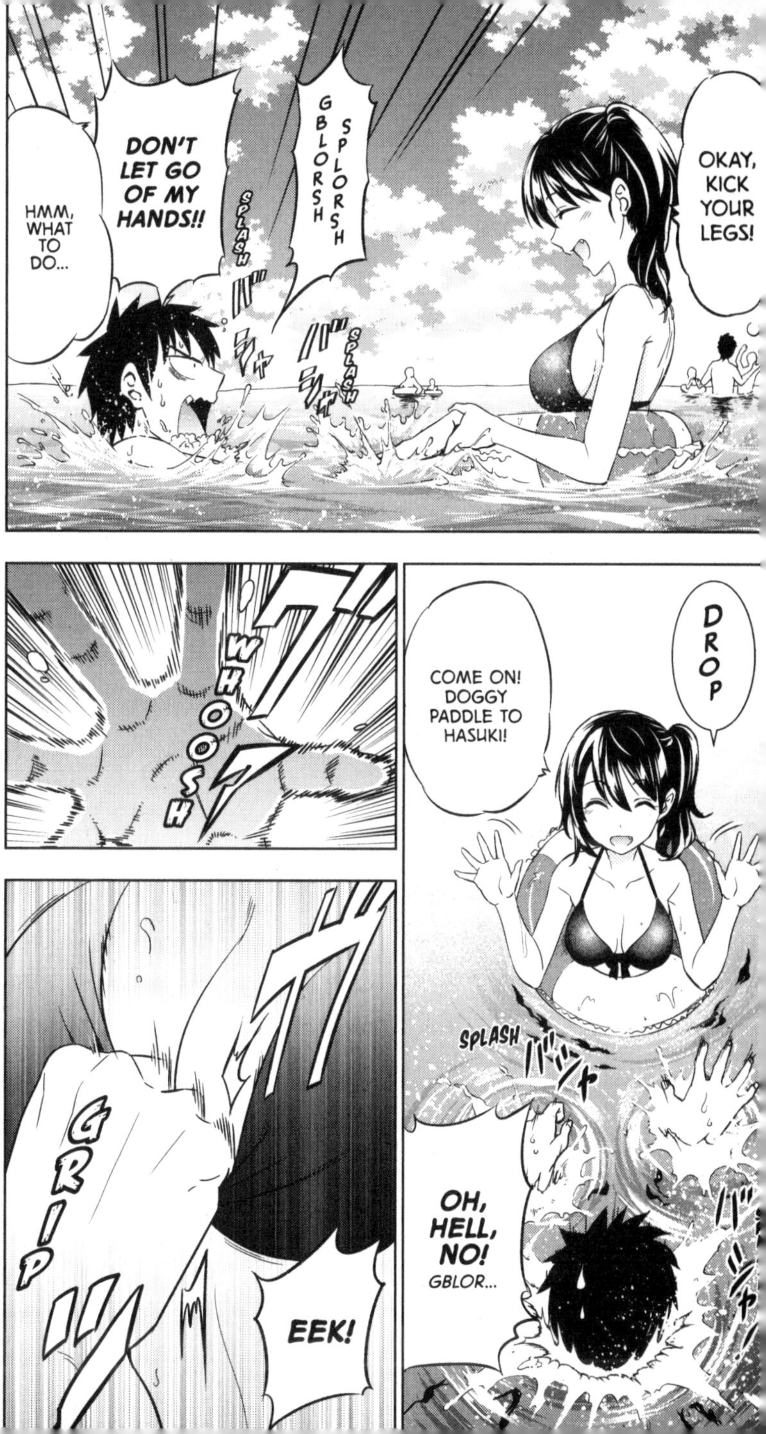

OKAY, KICK YOUR LEGS!
SPLASH
SPLORSH
GBLORSH
DON'T LET GO OF MY HANDS!!
SPLASH
HMM, WHAT TO DO...
DROP
COME ON! DOGGY PADDLE TO HASUKI!
SPLASH
OH, HELL, NO!
GBLOR...
WHOOOSH
GRIP
EEK!

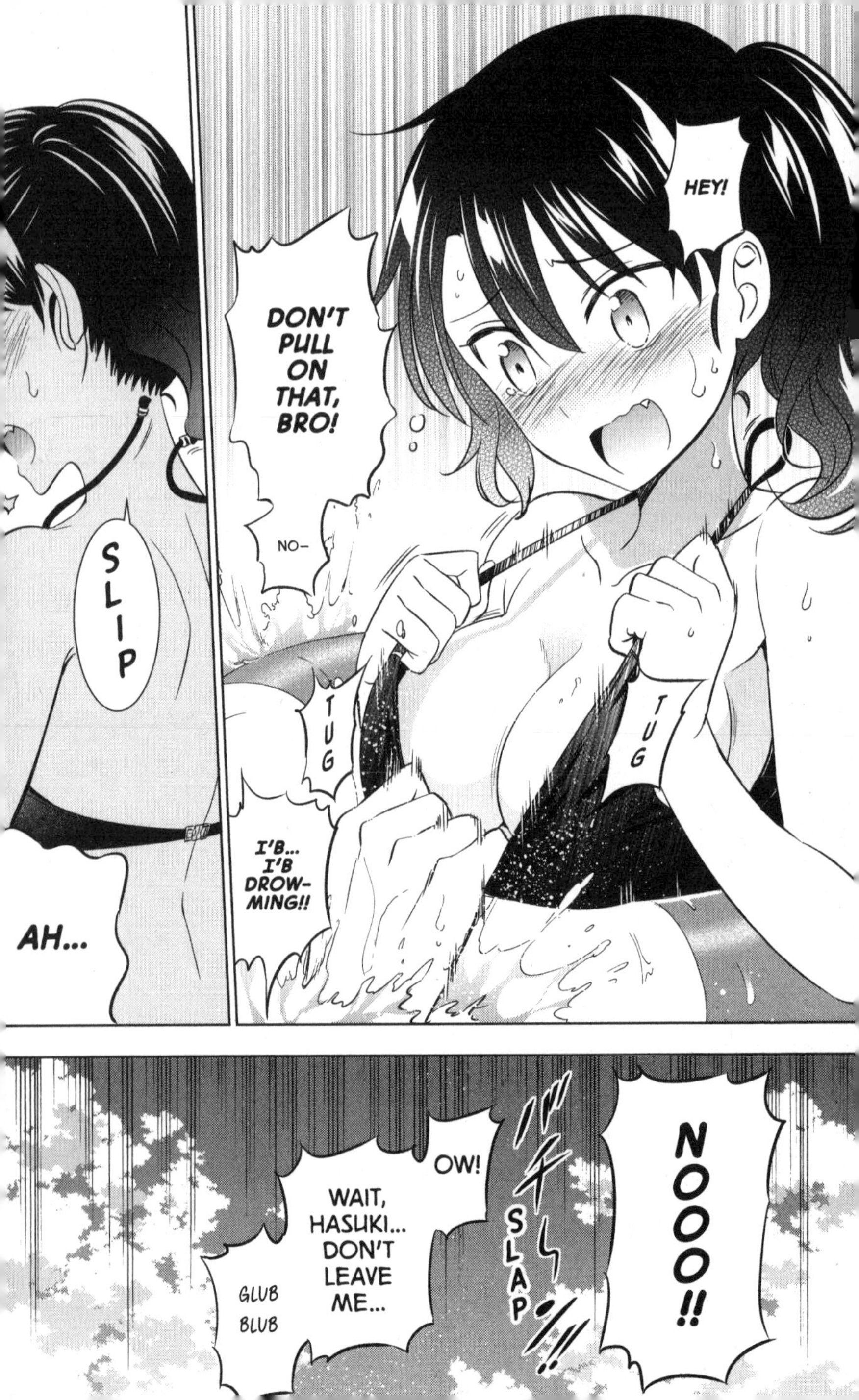
HEY!
DON'T PULL ON THAT, BRO!
NO–
TUG
TUG
I'B... I'B DROWMING!!
SLIP
AH...
NOOOO!!
SLAP
OW!
WAIT, HASUKI... DON'T LEAVE ME...
GLUB BLUB

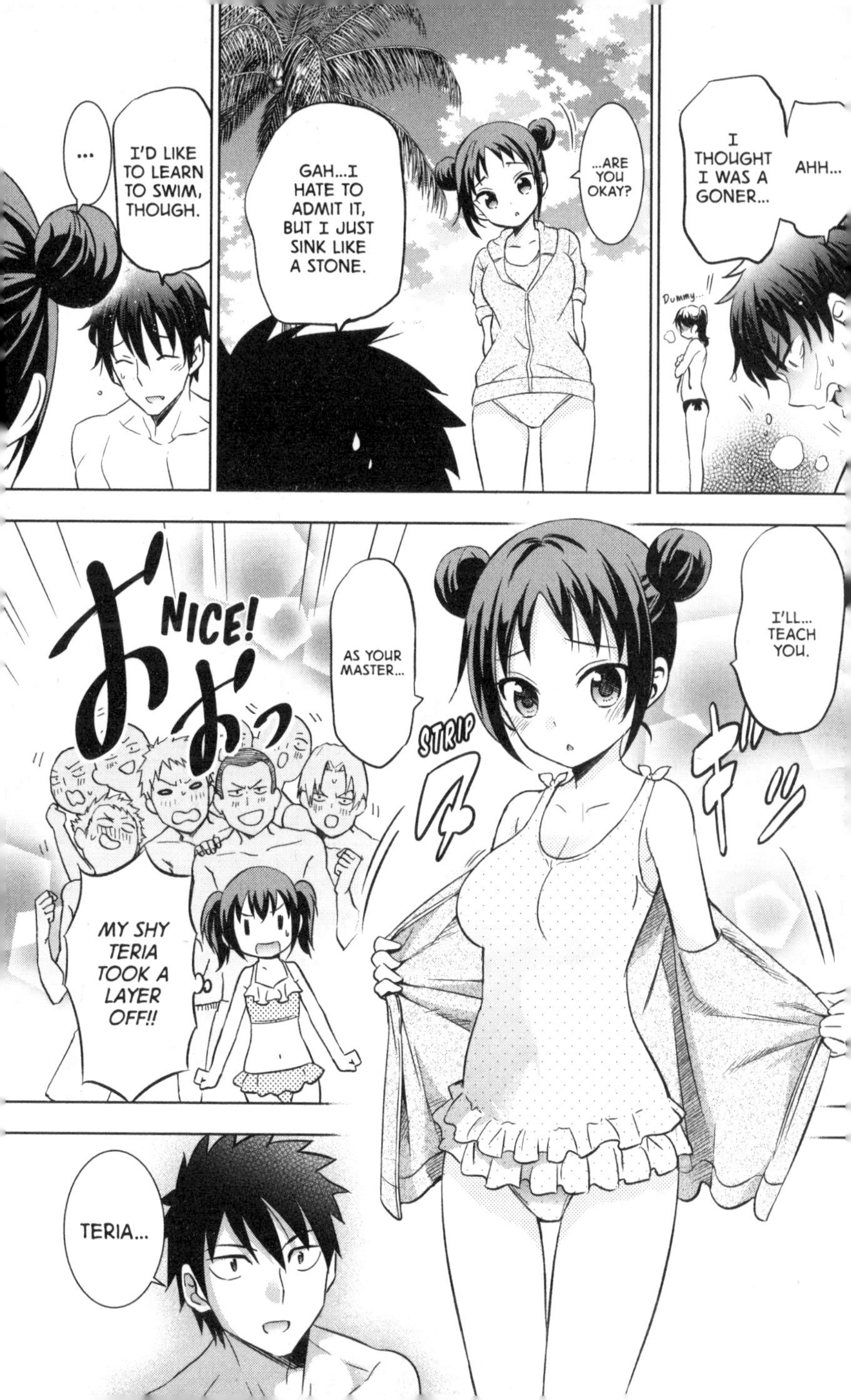
AHH...
I THOUGHT I WAS A GONER...
Dummy...
...ARE YOU OKAY?
GAH...I HATE TO ADMIT IT, BUT I JUST SINK LIKE A STONE.
I'D LIKE TO LEARN TO SWIM, THOUGH.
...
I'LL... TEACH YOU.
STRIP
AS YOUR MASTER...
NICE!
おおっ
MY SHY TERIA TOOK A LAYER OFF!!
TERIA...

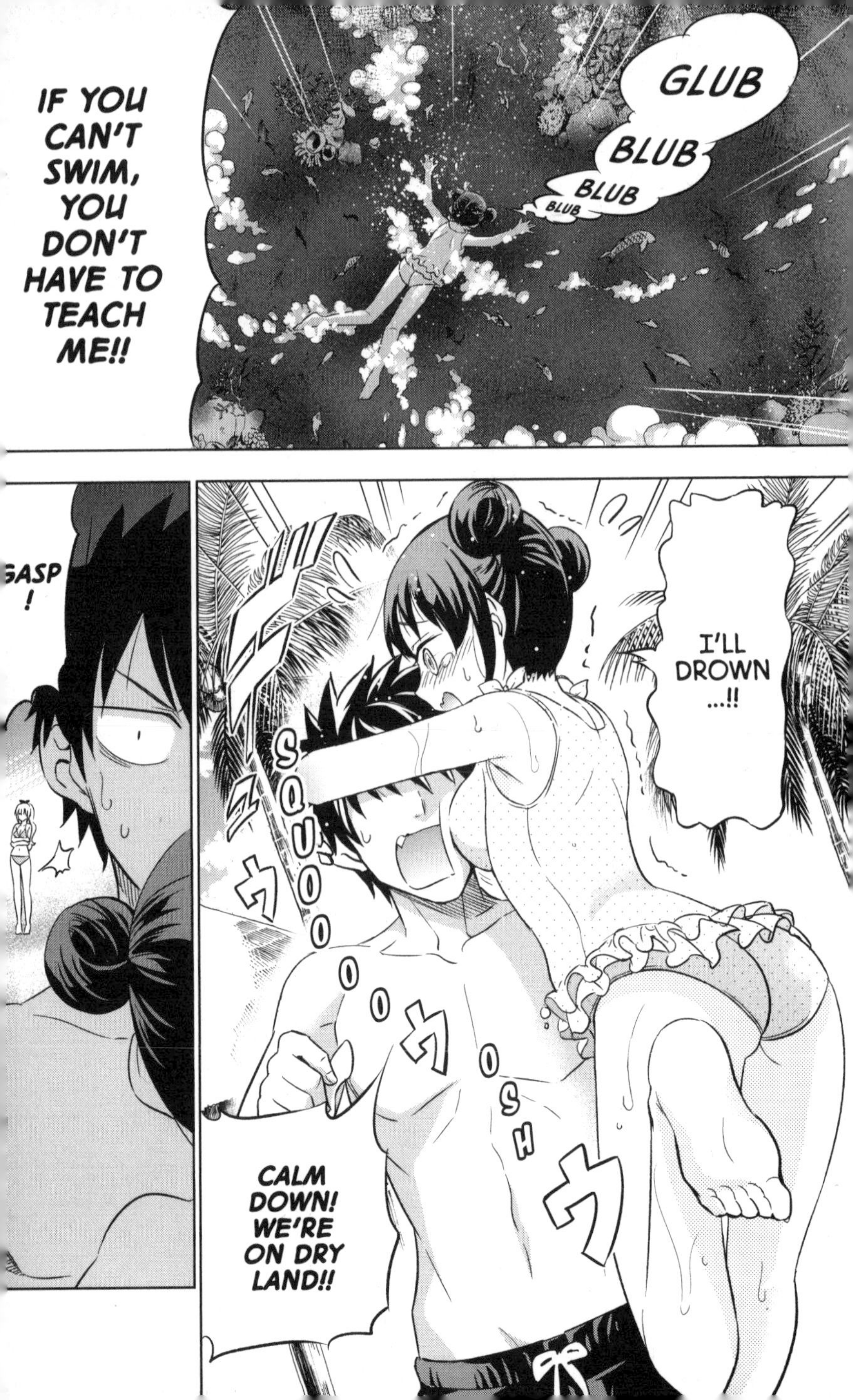
GLUB
BLUB
BLUB
BLUB
IF YOU CAN'T SWIM, YOU DON'T HAVE TO TEACH ME!!
I'LL DROWN ...!!
SQUOOOOOSH
CALM DOWN! WE'RE ON DRY LAND!!
GASP !

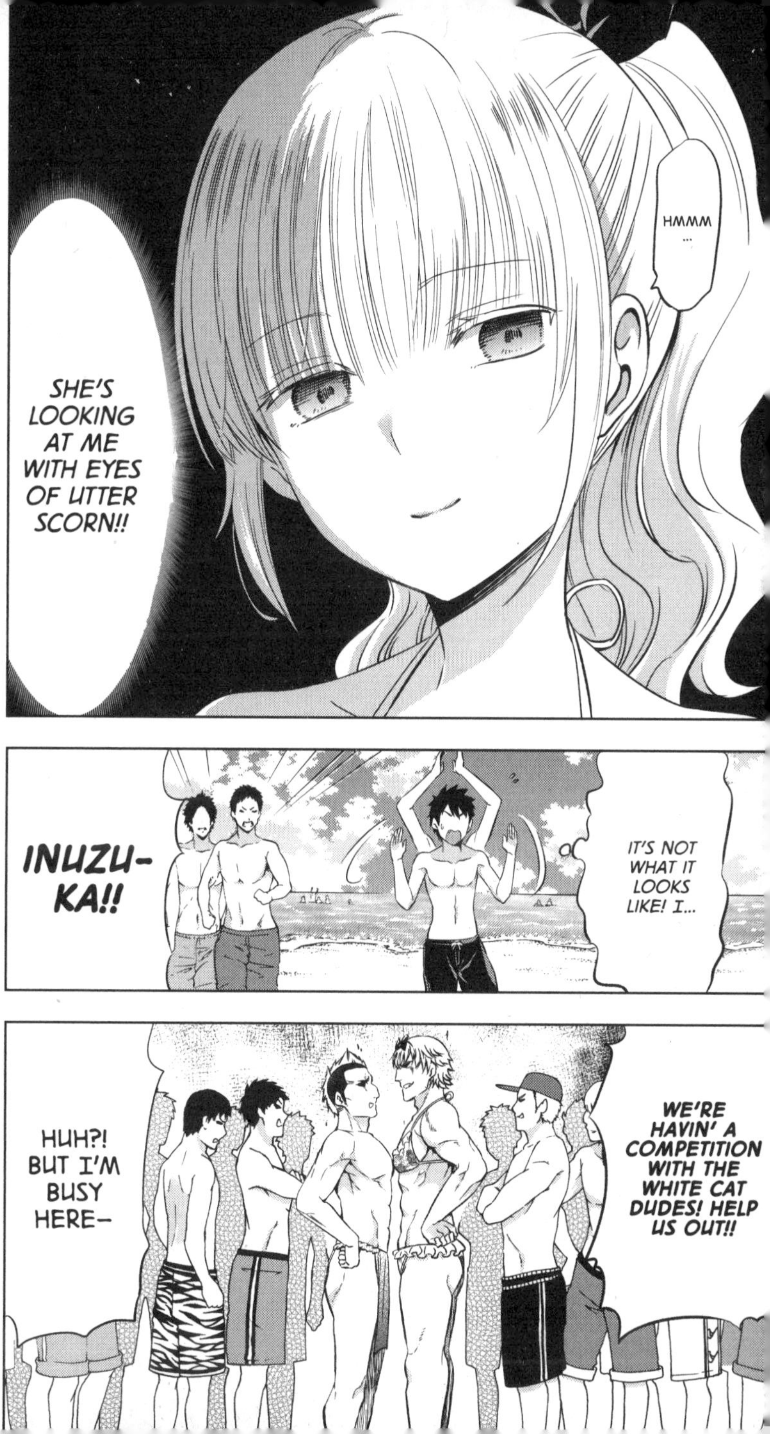
HMMM ...
SHE'S LOOKING AT ME WITH EYES OF UTTER SCORN!!
IT'S NOT WHAT IT LOOKS LIKE! I...
INUZU-KA!!
WE'RE HAVIN' A COMPETITION WITH THE WHITE CAT DUDES! HELP US OUT!!
HUH?! BUT I'M BUSY HERE–

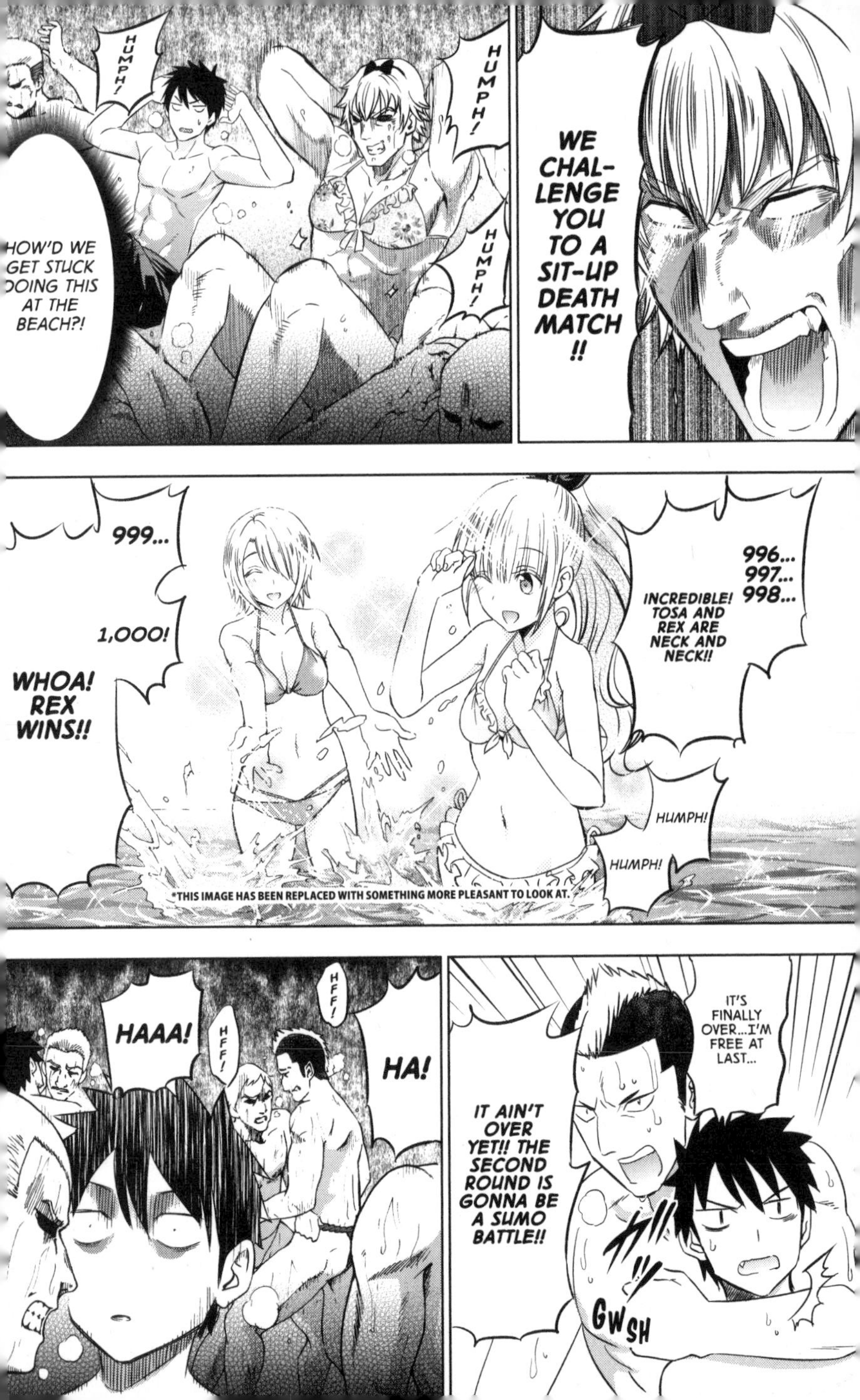
WE CHALLENGE YOU TO A SIT-UP DEATH MATCH!!
HUMPH!
HUMPH!
HUMPH!
HOW'D WE GET STUCK DOING THIS AT THE BEACH?!
996... 997... 998...
INCREDIBLE! TOSA AND REX ARE NECK AND NECK!!
HUMPH!
HUMPH!
999...
1,000!
WHOA! REX WINS!!
*THIS IMAGE HAS BEEN REPLACED WITH SOMETHING MORE PLEASANT TO LOOK AT.
IT'S FINALLY OVER...I'M FREE AT LAST...
IT AIN'T OVER YET!! THE SECOND ROUND IS GONNA BE A SUMO BATTLE!!
GWSH
HA!
HFF!
HFF!
HAAA!

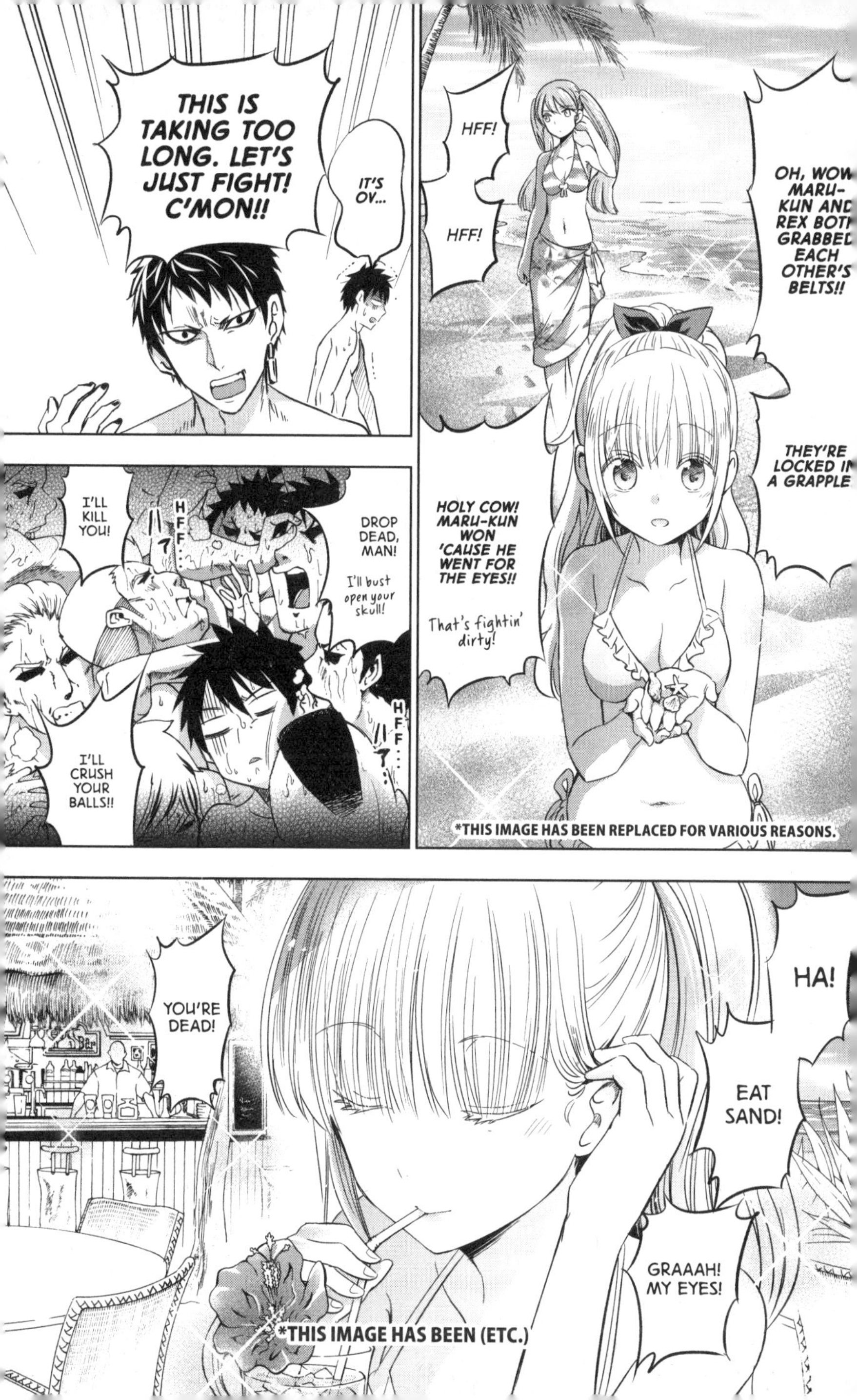
OH, WOW MARU-KUN AND REX BOTH GRABBED EACH OTHER'S BELTS!!
HFF!
HFF!
THEY'RE LOCKED IN A GRAPPLE
HOLY COW! MARU-KUN WON 'CAUSE HE WENT FOR THE EYES!!
That's fightin' dirty!
*THIS IMAGE HAS BEEN REPLACED FOR VARIOUS REASONS.
THIS IS TAKING TOO LONG. LET'S JUST FIGHT! C'MON!!
IT'S OV...
DROP DEAD, MAN!
I'll bust open your skull!
HFF...
I'LL KILL YOU!
HFF...
I'LL CRUSH YOUR BALLS!!
HA!
EAT SAND!
GRAAAH! MY EYES!
YOU'RE DEAD!
*THIS IMAGE HAS BEEN (ETC.)

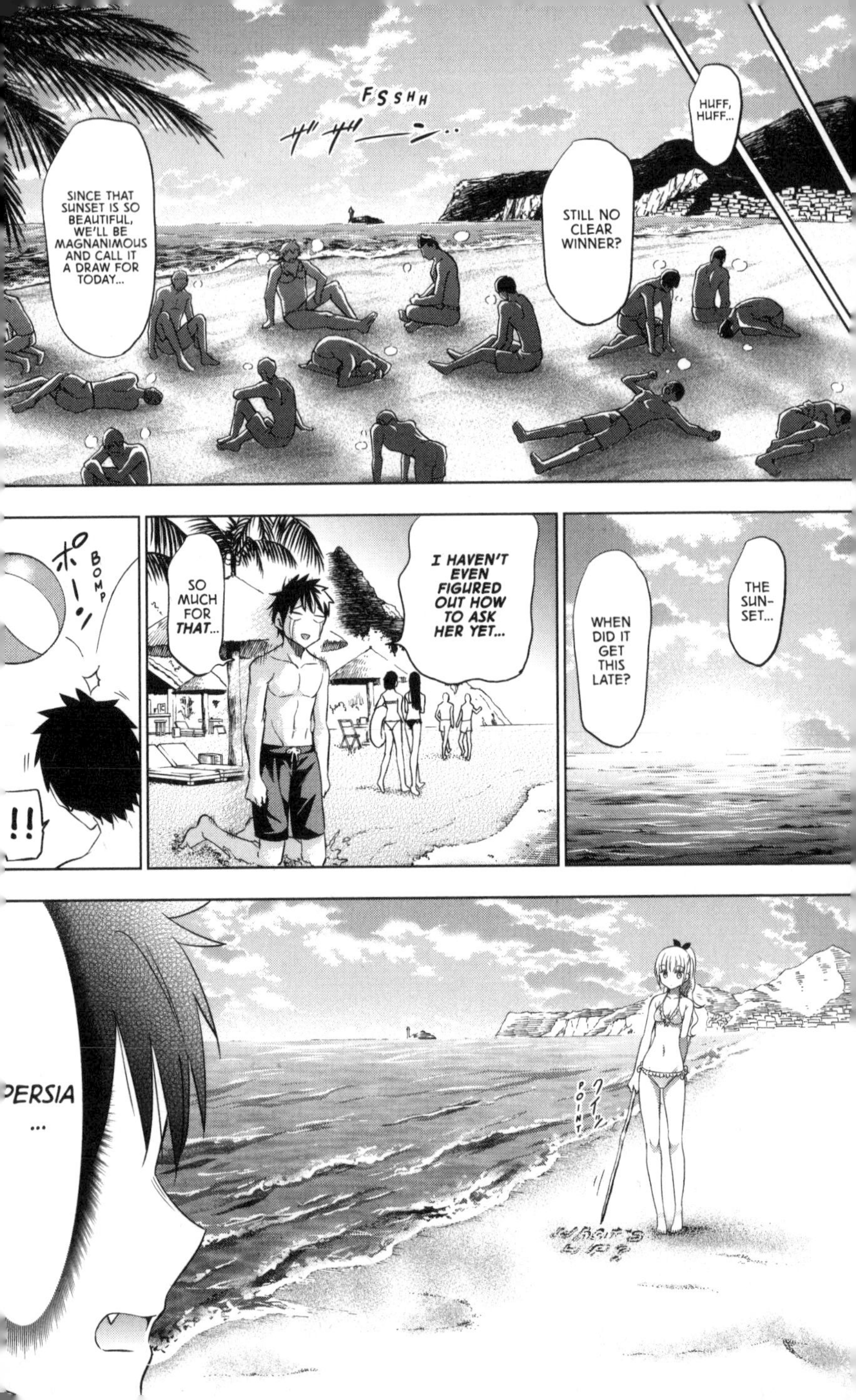
HUFF, HUFF...
FSSHH
STILL NO CLEAR WINNER?
SINCE THAT SUNSET IS SO BEAUTIFUL, WE'LL BE MAGNANIMOUS AND CALL IT A DRAW FOR TODAY...
THE SUN-SET...
WHEN DID IT GET THIS LATE?
I HAVEN'T EVEN FIGURED OUT HOW TO ASK HER YET...
SO MUCH FOR THAT...
BOMP
!!
PERSIA ...
POINT

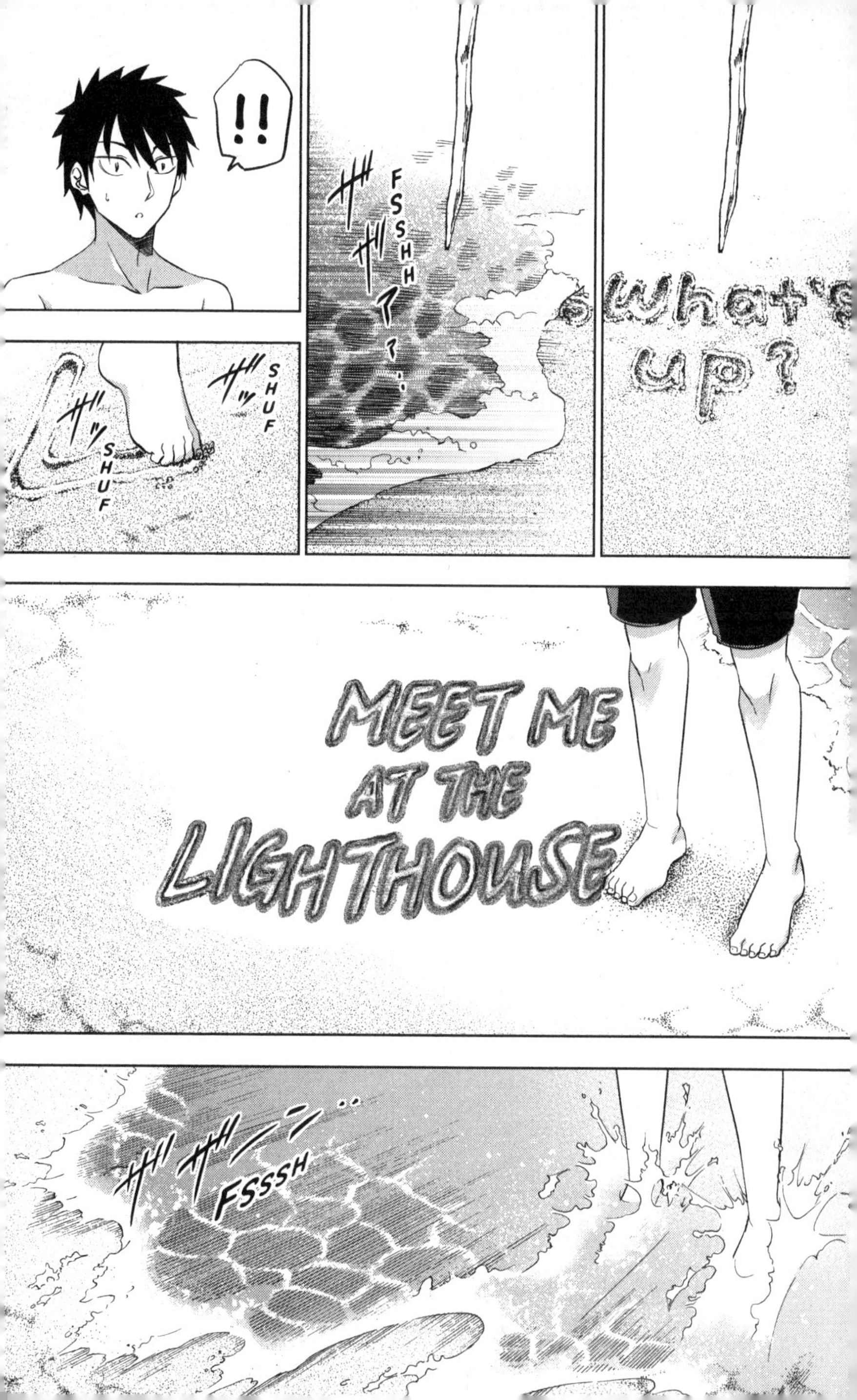
what's up?
FSSHH
!!
SHUF
SHUF
MEET ME AT THE LIGHTHOUSE
FSSSH

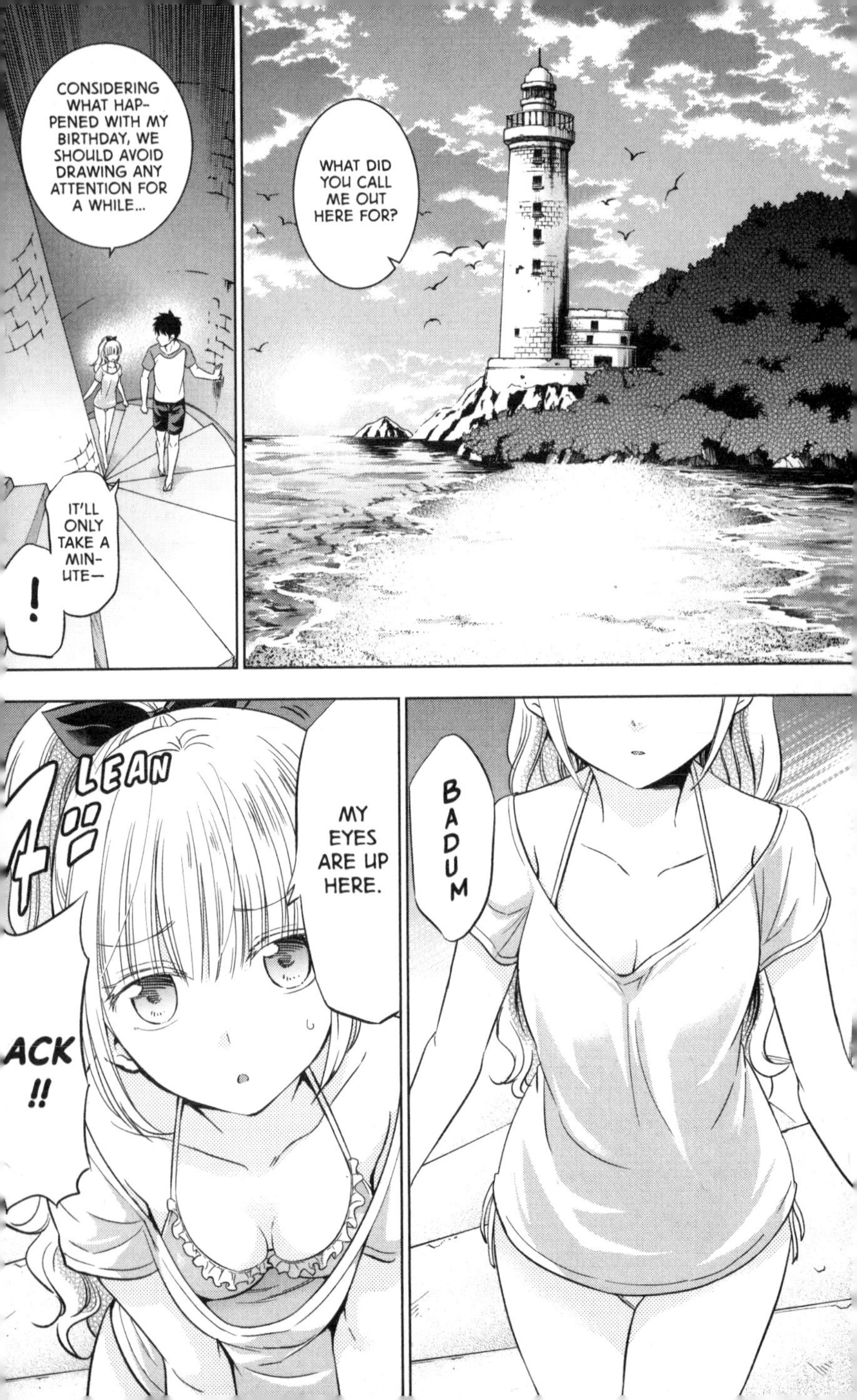
WHAT DID YOU CALL ME OUT HERE FOR?
CONSIDERING WHAT HAP-PENED WITH MY BIRTHDAY, WE SHOULD AVOID DRAWING ANY ATTENTION FOR A WHILE...
IT'LL ONLY TAKE A MIN-UTE—
!
BADUM
MY EYES ARE UP HERE.
LEAN
ACK !!

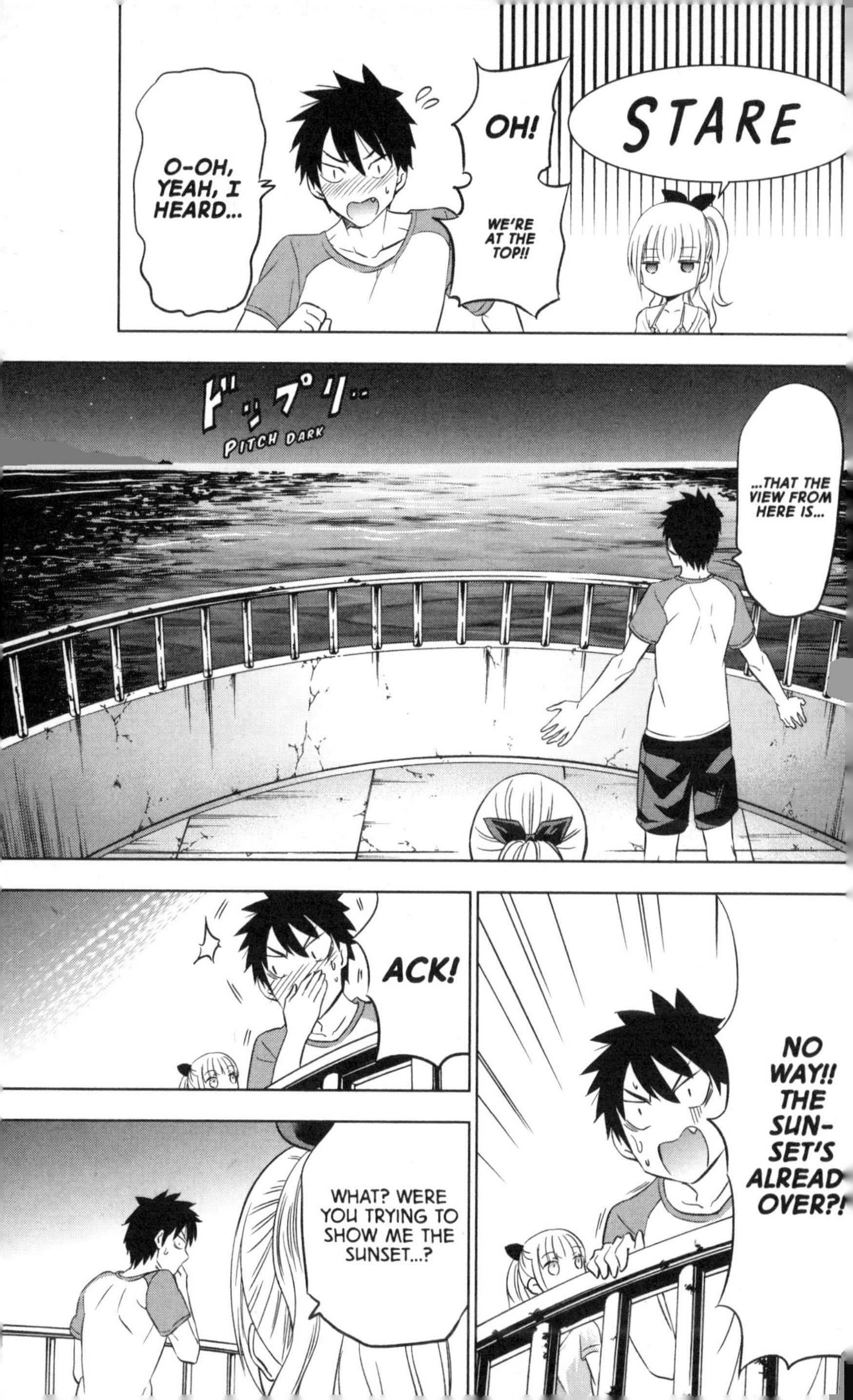
STARE
OH!
WE'RE AT THE TOP!!
O-OH, YEAH, I HEARD...
...THAT THE VIEW FROM HERE IS...
ドップリ‥
PITCH DARK
NO WAY!! THE SUN-SET'S ALREAD OVER?!
ACK!
WHAT? WERE YOU TRYING TO SHOW ME THE SUNSET...?

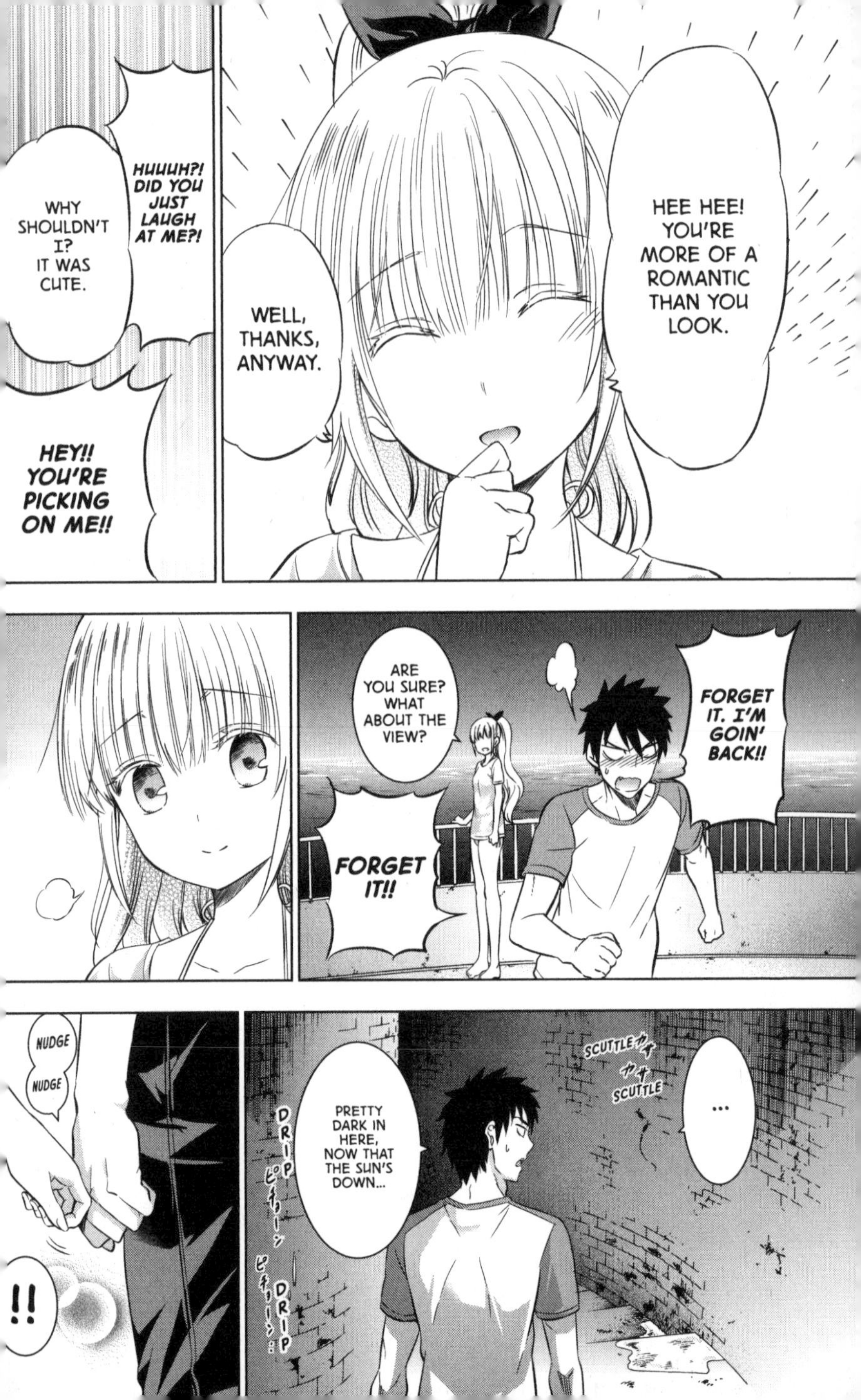
HEE HEE! YOU'RE MORE OF A ROMANTIC THAN YOU LOOK.
WELL, THANKS, ANYWAY.
HUUUH?! DID YOU JUST LAUGH AT ME?!
WHY SHOULDN'T I? IT WAS CUTE.
HEY!! YOU'RE PICKING ON ME!!
FORGET IT. I'M GOIN' BACK!!
ARE YOU SURE? WHAT ABOUT THE VIEW?
FORGET IT!!
SCUTTLE
SCUTTLE
...
PRETTY DARK IN HERE, NOW THAT THE SUN'S DOWN...
DRIP
DRIP
NUDGE
NUDGE
!!

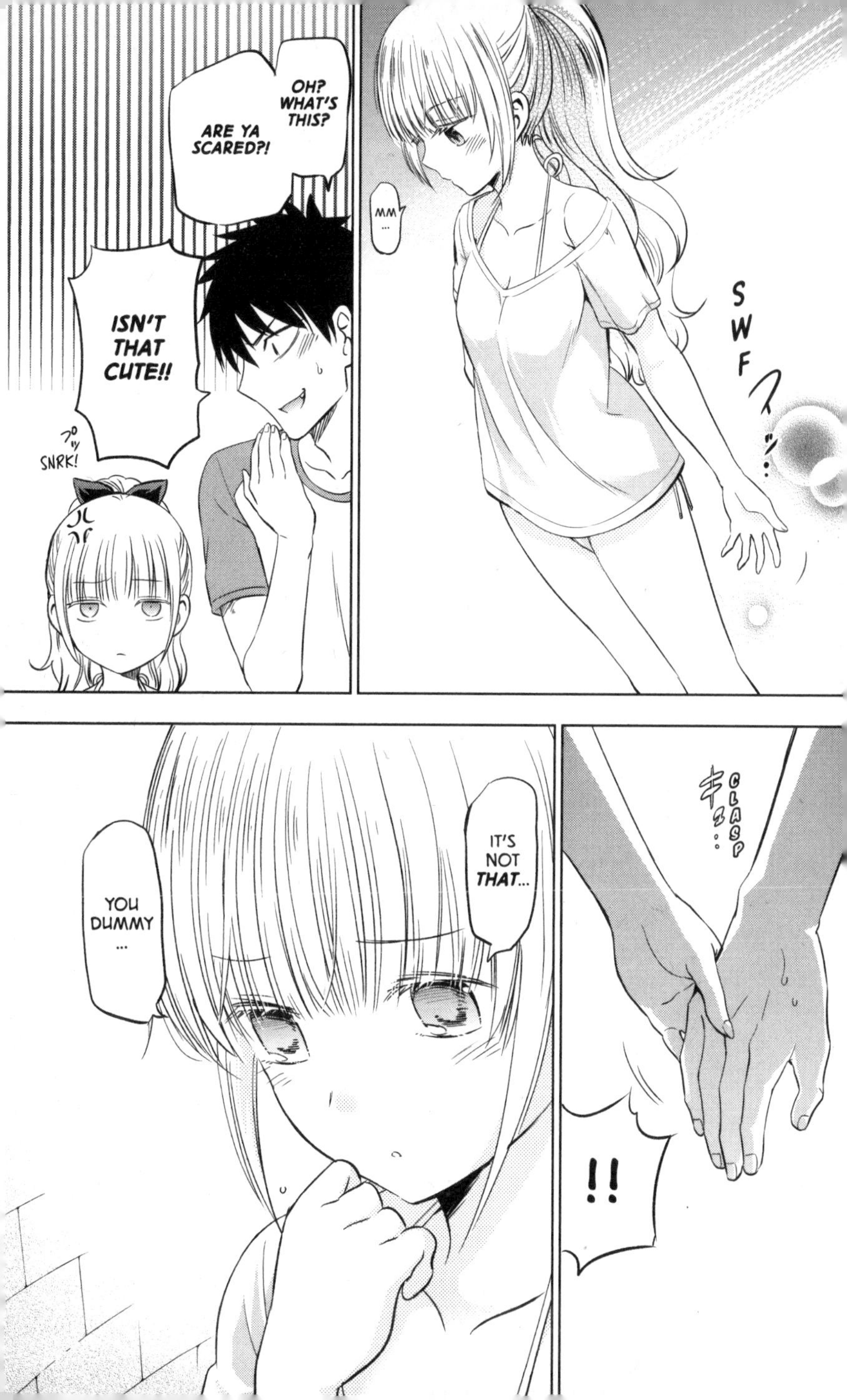
MM...
SWF
OH? WHAT'S THIS?
ARE YA SCARED?!
ISN'T THAT CUTE!!
SNRK!
CLASP
!!
IT'S NOT THAT...
YOU DUMMY...

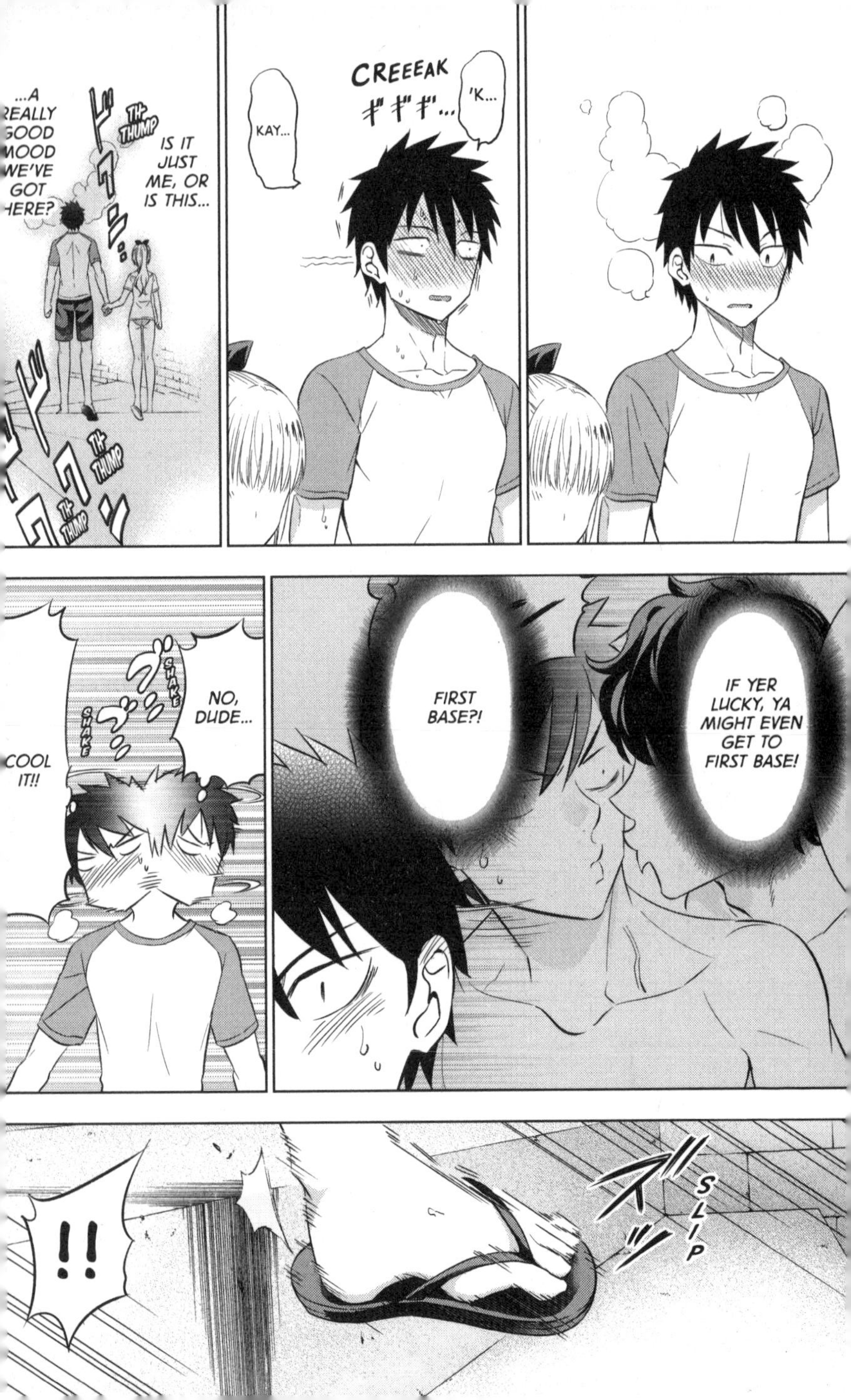

'K...
CREEEAK
ギギギ...
KAY...
IS IT JUST ME, OR IS THIS...
TH-THUMP
...A REALLY GOOD MOOD WE'VE GOT HERE?
TH-THUMP
TH-THUMP
IF YER LUCKY, YA MIGHT EVEN GET TO FIRST BASE!
FIRST BASE?!
NO, DUDE...
SHAKE
SHAKE
COOL IT!!
SLIP
!!

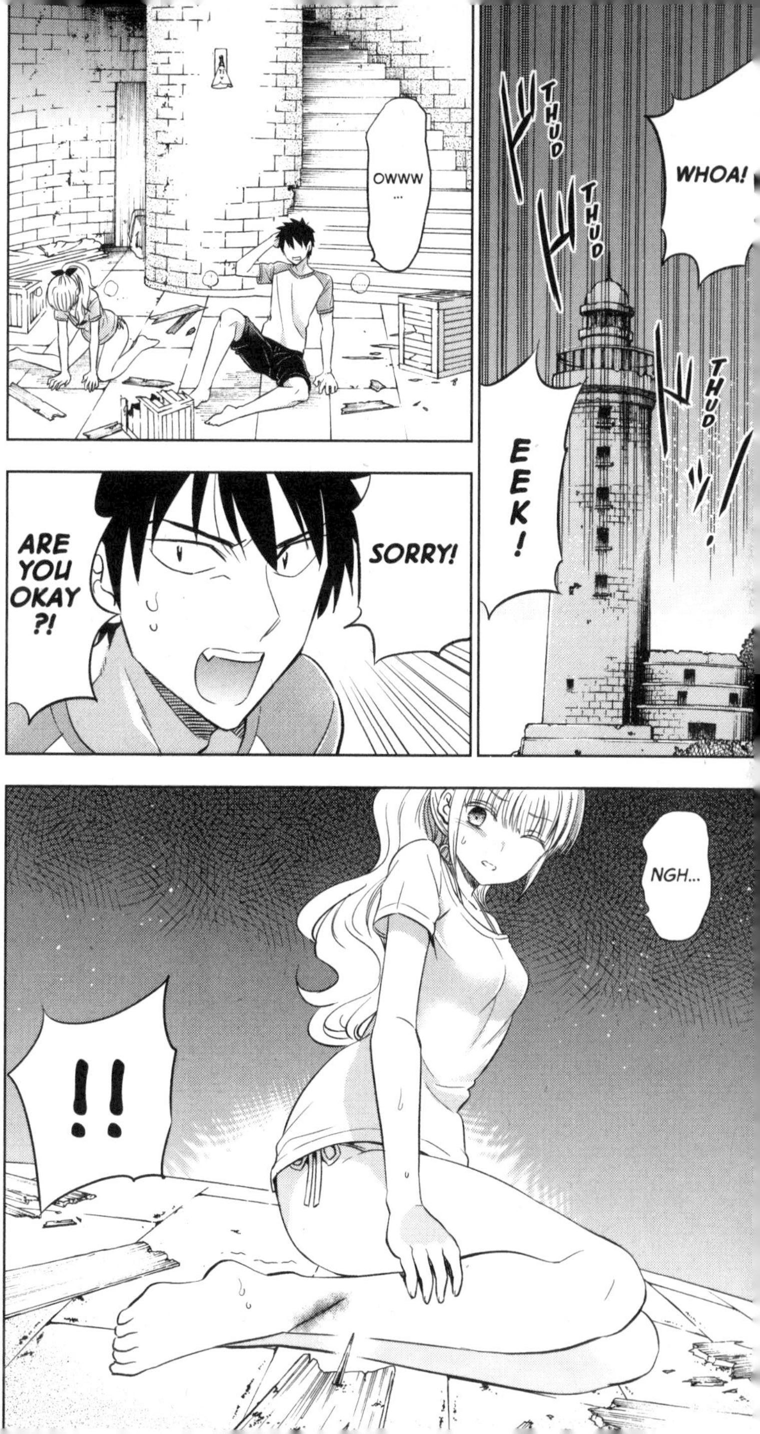
WHOA!
THUD
THUD
THUD
EEK!
OWWW...
SORRY!
ARE YOU OKAY?!
NGH...
!!

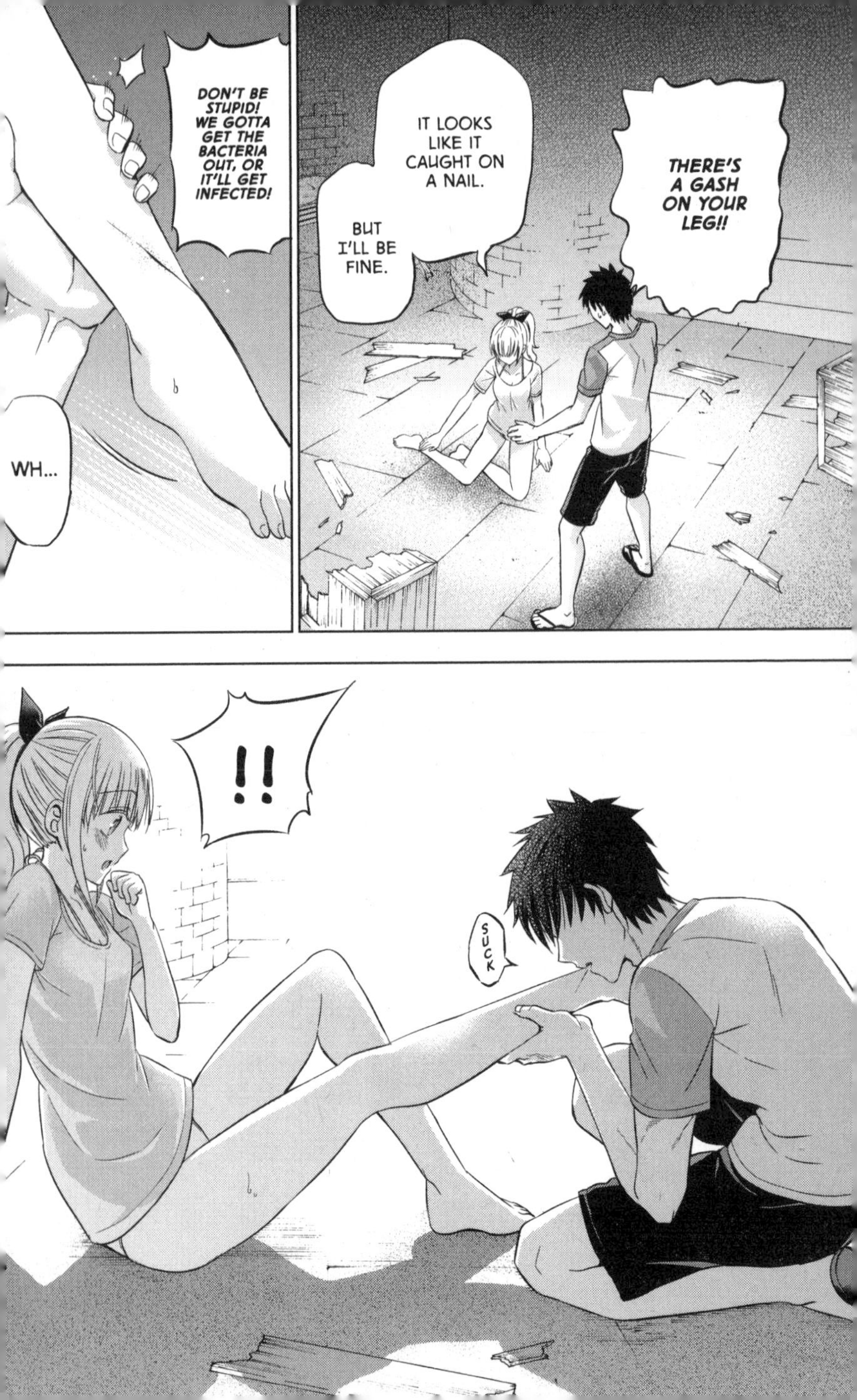
THERE'S A GASH ON YOUR LEG!!
IT LOOKS LIKE IT CAUGHT ON A NAIL.
BUT I'LL BE FINE.
DON'T BE STUPID! WE GOTTA GET THE BACTERIA OUT, OR IT'LL GET INFECTED!
WH...
!!
SUCK

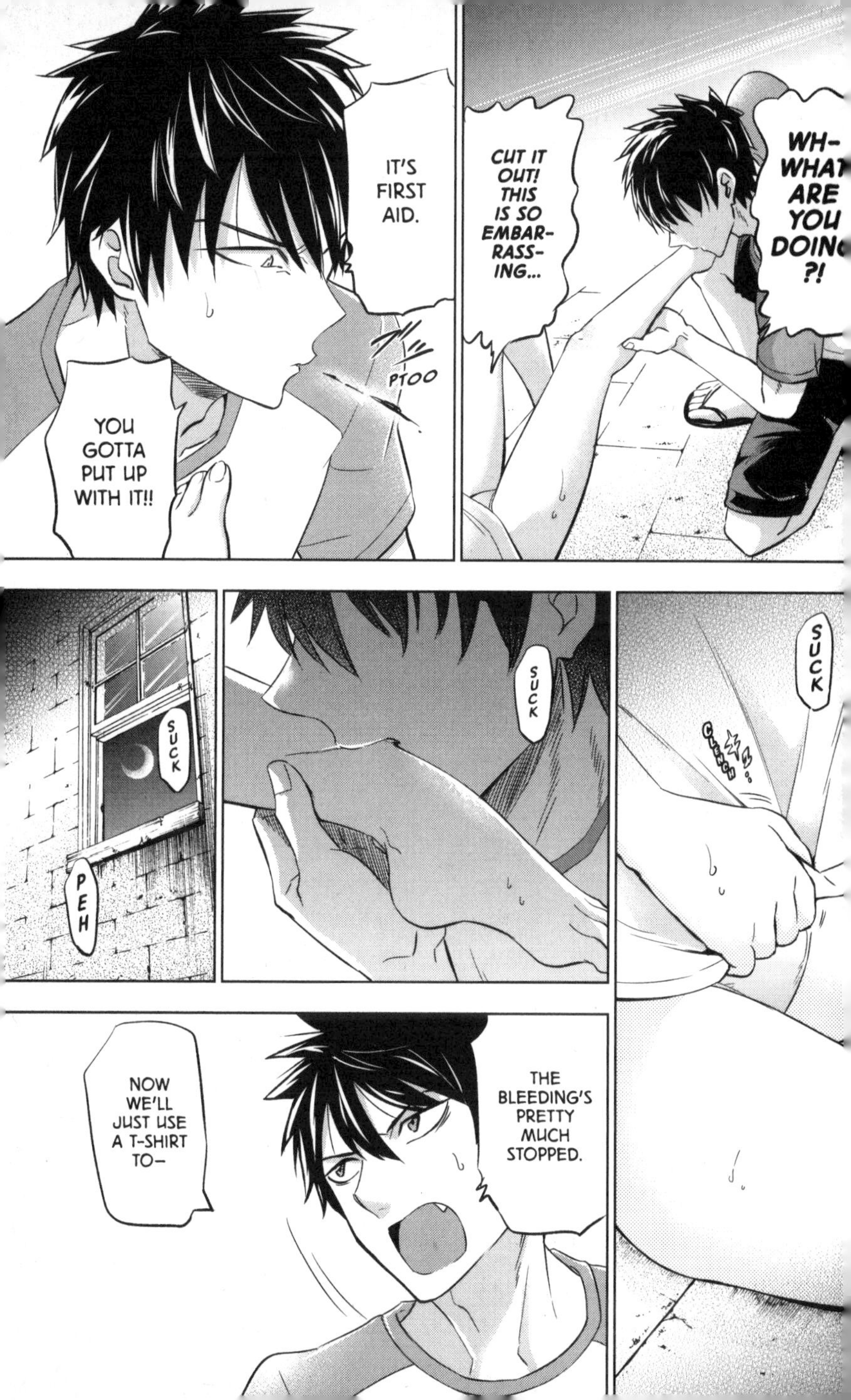
WH- WHAT ARE YOU DOING ?!
CUT IT OUT! THIS IS SO EMBARRASSING...
IT'S FIRST AID.
PTOO
YOU GOTTA PUT UP WITH IT!!
SUCK
CLENCH
SUCK
SUCK
PEH
THE BLEEDING'S PRETTY MUCH STOPPED.
NOW WE'LL JUST USE A T-SHIRT TO–

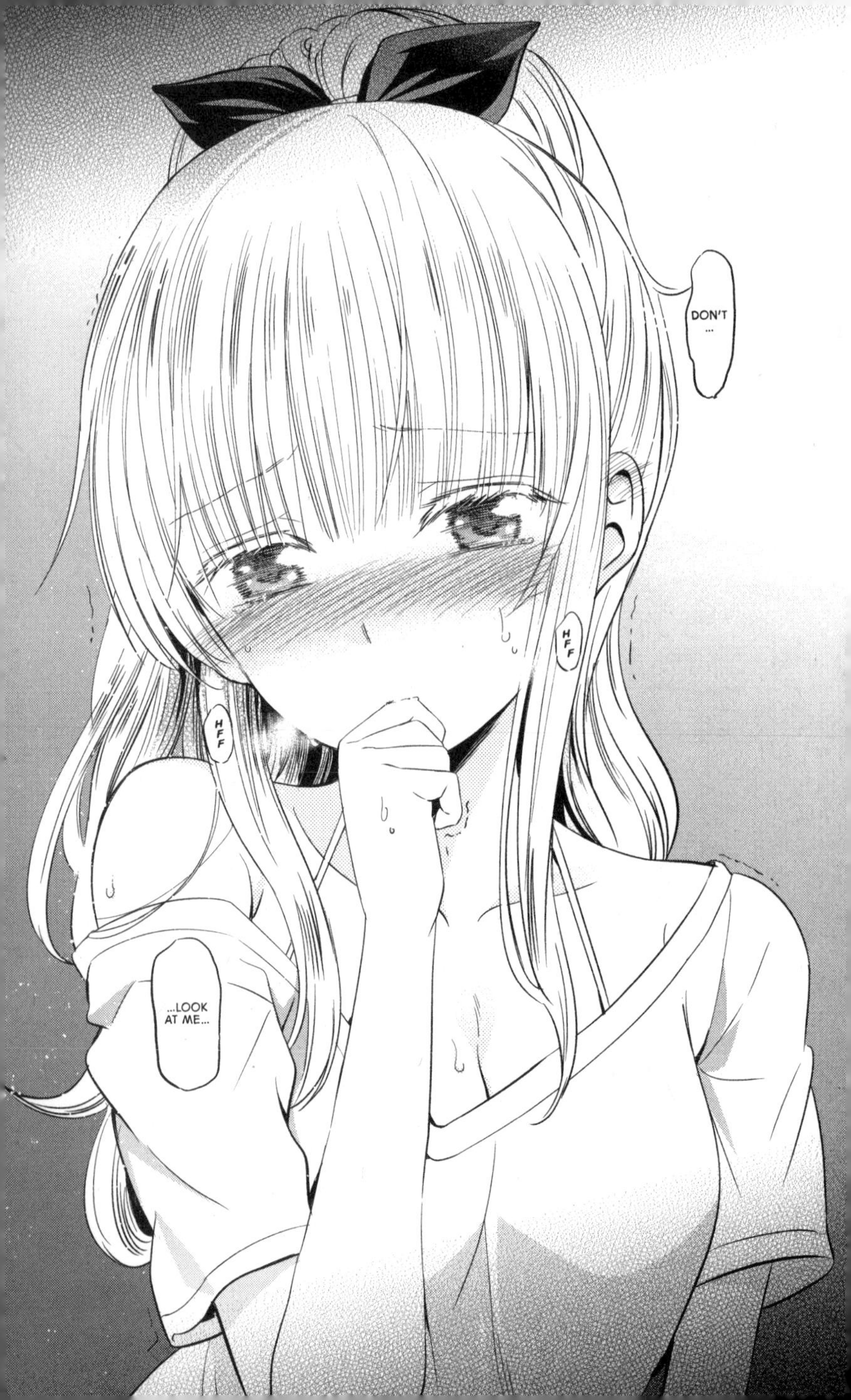
DON'T ...
HFF
HFF
...LOOK AT ME...

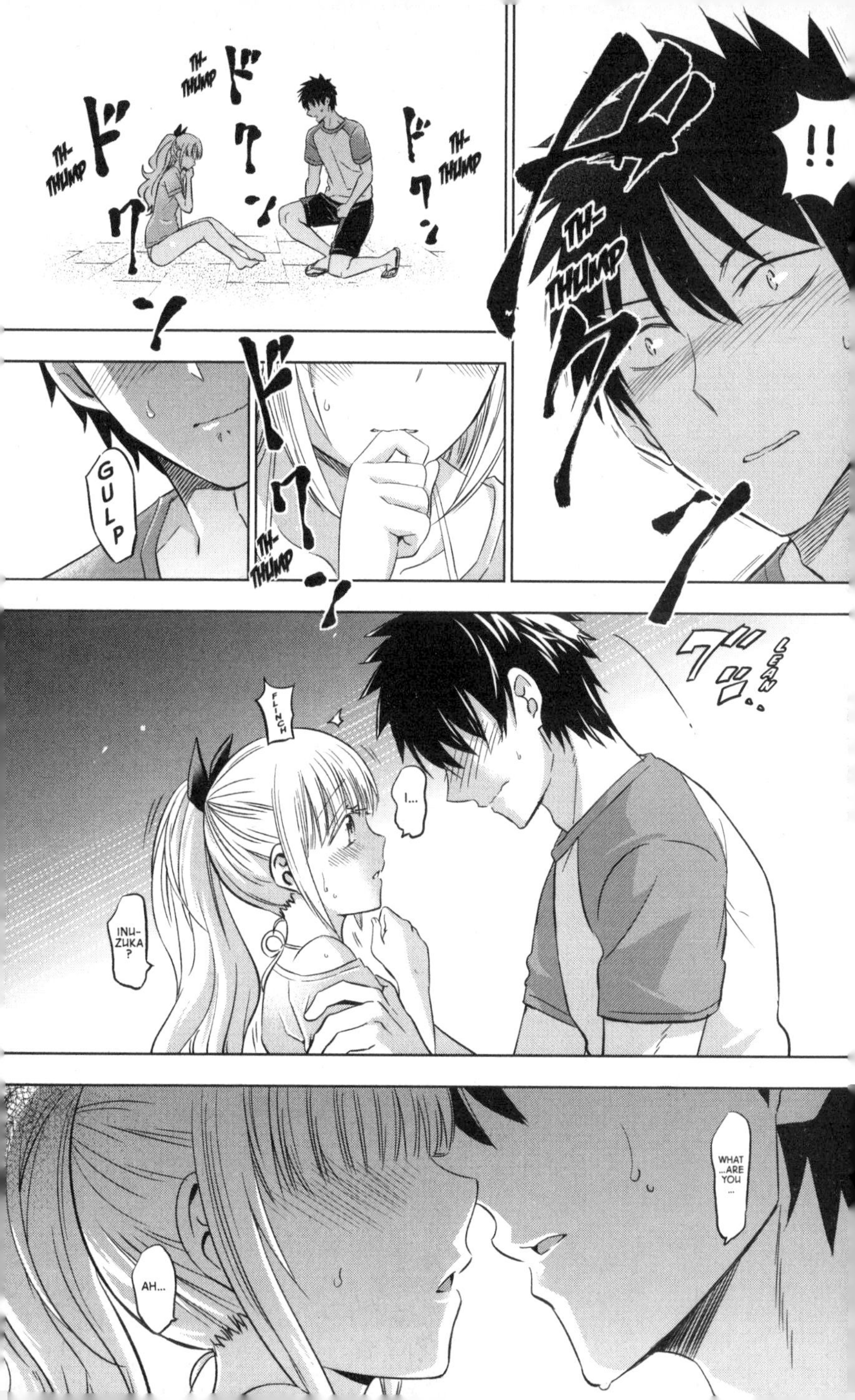
!!
TH-THUMP
TH-THUMP
TH-THUMP
TH-THUMP
TH-THUMP
GULP
LEAN
FLINCH
I...
INU-ZUKA?
WHAT ...ARE YOU ...
AH...

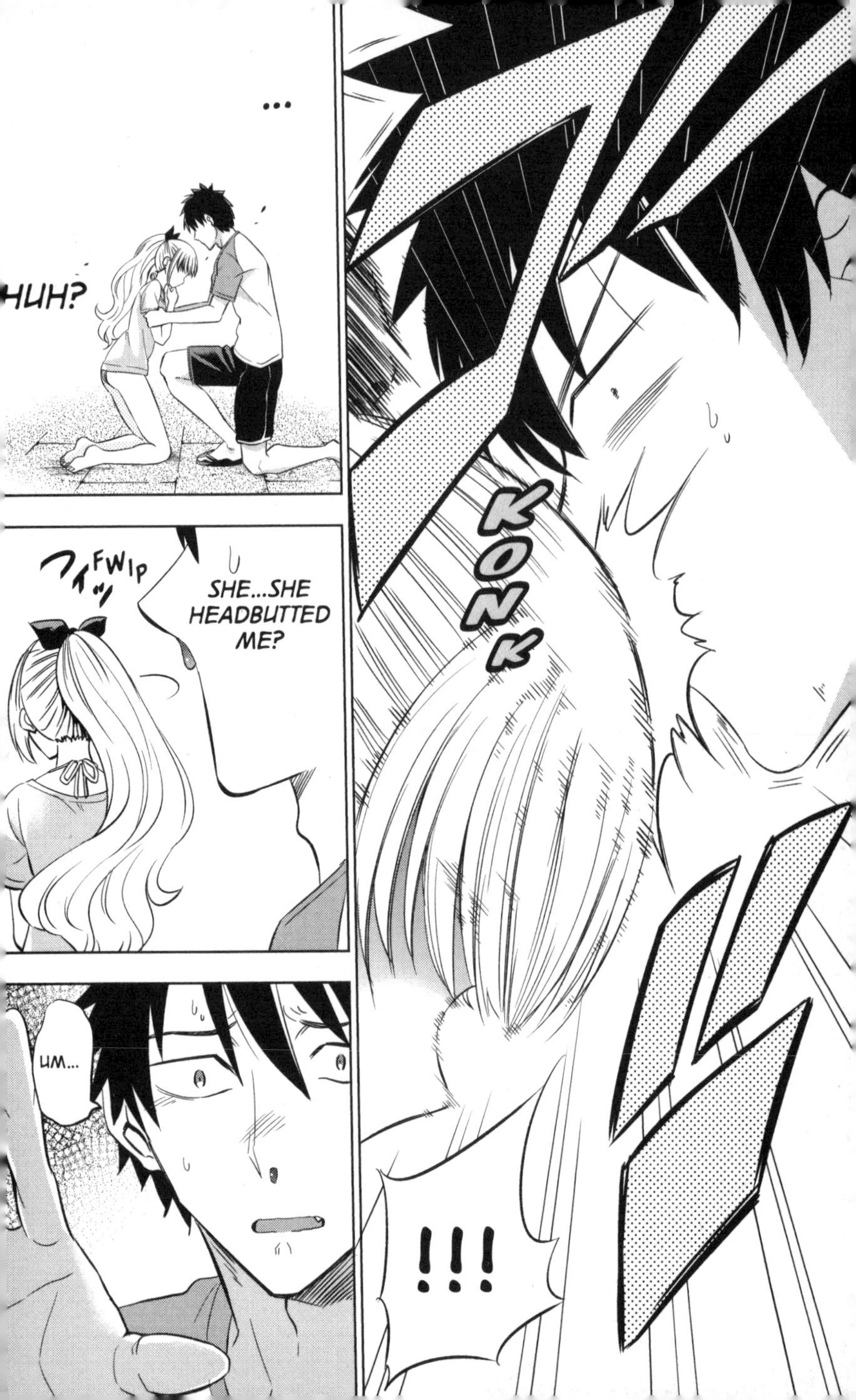
KONK
!!!
...
HUH?
FWIP
SHE...SHE HEADBUTTED ME?
UM...

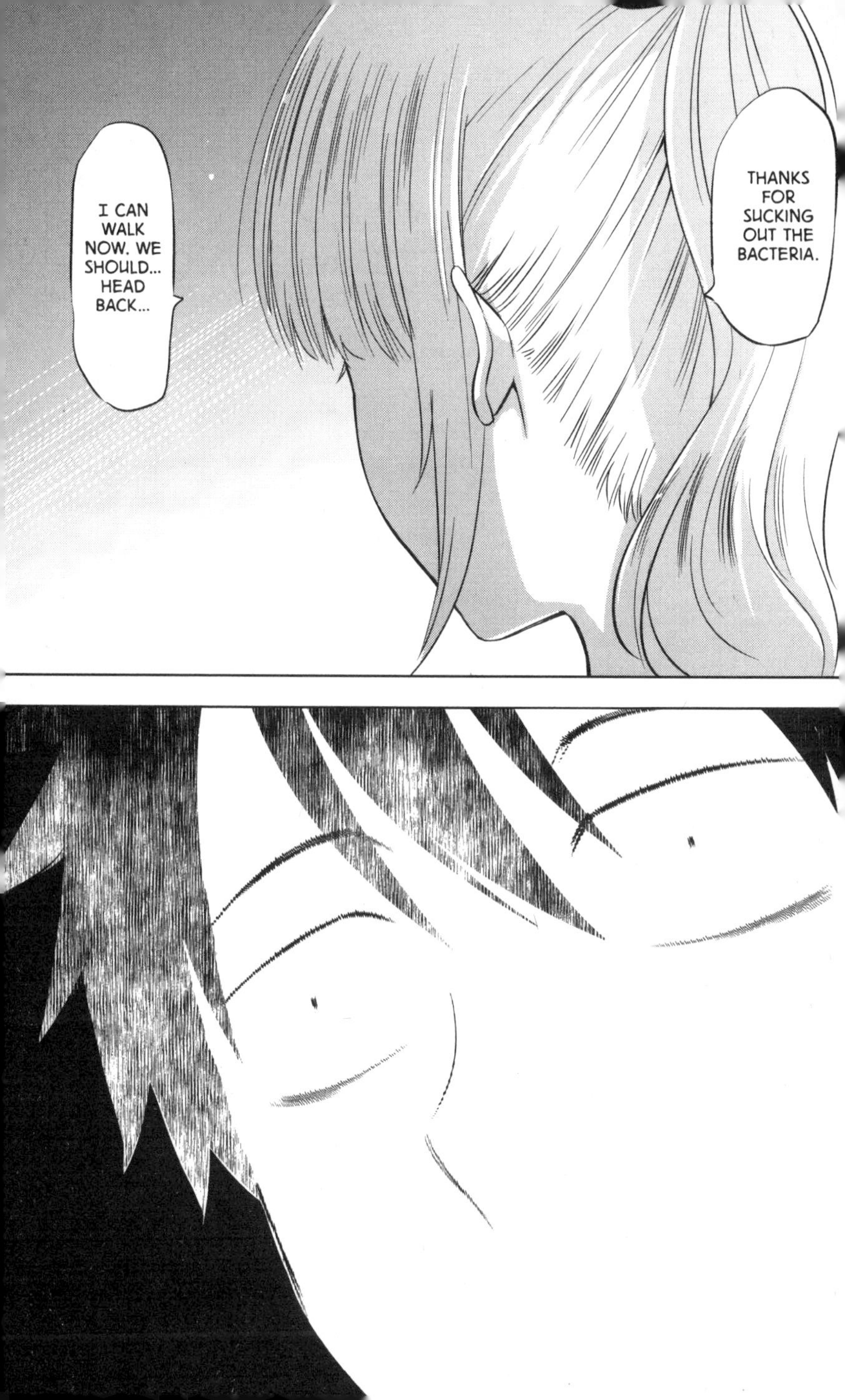
THANKS FOR SUCKING OUT THE BACTERIA.
I CAN WALK NOW. WE SHOULD... HEAD BACK...

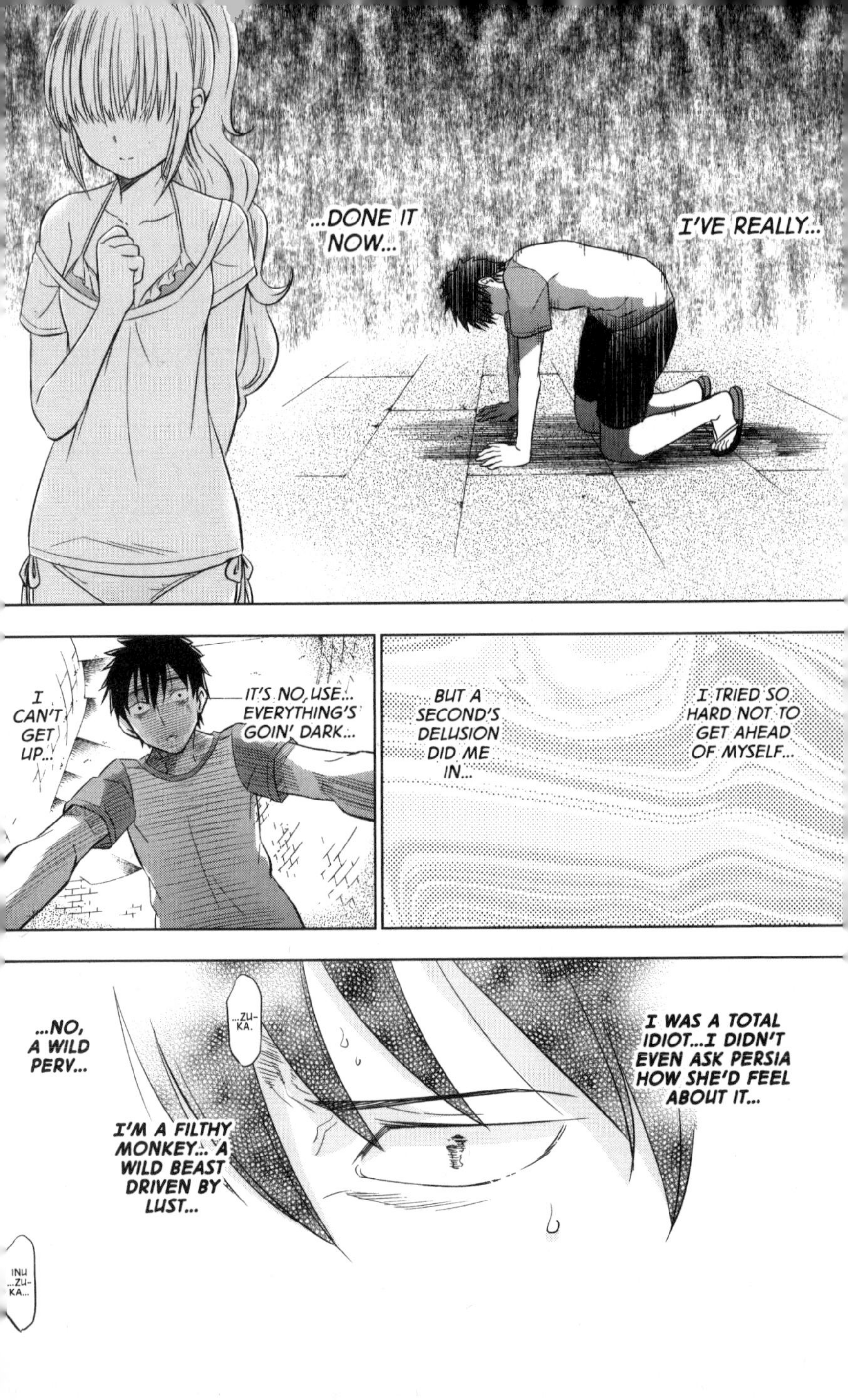
I'VE REALLY...
...DONE IT NOW...
I TRIED SO HARD NOT TO GET AHEAD OF MYSELF...
BUT A SECOND'S DELUSION DID ME IN...
IT'S NO USE... EVERYTHING'S GOIN' DARK...
I CAN'T GET UP...
I WAS A TOTAL IDIOT...I DIDN'T EVEN ASK PERSIA HOW SHE'D FEEL ABOUT IT...
...ZU-KA.
...NO, A WILD PERV...
I'M A FILTHY MONKEY... A WILD BEAST DRIVEN BY LUST...
INU ...ZU-KA...

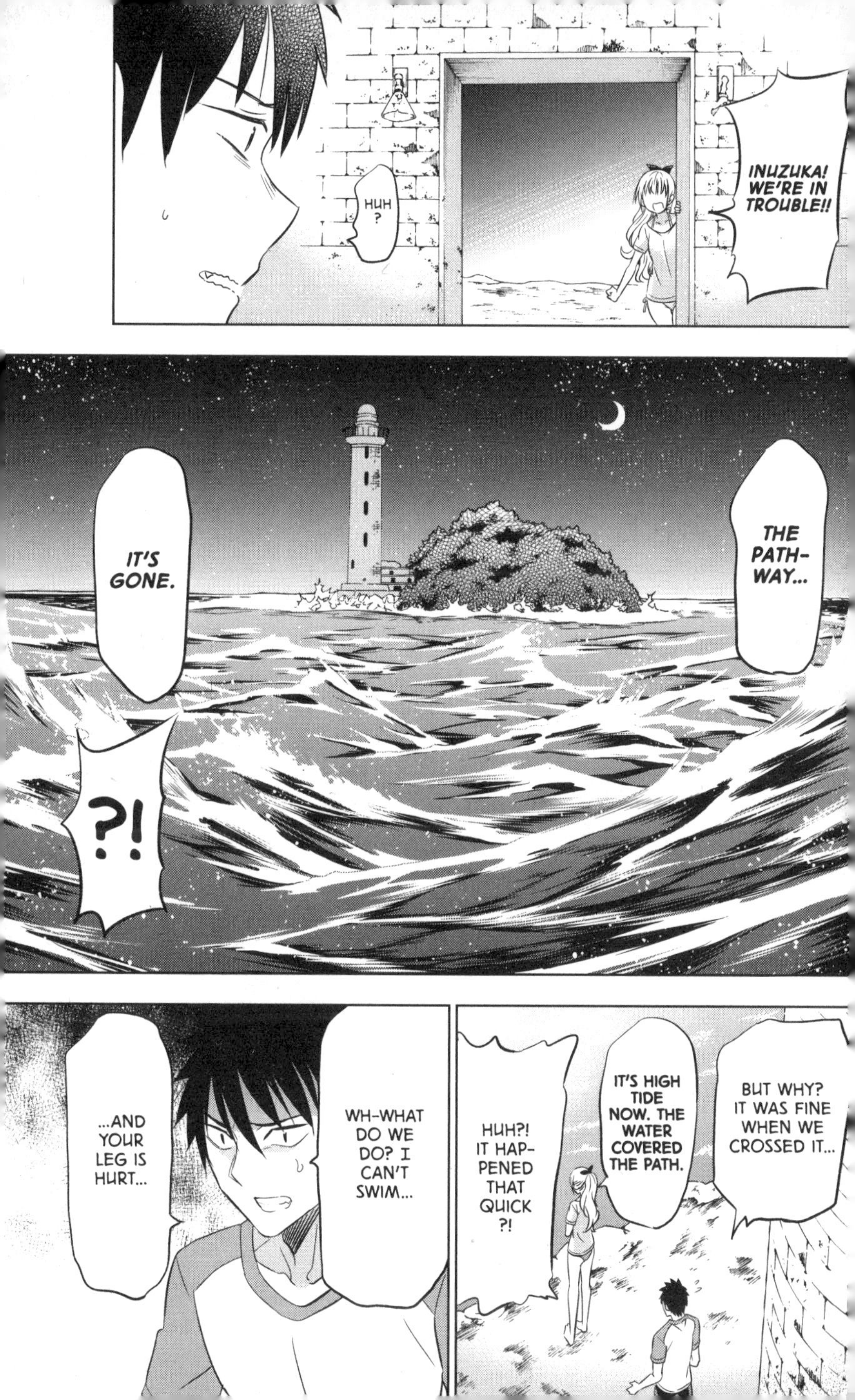
INUZUKA! WE'RE IN TROUBLE!!
HUH?
THE PATH-WAY...
IT'S GONE.
?!
BUT WHY? IT WAS FINE WHEN WE CROSSED IT...
IT'S HIGH TIDE NOW. THE WATER COVERED THE PATH.
HUH?! IT HAP-PENED THAT QUICK?!
WH-WHAT DO WE DO? I CAN'T SWIM...
...AND YOUR LEG IS HURT...

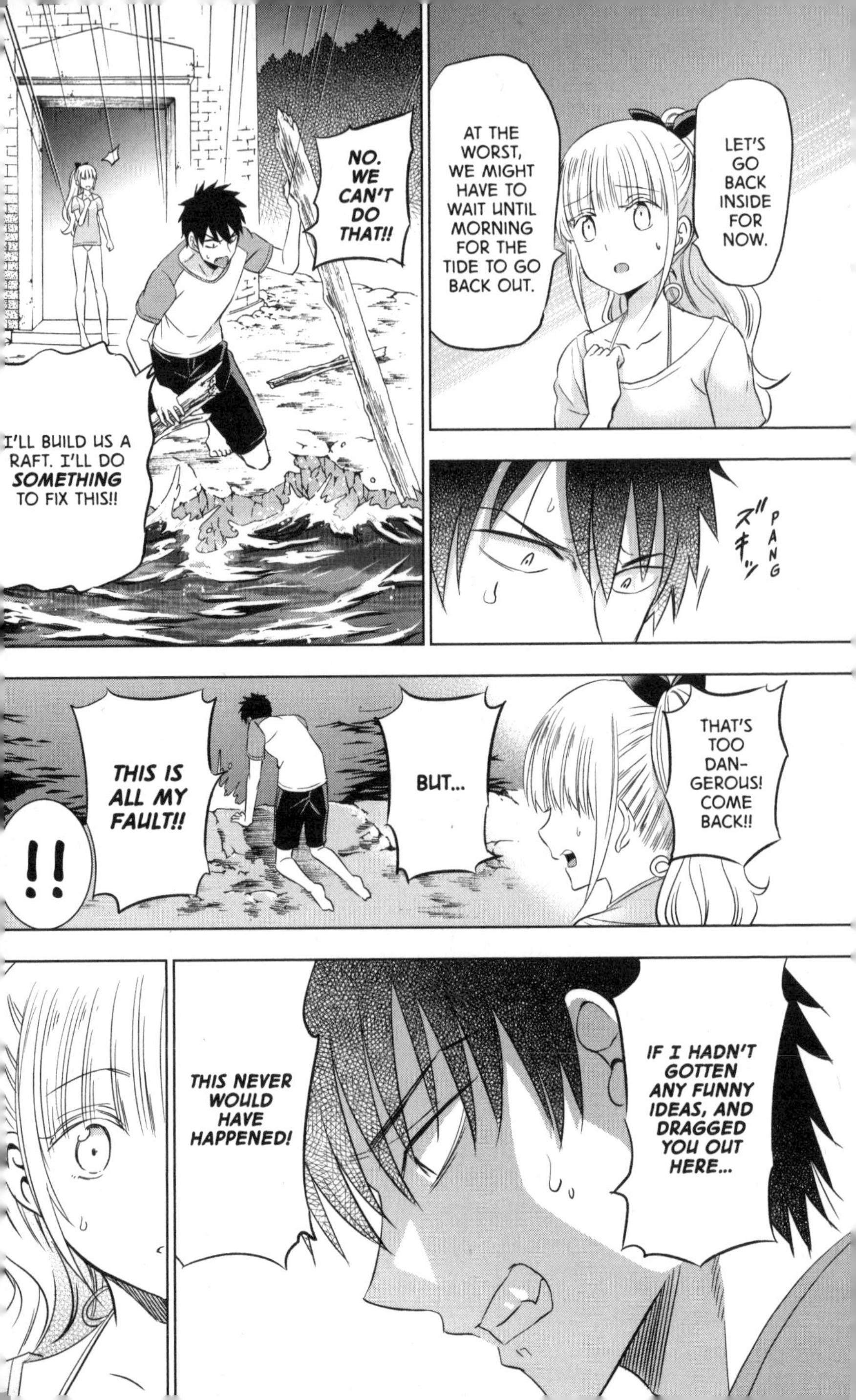
LET'S GO BACK INSIDE FOR NOW.
AT THE WORST, WE MIGHT HAVE TO WAIT UNTIL MORNING FOR THE TIDE TO GO BACK OUT.
ズキッ
PANG
NO. WE CAN'T DO THAT!!
I'LL BUILD US A RAFT. I'LL DO SOMETHING TO FIX THIS!!
THAT'S TOO DAN-GEROUS! COME BACK!!
BUT...
THIS IS ALL MY FAULT!!
!!
IF I HADN'T GOTTEN ANY FUNNY IDEAS, AND DRAGGED YOU OUT HERE...
THIS NEVER WOULD HAVE HAPPENED!

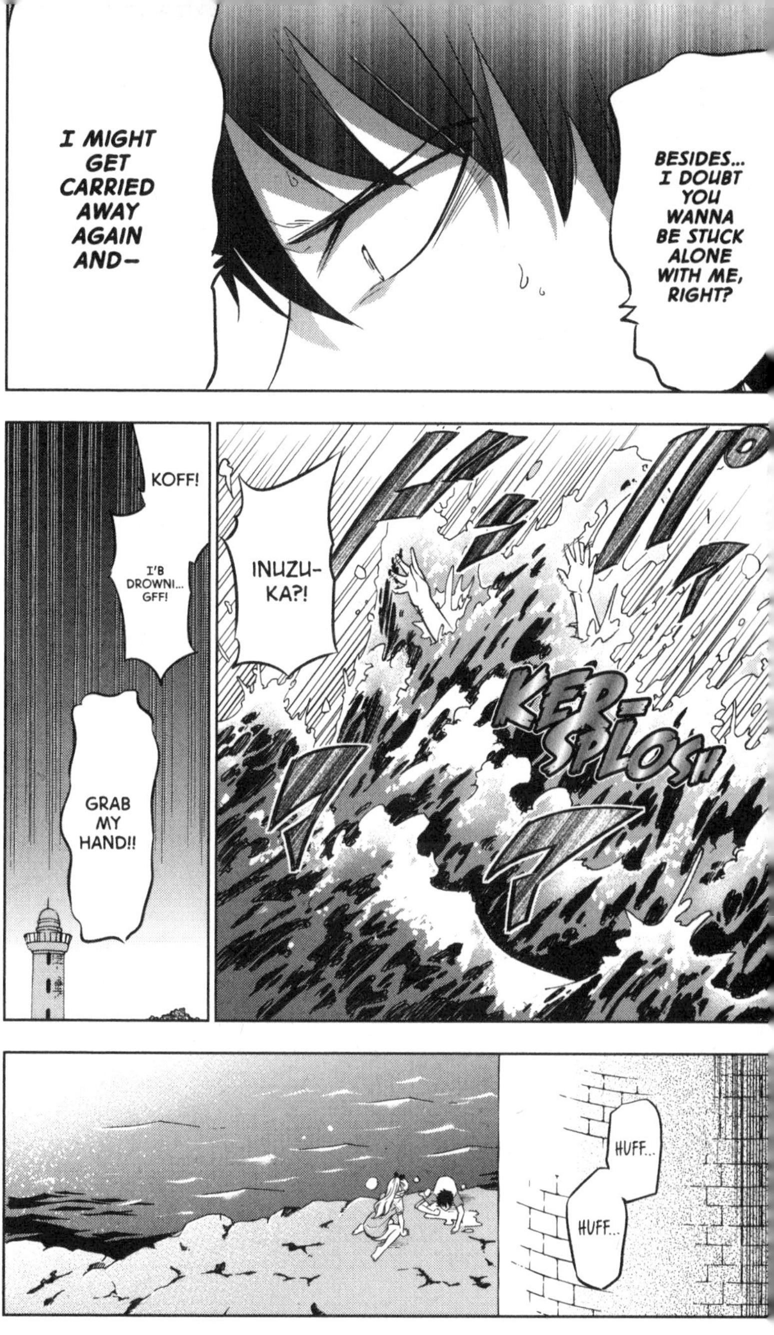
BESIDES... I DOUBT YOU WANNA BE STUCK ALONE WITH ME, RIGHT?
I MIGHT GET CARRIED AWAY AGAIN AND–
INUZU-KA?!
KER-SPLOSH
KOFF!
I'B DROWNI... GFF!
GRAB MY HAND!!
HUFF...
HUFF...

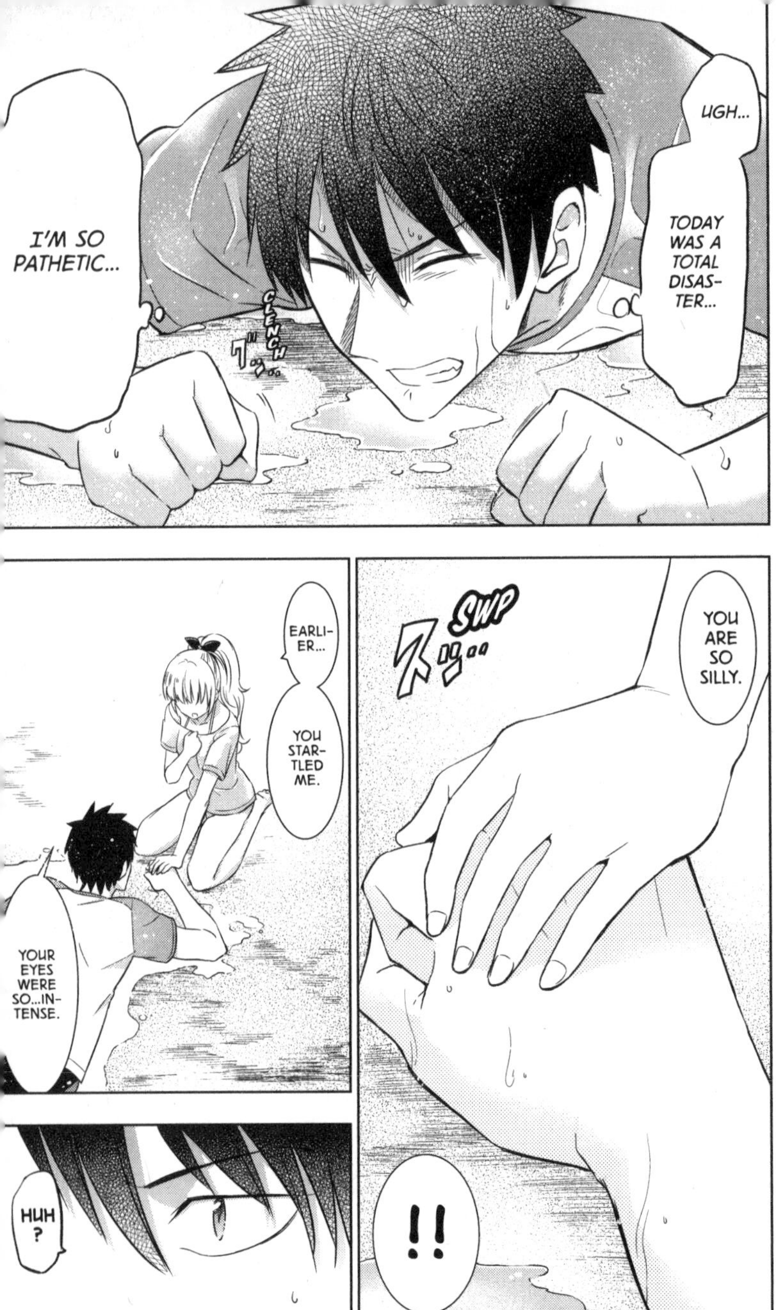
UGH...
TODAY WAS A TOTAL DISAS-TER...
CLENCH
I'M SO PATHETIC...
YOU ARE SO SILLY.
SWP
!!
EARLI-ER...
YOU STAR-TLED ME.
YOUR EYES WERE SO...IN-TENSE.
HUH?

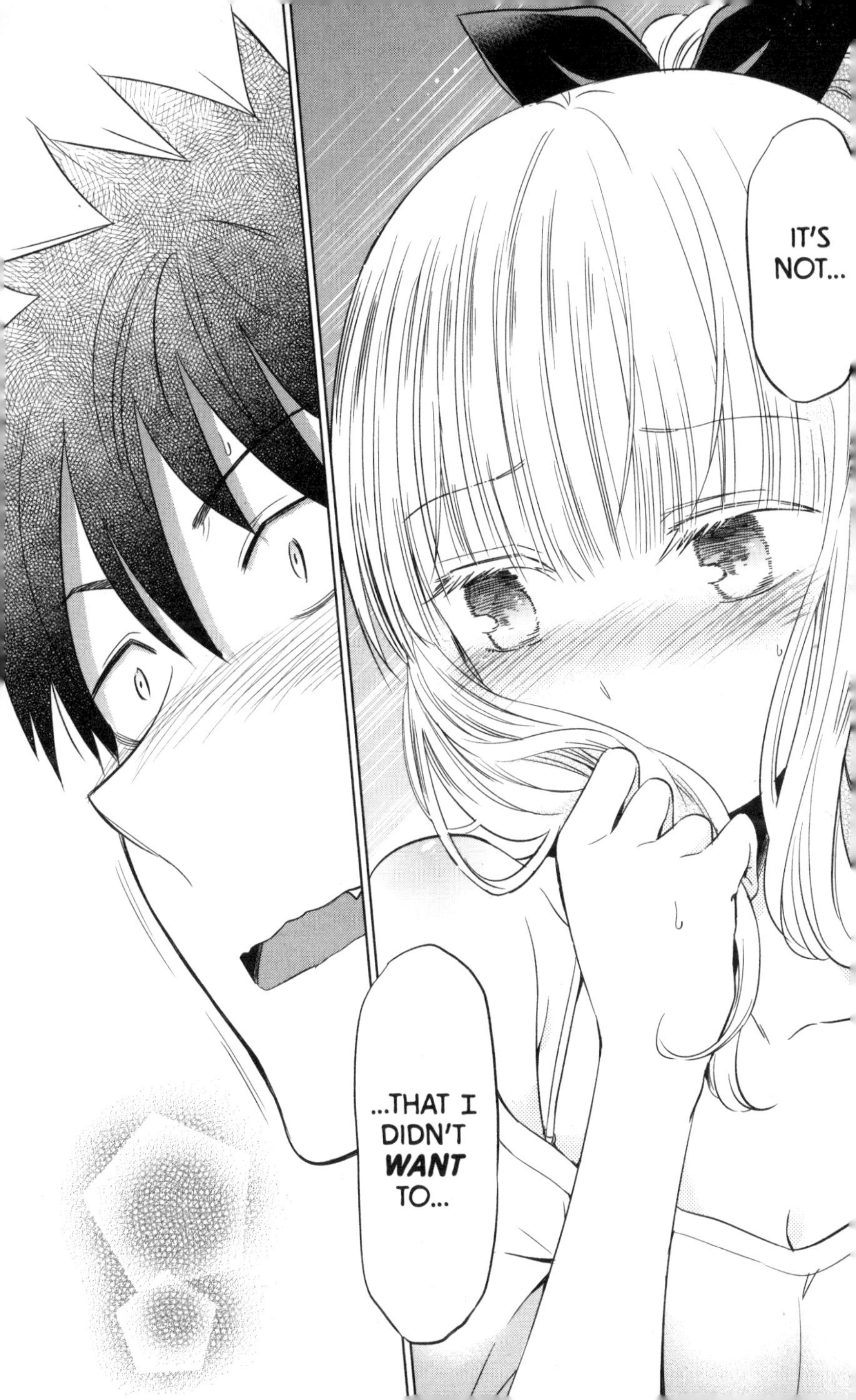
IT'S NOT...
...THAT I DIDN'T WANT TO...

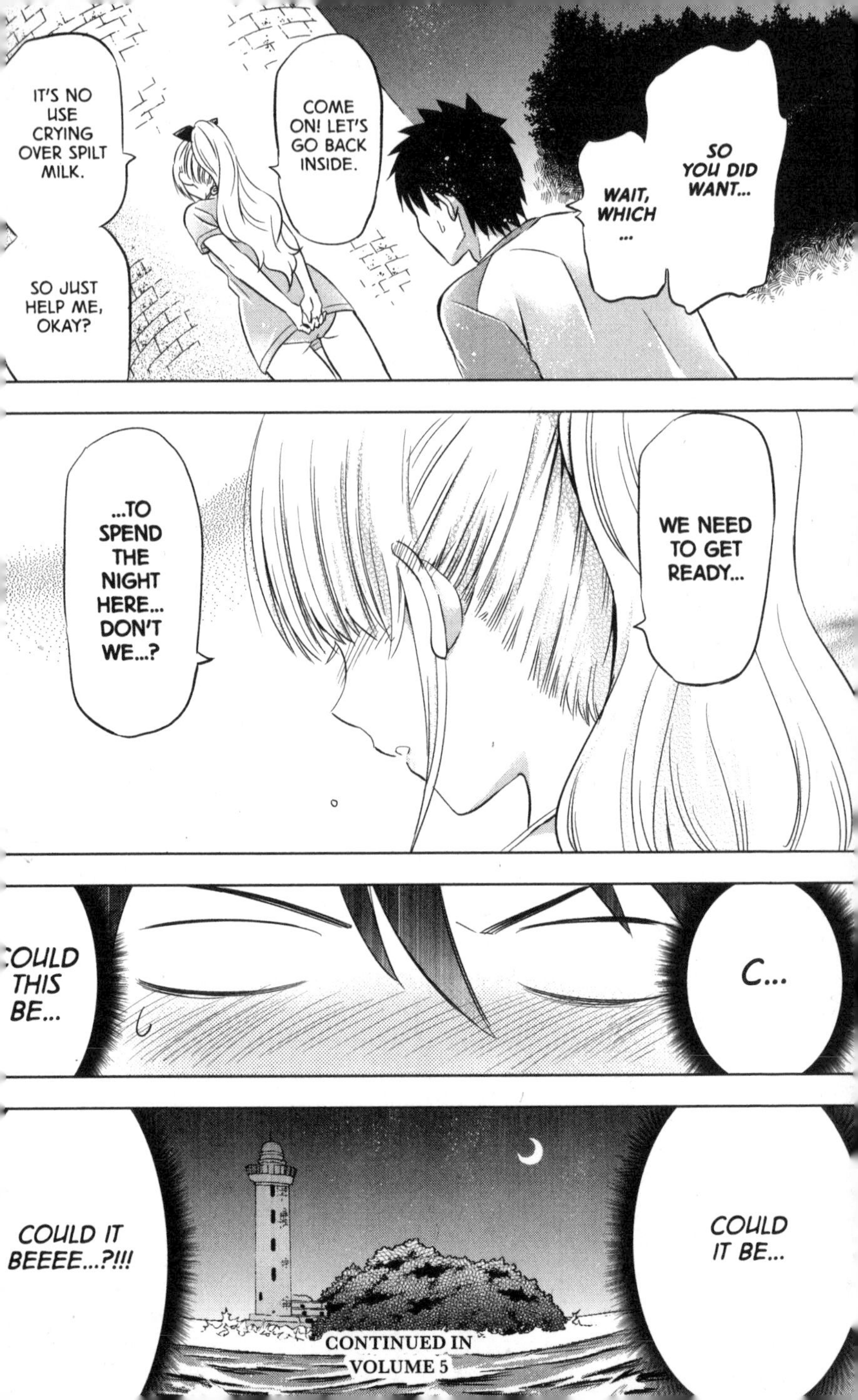
SO YOU DID WANT...
WAIT, WHICH ...
COME ON! LET'S GO BACK INSIDE.
IT'S NO USE CRYING OVER SPILT MILK.
SO JUST HELP ME, OKAY?
WE NEED TO GET READY...
...TO SPEND THE NIGHT HERE... DON'T WE...?
C...
COULD THIS BE...
COULD IT BE...
COULD IT BEEEE...?!!!
CONTINUED IN VOLUME 5

BONUS PAGE: REX'S SECRET

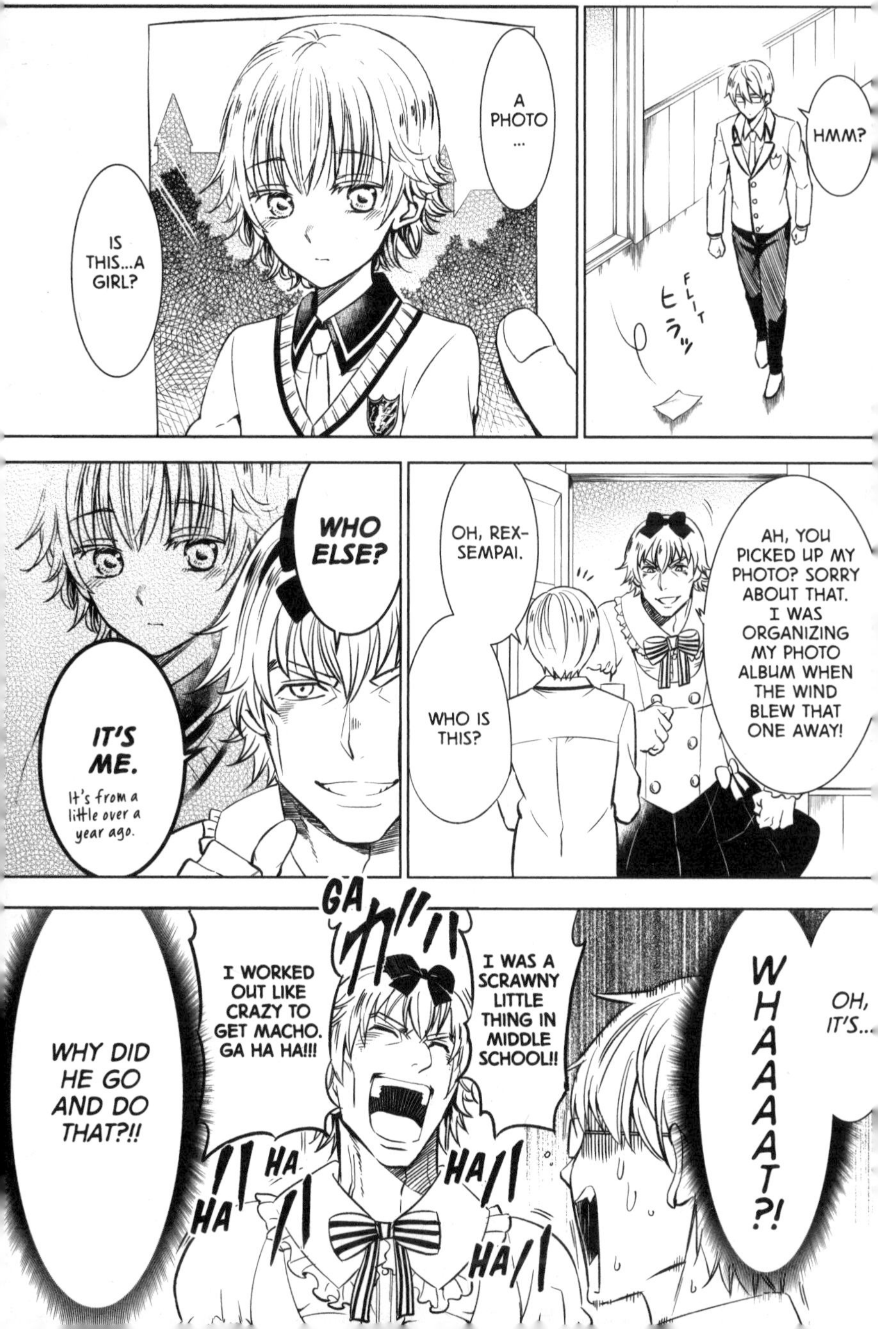
HMM?
FLIT
A PHOTO ...
IS THIS...A GIRL?
AH, YOU PICKED UP MY PHOTO? SORRY ABOUT THAT. I WAS ORGANIZING MY PHOTO ALBUM WHEN THE WIND BLEW THAT ONE AWAY!
OH, REX-SEMPAI.
WHO IS THIS?
WHO ELSE?
IT'S ME.
It's from a little over a year ago.
OH, IT'S...
WHAAAAAT?!
GA
I WAS A SCRAWNY LITTLE THING IN MIDDLE SCHOOL!!
I WORKED OUT LIKE CRAZY TO GET MACHO. GA HA HA!!!
HA
HA
HA
HA
WHY DID HE GO AND DO THAT?!!

HEIGHT REFERENCE CHART

height chart

*This is only a rough idea. Height differences may vary depending on the panel. Thanks for your understanding.

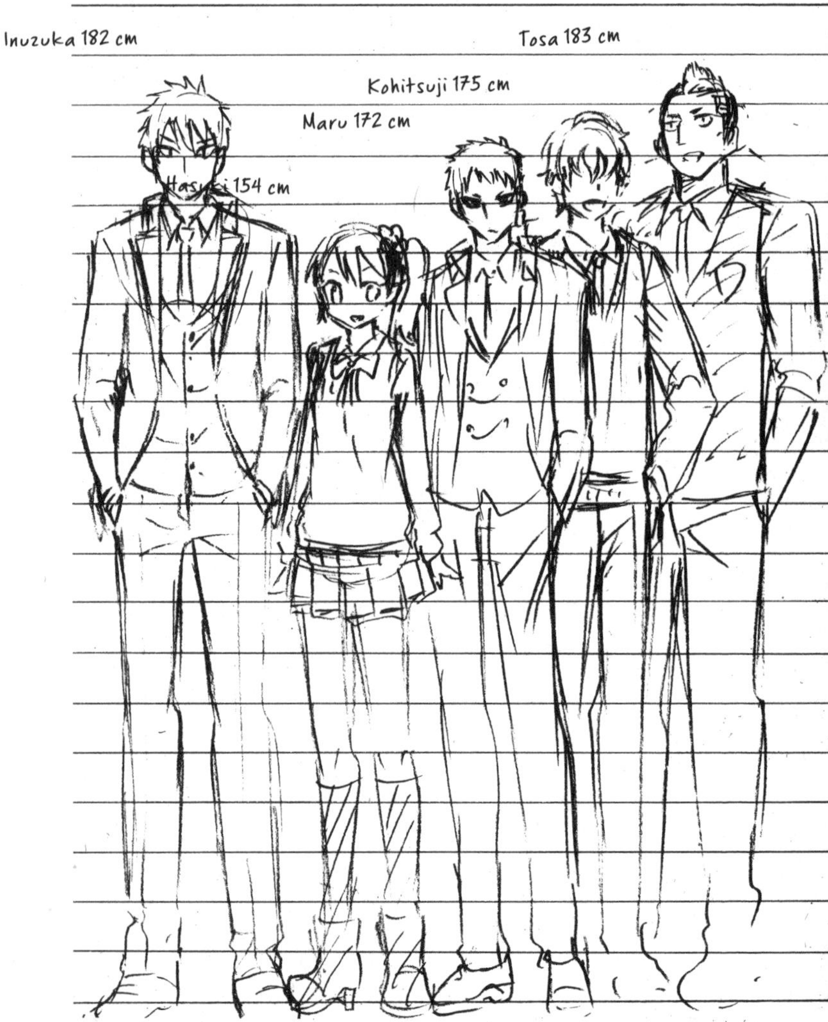
Inuzuka 182 cm
Tosa 183 cm
Kohitsuji 175 cm
Maru 172 cm
Hasuki 154 cm

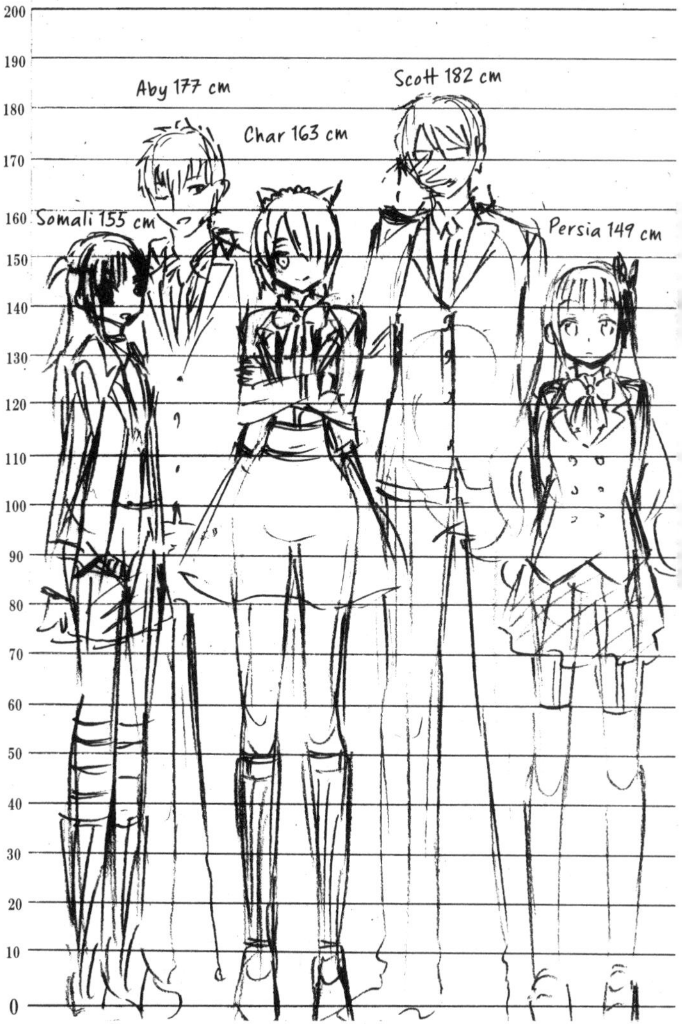
200
190
180
170
160
150
140
130
120
110
100
90
80
70
60
50
40
30
20
10
0
Aby 177 cm
Scott 182 cm
Char 163 cm
Somali 155 cm
Persia 149 cm

AFTERWORD

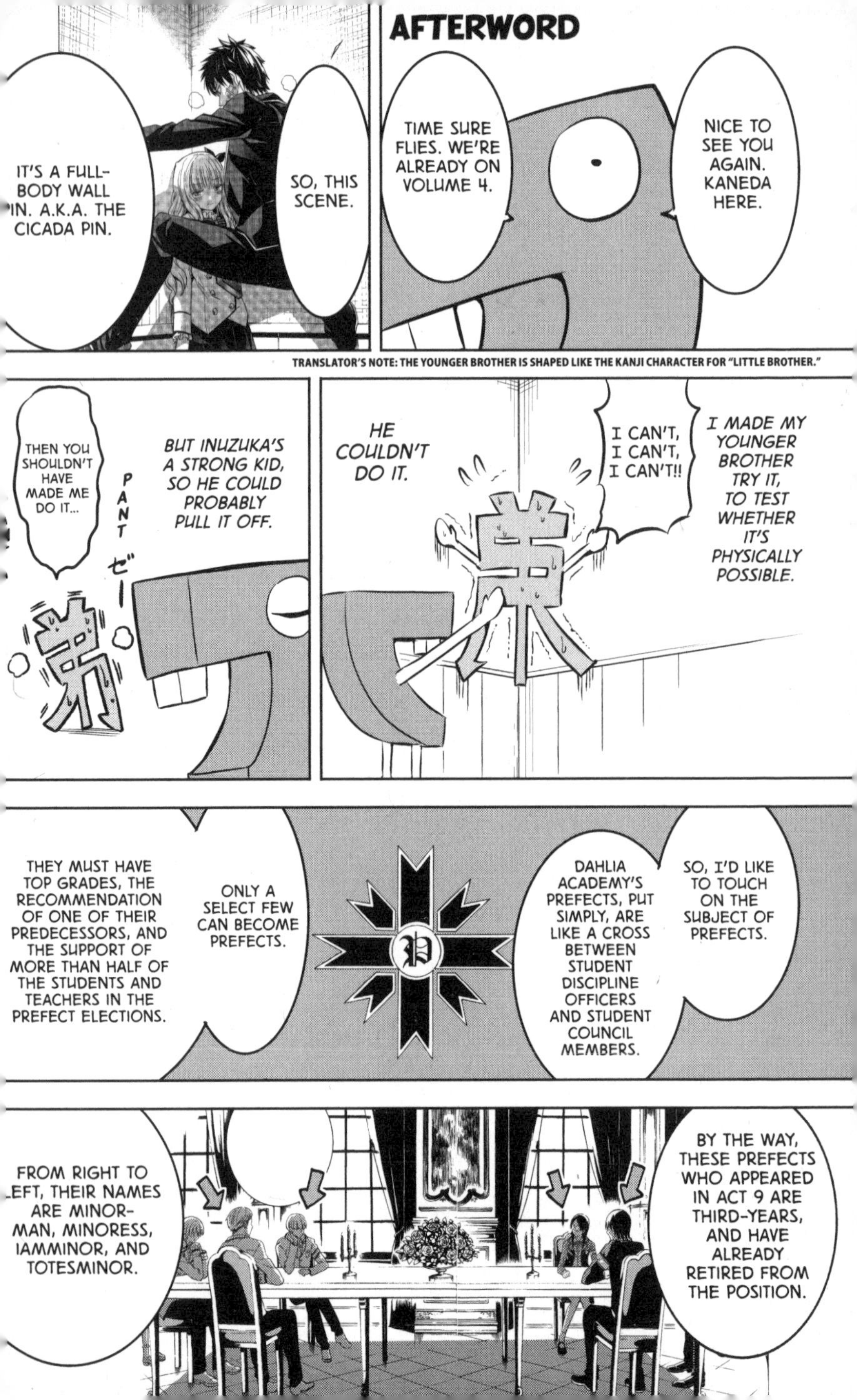
NICE TO SEE YOU AGAIN. KANEDA HERE.
TIME SURE FLIES. WE'RE ALREADY ON VOLUME 4.
SO, THIS SCENE.
IT'S A FULL-BODY WALL IN. A.K.A. THE CICADA PIN.
TRANSLATOR'S NOTE: THE YOUNGER BROTHER IS SHAPED LIKE THE KANJI CHARACTER FOR "LITTLE BROTHER."
I MADE MY YOUNGER BROTHER TRY IT, TO TEST WHETHER IT'S PHYSICALLY POSSIBLE.
I CAN'T, I CAN'T, I CAN'T!!
HE COULDN'T DO IT.
BUT INUZUKA'S A STRONG KID, SO HE COULD PROBABLY PULL IT OFF.
PANT ゼー
THEN YOU SHOULDN'T HAVE MADE ME DO IT...
SO, I'D LIKE TO TOUCH ON THE SUBJECT OF PREFECTS.
DAHLIA ACADEMY'S PREFECTS, PUT SIMPLY, ARE LIKE A CROSS BETWEEN STUDENT DISCIPLINE OFFICERS AND STUDENT COUNCIL MEMBERS.
ONLY A SELECT FEW CAN BECOME PREFECTS.
THEY MUST HAVE TOP GRADES, THE RECOMMENDATION OF ONE OF THEIR PREDECESSORS, AND THE SUPPORT OF MORE THAN HALF OF THE STUDENTS AND TEACHERS IN THE PREFECT ELECTIONS.
BY THE WAY, THESE PREFECTS WHO APPEARED IN ACT 9 ARE THIRD-YEARS, AND HAVE ALREADY RETIRED FROM THE POSITION.
FROM RIGHT TO EFT, THEIR NAMES ARE MINOR-MAN, MINORESS, IAMMINOR, AND TOTESMINOR.

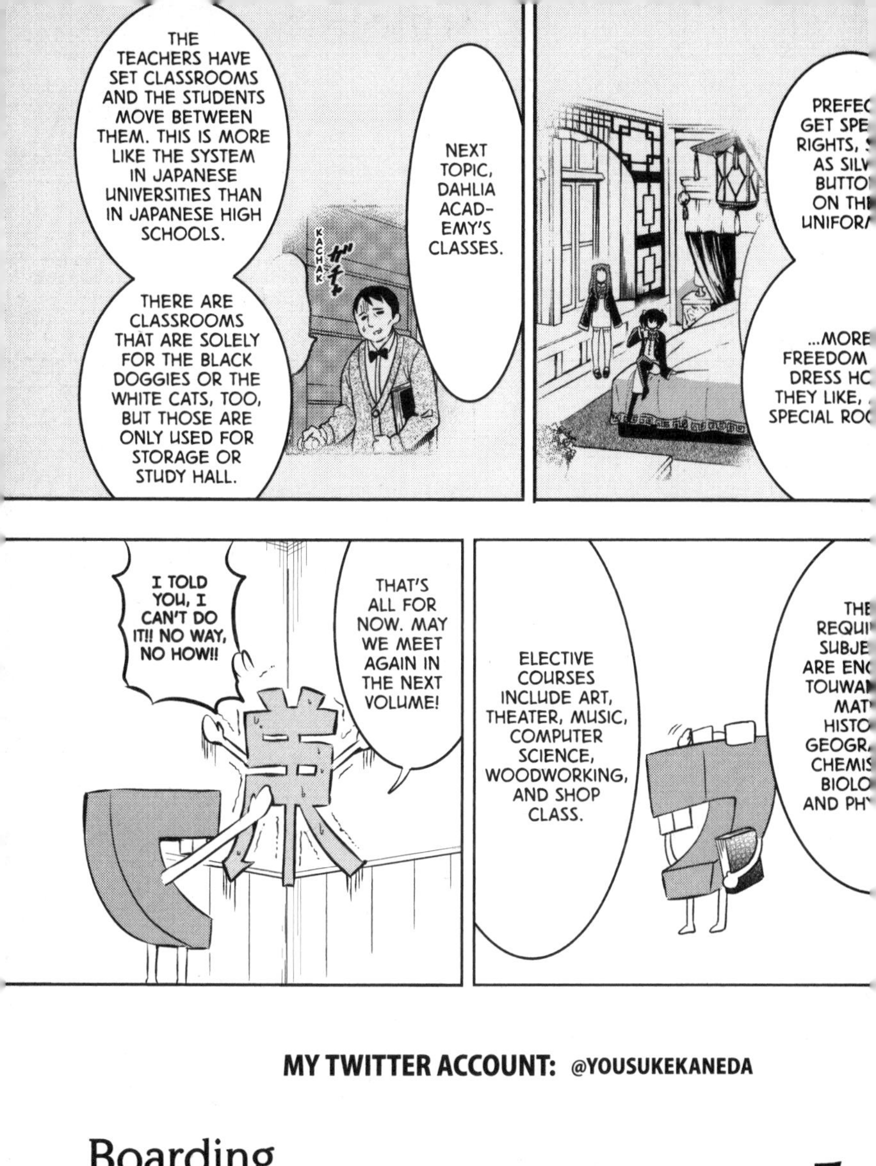
PREFEC GET SPE RIGHTS, AS SILV BUTTO ON TH UNIFOR
...MORE FREEDOM DRESS HC THEY LIKE, SPECIAL ROC
NEXT TOPIC, DAHLIA ACAD-EMY'S CLASSES.
KACHAK
THE TEACHERS HAVE SET CLASSROOMS AND THE STUDENTS MOVE BETWEEN THEM. THIS IS MORE LIKE THE SYSTEM IN JAPANESE UNIVERSITIES THAN IN JAPANESE HIGH SCHOOLS.
THERE ARE CLASSROOMS THAT ARE SOLELY FOR THE BLACK DOGGIES OR THE WHITE CATS, TOO, BUT THOSE ARE ONLY USED FOR STORAGE OR STUDY HALL.
THE REQUI SUBJE ARE ENC TOUWA MAT HISTO GEOGR CHEMIS BIOLO AND PH
ELECTIVE COURSES INCLUDE ART, THEATER, MUSIC, COMPUTER SCIENCE, WOODWORKING, AND SHOP CLASS.
THAT'S ALL FOR NOW. MAY WE MEET AGAIN IN THE NEXT VOLUME!
I TOLD YOU, I CAN'T DO IT!! NO WAY, NO HOW!!

MY TWITTER ACCOUNT: **@YOUSUKEKANEDA**

Boarding School *Juliet* **VOLUME 5**

A Kodansha Comics Trade Paperback Original.

Boarding School Juliet volume 4 copyright © 2017 Yousuke Kaneda
English translation copyright © 2019 Yousuke Kaneda

Published in the United States by Kodansha Comics,
an imprint of Kodansha USA Publishing, LLC, New York.

Publication rights for this English edition arranged through
Kodansha Ltd., Tokyo.

First published in Japan in 2017 by Kodansha Ltd., Tokyo, as
Kishuku Gakkou no Jurietto volume 4.

ISBN 978-1-63236-754-9

Printed in the United States of America.

www.kodanshacomics.com

9 8 7 6 5 4 3 2 1

Translation: Amanda Haley
Lettering: James Dashiell
Editing: Erin Subramanian and Paul Starr
Kodansha Comics edition cover design: Phil Balsman